Frederic Seebohm

The Tribal System in Wales

Being Part of an Inquiry into the Structure and Methods of Tribal Society

Frederic Seebohm

The Tribal System in Wales
Being Part of an Inquiry into the Structure and Methods of Tribal Society

ISBN/EAN: 9783337060602

Printed in Europe, USA, Canada, Australia, Japan

Cover: Foto ©Suzi / pixelio.de

More available books at **www.hansebooks.com**

THE TRIBAL SYSTEM

IN WALES

BEING PART OF AN INQUIRY INTO
THE STRUCTURE AND METHODS OF TRIBAL SOCIETY

BY

FREDERIC SEEBOHM, LL.D., F.S.A.

LONDON
LONGMANS, GREEN, AND CO.
AND NEW YORK
1895

PREFACE.

THIS volume contains the first part of an essay which may be described as an amplification of the very imperfect sections on the Welsh Tribal System published more than ten years ago in my 'English Village Community.'

It is confined to an attempt to understand the *structure* of tribal society in Wales. The *methods* of tribal society in Wales and the extension of the inquiry to other tribal systems are left to form the subject of another volume. It seemed best to print this part of the essay separately, so that the Welsh evidence might be considered on its own merits, without the subject being involved at this stage in the greater difficulties which arise so soon as the ground covered by the remarkably full and detailed Welsh documentary evidence is departed from.

The methods of the Welsh tribal system come, indeed, more or less, within the range of this documentary evidence, and might well add, incidentally, great strength to some of the conclusions as to the structure of tribal society in Wales. But as it is mainly through comparison of the Welsh methods

in detail with those of neighbouring systems that
the links are obtained by which the connections are
established, it seems best to leave the consideration
of the Welsh methods to that part of the inquiry
which is relegated to another volume.

The documentary evidence above referred to
will be found, I think, to justify the stress laid upon
the Welsh system as a stepping-stone to wider knowledge. So much of it is unpublished, and remains
in manuscripts not easily accessible to the general
student, that it became necessary to print at full
length in the Appendices the passages most relied
upon, as leading up to an understanding of the
Welsh Codes, and to the establishment on a firm
basis of the main facts of tribal customary law.

For the careful transcription and the correction
of the proof-sheets of these copious extracts I have
to thank the care and skill of Mr. W. K. BOYD.

The value of the several manuscripts for the
purpose in hand will become evident as the inquiry
proceeds, especially that of the Denbigh Extent, an
original copy of which, through the kindness of
Colonel HOWARD, of Wygfair, has been placed
entirely at my disposal. An Extent which enters
so fully into detail, and describes survivals of the
tribal system actually at work throughout a considerable district at the time of the English conquest of North Wales, could not fail to afford the
best possible ground from which to proceed to the
study of the customary law contained in the Codes.

As regards the Codes and legal treatises contained

in the 'Ancient Laws of Wales,' I will not forestall what is said in the text further than to express the belief that they will be found to fall into their right place when regarded as links in the chain of evidence as to the character of tribal custom which existed both before and after them.

Respecting the earlier evidence great caution is no doubt necessary. I cannot pretend to have said the last word upon a subject so difficult. But I have done my best to place the reader in the position to draw his own conclusions by giving careful transcriptions of the original text of the documents chiefly relied upon, side by side with the translations. And I trust their interest and importance will justify the use I have made of them.

I am much indebted to the officials in the Public Record Office and the Manuscript Department of the British Museum for help ungrudgingly given in connection with the documents under their charge.

I have not often in this volume referred to the conclusions of previous inquirers, because I was unwilling to appear in any way to write in a controversial spirit ; but this is no reason why I should not here fully acknowledge the value of Mr. A. Neobard Palmer's excellent work, all the more striking because it has been confined mainly to facts which have come within his own local knowledge and researches. Nor have I neglected to consult the more extended, but at the same time more speculative, work of the late Mr. H. Lewis.

I am aware that to the Celtic scholar the work

of an economic inquirer, making no pretence to a knowledge of the Welsh language, will in itself have the appearance of presumption. But if his taste should be offended by the avoidance of any attempt to translate the spelling used in the documents into modern Welsh, and by the use of English plurals to words which in such a connection become technical terms, his anger will, I hope, be disarmed by the candour with which the writer's ignorance of the language is frankly confessed.

I have to thank my friend, Professor Rhys, for many useful hints given, and the avoidance thereby of some of the linguistic pitfalls to which a stranger to the Welsh language was necessarily liable.

I trust that shortcomings of the kind above alluded to will not prevent the reader from appreciating the full weight of whatever economic conclusions may be legitimately drawn from the evidence itself.

It is not necessary to dwell upon the value of a substantial knowledge of the facts of one tribal system as a key with which to unlock the riddles of others. Nor is it necessary to point out the importance of a knowledge of the Tribal System, wherever found, as an almost universal factor in the early development of European society, and in the formation of mediæval institutions.

In conclusion, I wish to acknowledge the invaluable and constant help I have received from my son, whose study of the remains of the tribal system amongst the Greeks will, I hope, shortly be published, and form a useful contribution to the subject.

I have also to express my gratitude for the encouragement received from other fellow-workers in Economic History in the course of the studies which have resulted in this volume.

F. S.

THE HERMITAGE, HITCHIN:
March 1895.

CONTENTS.

CHAPTER I.

THE LAND SYSTEM IN ANGLESEY, AS DESCRIBED IN THE EXTENTS.

CHAPTER II.

THE DENBIGH EXTENT OF 8 EDWARD III. THE WELES AND GAVELLS OF TRIBESMEN.

CHAPTER III.

THE STRUCTURE OF TRIBAL SOCIETY.

CHAPTER IV.

THE STRUCTURE OF TRIBAL SOCIETY—(continued).

CHAPTER V.

THE RELATION TO THE TRIBE OF STRANGERS IN BLOOD.

CHAPTER VI.

CHIEFTAINSHIP IN THE TRIBE.

CHAPTER VII.

THE TRIBAL SYSTEM AND THE CHURCH.

CHAPTER VIII.

APPENDICES (see SEPARATE TABLE OF CONTENTS)

LIST OF MAPS.

CHAPTER I.

THE LAND SYSTEM IN ANGLESEY, AS DESCRIBED IN THE EXTENTS.

I. THE CYMWDS AND CANTREFS OF ANGLESEY.

In order to secure a firm basis from which to work backwards from the known to the unknown, it is proposed to commence the inquiry by the examination of a typical and well-known Welsh district as described in the various surveys or Extents made since the final conquest of North Wales.

The Isle of Anglesey presents a convenient geographical area for the purpose, and the so-called Manor of *Aberffraw*, on the south coast of it, a remarkably good example of a so-called 'manorial' unit.

Several Extents of the island are extant in the Public Record Office and elsewhere, the earliest being made in 22 Edward I. (A.D. 1294) only a few years after the conquest.[1]

The Isle of Anglesey, according to the Extents, was divided into three *cantrefs*, each of them embracing two *cymwds*.[2]

In each cantref a chieftain's residence, called a

---

[1] See Appendix A.

[2] The cantref of *Aberffraw* included the two cymwds of *Malltraeth* and *Llivon* or *Lywan*.

manor, formed a centre for the dependent *villæ* or hamlets scattered over the area of the two cymwds.

The Manor of Aberffraw was one of these central manors, and is of special interest as the royal seat, from early times, of the Princes of North Wales (successors of Cunedda and his sons), till the final defeat of Prince Llewelyn and the annexation to England in 1282.

These describe services before the conquest.

The earliest Extents describe the condition of things on the so-called Manors of Anglesey after the conquest. But from the result of a petition made in the year 1305, and repeated in 1314, it appears that the services mentioned in the survey of 22 Edward I. were the services *before* the conquest— *i.e.* the services by ancient Welsh custom under the native Welsh princes, and not fresh ones imposed after the conquest. In this petition the villeins of the Manor of Penros complained that a mistake had been made in the former 'Extent,' and the answer to the petition was the grant of a new inquiry to be made on the spot by the Justice of North Wales, 'who caused to come before him the best people to know and certify to him what were the customs and services which the said villeins made and ought to make in the time of the Princes of Wales.'[1]

The services, therefore, described in the earliest Extent, although it was made after the conquest, may be taken as the services of the tenants under Llewelyn and his predecessors.

The cantref of *Rhos* included the two cymwds of *Menay* and *Tyndaethwy*. The cantref of *Kemmeys* contained the two cymwds of *Talybolion* and *Turkelyn*.

[1] *Rolls Parl.* 8 Ed. III. i. 308, and small parchment schedule sewn on to the Roll of the Survey of 1294, and see Appendix A c.

I. of ANGLESEY
Showing
CANTREFS & CYMWDS
English Miles.

Opposite p. 2.

F. S. Weller.

So far everything is clear.

But the Extent was taken by Norman officials, who saw what was to be seen with Norman eyes, and recorded such facts as they found in the legal Latin of Norman lawyers with an admixture of such Welsh terms as defied easy translation.

When, therefore, in their description of the four head 'manors,' as they called them, of the cymwds and cantrefs of Anglesey, an attempt was made to press them into the mould of Norman common forms, it is very likely, indeed, that they made too rapid a generalisation of their main features according to *a priori* conceptions of what a manor ought to be, and it becomes needful to discriminate between the facts and the terms in which they may be stated.

The Extent which enters most fully into details, included in the ' Record of Carnarvon,' affords at once an instance in point. It was made not only after the conquest, but also unfortunately after the Black Death, and thus after the rearrangements and alterations inevitably following a great depopulation. It contains many incidental marks which show that Wales had suffered with the rest of the world in this great catastrophe.

The makers of this Extent describe the head manors of the cantrefs of Anglesey as *de trina natura*, and, knowing the Welsh love of triads, this might at first sight be taken as a specially Welsh characteristic. But closer examination leads to the conclusion that the surveyors were using terms of their own, and classifying the tenants under three heads for purposes of their own, rather than describing a triple constitution necessarily belonging to the Welsh system under Welsh chieftainship. It is well to clear out of the way at the outset this otherwise misleading generalisation of the makers of the ' Record of Carnarvon.'

Both the *Manerium de Kemmeys* and that of *Penros* are stated to be *de trina natura*—*i.e.* there are said to be in them people called [1]—

> 1. *Gwir Male,* or people paying ' mal,' or money tribute.
> 2. *Gwir Gweith,* or people doing services or work.
> 3. *Gwir Tir Borth,* or people on ' Board land.'

These two manors are the centres of the two cymwds of *Talybolion* and *Turkelyn* combined in one cantref, and are therefore probably described in the same terms by the same hand. But the manor of *Rosfair*, in the cymwd of *Menay*, though also described as *de trina natura*, is said to contain the following three classes of tenants,[2] viz.—

> 1. *Puri Nativi vocati mairdreve.*
> 2. *Alii Nativi qui se dicunt esse liberos nativos.*
> 3. *Alii Nativi vocati Gardynemen.*

If the *liberi nativi* of Rosfair be taken as equivalent to the *Gwir Male* of Kemmeys and Penros, and the *puri nativi* of Rosfair as equivalent to the *Gwir Gweith* of the other manors, still the *trina natura*, as a uniform system, breaks down in the third class. The tenants on *tir borth* hold ' gavells,' and pay from 12*s.* 7*d.* to 13*s.* 4*d.* each, and 5*s.* relief and 2*s. amobr*, while the *Gardynemen* of Rosfair pay only from 8*d.* to 2*s.* each, and their relief is only 2*s.* and *amobr* 2*s.*

---

[1] *Record of Carnarvon*, pp. 63, 64, and p. 70.　　　[2] *Id.* p. 83.

There is apparently no analogy between the Rosfair cottagers with gardens and the tenants on ' *tir borth* ' of the other manors with their ' gavells,' and a further examination into the details leads to the conclusion that the ' triple nature ' of these manors is one of Norman classification, and did not represent a real feature of the Welsh tribal system.

Whilst declining, therefore, to be misled by the too rapid generalisation of the Norman makers of the Extent contained in the ' Record of Carnarvon,' and still recurring again and again to it for valuable details, we turn to the earlier Extent [1] of 22 Edward I. as that most likely to represent the condition of Anglesey before the conquest.

In the description of the manors this Extent makes no mention of the *trina natura*, but English manorial precedents are nevertheless closely followed.

II. THE SO-CALLED MANOR OF ABERFFRAW.

Commencing with the Prince's own manor of Aberffraw, we get an unbiassed and direct introduction into our subject.

The village of Aberffraw is placed at the mouth of the river *Ffraw* just where it ceases to be tidal and begins to pass through a triangular reach of sands into the sea.

The Aberffraw mill is placed on the river, where doubtless it has always been, just above high tide.

---

[1] Chapter House, County Bags, Wallia, Box 143 B, No. 34. *Extent of Anglesey*, 22 Ed. I. (13 Mch. 1294), Public Record Office, now | Rentals and Surveys, Roll, 768. Another copy, Rentals and Surveys, Roll, 769. And see App. A a.

The church is ancient, for it contains a fine old Norman arch and stands on an ancient site on the high ground above the river. Near to this was the palace of the Welsh princes. Between this and the river lie now, as centuries ago, the little strips or gardens of the cottagers, now called ' lleiniau,' and divided by turf balks.

The territory included in what was called the manor in the Extents was divided into two parts by the river *Ffraw*, and the broad, sandy, and marshy tract on the east side of it (called the *Tywyn Aber- ffraw*) runs far into the land, nearly up to the ' *Llyn Coron*,' from which the *Ffraw* river flows.

There was a second mill on the stream above the Llyn called *Dyndroval*, and a third on another stream N.W. of Aberffraw called *Melin-y-Bont*.

The western portion of the manor lies behind the site of the palace, and forms a blunt promontory between the Ffraw river and the next bay. It also extends to the north a few miles inland.[1]

The eastern portion makes a similar promontory between the *Tywyn Aberffraw* and the tidal estuary of the river *Cefni*. But this eastern part of the manor is abruptly cut off from extension inland by the parish of St. Cadwaladr, which, apparently from the sixth or seventh century, by grant of the ancestors of the Welsh princes, was handed over to the Church, and freed from tribal or other secular services to them.

One of the features of the position of the manor

---

[1] The boundaries are given at the end of the Survey of 1608, Land Revenue, Record Office, | Ancient Surveys, vol. 17 (24), f. 62.

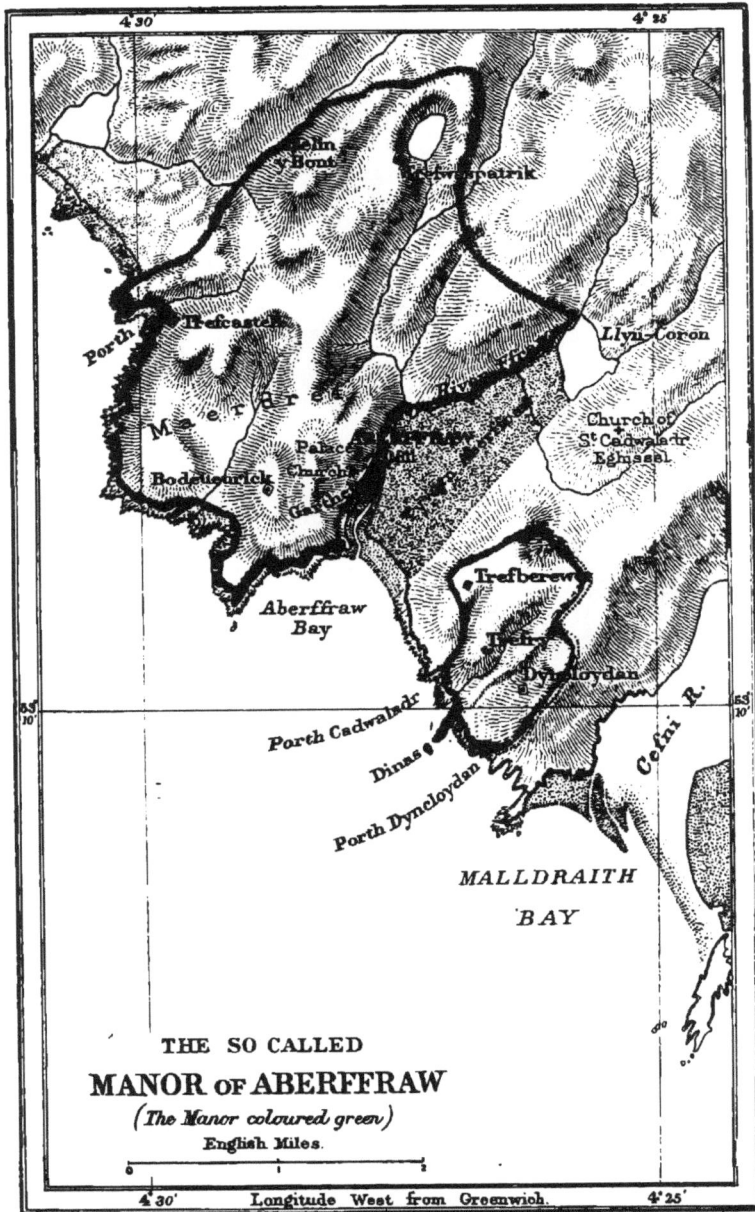

THE SO CALLED

MANOR OF ABERFFRAW

(The Manor coloured green)

English Miles.

Longitude West from Greenwich.

F. S. Weller.

of Aberffraw is the access to the sea all along the
rocky coast for small boats in the numerous ' porths '
or natural harbours running up between ridges of
rock and ending in a sandy beach.

The parish of Cadwaladr has its own little porth Porths
and places
of refuge.
—*porth Cadwaladr*—and each member of the manor
near the coast had its own porth in the same way
bearing its name. It sometimes also had its own
place of refuge for cattle in a rocky peninsula
running out into the sea, called a *dinas* and bearing
its name.

There are several manuscript Extents or surveys The
several
Extents
of the Manor of Aberffraw more or less in detail
and bearing date 1294, 1339, 1351, 1352 ('Record
of Carnarvon'), and 1608 (see Appendix A).

The various members or hamlets of the manor
are, with little exception, traceable throughout this
remarkable series, and they are still easily recognised
on the ground and on the Ordnance map in the
names of the most substantial farmhouses of the
modern estates.

The Extents before the Black Death describe first The
demesne.
The
Maerdref
and
Garthey.
what in the Domesday Survey would have been
called the lord's *demesne*, including 5 carucates of
land, 3 mills, 2 meadows, and the fishery. This
demesne land embraced what the later Extents
describe as the hamlets of *Garthey* (consisting of
14 gardens near the church), of *Maerdref* (the *tref*
under the *land maer* of the Welsh Codes—the
home farm of the manor), and *Trefcastell.*[1] The

---

[1] Trefcastell is described in the Extent of 1851 as part of the *terra dominica.* Its tenants at that time occupied one of the carucates.

continuity as between the Extents may be thus stated :—

1608	1352 *Record of Carnarvon*	1351	1339	1294
Garther and *Mayerdref*	*Garthey* *Mairdref*	4 carucates 3 mills 2 meadows	5 carucates 3 mills 2 meadows	5 carucates 3 mills 2 meadows
Treffcastell	*Drefcastell*	piscaria *Trefcastell* occupying 5th car.	piscaria	piscaria

The free tenants.

Under the head of free tenants are the following holdings described in the 'Record of Carnarvon' as 'Weles' (literally 'beds'), being tribal homesteads :—

1608	1352	1351	1339	1294
Free tenants	(Free Weles) Wele Porthorion Wele Simond Wele Bodeueurik Wele Trewaspadrik Gavel Sayr	— — Bodeueryk Trewaspatrik —	— — Bodeueuryk Trewaspatrik —	— — Bodeueurick Trefwaspatryk —

The un-free out-lying hamlets.

Lastly the *unfree and outlying hamlets*, not on the demesne, but situated on the other side of the river in the eastern portion of the manor, were as follows :—

1608	1352	1351	1339	1294
Treberfeth Trefry Tinlloydan Keventreffro	Drefberneth Trefry Dynloidan Kendrefrowe	Trefberwet — Dynthladan Keuentrefau	Trefberwyth — Dynthlodan Keuyntreffrau	Trefberewet — Dyncloydan Weuentefraw

It is curious to notice that the Norman officials just after the conquest confine themselves to Norman terms, and that such Welsh terms as 'Garthey' and 'Maerdref' and 'Weles' and 'Gavells' seem to revive in the Extents made after the Black Death.

This is explained by the remarkable tenacity of Welsh custom and the extraordinary continuity secured by it from one Extent to the other for 300 years after the conquest.

These surviving terms help to bridge over the periods before and after the conquest, and so to connect the Codes and the Extents.

One feature common to both is the location of the free and bond tenants in separate hamlets or groups of homesteads. Each class of hamlets must therefore be separately examined.

III. THE FREE TENANTS OF ABERFFRAW.

The free tenants are described in the 'Record of Carnarvon' as occupying *Weles.* We shall see hereafter that the *wele*[1] or *gwely* was, strictly speaking, rather the family or kindred occupying the hamlet than the hamlet itself, and that mostly a hamlet was occupied by several *weles.*

In the Extents the old food rents of the free tenants or *weles* had already been commuted into money payments. And these money payments were evidently treated as not charges upon persons but permanent charges upon the holdings in occupation at the time of the conquest. They were scrupulously respected by the conquerors, and have mostly been left unaltered from that time to this. The amounts of these rents are practically the same, even to the small details, in the Extent of 1294 and that of 1339 half a century later. And comparing these with the later surveys and Extents the evidence is

---

[1] Pronounced ' *welly* ' as ' *gwely.*'

conclusive of the literal truth of the historical statement that the rents of the free tenants remained
unaltered by the conquest of Wales.

The rents of free tenants.

The rents of the free tenants in the Extent of
1294 are stated as follows :—

	£	s.	d.
Of Aberffraw itself . . .	1	9	8
Of Bodeueurick . . .	0	15	11
Of Trewaspatrik . . .	0	10	0
	£2	15	7

They are the same in the Inquisition of 1339.
They are the same in the Extent of 1351 after the
Black Death.

They are the same in total in the 'Record of
Carnarvon' in 1352, though somewhat vàried in the
classification of them and increased by two additional
items.

The record commences with the statement that
there were 4 *free weles*, viz. :—

	£	s.	d.
Wele Porthorion paying . . .	1	1	0
Wele Simond ,, . .	0	3	2
Wele Bodeueurik ,, . .	0	17	11
Wele Trefwaspadrik ,, . .	0	13	6
	£2	15	7

exactly the old amount ; to which are added :—

	£	s.	d.
Gavell Sayr (carpenter's gavell)	0	3	8
4 bovates (escheat) . . . {	0	3	6
	0	1	0
Making the total . .	£3	3	9

They remain the same for centuries.

Finally in the Survey of 1608 the *Summa Totalis*
of the 'Rents of Assize of Free Tenants' = 3*l.* 3*s.* 9*d.*

These money payments are the amounts into

which the ancient food rents of the free tribesmen were commuted, and the continuity, as already pointed out, shows that they were regarded as charges on particular lands or holdings, and not personal charges. Many of them are still payable as ancient quit rents throughout North Wales.

Besides these money payments there were, however, customary services. Although the Extent of 1294 mentions no services beyond the money rents of the free tenants, there is other evidence that services were due from them. These are set out at length in the ' Record of Carnarvon.' [1]

The *Wele Porthorion* (or Homestead of the Gate-keepers) did suit at the Courts of the cymwd and cantref. The *heredes* of it were liable to payment of a fine or relief of 10*s.* on the entry of a new tenant, and an *amobr* of the same amount on the marriage of their daughters. For their grinding they went to the Prince's mill at Aberffraw. There they ground their wheat and malt without toll, and all other grain at a toll of $\frac{1}{30}$ measure. And they made and repaired one *vechme* of the wall of the lord's manor house on one side of the gate and another *vechme* of wall on the other side of the gate. And if the Prince were at home they had from him meat and drink for nine men whilst making the wall.

The *heredes* of *Wele Simond* were liable to the same suit at Court and mill, and the same amounts of *relief* and *amobr*, but did no work on the wall.

The *heredes* of *Wele Bodeueurik* (if the early spelling *Bodeueurik* may be trusted, possibly the Home-

---

[1] *Record of Carnarvon,* p. 48.

CHAP. I.   stead of the Smith—literally, of the *Goldsmith*) and
the *Wele Trewaspatrick* paid the same suit and relief
&c., and instead of work on the wall were liable to
the *kilgh hebbogothion* or service in connection with
the hawking expeditions of the Prince or his chief
falconer.

Of the
carpenter.

The *heredes* of the *Gavell* of the *Sayr* or carpenter
were liable to the same *relief* and *amobr*, but not
liable to the work on the palace wall or the hawking
service.

These homesteads seem to be those of officers
of the Court, and may well have been direct survivals of the times before the conquest.

They are
officers
of the
Prince.

The amount of the payment for relief (the Norman
equivalent for the Welsh *ebediw* or death fee) and the
amobr or maiden fee payable on marriage or incon-
tinence, viz. 10*s.*, suggests that these free tenants
on the demesne were subordinate officers of the
Court holding their land upon free tenure for their
services.[1]

The holding of the *Porthorion* or gatekeepers at
the Porter's Lodge was probably a survival from
before the conquest.   Though no prince now lived at
the Palace of Aberffraw, its walls were not at once
allowed to decay.   It continued as a Court and a
prison if not as a palace.   The porter (*porthaur*)
under the Venedotian Code was an important official.
He had his dwelling in the gateway, and had charge
of the great gate,[2] and in his house lodged the King's

---

[1] The *ebediw* and *amobr*
of the principal officers of the
palace were 20*s.*, of the subordinate officers 10*s.*, of inferior persons 5*s.*—*Ancient Laws of Wales,*
ii. p. 609.

[2] *Venedotian Code, id.* i. p. 26.

and the Queen's ' door-wards.'[1] He was to summon
the men of the *Maerdref* to work. His land and the
land of the door-wards were free by reason of their
office, and having the responsibility of the gate it was
natural (though not stated in the Code) that the
responsibility of keeping the wall on both sides of
the gate in repair should rest upon the gatekeepers
and be attached to their land.[2]

The smiths and the carpenters may also well be
survivals. According to the Venedotian Code, the
smith of the Court had to do all needful work for
the palace (except certain things) and had his land
free on account of his office. His work could hardly
be dispensed with, whether the shoeing of horses or
the mending of the ploughs of the *Maerdref*, or of
the hinges of the gates, or the fastening or unfastening
of the prisoners' chains, all of which were items of
his duty under the Codes.[3]

There is a small fragment of the Court Roll of
Aberffraw, dated 1346, at the Record Office,[4] which
shows that the porters still had charge of the prison,
for it contains an entry of a fine on the porters for
allowing prisoners to escape.

The examination of another Extent will elicit
further information respecting the free tenants or
successors of the Welsh free tribesmen. The Extents

---

[1] *Venedotian Code*, *id.* i. p. 46.
i. p. 57.

[2] *Id.* i. p. 66 &c.

[3] *Id.* i. p. 72, 14, &c. There
were Smiths on other manors, as
well as other officers. Thus on
the manor of Penros in Anglesey
there were *gavells* of the Carpenter (*Sair*), of the Smiths (*Govent*),
of the Gatekeepers (*Porthorion*)
and of the Squires (*Huysorion*).

[4] *Crt. Rolls*, Bundle 215. No. 13
(Record Office). See App. A d.

of Aberffraw reveal mainly the relations to the chieftain of those who were subordinate court officials.

IV. THE SO-CALLED 'VILLANI' AND 'NATIVI' OF ABERFFRAW.

Some of the so-called *villani* or *nativi* of the Extent of 1294 were located on the *demesne land* of the Prince, and others in detached hamlets.

The demesne, according to the Extent of 1294, consisted of five carucates and two meadows.

The villani or nativi of the Maerdref. From the other Extents we learn that it included the hamlets of the *Maerdref* and *Garther* and *Trefcastell*.

The services of the tenants of all these are described under the heading *The Villani of Aberffraw*, *i.e.* the villani of the demesne, as apart from the outlying hamlets in which other groups of *villani* were placed.

The cottiers' gardens. The gardens of the *villani* or cottier tenants included under the head *Garther* in the later surveys can hardly be other than those already mentioned as still divided by their turf balks and lying under the shadow of the church and formerly under the palace walls, close to the village where their ' cubiculi ' or cabins were huddled together very much as the cottages are now in the present village.

They are described in the ' Record of Carnarvon ' as consisting of[1] :—

> 14 gardens of *terra nativa* paying rents varying from 16*d.* to 7*s.* They did suit at the lord's mill at Aberffraw. They pay on account of *staurum*, and do carriage service. [There is no mention of *relief* or *amobr.* Probably they were people too small to have to pay on these accounts.]

[1] *Record of Carnarvon*, p. 49.

The rest of the demesne consisted of the *Maerdref* and *Trefcastell* with the five carucates (say 600 acres) of land. The *Maerdref* was the Prince's home farm, and *Trefcastell*, with the one carucate attached to it in the later Extents, was probably the central farm homestead of the demesne. It now survives as a substantial stone-built farmhouse with stone farm buildings forming a square behind it. It stands close by the *porth* at the extreme western edge of the Manor. The porth is a remarkably good one, affording more shelter and room than any other, and, as the name probably implies a stone-built homestead above the ordinary strength, it will be hardly wrong to consider *Trefcastell* as the farm homestead of the *Maerdref* cultivated by the ' *villani* of Aberffraw ' under the management and responsibility of the ' *land maer* ' of the Welsh Code.[1]

As we have seen, the porter was to summon the men of the *Maerdref* to their work, showing perhaps that they lived in the village close to the palace gates.

But it was the *land maer* who had to superintend the ploughing and who was generally responsible for the services of the men of the *Maerdref*. The following is the general description of their services in the Venedotian Code :—[2]

> ' The men of the maertrev are to make a kiln and a barn for the King, and to supply them when it may be necessary. They are to pay the tunc (money dues) of their land into the hand of the land maer, and they are to support him twice in the year. They are to thresh, to kiln dry, to reap, and to harrow, and to

---

[1] *Venedotian Code*, i. p. 68. Trefcastell was described in the *Record of Carnarvon* as in the hands of tenants who paid 60*s.* of rent, and the same rent was named by the Crown on the sale to the City of London in 1628.

[2] *Id.* i. p. 194. The word translated ' King ' is *brenhin*, meaning the Prince or head chieftain.

mow hay, and provide straw, and fuel for the fire, as often as the King visits the Court, and when the King comes to the Court they are to present the King, according to their ability, either with sheep, or lambs, or kids, or cheese, or butter, or milk.'

Services of the men of the Maerdref.

Let us compare this general statement of these services with those described in the Extent. The latter inform us how at the date of the conquest the *land maer* of Prince Llewelyn regulated his *Maerdref* at Aberffraw in order to supply the wants of his palace and household.

The services of the men of the *Maerdref* and *Garthey*, as described in the Extent of 1294, may be summarised thus :—

First, their ' rents of assize ' [*i.e. tunc*] amounted to	8*s.* 8*d.*
Second, they had to supply 10½ crannocs of wheat.	
8 ,, oatmeal.	
4 ,, barley meal.	
And these dues were valued at	48*s.* 7*d.*

[These, apparently, were paid from the results of their joint ploughing, which it was the land maer's duty to regulate.]

Group of nine *villani*

Then there was a group of 9 villani who rendered jointly the milk of 3 cows, 4½ sheep, 9 lambs, butter, 150 eggs, 27 hens, valued at   16*s.* 8*d.*

and of six,

There was another group of 6 tenements (then empty), but from which had been due jointly 3 sheep, 6 lambs, 9 hens, butter, 100 eggs, valued at   5*s.* 1*d.*

and of nine,

There was another group of 9 villani, rendering jointly 27 hens worth   2*s.* 3*d.*

Also 3 days' work at cutting corn, receiving each a loaf a day =   2*s.* 3*d.*

The villani, as a body, also had to supply fire and straw in the Royal Court, worth   30*s.* 0*d.*

and of fifteen.

Besides this, a group of 15 villani had to find in the autumn 300 day-works, by which [in addition to 80 day-works found by the *villani forenseci* of the cantref] the land of the *maerdref* was tilled   66*s.* 9*d.*

Also 600 day-works of men and horses at harrowing   75*s.* 0*d.*

The villani also had to find 10 crannocs of oats for the horses   6*s.* 8*d.*

Making the total value of their payments and services   £18 1*s.* 6*d.*

This shows clearly that the so-called villein payments and services were regarded, like those of the
free tenants, as due from the land or groups of holdings and not as personal charges upon single occupants.

The 'Record of Carnarvon' gives the further information that the *villani* of the *maerdref*

> 'do suit at the lord's mill of *Bout* (*i.e.* Bont) and *Traith.*
> [The demesne land lying west and north of the village, the mill
> of *Bont* would be their nearest mill.] Further, they carry timber
> and millstones within the Isle of Anglesey at their own charges.
> And they do joint work on the watercourse of the said mills. And
> they pay for relief and amobr 2s., if able, but not otherwise.
> And they pay Kilgh Raglot. And they do the lord's carrying.
> And they pay a share of *staurum*, and nothing more.' [1]

These actual services of the so-called *villani* of
Aberffraw correspond remarkably closely with the
services normally due from the *aillts* and men of
the Prince's *maerdref* as described in the Venedotian
Code above cited.

There is another point mentioned in the 'Record
of Carnarvon' requiring attention, viz. the tenure of
these tenants of the *maerdref*.

The Extent of 1294 has already disclosed that
the *villani* of the *maerdref* were arranged in groups.
There were two groups each of nine *villani* making
certain contributions. There was another group of
fifteen *villani* who had jointly to find 300 day-works.
These groups suggest very strongly arrangements for
joint liability.

But an entry in the 'Record of Carnarvon' is more
explicit. It runs thus [2] :—

> There is [in Aberffraw] another hamlet called *Mairdref*. And
> it is of such a nature that if there were only one sufficient tenant
> he would be charged with the whole rent.'

---

[1] *Record of Carnarvon*, p. 49.   [2] *id.*

C

In other parts of the ' Record of Carnarvon,' land under this joint liability is said to be *de natura de trefgevery*, and this at once connects it with the normal form of *villein tenancy* (if for the present we may so call it) in the Welsh Codes.

The Venedotian Code[1] states that the ' maer and canghellor are to regulate the King's *aillts* upon their *tyr kÿurÿw*[2] or *register land*.' And in another passage it states as follows :—

> ' Geldable land is not to be divided between brothers, but the maer and canghellor are to share it equally between all in the trev, and on that account it is called *tir kÿurÿw*. And there is to be no extinguished erw (*i.e.* escheated to the lord) in the register land ; but if there be an erw of that description in it the maer and canghellor are to share it in common among all, to one as well as to another, and no one is to remove from his legal tyddyn (or homestead) if an equivalent can be obtained for it of other land.
>
> ' And as we have said above respecting the other, so the maer is to proceed as to the land of the *maertrev*, leaving everyone in his tyddyn according as he best may.'[3]

From these passages it appears that the land of the *maerdref* was of the nature of such regulated land (*i.e.* in the nature of *trefgevery*). All the *aillts*, whether of the *maerdref* or of separate hamlets, were to be thus regulated, and those of the *maerdref* of the Prince were to be regulated by his *land maer*.

Accordingly, the ' Record of Carnarvon' describes not only the *maerdref*, but also the outlying hamlets of *nativi* as of the nature of *trefgevery*.

To these outlying hamlets attention may now be turned.

---

[1] i. p. 191.

[2] See ii. p. 293, where a *tref* of such regulated land is called *tref gyffry*.

[3] *Venedotian Code*, i. p. 169.

V. THE OUTLYING HAMLETS OF ABERFFRAW.

Passing now from the demesne and western portion of the manor to what are called in the Extents the Hamlets of the manor, they are thus described in the Extent of 1294 :—

The Hamlet of *Trefberewet* is described as a group of nine *villani* rendering :—

Group of nine villani,

	£	s.	d.
In rents	0	9	8
4 crannocks of barley meal .	0	5	4
9 sheep	0	4	6
9 lambs	0	1	6
Butter	0	2	3
180 eggs	0	0	7
9 hens	0	0	9
Work, 161 days . . .	1	16	2½
	£3	0	9½

From the 'Record of Carnarvon' we learn that this hamlet was of the nature of *trefgevery*, and there is mention also of their services :—

holding in trefgevery.

> The tenants did suit to the Aberffraw mill, did carrying of timber and millstones to the mill, repaired the ditch, and did joint work at the watercourse [just as the men of the *maerdref* did at the mill of *Bont*], and they paid *propartem stauri*, and they did carriage service for man and horse at 2*d.* They paid for *relief* and *amobr* 5*s.*, and *kilgh hebbogothion*.[1]

The dues from the Hamlet of *Dyncloyden* are described in the Extent of 1294 thus :—

---

[1] *Record of Carnarvon*, p. 49.

	s.	*d.*
Rent of one villein, viz. of *David Hibernicus*, who pays half of corn and milk, which is called *merionyth* [1].	2	0
The sons of Gregory ap Llewellyn pay :—		
1 cran. wheat, 4 cran. oats	8	6
2 sheep	1	0
2 lambs	0	4
Butter	0	6
40 eggs	0	1½
6 hens	0	6
30 days' work	8	9
De *Pellipariis*, ½ cran. barley meal, ½ sheep, ½ lamb, 10 *cunæ* of butter, and ½ hen	1	1½
7 days' work	0	11¼
	18	9¼

The 'Record of Carnarvon' describes this hamlet as *de terra nativa domini*, and the tenants as doing the same services as those of the hamlet of *Trefberewet*. The farm still bearing the name of *Dynloidan* lies near the sea, and has its own 'porth' and 'dinas' as already mentioned.

The dues from the Hamlet of *Weuentefrau* were :—

	s.	*d.*
Rent of *villani*	3	4
1½ lamb, 30 *cunæ* of butter, 5½ hens, 1 *istor bladi*, 18 days' work	1	6½
	4	10½

They answer as to meryonnyth with the *villani* of *Trefberewet*.

This hamlet, under the name of *Kendrefrowe*, is described in the 'Record of Carnarvon' as of the

---

[1] A somewhat similar custom of letting out cattle to tenants for the summer, reserving as rent a share in the milk, is still known in some parts of Wales, under the very similar name of *maeruriaeth*, or *cadw havod*. See Mr. L. Thomas's *Report on Labour in Wales*, b. ii. p. 64. See also use of the word *maeronaeth* for 'dairy-farming,' in *Welsh Laws*, ii. p. 515, and of the word *maerty* in Monmouthshire for dairy-house.

nature of *trefgevery*, like the *maerdref* and *Tref-berewet*, and as doing similar services.

Finally, there is a clause which states that all the *villani* of the Prince of Aberffraw pay every year for the work of the animals of the house 2*s.*

All these outlying hamlets appendant to Aberffraw were thus *villein* hamlets, according to the Extents, regulated by the Prince's officers, and in a special way connected with the Prince's estate or manor, more so apparently than were those of the rest of the cantref.

VI. DUES AND' SERVICES FROM THE REST OF THE CANTREF.

The rest of the cantref—*i.e.* the territory outside the boundaries of the Prince's manor or estate, and scattered over the two cymwds—consisted of what are called in the survey *villæ*, which seem to be groups of homesteads, some of them of free tenants and some of them of *villani*, and occasionally of both.

Separate villæ of free tenants and villani.

The *free tenants* and *villani* of these *trefs* or *villæ* paid as under :—

	£	*s.*	*d.*
In rents of assize from free tenants . . .	36	4	8
In rents, corn, oatmeal, butter, eggs, hens, &c., and for the '*potura*' of 1860 men and 403 horses and of dogs, from villein tenants, amounting in value to	23	6	0
The *villani* of the cantref also furnished special dues, and gave a day's ploughing once a year, valued at	4	6	11
The perquisites of the Court amounted to . .	2	0	0
Making a total of	£65	17	7

VII. THE RELATIVE BURDEN OF THE DUES AND SERVICES.

Giraldus Cambrensis described Anglesey as containing the best corn-growing land in Wales.[1]

The Welsh, he says, ploughed for their oats in March and April, and for wheat in summer and winter, yoking to their ploughs seldom fewer than four oxen. The four oxen were yoked abreast, as in the Isle of Man and in Scotland, and Giraldus mentions that the driver walked backwards in front of the oxen, as was the case also in Scotland.[2]

Bearing in mind that Anglesey was an agricultural as well as pastoral district, some light may be obtained from a comparison of the number of cattle in the manor and hamlets of Aberffraw, according to an assessment to a ' Fifteenth ' made early in the fourteenth century,[3] and in the parish of Aberffraw in 1893, according to the Agricultural Returns.

In the fourteenth century there were in all sixty-eight holdings of persons having cattle. Probably there are not as many at the present time.[4]

Only seven of these in the fourteenth century possessed a full yoke of four or more oxen; the rest must, therefore, have joined with others in the ploughing, unless they used horses or cows to make up the plough team.

---

[1] *Descr. Kamb.* C. I. vi.

[2] C. I. viii. and xvii., and see Train's *Isle of Man*, ii. p. 24.

[3] Treasury of Receipt, Miscell. $\frac{4A}{4}$, Public Record Office. Now Lay Subsidy $\frac{242}{44}$. See Appendix A f.

[4] In 1890 the number of small agricultural holdings under 50 acres, but excluding allotments, was 43.

The numbers of cattle, horses, and sheep at the two dates were as follows :—

		1820–40	1893
Oxen . . .	(valued at 5*s.* per head)	137	
Cows . . .	„ 3*s.* 4*d.* „	262	
Averia,[1] 3 yrs. old	„ 2*s.* 6*d.* „	38	
„ 2 „ .	„ 2*s.* „	91	
Total of cattle	. . . .	——528	1,711
Horses . .	„ 5*s.* „	71	
Jumenta (Mares)	„ 5*s.* „	36	
Total of horses	. . . . .	——107	242
Sheep . . .	„ 6*d.* „	735	2,913
Total . .	. . . . .	1,370	4,866

As regards the kinds of corn grown, it has already been seen that the payments of the *nativi* included wheat, oats, and barley.

On the day when the record above mentioned was made the quantities of these three kinds of corn on hand were as follows :—

115 crannocs of wheat valued at 2*s.* 6*d.* per crannoc.
307   „   oats   „   2*s.*   „
70   „   barley   „   1*s.* 4*d.*   „
492 crannocs in all.

It is obvious, therefore, that oats were the chief crop on the Aberffraw manor in the fourteenth century.

The total value of the cattle and corn calculated at the above prices amounted to 188*l.*

It is most likely that for purposes of taxation the assessment would be made after harvest before the produce was consumed. Perhaps, therefore, it would be fair to take the total as representing the capital of the tenants in cattle and corn after harvest, and probably there would not be much other capital, for

Oats the chief crop.

Value of cattle and corn

---

[1] Cattle.

Chap. I.

repre-
senting
the chief
part of
the
tenant's
capital.

otherwise the assessors would have taken care to include it in their valuation, the fifteenth of which was to be taken as the tax.

What proportion, then, did the value of the dues and services bear to the amount of their capital in cattle and corn thus ascertained?

The value of the dues and services of the tenants of the manor of Aberffraw, according to the Extent of 1294, roughly summarised, amounted to the following :—

	£	s.	d.
Money payments of free tenants . . .	2	15	7
„ *villani* . . .	1	9	2
Payments in kind by *villani*	6	17	4
Value of services in work by the *villani* .	9	19	6
Total	21	1	7

The amount of the annual dues and services was, therefore, about one-ninth of the capital of the tenants in cattle and corn.

This rough estimate, however, must only be taken for what it is worth. For it must be remembered

Only a
part of
the
Prince's
income
from the
manor.

that no distinction is made between different classes of tenants, and that these dues and services were only a part of the income of the Prince from his so-called manor.

The following is a summary of the value of the manor in the Extent of 1294 :—

	£	s.	d.
5 carucates of land in the *maerdref* and demesne	7	10	0
The three mills produced 60 crannocs . .	6	0	0
The fisheries	0	15	4
Value of pasture	1	0	0
Perquisites of the Court	2	0	0
	£17	5	4
Dues and services of tenants . . .	21	1	7
	£38	6	11

Adding to this sum the revenue of the Prince from the rest of the cantref in which his royal residence was placed—viz. 65*l.* 17*s.* 7*d.*, towards which free tenants contributed rather more largely than the *nativi*, the total revenue of the Prince from the cantref amounted to 104*l.* 4*s.* 6*d.* The amount annually received from the three cantrefs of Anglesey was 483*l.* 10*s.* 11*d.*

Chap. I.
Total
revenue
from the
cantref,
and from
the whole
of
Anglesey.

VIII. SUMMARY OF THE EVIDENCE OF THE ANGLESEY EXTENTS.

The evidence of the extents of Anglesey taken alone may be summarised as follows :—

The Prince of North Wales had rights, which may be termed *Royal* rights, of progress, &c., for himself and his retinue, chief falconer, &c., over the cymwds and cantrefs of the whole of Anglesey, except in those cases in which portions may have been handed over by him or his ancestors to religious uses.

The
Prince's
rights of
progress,
&c.

The Prince had his own particular so-called manor, with its palace, courts, and demesne land. His home farm or *maerdref*, was worked by the so-called villein tenants of Aberffraw living close by his palace.

His
' manor.'

There were free tenants—some of them free by reason of their office, others free tribesmen settled on the estate—from whom he had money rents in lieu of the old food rents and services.

Free
tenants.

There were also groups of villein tenants on outlying parts of the manor holding in *trefgevery* like those of the *maerdref*.

Villein
tenants.

Scattered over the two cymwds of the cantref, were hamlets of free tenants, and other hamlets of villein tenants, all contributing rents and services, and the latter supplying provisions and day-works. The villein hamlets were apparently held, as a rule, in *trefgevery.*

A 'manor' in each cymwd, with its courts.

In each of the other cantrefs or cymwds there was also a so-called manor, with its courts, forming a centre for legal proceedings, as well as for the performance of services and payment of dues. And all the *villæ* or hamlets within the cantref were under the jurisdiction of its courts, excepting those under ecclesiastical exemption from secular services. But it does not appear from the Extents that there were usually outlying hamlets specially annexed to these manors, as in the case of the Prince's own manor of Aberffraw.

Each cymwd or cantref was thus an organised geographical and judicial unit, and where the Prince himself did not occupy the palace, or use it as a hunting lodge in his annual progress, it was probably occupied by a subordinate chieftain; but on this point, as all the rights of the chieftains were transferred in lump to the Prince of Wales, the Extents naturally throw little light.

Services not personal, but attached to the holdings.

Lastly a remarkable feature, prominent throughout the Extents, is the emphatic way in which the dues and services of both free and villein hamlets were regarded, not as personal services, but as attached to particular holdings or hamlets, so that they remained untouched either by the confiscations on the conquest or by the depopulation of the Black Death, and continued exactly the same for centuries after the conquest, till they came to be regarded as permanent quit rents, some of which are still col-

lected by the collectors of the Crown revenues under
the Department of the ' Woods and Forests.'

It may be added that the distinction between the free and villein hamlets was so deep and so marked that it was retained long after the conquest, and even long after the services of the bond hamlets had become commuted into fixed money rents. Even now, in the annual returns made to the ' Woods and Forests,' in some cases the rents of two classes of holdings, conjecturally, of the free and bond holdings of a district, are not only returned in separate lists, but even collected by officers with different names, the presumably free rents being collected and accounted for by a ' *beadle* ' and the others by a ' *prepositus* '; the latter being possibly the successor of the *land maer* of the Welsh codes, in the Latin version of which the word is translated *prepositus*.[1]

---

[1] I have to thank Mr. Russell Sowray, late of the ' Woods and Forests,' for this information. The return of 1892, from the Manor or Lordship of Harnuiniog, in Cardiganshire, is an instance of this.

CHAPTER II.

THE DENBIGH EXTENT OF 8 *EDWARD III. THE WELES AND GAVELLS OF TRIBESMEN.*

I. THE VALUE OF THE DENBIGH EXTENT.

CHAP. II. BEFORE proceeding to the direct evidence of the Codes and legal treatises—some of them of doubtful dates and authority—it is worth while to examine whether some further facts may not be obtained from the Extents as regards the structure of the tribe itself and the relation of the tribe and its kindreds to the land.

Further evidence required. The Anglesey Extents have given a pretty clear view of the scattered hamlets, some of them occupied by free tribesmen and others by so-called *villani* or *nativi*. They have naturally disclosed the relations of both classes of tenants to the chieftains, and the geographical arrangement of the hamlets in cymwds and cantrefs, rather than the internal structure of the tribe itself.

They have, indeed, disclosed that the free hamlets were occupied by *weles* and *gavells*—whatever these may have been—and that their 'heredes' were so and so, but we have yet to learn what a *wele* was

and what a *gavell* was, and in what relation each of
them stood to the tribe or the kindreds of which it
was composed.

Can this knowledge be obtained from the Extents?
If it could, it might prove an invaluable key to the
true understanding of the Codes.

It is worth while, therefore, to examine whether
the Extents afford actual examples from which may
be discovered what the *weles* and *gavells* of the free
tribesmen were.

The earliest Anglesey Extents are deficient in
detail, and do not supply the information.

The 'Record of Carnarvon,' as we have seen, is
much more ample in its details, but it has the great
disadvantage of having been made not only after the
conquest of Wales, but also after the ' Black Death.'
That great pains were taken to fulfil the terms of
the engagement that, with certain exceptions, the
services of free tenants and other Welsh customs
should remain unaltered by the conquest, has been
abundantly shown. But the devastations of the
Black Death were limited by no such condition,
and may well have played havoc with tribal arrangements.

Moreover, the Anglesey and Carnarvonshire district was, we are told by Giraldus Cambrensis, exceptionally *agricultural* in character, and may, therefore,
have advanced, before as well as after the conquest,
further than some other districts on the lines of
approach to the manorial system.

What is required, therefore, is a survey of a
pastoral district, in full detail, and made before the
'.Black Death.'

CHAP. II.

The Denbigh extent gives the required evidence.

The district included in the extent.

The Extent of the Castle and Honour of Denbigh,[1] made in 8 Edward III., seems to be the only one which meets the requirements of the case. It was made before the 'Black Death.' It relates to a mainly pastoral district which continued to a large extent under the rules of ancient custom. It gives the name of every tenant, and has, moreover, distinct reference to the condition of things both before and after the final conquest of North Wales.

It is hardly possible to over-estimate the value of this Extent for the purpose in hand.

The annexed map will show at a glance the geographical conditions of the district.

Broadly speaking, it is bounded by the mountains surrounding the valley of the *Clwyd*, with its tributaries the *Istrad* and the *Aled*, embracing also the valley of the *Dulas* which enters the sea independently.

This district, like Anglesey, was divided into cantrefs, and each of its two cantrefs was divided into two cymwds. The cymwds took their names from the rivers. The cantref of *Rowaynok* contained the cymwds of the farther and hither[2] *Aled—Ughalet* and *Ishalet*—and the cantref of *Ros* contained the cymwds of the farther and hither *Dulas—Ughdulas* and *Istulas*.

---

[1] 'Extenta Castri et Honoris de Dynbeigh facta per Hugonem de Beckele et per recognitionem tenencium singularum villatarum anno regni Regis Edwardi tercii post conquestum octavo.' Harleian MSS. 3632, B.M. A still older copy, if not the original, through the kindness of Colonel Howard, of Wygfair, is at present in my possession, as well as a careful transcription, for which I have to thank the patient labour of Mr. W. K. Boyd. There is an imperfect copy at the Land Revenue Record Office, No. 6 Whitehall.

[2] Literally 'above' and 'below.'

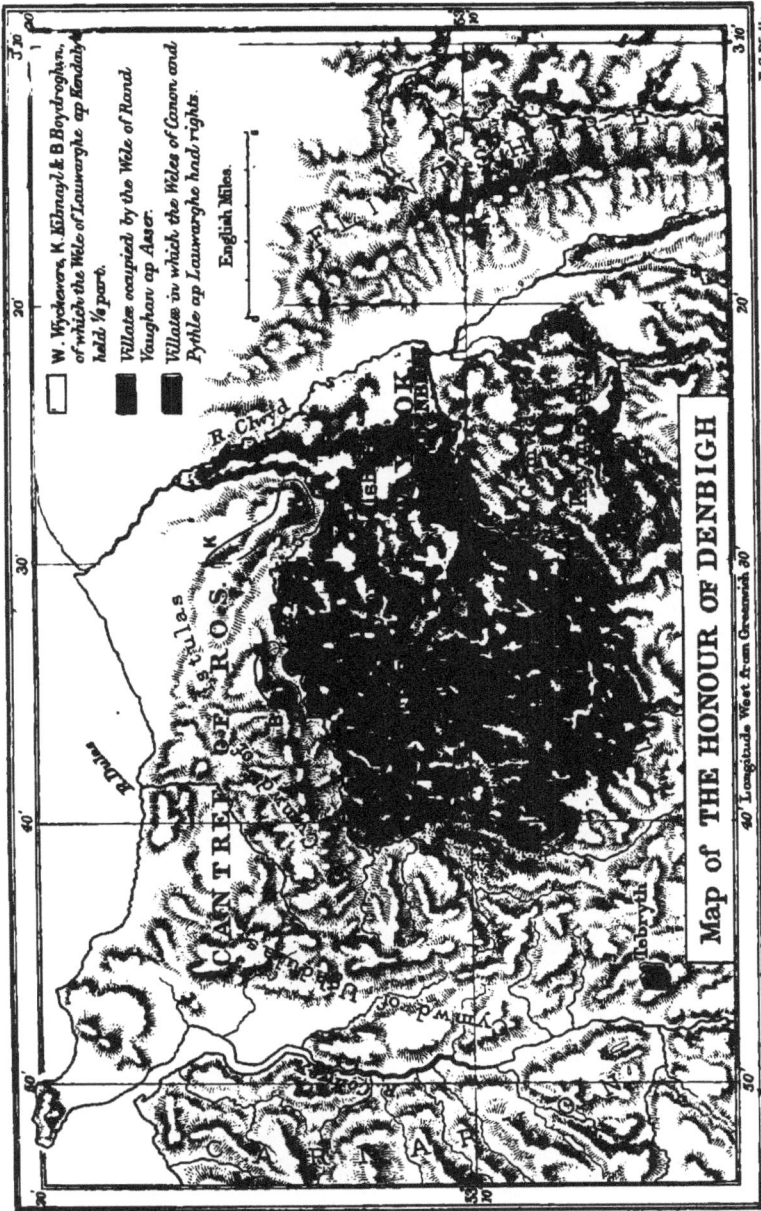

Map of THE HONOUR OF DENBIGH

W. Wychawm, K. Kilmayl & B. Boydroghun, of which the Wele of Iauwarghe ap Kendaly held Va part.

Villate occupied by the Wele of Rand Vaughan ap Asser.

Villate in which the Weles of Canon and Pyhtle ap Iauwarghe had rights.

English Miles

40′ Longitude West from Greenwich 30′

R. Clwyd

R. Conwy

CANTRED OF ROS

CANTRED OF RUVONIOK

F. S. Weller.

Finally, the single cymwd or half-cantref of CHAP. II. *Kaymerghe* completed the district.

II. THE *WELE* OF LAUWARGHE AP KENDALYK.

The Extent describes the tenants of each villata both before the conquest and also after the disturbances which followed it.[1]

The free tribesmen are called in the survey *priodarii*, a name which we shall find familiar to the Codes, being a Latinised form of the Welsh *priodorion*, or proprietors, thus making it clear that in their case the survey is dealing with free tribesmen.

The *weles* are of free *priodarii.*

These *priodarii* are said to hold in *weles* and *gavells*.

Turning first to the description of the villata of *Wyckewere*, now Wygfair, in the *cymwd* of Ros-Isdulas, it begins by stating that in the time of the Princes before the Conquest it consisted of eight *weles* or *lecta*, viz. :—

The villata of Wygfair occupied by eight *weles*.

1. Wele Lauwarghe ap Kendalyk (freemen).
2. Wele Moroyth (⅔ freemen, ⅓ *nativi*).
3. Wele Pridith Mogh do.　　do.
4. Wele Breynt
5. Wele Bothleyn } (all *nativi*).
6. Wele Moynou
    (These six extended over Wyckewere, and its hamlets Boydroghyn and Kilmayl).
7. Wele Anergh Cuyr Duyon } (all *nativi*).
8. Wele Thleythen
    (These two were in the hamlet of Boydroghyn only.)

The first of these *weles* is that of Lauwarghe ap Kendalyk. A summary of its contents is given on the opposite page in a tabular form, and the examination of this actual example of a *wele* cannot fail to be instructive.

That of Lauwarghe one of them.

---

[1] The passages from the Extent referred to in this chapter will be found in Appendix B. See Table of Contents of Appendix.

The Wele of Lauwarghe ap Kendalyk.

Father	Sons	Grandsons	Great Grandsons and others
1. Wele LAU-WARGHE ap Kendalyk	1. Wele *Risshard* ap LAUWARGHE	1. Gavell Madok ap *Risshard*	Gronou ap Madok Vaghan, and Eynon Routh his brother. Heylyn ap Eynon ap Risshard. Heilyn ap Gronou ap Eynon, Bleth and Ithel his brothers. Heilyn ap Eynon Gogh.
		2. Gavell Kendalo ap *Risshard*	Madok ap Heilyn ap Howel. Ithel ap Iorwerth ap Kendalo, Griffith and Tuder his brothers. David ap Kendalo ap Iorwerth. David Vaghan ap David ap Iorwerth, and Tuder his brother.
		3. Gavell Keñ ap *Risshard*	Keñ Vaghan ap Keñ ap Madok, Eynon his brother. Iorwerth ap Madok ap Iorwerth, and Ievan his brother. David Loyd ap Kendalo, and Iorwerth his brother. Madok ap Keñ ap Eynon, David and Ievan his brothers. Madok ap Eynon, Ada and David his brothers. Heylyn ap Eynon ap Risshard (as above in 1st gavel) and his 'nepotes.' $\frac{1}{4}$ *Escheat.*
	2. Wele *Moridyk* ap LAUWARGHE	Gavell *Moridyk* ap LAUWARGHE	Kendalo ap Madok. Eynon ap Groñou ap Griffith, Lauwarghe his brother. Iorwerth ap Lauwarghe ap Griffith. Madok ap Heylyn ap Griffith.
	3. Wele *Kendalo* ap LAUWARGHE	1. Gavell Iorwerth ap *Kendalo*	Gronou ap Eynon ap Madok. Eynon ap Iorwerth and Ievan his brother. Heylyn ap Eynon ap Howel.
		2. Gavell David ap *Kendalo* (called Gavel Kyloen)	$\frac{1}{4}$ Ithel ap Eynon ap Kendalo and Phelip his brother. $\frac{1}{8}$ *Escheat.*

Instead of the description of a holding of land with its boundaries we have here what is practically a pedigree, embracing the sons and grandsons and great-grandsons of Lauwarghe ap Kendalyk. The numerous successors of each of the grandsons were apparently not all of them great-grandsons at the date of the survey. There had been apparently some admission of outsiders among them, but the extent speaks of a time when such groups embraced *true heirs* only.

It will be seen that the whole kindred of the descendants of Lauwarghe to the fourth degree was, or had been, included in the *wele* bearing his name; the word *wele*, or *gwely*, as already hinted, meaning *bed*, and being accordingly translated by the Latin word *lectum*.

Lauwarghe himself was probably not alive, and therefore, presumably, the shares of the sons in the kindred were again called *weles*, and so also of the grandsons if by the death of their fathers they had become heads of households. But in cases where the parent was alive the sub-shares of children, according to the custom of gavelkind, were apparently not called *weles*, but *gavells*. The *gavell* is a division of a *wele*. At least, this is what the use of the terms seems to suggest as their meaning.

Thus, when we read that the villata of so-and-so consists of so many *weles*, the meaning seems to be, not that the land of the villata is divided into so many sections or estates, but that it is occupied by so many kindreds, or family groups. And when we read that the *wele* of so-and-so consists, or con-sisted when it was held *integre*, of so many *gavells*, we are to understand that it embraced so many subordinate families or sub-households of descendants.

The *wele*, therefore, of the original ancestor is a division not of the land, but of the tribe, and it remains outwardly one unit, with internal subdivisions among sons, grandsons, and great-grandsons; and thus also the subdivisions of the *wele* are subdivisions of the family group and not of the land.

This being so, the next point arises, what may be the relation of the complex unit to the land? Where and how are the numerous progeny of Lauwarghe ap Kendalyk located on land, and how are their possessions or rights described in the Extent?

The answer is that the *weles* of the *progenies* of the three sons of Lauwarghe are described as located in the *Villata de Wyckewere* with its two hamlets of *Boydroghyn* and *Kilmayl*. The *wele* of Lauwarghe originally, and when it was entire, occupied only one-sixth part of the whole villata, and so it did still, as described in the Extent, though now subdivided into the *weles* and *gavells* of his descendants.

This original *wele* of the common ancestor of the great-grandchildren thus held, apparently, an undivided share in the occupation of the district, or villata. And so it did still, though now subdivided into the *weles* of the sons and the *gavells* of the grandsons, and each of the latter at the time of the Extent embraced a numerous community originally of great-grandsons only, but since the conquest not strictly confined to them.

Thus classified still under the original *wele* of Lauwarghe ap Kendalyk, a community of a score or two of kinsmen held together as one family group an undivided one-sixth part, or share, in the occupation of the villata of *Wyckewere* and its hamlets.

This joint occupation by so numerous a body of kinsmen would have been complicated enough had the kindred of Lauwarghe been the only occupants of the villata. But it was still more complicated by the fact that the other five-sixths were shared in the same way in undivided shares, some by *nativi*, and others by more or less related kindreds, whose ties of blood with the kindred of Lauwarghe and with each other are not disclosed.

It is, perhaps, needful to assume that the actual homesteads, and inclosures round them, may have been held more or less in severalty, but it seems to be clear that, with this exception, the *weles* or family groups occupied *undivided* shares in what may be called the common rights of the villata.

This is confirmed by the description of the escheats to the lord, after the conquest, which are carefully recorded. These escheats were not of particular fields or portions of land, but fractions of such and such a *wele*, and such and such a *gavell*. Thus, a fourth part of the *gavell* of one of the grandsons of Lauwarghe was escheat, and five-sixths of another, and so on, according as fewer or more of the kindred had died *contra pacem*, or had otherwise forfeited their rights.

The total of escheats to the lord within the villata was therefore an aggregate, not of definite actual areas or acres lying here and there, but of

Marginal notes:

CHAP. II.

The homesteads and crofts probably held in severalty.

The escheats were of fractions of rights, not of land,

Chap. II. a series of undivided fractions, which, when put together, amounted to a considerable undivided share in the right of occupation in the whole villata; and so the only way in which an estimate of the lord's share in the villata could be arrived at by the surveyors was by working out the calculation as one of proportion, and then translating the result into acres, thus :—

	Acres
The Villata of Wyckewere contains in lands, woods, and wastes	1,072
The Hamlet of Kilmayl	160
The Hamlet of Boydroghyn of land, wood, and waste . . . . , . .	1,340
Sum total	2,573
And therefore the share of escheats of the lord *by true proportion* will be	1,638
Of which are allocated to diverse *priodarii* of *Lewenny* and *Astred Canon* in exchange for their patrimonies in the said villæ, certain proportions of divers tenants in Wyckewere, who have died ' contra pacem,' whose proportions ought to contain 176 acres of land, wood, and waste	176
And so there are over of the shares of the lord .	1,462

The lord seems ultimately at a recent date to have taken not quite one-third of this estimated acreage into his own hands, in order to let it out in lots of a few acres each to tenants, many of them Englishmen, at money rents on the English system.

and so, therefore, were the *weles* and *gavells*. But the point of importance is that if the escheats were undivided shares of common rights so must also have been the shares of the *weles* and *gavells*, of which the escheats were undivided fractions.

III. THE WELES OF CANON AP LAUWARGHE AND PYTHLE AP LAUWARGHE.

Passing now to another example, we find the *progenies* of apparently two other sons of Lauwarghe located in another cymwd. It is possible that they may be sons of another Lauwarghe, but it is hardly likely, as no distinguishing name is given in the Extent. They may therefore be offshoots from the original *wele* of Lauwarghe ap Kendalyk, but of this we cannot be sure.

Their *progenies* are described in summary on the next page, and also those of the other kindreds sharing with them in the villata of *Prees.*

Following the *progenies* of each son separately a glimpse may perhaps be obtained of the way in which the family groups were located on land, and shifted according to tribal needs or arrangements.

The *progenies* of Canon ap Lauwarghe were located in the valley of the *Istrad,* not only in the villata of *Prees,* but also in the two other villatæ of *Astred Canon* and *Nanthyn Canon.*

According to the Extents of these three villatæ the *progenies* of Canon ap Lauwarghe held one-sixth share in the villata of *Prees,* to which were appendant grazing rights in a great tract of mountain waste, common to the tenants of the whole lordship. The whole villata of *Prees* paid 20*s.* of *tunc,* and the undivided sixth share of the *progenies* of Canon ap Lauwarghe in it contributed 3*s.* 4*d.* to the *tunc pound.*

They were the same family group with similar internal divisions into gavells wherever they had

VILLATA OF PREES with its Hamlets; paying 20s. 0½d. tunc, held in VI. parts, each paying 3s. 4d., viz.:—

I. Progenies of *Canon* ap Lauwarghe.	$\frac{1}{2}$ Gavell Lauwarghe Vaghan		in which are	Ithel Loyt ap Cadugan and 2 others.
	$\frac{1}{3}$ Gavell Iorwerth	ap *Canon*	"	Cadugan Bottum ap Ednon and 4 others.
	1 Gavell Iennaf	ap *Canon*	"	Keñ Kouth ap Iennaf ap Ririd and 8 others ($\frac{7}{15}$ escheat).
	1 Gavell Eignon	ap *Canon*	"	Iennaf Loyd ap Gronou ap Cadugan and 9 others ($\frac{1}{4}$ escheat).
	$\frac{1}{6}$ Gavell Meuric	ap *Canon*	"	Madok ap Eignon ap Keñ and 13 others.
	$\frac{1}{2}$ Gavell Nynyat	ap *Canon*	"	Madok ap David ap Eignon and 10 others ($\frac{5}{8}$ escheat).
	$\frac{1}{2}$ Gavell Kenewerth	ap *Canon*	"	Escheat (and therefore not mentioned in the other villate held by the *progenies* of Canon ap Lauwarghe).
II. Progenies of *Pythle* ap Lauwarghe.	1 Wele Iorwerth	ap *Pythle*	"	Eschent by death 'contra pacem.'
	1 Wele Ednowen	ap *Pythle*	"	2 holders ($\frac{7}{8}$ escheat).
	1 Wele Ithon	ap *Pythle*	"	1 holder ($\frac{3}{10}$ ")
	1 Wele Kennyngh	ap *Pythle*	"	7 holders ($\frac{3}{10}$ ")
	1 Wele Cadugan	ap *Pythle*	"	4 " ($\frac{3}{10}$ ")
	1 Wele Ednon	ap *Pythle*	"	2 " ($\frac{3}{10}$ ")
	1 Wele Bissard	ap *Pythle*	"	1 holder ($\frac{3}{10}$ ")
	1 Wele Genythlyn	ap *Pythle*	"	3 holders ($\frac{3}{10}$ ")
III. Progenies of *Runon* ap Cadugan ap Ostrouth.	1 Wele Kefuenerth	ap *Runon*	"	3 holders ($\frac{1}{4}$ escheat).
	1 Wele Tegwaret	ap *Runon*	"	3 holders (held whole).
	1 Wele Iorwerth	ap *Runon*	"	2 " "
	1 Wele Gronon	ap *Runon*	"	Escheat.–
	1 Wele Yarthur	ap *Runon*	"	2 holders and Magʳ. Hospitalis St. Johannis del Specii.
IV. Progenies of *Tenyth* ap Kendalo ap Cadugan.	1 Gavell Heilin	ap *Tenyth*	"	13 holders.
	1 Gavell Elyder	ap *Tenyth*	"	11 " ($\frac{1}{8}$ escheat).
V. Progenies of *Ithel* ap Cadugan ap Ostrouth.	2$\frac{1}{2}$ Gavells Lauwarghe	ap *Ithel*	"	4 holders (1 gavell escheat).
	2$\frac{1}{4}$ Gavells Ednon	ap *Ithel*	"	1 holder (2$\frac{1}{10}$ gavells escheat).
	2 Gavells Gilbert	ap *Ithel*	"	15 holders (1 gavell escheat).
VI. Sundry *free* weles and several in hands of *nativi*.				

rights of occupation, and so it was not necessary, according to the Extent, to inscribe all the names of the grandsons of Canon ap Lauwarghe in the survey of *Prees*, because they were already recorded at length under the heading of *Astred Canon*. Excepting their share of the *tunc* of *Prees* they did no other services at *Prees*. Their services of *pastus* &c. were recorded under the head of *Astred Canon* and rendered there only. But, besides their services, they originally paid 10*s.* of *tunc* in *Astred Canon*.

Chap. II.

with the same sub-divisions wherever they hold.

They also held as a family group, with the same internal divisions, the villata of *Nanthyn Canon* with its hamlet of *Pennankyng*, but in this they owed neither services nor *tunc*, because it was reckoned as appurtenant to *Astred Canon*.

The *progenies* of Pythle ap Lauwarghe, who were also located in *Prees*, were divided into the eight *weles* of his eight sons, and held as one family group one-sixth share in the occupation of the villata side by side with the *progenies* of Canon ap Lauwarghe and other kindreds, paying their due proportion of *tunc*; but instead of having a second and a third location in *Astred* and *Nanthyn* they had a second location in the distant villata of *Tebrith* and its hamlets in the cymwd of *Ros Uchdulas*, south of Llanrwst, in the extent of which villata their names were recorded over again in detail.

So also the *pro-genies* of Pythle.

But the *wele* of one son described as escheat in *Prees* is omitted altogether in *Tebrith*. The *weles* of two other sons are omitted for some reason or other undisclosed, and the *weles* of the five remaining sons are therefore the only ones recorded

CHAP. II. in *Tebrith.* The entry in Tebrith also contains the statement that 'all the tenants in the said villata and hamlets are free *priodarii* and not *nativi,* and they are called '*wyrion Pythle*' (*i.e.* grandsons of Pythle).

The *progenies* of Pythle like their kinsmen, the *progenies* of Canon, paid their contributions of 3*s.* 4*d.* to the *tunc pound* of *Prees.* At the same time they paid 20*s.,* *i.e.* the whole *tunc pound,* at *Tebrith,* where they had the whole villata to themselves, and also paid services.

The escheats again are of fractions of rights. Turning, as before, to the escheats, $\frac{1}{3}$ and $\frac{1}{18}$ part of the gavell of one of the sons of Canon, and $\frac{1}{4}$ of the gavell of another son, and $\frac{2}{3}$ of $\frac{1}{3}$ of the gavell of another son were escheat to the lord in the villata of *Prees.* The whole *wele* of one of the sons of Pythle, who died *contra pacem,* and $\frac{1}{5}$ and $\frac{1}{10}$ of the *weles* of the other seven sons of Pythle were escheat, so that in these cases also the escheated shares were fractional proportions of the undivided rights of the family group.

Thus the conclusion is arrived at that the *gavells* of the *progenies* of Canon ap Lauwarghe were undivided shares of rights in the several village communities of *Astred Canon, Nanthyn Canon,* and *Prees,* and the *weles* of the *progenies* of Pythle ap Lauwarghe undivided shares of rights in the villata of *Prees* and the distant villata of *Tebrith.* No doubt, as already stated, the kinsmen of each family group may have had the separate use of homesteads and crofts, but with this exception, if the words *wele* and *gavell* may be transferred at all from the family group to the holdings, they were substantially to all appearances bundles of undivided shares or

The *weles* and *garells* bundles of undivided rights.

rights of co-aration and pasture in the several villatœ.

Nor are these solitary instances. Three of the other sixths of the villata of *Prees* are respectively in the hands of the *progenies* of the three sons (or rather two sons and a grandson) of Cadugan ap Ostrouth.

The first of the sixths was held in five *Weles* by the five sons of Runon ap Cadugan and besides this sixth of *Prees* they paid *pastus* to the Prince in the villata of *Garth Kanannel* in the cymwd of Ros Uchdulas.

The second of these three was held by the *progenies* of Tenyth ap Kendalo ap Cadugan, and besides this sixth of *Prees* they paid *tunc* and did services for what they held in the villatœ of *Carueduenuth, Penporghethl*, and *Dyncaduell*.

The third of the three sixths was held by the *progenies* of Ithel ap Cadugan, and they also had rights in *Carueduenuth* and originally in *Dyncaduell* also.

IV. THE WELE OF RAND' VAGHAN AP ASSER.

The foregoing examples have sufficiently illustrated the position of *weles* of kinsmen located, along with others, in a single villata or holding fractional rights in several villatœ. It may be well to add yet another example showing how in some cases a kindred could occupy exclusively several whole villatœ as well as fractions of others. The following will answer the purpose. The entry in the survey is as under :—

' Be it known that there is a certain *progenies* of free tenants in this cymwd (of *Ughalet*), which is called the " progenies of *Rand' Vaghan ap Asser*," which said progenies hold in diverse

CHAP. II.   villæ of the cymwd, and held in the time of the Princes before
the conquest, viz. :—

> The whole villata of *Dennant.*
> The whole villata of *Grugor.*
> The whole villata of *Guylberyñ.*
> The whole villata of *Penglogor.*
> The whole villata of *Pennaualet.*
> Half of the villata of *Hendreuenuyth.*
> One third of the villata of *Prestelegot.*
> One thirteenth part of the villata of *Petrual.*

And all these said villatæ and parts of villatæ they held in
4 lecta, viz. :—

> Wele Ruathlon ap Rand'.
> Wele Idenerth ap Rand'.
> Wele Daniel   ap Rand'.
> Wele Kewret   ap Rand'.'

And there will follow concerning the proportion of tenure and
services of every *wele* and of every one of its *gavells* in each of
the several villatæ *seriatim* by itself.'

The *wele* or *progenies* of Rand' ap Asser was
thus subdivided into *weles* of sons, and each of these
again were divided into *gavells* of grandsons according
to the annexed statement. The family group in the
eye of the surveyors had become divided into groups
of grandsons, and they are described as the *priodarii*
holding the original *lectum* called *wele wyrion Rand'*
—*i.e.* the *wele* of the grandsons of Rand', and
wherever they hold, whether whole villatæ or fractions of villatæ, the original *lectum* or family group
is subdivided precisely in the same manner into
the same *weles* and *gavells* of the sons and grandsons of Rand'. But, again, the subdivisions of the
kindred did not imply any actual divisions in the
land.

The *priodarii* of this *wele* did all their services in
the villata of *Dennant,* and paid their proper propor-

tions of *tunc* in every villata in which they had
rights.

Wele Rand' *Vaghan* *ap Asser*	Wele *Ruathlon* ap Rand'	Gavell Guyon ap *Ruathlon* / Gavell Bleth ap *Ruathlon*	} 5 holders.
		Gavell Kewret ap *Ruathlon*	1 holder.
		Gavell Madok ap *Ruathlon*	5 holders.
	Wele *Idenerth'* ap Rand'	Gavell Iorwerth ap *Ienerth'*	8 holders.
		Gavell Madok ap *Idenerth'*	4 holders ⅛ esch.
		Gavell Allot' ap *Idenerth'*	4 „ ¾ „
		Gavell Tegwaret ap *Idenerth'*	1 „ ⅓ „
	Wele *Daniel* ap Rand'	Gavell Eignon ap *Dariel* (sic)	12 holders 7/14 esch.
		Gavell Cadugan ap *Danyel* (sic)	8 „ ⅝ „
	Wele *Kewret* ap Rand'	Gavell Grifro ap *Kewret*	escheat.
		Gavell Kenewrek ap *Kewret*	3 holders. ⅛ esch.

V. THE SHIFTING IN THE LOCATION OF THE KINDREDS AFTER THE CONQUEST.

Lastly, some additional light as to tribal methods of distribution may perhaps be got from what happened after the conquest.

There had been escheats, *e.g.* in *Wyckwere*, owing to the death of tenants *contra pacem*. These escheats threw into the lord's hands the vacant proportions. Henry de Lacy's policy was to extend into the neighbourhood of the Castle of Denbigh the English three-field system of husbandry. Already in neighbouring parishes (*Llanriadr* and others) the three-field system was at work with its plough-teams

CHAP. II. and bovates on the English fashion.[1] To accomplish his object and make for himself an English manor, he excluded the *progenies* of Canon ap Lauwarghe from *Astred Canon* and gave them exactly corresponding rights in *Wyckwere* by way of exchange. And he acted in the same way in the villata of *Llewenny*.

When it is considered how complex were the rights of the tribesmen *inter se* in these cases, and yet how easily the exchanges were made, it becomes clear that the complexity lay in the structure of the kindreds and not in the facts of the husbandry.

These exchanges easily made,

The cattle and the ploughs of, a kindred could be moved with ease from one part of the country to another, and some of them placed in one villata and some in another, even in different cymwds and cantrefs, without interfering with the intricate family rights of the members of the kindred *inter se*, which easily followed the cattle and the ploughs wherever for the time they might be.

and so might have been under the tribal system.

And thus these shiftings and redistributions of the kindreds on the land after the conquest may illustrate the ease with which the chiefs of kindred could move the kindreds and families about under the tribal system whenever changes in population might require it. But they do more than this. They give point and clearness to the conception of the landholding kindreds, each holding together as one family unit with its own tribal rights as against

---

[1] *Record of Carnarvon,* p. 112 and pp. 109-110. The Villa of *Llanreadur* was held by 4 groups of tenants, which each held 4 bovates, *i.e.* half the full plough team. And *Llech* by 4 groups, each with 8 bovates or full plough teams. *Llandulas* was held by 3 groups, each with 12 bovates.

other kindreds in this villata or that, and sometimes even in different cymwds. They oblige us to picture them as communities of graziers of cattle with rights of grazing by tribal right or tribal arrangement in different parts of the district, each community, with, it may be, its score or two of kinsmen, forming a complex unit, one in its relations to the other kindreds, but nevertheless with intricate internal hereditary and family divisions and rights known intimately, doubtless, to the elders of the kindred, but far too intricate to be of interest to the makers of the Extent.

The kindreds family groups of graziers.

One point of importance may, however, be gathered from the Extent as regards these family rights.

It will have been noticed that in all the cases cited the kindred seems to have stopped with the greatgrandsons of the common ancestor, of whose *wele* they held their undivided shares or gavells.

The group went no further than greatgrandsons.

The following passage from the Extent seems to explain this :—

> A son of a free *priodaur* after the death of his father shall give to the lord for his *relief*, before he possesses his inheritance, 10s.
>
> A brother or nephew or cousin within the 3rd grade, and in the 3rd grade, shall give for his *relief*, after the death of his antecedent, before he obtains his inheritance, 20s.
>
> Beyond the 3rd grade there is no right of inheritance amongst them, but the land shall be escheat to the lord for default of heirs.[1]

The importance of this rule in the tribal system will become apparent when the evidence of the Codes is examined.

And turning from the groups of kinsmen to the

---

[1] See Appendix B. i.

geographical areas or land-units, called in the surveys *villatæ*, in which they had rights—sometimes sole and exclusive, but more often concurrent with other groups of kindreds in fractional shares— we are forced to consider the *villata* rather as a unit of husbandry and of the grazing of so many cattle than as a 'village community' of the English type.

The villatæ were units of occupation.

The numerous *progenies* of Canon or Pythle ap Lauwarghe obviously cannot all live in every villata in which they have rights and in which their cattle are placed to graze. Where, then, are the homesteads? In which of the villatæ?

It is when we are forced by the surveys to ask such questions as these that we fully appreciate the value of the description of Welsh habits in the twelfth century by *Giraldus Cambrensis*.

The homesteads easily built and removed.

His statement becomes very significant that the houses of the Welsh tribesmen were not built either in towns or even in villages, but scattered along the edges of the woods. Quite as important is the remark that to his eye they seemed mere huts made of boughs of trees twisted together, easily constructed, and lasting scarcely more than a season. They consisted, he says, of one room, and the whole family, guests and all, slept on rushes laid along the wall with their feet to the fire, the smoke of which found its way through a hole in the roof.[1]

Summer and winter homesteads.

The Welsh tribesmen, in fact, like other pastoral people, had two sets of homesteads. In summer

---

[1] *Descr. Wall.* I. c. x. and cxvii. The peasants of the villages on the south coast of the Isle of Achill, even to the present day, have duplicate cabins in the summer village on the higher slope of the mountain, the whole of this village being unoccupied in winter.

their herds fed on the higher ranges of the hills and
in winter in the valleys. So they themselves, following their cattle, had separate huts for summer and
winter use, very much as was also the custom in the
Highlands of Scotland and is still the case in the
higher Alpine valleys.

Dispelling, therefore, from the word *villata* all
ideas which hover around its use as the equivalent of
the 'village community,' the picture given by the
Extent, taken together with the information of
Giraldus Cambrensis, of the scattered pastoral life
of the groups of kinsmen becomes much more intelligible. The geographical units called *villatæ* are
evidently the fixed and permanent units. The
groups of kinsmen and their herds of cattle are the
movable elements in pastoral life under tribal arrangements ; and the complexity of rights within the
kindred, whilst subject probably to inflexible tribal
rules fixed by immemorial custom, follow the kindreds wherever they go and however much they may
be scattered.

The kin-
dreds and
their herds
the mov-
able ele-
ment in
tribal life.
The
villatæ
the fixed
units.

The meaning and significance of these tribal
arrangements can only be fully appreciated when
the descriptions given of the structure of tribal
society in the Codes and other legal traditions have
been studied. But, on the other hand, it will be
readily admitted that we should have approached
their study at great disadvantage had the previous
examination of the actual examples of *weles* and
gavells, furnished by the Denbigh Extent, been
omitted.

VI. THE GWELY IN SOUTH WALES.   EXTENT OF THE LANDS OF ST. DAVID'S.   A.D. 1326.

CHAP. II.

Now that it is known what the *weles* of the tribes-men were, the question arises over how wide an area mention of them is found in the Extents.

Weles prevalent through-out North Wales.

They were not confined to Denbighshire.   The Extents contained in 'The Record of Carnarvon' testify to their prevalence throughout Anglesey, Carnarvonshire, and Merionethshire.   The addition of Denbigh nearly completes the number of modern counties included in the district conquered by Edward I., and dealt with by the Statute of Rothelan. This district is that to which the Venedotian Code mainly applied.   There is corresponding evidence for South Wales though not of so full and complete a character.

Extent of the lands of St. David's.

The lands of the Bishop of St. David's were scattered over three or four counties, and an Extent was made of them in the year 1326,[1] which though not nearly so rich in details as that of Denbigh, gives, nevertheless, valuable evidence.

The Extent shows that English influences had long been at work in South Wales and especially in Pembrokeshire.   The prevalence of carucates and bovates in the scattered agricultural hamlets of Pembrokeshire and other counties indicates that in many districts the tribal system had given way to settled agriculture and English methods.   But in

---

[1] British Museum *Additional MSS.* No. 34135 : — ' Extenta omnium terrarum et reddituum domini episcopi Menevensis facta per magistrum David Fraunceys Cancellarium Menevensem tempore venerabilis patris domini David Martyn, Dei gracia episcopi loci.   Anno Domini Millesimo CCC[mo] vicesimo sexto.'   See Appendix C.   For a copy of this Extent I am indebted to the labour of Mr. W. K. Boyd.

the district through which the River *Teifi* flows between Cardiganshire and Carmarthenshire, the Extent
discloses interesting survivals of tribal holdings of
the same type as those of Denbighshire, though not
described with the same completeness of detail.

Thus at *Keuendeneuyth*, in Carmarthenshire [1] :—

Gweles of the stirps of so-and-so, in Carmarthen-shire.

> ' They (the jurors) say that there are there four *lecti*, com-
> monly called *gwele*, and of the first *gwele* is the stirps (*stipes*)
> of Gruff. ap Gilbert, and of the second *gwele* is the stirps of
> Isac ap Ithua, and of the third *gwele* is the stirps of Gronou ap
> Graylwyn, and of the fourth *gwele* is the stirps of Cadogan ap
> Donandwr, and each *gwele* renders to the lord 2s. by the year at
> Michaelmas.'

At *Henllan*,[2] in Cardiganshire, there was one
lectus of which three persons named and their co-
portioners were tenants. And at *Bangor* [3] there were
four *lecti*, three of them being called *Gwely Oyrion
so and so*, *i.e.* of the *grandsons* of the original holder.

Lecti in Cardigan-shire.

In the villa of *Landewybreuy*,[4] the lord had a
house, and in what is called the '*Patria de
Landewybreuy* '—there were, according to the jurors,
eight *lecti qui vocantur Gwely*, and of each of these eight
lecti it is stated that there are such and such persons
(in all cases but one the number being three), and
descendants from them (*descendentes ab eisdem*).
And it is added ' all the aforesaid hold *per antiquam
tenuram*, viz. *per ach et Edrit*' ; *i.e.* 'by kin and
descent,' the Welsh words used for this phrase in the
Dimetian Code being ' *o ach ac etryt.*' [5]

Gwelys of three persons and their descendants holding by ancient tenure of 'kin and descent.'

In *Garthely* [6] there was only one *lectus vocatus*

---

[1] Fol. 41.
[2] Fol. 36D.
[3] Fol. 37.
[4] *Llandewybrevi.* Fol. 33, 34.

[5] i. p. 396, and ii. p. 777, *Leges Wallice*, '*per hach et edryt.*'
[6] Fol. 35.

CHAP. II.   *Gwely,* and this again was of three persons named *et descendentes ab eisdem.*

In *Llannon,*[1] there was only one *lectus,* and this also was of three persons *cum sequela et descendentibus ab eisdem.*

Gweles in Brecon-shire,   In *Glascom* in the Archdeaconry of Brecon there were three *lecti qui vulgo vocantur Gwele.* And each was that of a *stirps* and descendants from it.[2]

and in Gower.   The Bishop of St. David's also had land at *Landewy* and *Langevelach,* in Gower, in Glamorgan-shire. In the latter place there were recorded under the head 'Liberi' seven *lecti qui vulgo vocantur Gwele.*[3]

This evidence of the Extent of St. David's, there-fore, extends the mention of these holdings to four counties of South Wales, and there is no reason to suppose that the same system was not once prevalent in other districts of which there do not happen to be surveys.

---

[1] Fol. 36.

[2] Fol. 52.

[3] Fol. 51.   And see *Cambrian*

Archæological Association, The Lordship of Gower, part ii. p. 192.

CHAPTER III.

THE STRUCTURE OF TRIBAL SOCIETY.

I. NATURE OF THE EVIDENCE OF THE CODES AND TRADITIONS.

PASSING now from the firm ground of the surveys to the more debatable ground of the Codes and the legal traditions classed together in the second volume of the 'Ancient Laws of Wales,' it is necessary at once to disclaim any attempt to settle or even adequately to criticise the dates or authority of the several MSS. or of the traditions out of which they may have sprung.

The surveys have made it clear that upon the conquest of North Wales there was existent, and inextricably interwoven into Welsh polity, a mass of tribal custom which even Norman phraseology and classification could neither force into ordinary manorial grooves nor ignore. And it would be idle to dream that a body of custom of this kind could have been of recent or rapid growth. Rather must it be regarded as an axiom in economic history that a condition of rural polity such as the surveys disclose could not be other than the result of traditional and immemorial usage. And when it is considered how tenacious and stubborn was the Welsh adherence to custom, that even long generations of Christian or ecclesiastical influence had failed to Christianise the tribal law of marriage; that (according to the Venedotian Code) 'the law of the Emperor and the law of the Church' combined could not force Howell the Good to alter tribal custom so far as to disinherit illegitimate sons; and that even Edward I. on the final conquest could not force upon the Welsh tribesmen the law of primogeniture—when this continuity of stubborn tribal habit is considered, it becomes clear that it must have been ingrained in the very structure of tribal society.

Welsh tribal custom survived into the era of codes and surveys.

Instead, then, of entering into critical examination of the dates of MSS. and the authority of the so-called 'Triads' and other legal traditions—which must be left to the labours of the Celtic scholar—and instead of being tempted to exaggerate the antiquity of the evidence, the wiser course in this practical inquiry will be fully to realise that the value of the evidence of Welsh tribal life does not lie in its antiquity. It rather lies in its being the latest and most modern instance in Western Europe of a tribal system which, having held its own till the era of codes and surveys, is unique in the fact that it can be examined in a way no other tribal system of Western Europe can be, excepting, perhaps, that of Ireland.

There is, however, one direct link between the surveys and the Codes which is worth mentioning.

In the Statute of Rothelan (A.D. 1284—*i.e.* ten years only before the date of the earliest Extent of

A.D. 1294) it is stated that upon the final conquest of North Wales, before a single survey had been made, the king, Edward I., 'wishing that his newly acquired Welsh lands should be governed under proper laws, to the honour of God, and that those just received under his rule should be dealt with by fixed laws and customs under his peace . . . caused the laws and customs of those parts hitherto used, to be recited before him and the nobles of his realm, the which having been diligently heard and fully understood, certain of them by counsel of the said nobles were annulled, certain were permitted, and certain were corrected, and also certain others were ordained to be added and enacted.'

Now, there is, in the British Museum,[1] a MS. of the Venedotian Code, not by any means the earliest MS. of it still extant, which at the end has a note mentioning Anianus, the Bishop of St. Asaph, who was probably one of the nobles before whom the Welsh laws and customs were recited. And thus it may well be the very copy of the Code used before the King and his nobles at Rhuddlan.

The wiser course, therefore, will be to rely chiefly on the mutual support given to each other by the Codes and the surveys. The facts of the surveys are sure. If the Codes contain a body of customary law which in natural course would produce the condition of things described by the surveys, their authenticity will be substantially confirmed. And, again, if the legal traditions of more doubtful date and origin supply reasons, in tribal sentiment or in

---

[1] Cott. *Titus*, D. ii.

more or less archaic details of custom, for the legal rules of the Codes, they themselves become evidence which cannot be wholly ignored.

It cannot be doubted that they throw valuable light of this kind, and all we can do is to use discrimination and not to rely too exclusively upon them in cases where they stand alone or seem to contravene better evidence with a suspiciously unhistoric motive.

The reader will readily discriminate between the different sources of evidence from which quotations are made as, whenever the two volumes of the 'Ancient Laws of Wales' are cited, references to Vol. I. are to the Codes, whilst those to Vol. II. embrace the other miscellaneous documents and the Latin versions of the Codes.

II. THE DISTINCTION BETWEEN TRIBESMEN AND NON-TRIBESMEN PRIMARILY ONE OF BLOOD.

Tribesmen and non-tribesmen.
At first sight there is great confusion in the classes of men mentioned in the ancient Welsh laws—of tribesmen, *uchelwrs*, *breyrs*, and *innate boneddigs*; of *non*-tribesmen, *taeogs*, *aillts*, *alltuds*, &c. The confusion vanishes only when the principle is grasped underlying the constitution of tribal society. And this principle would apparently be a very simple one if it could be freed from the complications of conquest and permanent settlement on land and from the consequent inroads of foreign law, custom, and nomenclature.

To begin with, there can be little doubt that the ruling principle underlying the structure of tribal

society was that of blood relationship among the free
tribesmen. No one who did not belong to a kindred
could be a member of the tribe, which was, in fact,
a bundle of Welsh kindreds. Broadly, then, under The dis-
tinction
one of
blood.
the Welsh tribal system there were two great classes,
those of Cymric blood and those who were strangers
in blood. There was a deep, if not impassable, gulf
between these two classes quite apart from any
question of land or of conquest. It was a division
in blood. And it soon becomes apparent that the
tenacity with which the distinction was maintained
was at once one of the strong distinctive marks of
the tribal system and one of the main secrets of its
strength. There were, indeed, if we may believe
later tradition, in South Wales at least, bridges
across the gulf, but they were such as to emphasise
the hard fact of its existence and to prove not only
its breadth but its permanence.

Two of these bridges may be alluded to at once In S. Wales
strangers
become
by way of illustration :

(1) Residence in Cymru, according to the tradi- Cymry
at ninth
genera-
tion,
tions of S. Wales, made the descendant of a stranger
at last a Cymro, but not until continued to *the ninth
generation.*[1]

(2) Intermarriage with innate Cymraeses genera- or by inter-
marriage
at fourth.
tion after generation made the descendant of a
stranger an innate Cymro in the *fourth* generation.
In other words, the original stranger's great-grandson, whose blood was at last seven-eighths Cymric,
was allowed to attain the right to claim the privileges
of a tribesman.[2]

---

[1] *Ancient Laws of Wales*, ii. p. 504.   [2] ii. pp. 504-7.

Such being the width of the gulf which divided the stranger in blood from the free-born Cymro, the next point to be noticed at the outset is the nature of the disabilities which resulted from the want of tribal blood.

Dis-
abilities of
strangers
in blood.

It is remarkable that these disabilities were apparently not so much the subjection to severer services and dues, as the natural results of *the* want of the blood-ties which bound tribesmen together into so tightly moulded a community.

The evidence of a stranger in blood was of no worth against a Cymro.[1]

Whilst every tribesman, head of a household, must have his ' sword and spear and bow, with twelve arrows in the quiver ' always ready at a moment's notice, weapons were not allowed to any stranger or *aillt* until the third descent.[2]   And neither horsemanship nor hunting were free to any but an innate Cymro.[3]

Without his lord's consent the *taeog* was to be neither a scholar, a smith, nor a bard.[4]   But if the lord were passive till he were tonsured as a scholar, or till he had set up a smithy of his own, or till he had graduated in song as a bard, he was free.[5]

The reason
for them.

The traditional reason for these disabilities, given in the *Triads*, was to keep the stranger class unorganised and weak ; ' to guard against treachery and ambush ' ; ' to prevent the plotting of strangers and their adherents, lest *alltuds* obtain the lands of the innate Cymry.' [6]

---

[1] i. p. 152.
[2] ii. pp. 557 and 515.
[3] ii. p. 515.

[4] i. p. 79.
[5] i. p. 436.
[6] ii. pp. 505 and 557.

These explanations are naturally not given in the Codes, but on such a point even a later tradition is not without value.

Lastly, there were special and exceptional cases in which kinship was allowed to the stranger in blood—exceptions which prove the rule, because they rested upon the hypothesis that an artificial tie of blood had been formed which might fairly be considered as strong as the natural tie.

The following typical examples are taken from a MS. of additional laws of about A.D. 1400.[1] Whether ancient tradition or indicating later relaxation of the strictness of tribal rules, they are equally instructive :— *Examples of artificial kinship.*

If a person be killed and his kindred shall not obtain right, and his kinsmen proceed to avenge their kin, and they deem their number small, and if a stranger come and proceed along with them upon the *privilege of kin (ar vreint car)*, saying ' I will go along with you to avenge your kin (*car*), and will take upon myself the slaughter and blood of him whom ye also shall take upon yourselves,' and they kill one or more, on account of their kin (*kar*), such stranger obtains the privilege of kin (*ar vreint kar*).

If his travelling companion sees his enemies and says to him ' See'st thou ? See'st thou yonder men who will have me ? and since there is no kin (*kar*) with me they will have me cheap!' says his stranger companion, ' I will fight along with thee, and I will take upon myself the blood of such as thou shalt take upon thyself,' and he escape because of that, that stranger acquires the privilege of a kin (*kar*) to him.

If a person be condemned to lawful wager of battle, either for land and soil, or for any crime, and he should dread in his heart entering into personal combat, and a stranger should arise and say to him, ' I will go in thy stead to combat,' and he should escape thereby, such stranger acquires the privilege of a brother to him, or nephew, the son of a sister (*nei vab chwaer*) to receive galanas, or to pay it for him.

---

[1] ii. pp. 313-315.

Now, in all these cases the word for kin is *car* or *kar*, and so, in the reverse case of a tribesman losing or forfeiting the privilege of kin, he became a *car-shattered* or *kin-wrecked* person—a person who had broken his kin and put himself for a time or in part into the position of a stranger in blood.[1]

It would seem as though the tie of kin was a tie of nature, too strong to be broken for ever, except in extreme cases. In one sense, ' once a kinsman, always a kinsman.'

The following is from the Gwentian Code :—

> Three persons hated by a kindred : a thief, and a deceiver, and a person who shall kill another of his own kindred; since the living kin (*car*) is not killed for the sake of the dead kin (*car*) everybody will hate to see him.[2]

Such a criminal as the last-mentioned, whose crime, being within his own kindred, was outside the law of *galanas* or ' blood-fine,' could not be slain. He might, however, with the consent of his kindred, relinquish the privilege of kinship. In such a case,

---

[1] The *car-shattered* person has hitherto been considered as a *waggon-shattered* person; but as to the word *car* compare *kerennyd* = relationship (*Venedotian Code*, i. pp. 220 and 230), *kar* and *car* = relative (*Gwentian Code*, i. pp. 774, 778, and 780), *karant* = relations (do., p. 780). And (ii. 638), under the head *Am Geraint* = of relations, are the three following paragraphs, which clearly prove that the *car* of the car-shattered person was his *kinship*, and not his waggon :—

' There are three kinds of relatives (*car*) on the side of the father, among whom land is shared : a brother, a cousin, and a second cousin.

' Three relations (*tri char*) on the side of the mother who share land with their relatives (*ac eu car*): an uncle, the mother's brother, a mother's cousin, and a cousin to himself, where a person shall obtain land by maternity.

' There are three car-shattered persons (*tri char llywedroc*) : son of an alltud by a Cymraes; a taeog accepted into the service of a person ; and a wealthy person by inheritance on the land of another.'

[2] i. 791.

he became a kin-wrecked man, but the rights of the descendants of such a person, including their rights of inheritance in the tribe, were protected for nine generations—' till the ninth man.'

Thus, according to the Venedotian Code :—

> If the ninth man come to claim land his title is extinguished, and that person is to raise an outcry that from being a proprietor (*priodawr*) he is becoming a non-proprietor, and then the law listens to that outcry, and assigns to him a shelter [or a free tribesman's *kyfran* or portion], and that outcry is called ' an outcry *over the abyss.*' [1]

What is this terrible ' cry over the abyss ' but the last despairing cry of a kinsman on the point of losing for ever, for himself and his descendants, his rights of kinship?

By one thing alone could the tie of kinship be absolutely broken—viz. by a man's *life being forfeit* for crime, such as murder of his chief of kindred. For such a criminal the gulf was opened and could only be bridged by his descendants, as in the case of strangers in blood, in the ninth generation, or by repeated intermarriage with innate Cymraeses in the fourth generation.[2] And this only in South Wales !

How the tie of kinship broken.

In such a case the criminal was banished from Cymru, and ' it was required of every one of every sex and age within hearing of the horn to follow that exile, and to keep up the barking of dogs, to the time of his putting to sea, until he shall have passed three-score hours out of sight.' [3]

Thus, though the makers of the mediæval surveys naturally described the two classes of tribesmen and

---

[1] i. 173, and see ii. 277 and 689.
[2] ii. p. 505.
[3] ii. p. 478, and cf. *Ancient Laws of Ireland*, iii. c. vii.

non-tribesmen as ' free ' and ' bond,' or as *liberi* and *villani* or *nativi*, according to English manorial usage, the real dividing line between them under the tribal system turns out to be one of blood. It is true that the Welsh versions of the Codes themselves occasionally use the loan-word ' villein ' in a vague sense for the stranger classes, but they never seem to forget that the real missing link between them and tribesmen is the tribal one of blood.

Grades of blood relationship belong to early stages of the tribal system.

The connection of both classes with land introduces, no doubt, at first sight, a complicating element into tribal society ; but one strong indication that the tie of blood relationship had always lain at the root of tribal society from its early stages before it became finally settled upon land is the fact that when anything like proprietorship of land came into the tribal life it was forced, like everything else, into a tribal mould.

Whatever, for example, may have been the relation of the kindreds to land in the Denbigh Extent, the *weles* and *gavells* were moulded by blood-relationship. And we have seen that they were limited by the rules of tribal inheritance within the range of the fourth degree of descent.

The meaning of these rules and grades of kinship in the structure of the tribal community will next be examined, and then the light so gained may be thrown upon the further consideration of the position of the stranger classes.

III. THE KINDRED, AND ITS ORGANISATION.

The *innate boneddig* [1] was the fully freeborn Cymro, of pure Welsh blood, both on his father's and his mother's side, *without mixture of kin.* [2]

CHAP. III.

He belonged to a kindred (*cenedl*). And the Cymric tribe or nation was a bundle of such kindreds bound together and interlocked by common interests and frequent intermarriages, as well as by the necessity of mutual protection against foreign foes.

The tribe a bundle of kindreds.

The whole tribe or federate country (*gwlad*) under the head king (*brenhin penraith*) was regarded as the supreme kindred (*cenedl benbaladr*).[3]

This acknowledgment of a common country and supreme kindred, whether a late or early conception, had this result : that a Cymro was a Cymro wherever he went within its bounds, whilst preserving his particular privilege in respect to land only in the territory of the chief of kindred under whom he was born. Even the *kin-shattered* man, therefore, had not necessarily ceased to be a free tribesman, and was not without a country.[4]

Confining attention at present to the lesser kindreds, the kindred proper, which was an organised unit, having its own 'chief of kindred' (*pencenedl*) and other officers, was the kindred embracing the descendants of a common ancestor to the ninth degree of descent—*i.e.* the same number of generations as that through which the stranger in blood

The kindred to the ninth degree of descent.

---

[1] Bon = stem, stock ; bonedd = stock, pedigree ; boneddig = having a stock or pedigree.

[2] i. pp. 179 and 509.
[3] ii. p. 503.
[4] ii. p. 503.

CHAP. III. must pass before he became a Cymro under the tribal rules of South Wales.

The chief of kindred.
According to the Venedotian Code, the chief of kindred must not be either a *maer* or *canghellor* of the Prince, but an *uchelwr* of the country, and his claim must not be by maternity. He was entitled to 24*d.* for every woman brought by marriage into the kindred, and 24*d.* from every youth admitted by him to the kindred.[1]

And he had to pay 1*l.* yearly[2] to the lord, or higher chieftain, to whom he was thus placed in a semi-feudal relation.

He was assisted by other officers. The Gwentian Code mentions as indispensable the *representative* (*teispan tyly*), the *avenger* of the kindred (*dialwr*) and the *avoucher* (*ardelwr*).[3]

Organisation of the kindred.
The Triads thus enlarge upon the organisation of the kindred :—

> Three indispensables of a kindred : its *chief of kindred* (*pencenedl*), its *avenger* (*dialwr*), and its *representative* (*theisbantyle*).
>
> A *chief of kindred* is to be the oldest efficient man in the *kindred to the ninth descent*, and his privilege and office are to move the country and court in behalf of his man, and he is the speaker of his kindred in the conventional raith of country and federate country, and it is the duty of every *man* of the kindred to listen to him, and for him to listen to his *man*.
>
> The *avenger of a kindred* leads it to battle and war as there may be occasion, and he pursues evil-doers, brings them before the court, and punishes them according to the sentence of the court and judgment of the country.
>
> The *representative* is the mediating man—in court, and in congregation and in combat, and in every foreign affair. He is to be one of the wise men of the kindred by raith of chiefs of households (*penteuluoedd*) in the kindred, and be a coadjutor

---

[1] i. pp. 190 and 553.
[2] i. p. 557.

[3] i. pp. 785 and 791.

with the chief of kindred in every raith and convention of country; and he is to be elected by the raith of his kindred to the ninth descent by lot, *i.e.* by tacit vote.[1]

We are reminded, therefore, that the organisation of the kindred existed for defence and border warfare, as well as for the maintenance of legal rights.

If the Venedotian Code mentions the semi-feudal relation of the chief of kindred to the lord or higher chieftain, it would seem from the Triads representing early or later tradition (whichever it may have been) that a kind of semi-feudal relation was established also between the chief of kindred and the men of the kindred.

Every kinsman to be a 'man and kin' to the chief of kindred.

> Three indispensables of a chief of kindred : being an efficient man, being the eldest of the efficient men of his kindred to the end of the ninth descent, and being the chief of a household (*penteulu*), or a man with a wife and children by legitimate marriage; *and every one of the kindred is to be a 'man' and a 'kin' to him (yn wr ac yn gar iddo).*[2]

This tradition seems to be corroborated by the statements of the Codes, but with the curious difference that, as we shall see, in the Codes the 'lord' takes the place of the 'chief of kindred,' suggesting (as often happens) that the later traditions sometimes hail from an earlier stage in tribal life than those described in the Codes.

Be this as it may, the next point arises, how and when the entrance into the kindred and the establishment of this relation of *man* and *kin* took place.

Beginning with the Codes, a distinction must be drawn between the reception of a son into the kindred and the accession of the son to the full rights of a tribesman in the kindred.

---

[1] ii. pp. 517-519. | [2] ii. p. 537, and see ii. p. 507.

As to the first, according to the Venedotian Code, in the case of a legitimate child the proof of kinship on the introduction of the child into the kindred was the oath of the mother in the church where the burial place of her people was, she placing her right hand on the altar and the relics, and her left hand upon the head of her child.[1]

The ceremony of formal reception is thus described in the Venedotian Code :—

> Thus a son is to be received as of kin. The father himself may receive him, after he is lawfully affiliated to him by his mother. If the father be not alive, the chief of the kindred with six may receive him, and those of the best men of his kindred, and thus he is to be received; the *chief of the kindred* is to take the hands of the child between his own hands, and give him a kiss, for a kiss is a sign of affinity, and then [the others are to do the same]. If there be no *chief of kindred*, twenty-one of the best men of the kindred, and the man who shall be in the place of the lord (*argluyd*) is to take the boy by his right hand, &c.[2]

As regards the attainment by the young tribesman of his full tribal rights, the following is from the Venedotian Code :—

> From the time when a boy is born until he shall be fourteen years of age, he is to be at his father's platter, and his father lord (*argluyd*) over him, and he is to receive no punishment but that of his father, and he is not to possess a penny of his property (*da*) during that time only in common with his father. . . . . since his father during that time is to be responsible for him for everything.
>
> At the end of fourteen years the father is to bring his son to the lord (*argluyd*) and commend him to his charge, and then the youth is to become his *man*, and to be on the privilege of his lord ; and he is himself to answer for every claim that may be made on him, and he is to have his *da* (*cattle* or property).
>
> From that age [fourteen] onwards, he is of the same privilege

---

[1] i. p. 207, and see also i. pp. 784-786.   [2] i. p. 214.

with an innate boneddig, for he has no privilege excepting his CHAP. III.
descent, as he ascends not to the privilege of his father till his
father's death.[1]

The completeness of the transference of the obligation for the son's maintenance from the father to the lord is shown further by the fact that on the son's death after attaining fourteen and leaving no child, the lord succeeds to his *da*, and not the father.[2]

Father not to maintain him after fourteen, but the lord.

And in another passage in the Venedotian Code it is explicitly stated that at fourteen a son is to be taken by the father to his lord, to become a man to the lord, and further it is added, ' and from that time forth he is to be supported by his lord.'[3]

A later development of this relation is mentioned in another treatise,[4] which states that a son is to become a lord's man at fourteen, and at twenty-one take land from his lord and do military service for him. This was a very natural extension of the older tribal relation, which, though one of kinship, also involved the common duty of mutual defence, and also participation in marauding enterprises in which kinsmen fought together under their chief of kindred.

Returning, however, from military service to the right of maintenance, which the young tribesman claimed at the age when he also became liable to discharge the tribesman's duties, many cases of analogy in the Codes would seem to imply that it involved his being supplied with cattle by his lord or by the chief of kindred. Whether agriculture or

The lord or kindred supplies him with cattle &c.

---

[1] i. pp. 203–205, and see the same point as to *villani*, ii. 868, in the Latin version of the laws.

[2] i. p. 203 and ii. p. 391.
[3] i. p. 91.
[4] ii. p. 211.

the grazing of cattle were the tribesman's means of support, oxen would be needed for his ploughing, and a share in the common herd of cattle to provide the meat and milk required to maintain him and his wife and children.

If so much as this be stated in the Venedotian Code, or is to be implied from its statements, the fact is very important, for whether it were the lord or the chief of kindred who had to supply the young tribesman on coming of age with his full tribal rights and cattle, it shows that he got them somehow from the tribe or kindred—*i.e.* from the lord, whose man he had become, whether a territorial lord over several kindreds, or the chief of his own kindred. In either case, his lord was the representative of the tribe or of the kindred ; which of the two hardly can matter much. If the lord were the higher chieftain of the greater kindred of which the tribesman's kindred formed a part, the young tribesman might well be *man* and *kin* to him as well as to the chief of his own kindred.

Passing now to the evidence of the Triads, as already said, it is quite possible that on such a point they may record earlier traditions than the Codes. Their statements do not seem, on the whole, inconsistent with the facts just learned from the Codes. Greater stress, however, is laid upon the bundle of tribal rights acquired by the tribesman at the age of fourteen. They present some graphic details, and, without leaning too much upon them, they may at least be listened to.

This bundle of rights is designated throughout the Triads by the curious word *cyvarwys*.

The word is not unknown to the Codes, and is used as an equivalent of what may be called a 'perquisite' or 'customary payment.' Thus, the chief of the household, who is a son of the Prince (*brenhin*), was to receive three pounds yearly from him as his *cyvarus*,[1] and the chief of song a bridal *cyvarus* from every maiden on marriage.[2] But the word is used in the Triads apparently for the provision granted by the tribe to the tribesman on his coming of age. It is thus defined in the Triads :—

> Three *cyvarwys* of an innate Cymro: five free erws; cotillage of the waste (*cyvar gobaith*) ; and hunting.[3]

And from another passage we learn that something like this was the usual provision made under the tribal system for those who had a right of maintenance, and who were therefore called *priodorion*. This passage shows that not only the 'innate Cymro,' but also the men of the Court by reason of their office, and, further, the clergy, had this right of maintenance, and so were *priodorion*.

> There are three sorts of *proprietors* (*priodorion*), viz. :— (1) Those naturally born free, (2) men of the court, and (3) clergy. The first of the three are called *laics*, and to them pertains the privilege of *location upon land* and *cyvarwys* . . . To the third class, or the clergy, there pertains the privilege of teachers, with an allowance to each from each plough within the district where he shall officiate as an authorised teacher, and his land of privilege free to him and his maintenance secured to him under the privilege of his services.[4]

Another triad describes the usual methods by which maintenance was provided for such persons, and applies the word *cyvarwys* to the maintenance :—

---

[1] i. pp. 15 and 358.
[2] i. pp. 389 and 679.
[3] ii. p. 516.
[4] ii. p. 547.

F 2

From three things are those who have free maintenance (*trwyddedogion*) to obtain their *cyvarwys*: (1) 5 *free erws*; and when that by any circumstance is not available, then (2) from a *plough penny*; and when that is not available, then (3) from a *spear penny*, or a spear charge, regulated by the occasion from every household of the kindred.[1]

Finally, the Triads confirm the Codes in stating that the innate Cymro attained his *cyvarwys*, or bundle of tribal rights, on coming of age :—

Three persons who pay *ebediw* without land; (1) a boy under 14, for it is then he is to enter upon cattle (*da*) of his own with tillage (*ardrethu*); (2) an innate boneddig; and (3) a *cyvarwysed* man.[2]

Another triad is as follows :—

Given to the tribesman on coming of age.

Three *original privileges of every native Cymro* (and also under the name of Cymro is included the Cymraes):—(1) *Cyvarwys* and fruition of five free erws under the privilege of his origin as an innate Cymro . . . (2) The privilege of bearing defensive arms . . . and (3) The privilege of raith under the protection of his chief of kindred: and *at the age of growth of beard they are bestowed on a Cymro, and upon a Cymraes when she shall marry.*[3]

If this passage means anything, it surely means that even during the lifetime of the parents the ' privileges of every Cymro' (including the cyvarwys of 5 free erws, &c.) attached to the son on his coming of age.

This, as we have seen, is consistent with the Venedotian Code, though the latter makes no mention of the 5 free erws, and does not apply the word *cyvarwys* to the bundle of rights which the new tribesman acquires when he becomes the acknowledged *man* of the chief of kindred or the higher lord.

Lastly, there is obviously something in this gift of the means of maintenance by the lord or the.

---

[1] ii. p. 548.
[2] ii. p. 575.

[3] ii. p. 503 and see i. p. 229.

chief of kindred to the youth on his coming of age, involving an idea or principle very much like that of *investiture.* He becomes 'man and kin' to the chief of kindred, and, entering thus upon a tribesman's responsibilities, he is invested by right with the *cyvarwys* or donation of the necessary provision for his tribal maintenance and the fulfilment of the tribesman's duties. Is it not possible that there may be something in the *cyvarwys* which is typical of the ceremony of tribal investiture?

CHAP. III.

The *cyvarwys* a kind of investiture of full tribal rights.

· If it be permissible on this point to travel outside the lines of the Welsh laws, there is a passage in the story of *Kilhwch and Olwen*, which is significant of the almost feudal character of the *cyvarwys*. *Kilhwch* confesses that he is not yet of an age to wed, but yet he wants *Olwen* for a wife. His father tells him, 'That will be easy for thee. Arthur is thy first cousin (*ceuynderw*). Go therefore unto Arthur, and ask him to cut thy hair, and ask this of him as a *cyuarwys*.' Then he goes to Arthur, and Arthur tells him he will give him whatever *cyvarwys* he may ask for. The youth thereupon asks him first to dress his hair. And Arthur takes 'a golden comb and scissors, whereof the loops were of silver,' and he dresses his hair. Then Arthur asks him, ' *Who art thou? For my heart warms unto thee, and I know that thou art come of my blood.*' He recognises that he is a first cousin (*keuynderw*), and promises to give him whatever he may ask for. Lastly, the youth asks for *Olwen* as his *cyvarwys*.[1]

Connected with ton sure, in the story of *Kil-hwch and Olwen.*

---

[1] Guest's *Mabinogion*, p. 219 *et seq. Red Book of Hergest* (1887), i. p. 105 *et seq.* See mention of land given by a *brenhin* to his man as a *cyvarwys. Ancient Laws of Wales*, ii. p. 857 and p. 397.

How easily the submission to tonsure, as the outward acknowledgment of rightful service to a chief of kindred on becoming his man, and the receipt thereupon of a *cyvarwys* from the lord might grow into something very much like the homage and investiture of feudal knighthood!

We shall see by-and-by that *tonsure* was the ceremony whereby a stranger in blood became the *aillt* or tonsured servant of a lord. But the point here is the connection of tonsure with the recognition of kinship, on the youth becoming 'man and kin' to a chief of kindred.

Kilhwch goes to Arthur, and demands tonsure and his *cyvarwys*, not only because Arthur is *King*, but also because he is *of his own kindred*, and probably also the chief of kindred to him. And the whole story turns on Arthur's recognition that the youth is of his kin. It would seem, then, that there was a tonsure for kinship and another tonsure for service, and most likely a distinction between the two.

Earlier instance of tonsure connected with kinship. Another, and perhaps older, illustration of the ceremony of tonsure, as the recognition of kinship, is found in the story related by Nennius of Vortigern and Germanus. Vortigern's son, whom he tried to fasten upon Germanus, at the suggestion of the latter, and to the great disgust of the former, takes a razor and scissors and comb to his real father— *i.e.* Vortigern—saying to him, '*Thou art my father; shave and cut the hair of my head.*'[1]

These traditional stories seem to add some colour

---

[1] Nennius, *Hist. Britan.*

to the suggestion that, in this matter at least, the Triads represent an older tradition than that of the Codes.

To sum up the evidence, it would seem, then, from the passages quoted from both the Codes and Triads, that the kindred included the descendants of a common ancestor to the ninth degree, and that this kindred was bound together not only by the tie of a common ancestry, but also by the tribal relation of each one of its members to the chief of kindred. This relation was that of being a 'man' to the 'chief.'

Nor had this relation apparently, in its origin, anything to do with land. It seems to belong to the essence of the tribal system itself, for the chief of kindred of the district was not necessarily the territorial lord.

And further, if we may trust the Triads, the chief of kindred had, besides those mentioned, duties of a paternal character to the young tribesmen. The youths who became his *men* at the early age of 14 not only became entitled to maintenance, but also to training.

And this training, we are told, was not merely military. The organisation of the kindred extended also to the provision of education in the domestic arts necessary to pastoral and semi-agricultural tribes.

There are three domestic arts, being primary branches—husbandry or cultivation of land (*aru tir*), dairy farming (*maeronaeth*) and weaving, and the chiefs of kindreds (*pencenedlocdd*) are to enforce instruction in them. . . .[1]

---

[1] *Ancient Laws of Wales*, ii. p. 515.

CHAP. III.

The seven
elders the
guardians
of kinship.
Associated with the chief of kindred, and acting as his coadjutors, were *the seven Elders of the kindred*,[1] whose duty it was to preserve by tradition the knowledge of kinship, and who had an important place in judicial proceedings, inasmuch as it was their duty, according to the Codes, to swear to the kin of anyone claiming by kin and descent.[2]

These Elders were ' Chiefs of Households ' within the kin, and were an important representative element in the organisation of the kindred. From one passage in the Triads, it would seem that the official *representative* of the kindred was in some cases chosen by them.

> Three raithmen of a kindred—its chief of kindred, its seven elders (*henadur*) as coadjutors of its chief of kindred, and its representative (*teisbantyle*), and he is a man of the kindred who shall be chosen on account of his wisdom and his literary knowledge, and to be chosen by lot or silent vote, of the elders of the kindred.[3]

Duties of
the ideal
chief of
kindred.
Finally, another of the Triads sums up the duties of the ideal chief of kindred in these graphic words :—

> Three things, if possessed by a man, make him fit to be a chief of kindred :—That he should speak on behalf of his kin and be listened to, that he should fight on behalf of his kin and be feared, and that he should be security on behalf of the kin and be accepted.[4]

IV. THE GRADE OF KINDRED TO THE FOURTH DEGREE OF DESCENT.

The Denbigh Extent has made us familiar with the group of descendants down to great-grandchildren,

---

[1] ii. p. 537.
[2] i. pp. 458 and 759.
[3] ii. p. 537.
[4] ii. p. 537.

or the fourth degree of descent, holding together as
a tribal unit of occupation under the name of the
wele of the common ancestor.

And the Denbigh Extent also supplied the statement that inheritance was allowed no further than to
the fourth degree. If there were no kindred within
that limit the lord took the inheritance by escheat.

Now, there is a passage in the Venedotian Code,
headed 'The Law of Brothers for Land,' repeated in
substance by the other Codes and also in other legal
treatises, to the following effect :—

> Thus, brothers are to share land between them: four erws
> to every *tyddyn* (homestead). Bleddyn, son of Cynvyn, altered
> it to twelve erws to the *uchelwr* and eight to the *aillt*, and four
> to the *godaeog* ; yet, nevertheless, it is most usual that four erws
> be in the tyddyn.
>
> [Here follows the measure of the erw.]
>
> If there be no buildings on the land, the youngest son is to
> divide all the patrimony (*trew y tat*), and the eldest is to choose,
> and each in seniority choose unto the youngest.
>
> If there be buildings the youngest brother but one is to divide
> the tyddyns, for in that case he is the meter: and the youngest
> to have his choice of the tyddyns : and after that he is to divide
> all the patrimony : and by seniority they are to choose unto the
> youngest : and that division is to continue during the lives of the
> brothers.

This refers to the division among brothers ; but the
family holding was not broken up by it, because the
division was not final. The sons of the brothers did
not claim *per stirpes*. They were first cousins, and
had the right to claim an equality of shares *per
capita*.

> And after the brothers are dead, the first cousins are to equalise
> if they will it : and thus they are to do: the heir of the youngest
> brother is to equalise, and the heir of the eldest brother is to
> choose, and so by seniority unto the youngest : and that distri-
> bution is to continue between them during their lives.

Chap. III.

Final
division
among
second
cousins
per capita.
This refers to the equalisation of the shares of the grandchildren who are first cousins. But still the family holding is not broken up. Yet another division is provided for, to. take place, when, presumably, all the grandchildren are dead. Then the great-grandchildren or second cousins finally divide equally *per capita.* ‚

> And if second cousins should dislike the distribution which took place between their parents, they also may co-equate in the same manner as the first cousins : and after that division no one is either to distribute or to co-equate. *Tir gwelyawc* is to be treated as we have above stated.[1]

In the Dimetian Code the same rules of division are stated as follows :—

> When brothers share their patrimony between them, the youngest is to have the principal tyddyn, and all the buildings of his father, and eight erws of land, his boiler, his fuel hatchet, and his coulter, because a father cannot give those three to any but the youngest son, and though they should be pledged they never become forfeited. Then let every brother take a homestead (*eissydyn*) with eight erws of land, and the youngest son is to share, and they are to choose in succession from the eldest to the youngest.
>
> Three times shall the same patrimony be shared between three grades of a kindred, first between brothers, the second time between cousins, the third time between second cousins; after that there is no propriate share of land.
>
> ·　·　·　·　·　·　·　·
>
> No person is to obtain the land of a co-heir, as of a brother, or of a cousin, by claiming it as heir to that one co-heir who shall have died without leaving an heir of his body ; but by claiming it as heir to one of his own parents who had been owner of that land until his death without heir, whether a father or grandfather, or great-grandfather, that land he is to have, if he be the nearest of kin to the deceased.[2]

Now, without inquiring at present whether the description of family rights contained in these pas-

---

[1] *Venedotian Code*, i. pp. 166–169.　*Tir gwelyawc* = land of *weles* or *gwelys*.
[2] i. p. 542-545.

sages was primarily applicable to actual ownership
by a family of particular land in the modern sense,
or whether it applied rather to the tribesmen's shares
or rights of occupation, grazing, and co-tillage in the
land of the tribe such as belonged to the *weles* of
the Denbigh Survey, there must surely be a close
connection between these *weles* or *gwelys* and the
tir gwelyawc of these passages.

They describe the internal rights of a family
holding of whatever kind it might be. And certainly
they seem to describe exactly what is necessary to
explain the care which is taken in the Survey to
keep up the memory of the successive divisions of
the original *wele*. In the case of the original *wele*
of Lauwarghe ap Kendalyk, there is, so to speak, the
external undivided unity preserved, but there is also
recognised the family division of the *wele* of a presumably dead ancestor into the several *weles* of his
sons. And, further, the division of these into the
weles or *gavells* of their sons, and so on. And if we
ask why the original *wele* remains externally undivided all the time till the family has grown into a
community of a score or two of descendants, this
passage from the Codes clearly seems to explain the
reason. So long as any one of the sons were alive
there was to be no internal or family division among
grandsons ; and until all the sons and grandsons had
died no final division was to take place among great-
grandchildren. And, therefore, the original *wele*
remains the external unit, till the division between
great-grandsons has been effected.

That the *wele* occupied both the homesteads, with
some land round them, which may have been, in a

This ex-
plains the
weles of
the sur-
veys em-
bracing
great
grand-
sons.

The *wele*
holds to-
gether till
the final
division
of rights
per capita
takes
place.

manner, held in severalty—*i.e.* in the exclusive occupation of the several families—and also the rest of the district held in common, in undivided shares, between various kindreds and families, does not necessarily prevent the term *tir gwelyawc* from embracing the whole.

Be this as it may, for the present we may conclude that, in the case both of particular ownership and tribal occupation of land, the limit of kindred to the fourth degree of descent was an important practical limit of family or tribal rights.

The same grade of kindred applied to strangers who intermarry with tribeswomen. It has already been incidentally mentioned that the rules regulating the attainment of tribal rights by the stranger in blood bring us again to the same limit or grade of kinship. The descendant of the stranger in blood, whose entrance into tribal rights has been hastened by repeated intermarriages, becomes a *priodawr* and the founder of a new stock or kindred in the fourth degree of descent.

Here, then, is an important line or limit marking a distinctive grade of kinship, and inclosing, as it were, a distinct group of kinsmen embracing great-grandchildren or second cousins.

It was the limit of certain responsibilities. For what other purposes did it exist?

There were three distinct responsibilities which were confined within this special grade of kinship—*i.e.* they were not extended to the wider kindred.

> Three things which are not to be done by any further of kin than a second cousin :—(1) To pay *saraad* with such as shall have nothing of their own to pay; (2) To pay cattle without surety with the son of an alltud by a Cymraes beyond the third kin; (3) To mutually uphold and keep each other's share with property and oath by those beyond second cousins, for [land] is not to be shared further.[1]

---

[1] ii. p. 657, and see i. pp. 208–10.

Now, what were these three things?

First. The *saraad* was the payment for insult or injury short of homicide. Kinsmen as far as second cousins had joint responsibility to the injured person for the crimes of their kinsman, and no kinsman beyond this grade was responsible unless the crime amounted to homicide.[1]

Secondly. Kinsmen within this grade were responsible for the marriage of daughters.[2] As a rule, the daughter did not inherit family land with her brothers, but she was entitled to her *gwaddol*, or marriage portion,[3] which she took with her on marriage, and took back again in case she separated from her husband within seven years. After that, if the marriage continued, the husband and wife were jointly entitled to the combined chattels of both.[4] But the kinsmen's duty to her did not stop here.

She was entitled to be married to a free tribesman, so that her sons might have full tribal rights.

But if this responsible family group gave the daughter away to a non-tribesman, who was not a member of a family or kindred, so that her sons could not receive inheritance in tribal rights from their father, then they had not fulfilled their responsibility to her.

The sons could in such a case have no inheritance from their father, and, therefore, tribal law gave them

---

[1] i. pp. 231 and 703.

[2] So in the tale, 'Kilhwch and Olwen,' *Red Book of Hergest* (1887 ed.), i. p. 119; Guest, p. 234. When Yspaddaden Penkawr is asked to give his daughter in marriage, he answered, 'Her four great-grandmothers and her four great-grandsires are yet alive; it is needful that I take counsel of them.'

[3] One half of a brother's share in chattels, i. p. 99.

[4] i. p. 523.

CHAP. III.

Right of their sons by maternity in some cases.

an inheritance by right of maternity in the family rights of the group who had given their mother away to a stranger.[1]   And, further, as the sons would have no kinsmen on their father's side to be responsible for them, tribal law threw the responsibility on the mother's kindred.   They became responsible for the *saraad* of their kinswoman's sons in case they committed crime.   This was called 'payment of cattle without surety,' because (as explained in the Venedotian Code) no bond of suretyship was necessary, and 'with cattle every payment formerly was made.'[2]

The *third* point refers to the final division of *tir gwelyawc* among second cousins.   After this there was no further joint occupation, but only what may be described as joint warranty of their common title in case it was disputed.

In all three cases the limit of responsibility was that of the fourth degree of descent—the great-grandsons of a common ancestor—and there was no liability beyond it.

V. THE GRADE OF KINDRED TO THE SEVENTH AND NINTH DEGREES.

Middle grade to seventh degree of descent.

Passing now from the definite grade of kindred confined to the fourth degree or second cousins, it is at first sight more difficult to comprehend exactly the meaning of the middle grade of kindred—*i.e.* the grade extending to the seventh degree of descent, or fifth cousins, which was the grade primarily re-

---

[1] *Venedotian Code,* i. p. 97. | 98 and 553, and ii. pp. 12 and
[2] i. pp. 208-212, and see i. pp. | 328.

sponsible for the crimes of its kinsmen as regards
homicide.

There is some confusion in the Codes in the method of counting degrees of relationship and in the statements of the exact degree of kinship to be included in this middle grade; but there seems to be reason in the inference that the limit of the seventh degree of descent in the case of responsibility for homicide was based upon the principle that the greater crime involving heavier payments necessitated a wider area of responsibility.

But the full responsibility of the kindred for the *galanas,* or payment for homicide, did not end with the kindred within the seventh degree of descent.

In the Venedotian Code there are two versions as to the payment of *galanas.*

The first[1] makes the amount fall in thirds. One-third fell on the murderer and his father and mother, if living; two-thirds fell on the kindred. Of the first third the murderer and his children were to pay two parts, and his father and mother the other part—the father paying twice as much as the mother.

The kindred on whom the other two-thirds fell was defined as 'from maternity to maternity unto the seventh descent.'

This exhausts the *galanas,* but there is still the further provision of the 'spear penny,' in aid of the murderer, in case of his default in paying his share. The deficiency in this case was to be gathered from the kindred beyond the seventh descent, or fifth

[1] i. p. 223.

CHAP. III. cousins.   And thus, according to the Venedotian
Code, it was to be obtained :—

> The murderer is to take a servant of the lord, carrying with
> him a relic, and wherever he shall meet with a person beyond
> the seventh degree of kindred, let such person take his oath that
> he is not descended from any of the four kindreds from which
> the other is descended, and unless he take that oath, let him pay
> a spear penny, and if he take the oath he is to be exempted.[1]

The other Venedotian version may be summarised
thus :—

> The first third [of the *galanas*] falls on the murderer, and
> the mother and father and brothers and sisters with him, for
> those persons would receive with him a third of the *galanas* if
> paid to them, therefore let them pay so with him . . . (one-third
> of it on the mother and father, one-third on brothers and sisters,
> and one-third on the murderer, . . . males paying two parts and
> females one).
>
> The remaining two-thirds fall on the kindred (two parts of it
> on the kindred of the father and one part on the kindred of the
> mother).
>
> The kindred for this purpose is confined within the seventh
> man thus :—

1. Brother	= braut.
2. 1st cousin	= keuenderu.
3. 2nd cousin	= keuerderu.
4. 3rd cousin	= keẏuẏn.
5. 4th cousin	= gorcheẏuen.
6. 5th cousin	= gorchau.
7. Son of 5th cousin	= mab gorchau.

And then it continues :—

> If the murderer have nothing to pay with, it is right to give
> him a spear penny to assist him, and that shall be paid to him
> from the seventh man onwards : those seven men are brother,
> first cousin, second cousin, third cousin, fourth cousin, fifth cousin,
> and a kinsman, son of a fifth cousin,[2] and *since relationship can
> be no further counted, let them beyond that* pay to him a spear
> penny.   And the manner he shall collect a spear penny from the
> men he may find of his kindred, when he may not know how to

---

[1] i. p. 225.

[2] In the case of the son of the
fifth cousin, ' the father pays the
galanas for his son, and the son
does not,' i. p. 231.

trace his relationship to them, is to take a relic he may credit, and
when he shall meet with one of those men, let him take his oath
that he does not originate from his kindred, or pay him a
spear penny.[1]

There is here the same confusion in the description of the fifth cousin or seventh in descent—*i.e.* the great-grandson's great-grandson; but one thing is clear: *there are men of the kindred beyond what we have called the middle grade of kinship*, and these are to contribute the spear penny up to the ninth degree in descent—otherwise who are the remoter kindred by whom the spear penny is to be paid?

VI. THE REASON OF THE THREE GRADES OF KINSHIP.

The importance of the division of the kindred into the three grades of kinship makes it worth while to attempt to get a glimpse, at least, of the circumstances or facts of human nature out of which it arose. So remarkable a feature in the structure of tribal society must surely have had a rational and natural basis.

(margin: Natural basis of the three grades of kinship.)

Without travelling outside the knowledge derived from the Welsh laws, there are indications that it had a connection with the *hearth*.

There were two tribal chieftainships within the *cenedl*, or kindred—viz. that of the *pencenedl* and that of the *penteulu*, and under each chief of kindred were many chiefs of households.

The hearth (*aelwyd* or *ayluyt*[2]) was the centre of the house, and it was sometimes metaphorically used for the household.

(margin: The hearth and the mark of the kindred upon it.)

Three hearths (*aelwyd*) that are to make satisfaction on account of such as shall not be under fealty to the lord—that of the father, of an elder brother, and of a father-in-law.[3]

---

[1] i. pp. 225–227.   [2] i. p. 172.   [3] ii. p. 531.

G

The hearth, moreover, was the symbol of family ownership and inheritance. The right of the son on succession was to uncover the hearth of his father or ancestor. The legal term for the recovery by an ejected son of his patrimony was *dadenhudd*, or the uncovering again of the parental hearth. The term was a graphic one. The fire-back-stone, set up against the central pillar of the hut supporting the roof (*pentanvaen* = head-fire-stone), was a memorial or witness of land and homestead (*tir a thyle*), because it bore the *mark of the kindred* upon it.[1]

> There are three dead testimonies concerning land : (1) The witness of heirs as far as great-grandchildren (*gorwyron*), or beyond, is credited in court as to what they heard from their ancestors. . . . (2) Elders of country and kindred (*gwlad a chenedl*) as to what they know of kin and descent ; (3) The *fire-back-stone* of the plaintiff's father, or of his grandfather, or of his great-grandfather, or others of his kindred. . . .[2]

And the covering and uncovering of the fire had a picturesque significance.

Whether the fire were of wood or turf, the hearth was swept out every night. The next thing was to single out one particular glowing ember—the *seed of fire*—which was carefully restored to the hearth and covered up with the remaining ashes for the night. This was the nightly covering of the fire. The morning process was to uncover the ' seed of fire,' to sweep out the ashes under which it was hid, and then deftly to place back the live ember on the hearth, piling over it the fuel for the new day's fire. This was the uncovering of the fire, which thus from year end to year end might never go out. Anyone who has seen the process performed

---

ii. p. 523.   [2] ii. 561 and ii. 677 (*Leges Wallice*).

on a Celtic hearth will understand the natural
transition in the mind of the Welsh poet, Henry
Vaughan, in his lines on 'Sleep,' from the high-
flown metaphor—

> The pious soul by night
> Is like a clouded star. . . .

to the more homely one—

> Though sleep, *like ashes*, hide
> My lamp and life. . . .

and see at once the symbolic significance as well of
the *dadenhudd* as of the *curfew*.

The evidence of folk-lore might lead us further
to recognise important religious superstitions connected with the hearth. But even without this the
picture of the son, or grandson, or great-grandson,[1]
returning perhaps from exile to claim the paternal
homestead by uncovering again the ancestral hearth,
is graphic and solemn enough to emphasise for us
the importance of the Cymric hearth as, in a very
literal sense, the *focus* of the rights of kindred.

The hearth the 'focus' of the rights of kindred.

There is significance also in the bar to the
realisation of the exile's rights to the full recovery of
his patrimony, resulting from the existence on the
land where such was the case of 'occupiers who had
grown into *priodorion*,' and founded a family hearth
by occupation for four generations. In that case the
returning exile could not oust the actual occupant.
The fire-back-stone of the new occupant's family had
acquired the mark of a kindred upon it, and the two

---

[1] ii. p. 141. 'A person is not
to claim *dadenhudd*, except by
the hearth he himself shall uncover, or his father before him.
A person is not to claim *daden-*
hudd of land, although his grandfather or his great-grandfather
shall have been on the land, unless he mind to claim by kin and
descent.'

CHAP. III. claimants must therefore divide the land between them.[1]

Returning, then, to the consideration of the three grades of kindred from the point of view of the family hearth, the first two had obviously a foundation in the nature of things, inasmuch as they were bounded at one end by the reach of the actual sight and at the other end by the direct memory of a single person.

The ancestor may live to see great-grandsons, and remember his own great-grandfather.

The eldest living ancestor, as chief of the household occupying the principal homestead or *tyddyn*, and seated by the ancestral hearth, might well live to see growing up around it a family group extending to great-grandchildren.

On the other hand, looking backwards to his own childhood, he might well recollect his own great-grandfather sitting as head of the household at the same hearth, just as his great-grandchildren would some day hereafter remember him. Thus the

Memory and sight may well cover seven generations,

extreme natural reach of the knowledge of the head of the household might cover seven generations. If during this period the purity of the family blood had been duly preserved, the kindred within these natural limits would be a perfect kindred.

and tradition go back two more.

Finally, if family tradition went back two stages farther than actual memory, then it would embrace the larger kindred to the ninth degree of descent. And as, in all probability, amongst the various household hearths there would always be present and conspicuous that of the head of the kindred, the patriarch under whose chieftainship the groups of

---

[1] i. p. 173.

lesser kindreds were united into the larger kindred, CHAP. III.
tradition thus backed by outward and visible signs
would, in the course of ages, easily invest such tribal
rules with the force and strength of customary
law.[1]

That rules and grades of kinship thus ingrained Force of
in the structure of tribal life should be applied as custom.
they arose to other matters, such as the attainment
by strangers in blood of the privilege of kinship or the
acquirement of proprietary rights in land, and finally
that the same rules should mould the form of land
ownership, when at last attained, into a family holding by the kindred within the fourth degree—all this
was natural enough. And when we realise how
customary law in these further matters became thus,
in the same way, formed and fixed by the force of
constant repetition, backed by household and tribal
tradition, we begin to understand the tenacity with
which the tribal system everywhere was able to
maintain itself through centuries and even thousands
of years.

The tribal system of blood-relationship never
grew old. It was always forging new links in an
endless chain, and the links of kindred always over-
lapped one another.

Were Welsh tribal law historically isolated and The
alone, the account thus given of the structure of hearth
connected

---

[1] *Giraldus Cambrensis* mentions that the Welsh knew the
names of their ancestors to the
sixth or seventh degree, and sometimes further. Mr. A. N. Palmer
has referred me to the fact that as
late as the time of Norden's survey (A.D. 1620) of Abenbury, a
township adjoining Wrexham, a
gentleman of estate gave his name
as ' Humfridus ap Robert ap
Will'm ap Rob't ap David ap
Griffith ap Robert.' In this case
seven generations were represented in one man's name.

tribal society and of the grades of kinship might perhaps be accepted as sufficient in itself, and the hints given by folklore of still deeper religious and superstitious foundations for the sacredness of the hearth and the sacredness of kinship might perhaps be passed by unheeded.

But when the comparative method forces upon us the fact that in other tribal systems the hearth is surrounded with sacredness as the centre of the worship of ancestors, and that connected with that worship there were found in various tribal systems strangely similar grades of kinship, to shut our eyes to this wider view would be wilful blindness to facts which may throw back, even upon the Welsh tribal system, an important side-light.

When it is considered how large a part tribal religions have played in history by giving to tribal societies the tough tenacity which has enabled them to live through so many ages and to make and maintain such conquests as they have done—conspicuously in the case of the Jews and the Arabs—we may be thankful even to folklore for reminding us that the ties of Cymric blood relationship may have had religious sanctions long ago obscured, if not altogether obliterated by Christian and ecclesiastical influences.

CHAPTER IV.

THE STRUCTURE OF TRIBAL SOCIETY—(continued).

I. THE RELATION OF THE GRADES OF KINDRED TO THE OCCUPATION OF LAND.

THE foregoing considerations lead to the recognition of the extreme antiquity of the grades of kinship.

Rooted in the nature of things and moulded by the necessities and circumstances of tribal life, they in their turn seem to have controlled and forced into their mould any new elements which might enter from time to time within the range of tribal life and require adjustment to it.

One of these new elements was undoubtedly encountered, earlier or later, in connection with ownership and occupation of land.

The passage from nomad life to settled occupation involved the absorption, so to speak, of the new element into the tribal system.

It is not easy to attain a clear idea of how the problem as to land was solved.

It is easy enough to assume that whatever of land ownership grew up in the tribe was tribal ownership. But this, if strictly true, would carry us but a very little way into a correct understanding of the relation of the tribesmen to land.

It will not do to bring into the question the modern democratic view of a society in which equality of rights and shares settled every question. Such an idea was foreign to the tribal system.

Careful consideration of such facts as turn up incidentally in the surveys and Codes affords the only chance that a true understanding can be reached, and, after all, survivals of apparently conflicting principles may suggest that there is a misunderstanding somewhere needing further light to dispel it.

In the first place we must try to get behind the political or juridical arrangements, the cantrefs and the cymwds with their so-called manors in which representatives and officers of the chieftain maintained a kind of lordship approaching to the territorial and manorial type.

The kindreds to the ninth and fourth degree

Recognising the existence of this element and its importance and possible antiquity as belonging to the question of chieftainship (to be hereafter considered), and confining attention to the strictly tribal occupation of land, we have first to recognise the relation to land of both the greater kindred to the ninth degree and the lesser kindred to the fourth degree of descent.

The kindred to the ninth degree acknowledging a common ancestry and organised into a social or political unit under its chief of kindred, its representative, and its seven elders, was a clearly defined and separate group.

both related to land.

Within each of these greater groups of kindred were the lesser groups of kindred to the fourth degree of descent, embracing great-grandchildren or second cousins, each group forming a separate *wele* or *progenies* under the name of the great-grandfather, whether dead or alive, until the final division among second cousins when all the sons and the grandsons should be dead, and in the meantime divided into sub-*weles* or gavells, as the case might be, under their several heads of households or eldest living ancestor.

It is these lesser groups or *weles* that the Denbigh Extent represents as the tribal units of land occupation.

Were each of these *weles* the sole occupants of the district in which their members lived and in which their cattle were pastured, the head of the *wele* might be regarded as the landowner of the district, and a ring fence might be thrown round the land occupied by him and his *wele*. He would be the *tiriawg* or landed person in whom was vested the tribal proprietorship of the land occupied by the numerous members of his *wele*.

The head of a *wele* a *tiriawg* or landed person.

The fact that he and his *wele* were only joint participants with other *weles* in the tribal rights of the district in undivided shares (as in the case of Lauwarghe ap Kendalyk) ought not to blind our eyes to his position as a *landed* proprietor in the sense that in him were vested the tribal rights of his *wele*, so far as regards land occupation.

Externally viewed, he might well be regarded as *proprietor* of the *tyddyns* or homesteads occupied in severalty by himself and his descendants along with their crofts and cattle yards, and, besides these, of undivided and extensive rights of grazing jointly with other *weles*. When he, the original head of the *wele*, was dead, his sons would be the proprietors of the occupation rights of the same original *wele*, and when the sons were dead the grandsons would succeed them in the proprietorship.

Thus in the Denbigh Extent *Tebrith* was occupied by the *wele* of ' the grandsons of Pythle,' and so, too, the *priodarii* holding the original *wele* of Rand' ap Asser were grandsons, and the *wele* was called by the surveyors ' *wele wyrion Rand*'.'

Thus whoever was the head of the *wele* was a landed person and also a chief of household. And by virtue of this double position his so-called ' privilege ' was that of an *uchelwr* or *breyr*, and in South Wales he was as such a judge in the court of the cymwd or cantref.

> Every landed person (*tiriawg*) being a chief of household (*penteulu*) is a judge in South Wales.[1]

And again :

> A *breyr* is an innate landed person (*tiriawg*) who is a chief of household (*penteulu*) with privilege of a court of justice.[2]

The *uchelwr* or *breyr*, sometimes called a *gwrda*, was a man of responsibility, bound to afford protection and to secure justice out of court as well as in it.

> If a man take a woman clandestinely and bring her to the house of an *uchelwr* to sleep with her, and the *gwrda* do not take security for her *amobr*, let him pay it himself.[3]

It seems to be clear, then, that the *uchelwr* or *breyr* was a ' landed' person and a chief of household, and privileged in respect of his position as

---

[1] ii. p. 567.　　　　　[2] ii. p. 557.
[3] ii. p. 89.　See i. p. 205.

such. Every chief of kindred and every chief of a *wele* was thus in the sense above mentioned a landed and privileged person, with certain land occupied by himself and his family in severalty in *tyddyns* and crofts as well as with large grazing rights over sometimes several and distant districts.

At the same time, extensive rights of grazing implied wealth in the shape of herds of cattle. The possession of numerous oxen implied the lion's share in the produce of co aration. All this went with his being the landed head of his *wele*, and made him a powerful man. And yet, at the same time, his land-ownership, such as it was, could not be an absolute ownership. It was subject to the rules of ' *tir gueliawc.*'

To take an actual case, it would seem that under these rules Lauwarghe ap Kendalyk was during his life the only landed person in his *wele*. In him its rights as to land were vested.

He was the *penteulu*, and probably the *uchelwr* of the *wele*, and the only one. All his descendants, members of the *wele*, were, as to the land, in a subordinate position, with rights of maintenance only, which rights of maintenance, however, implied rights of grazing cattle in the common herd and co-aration with fellow tribesmen.

The young tribesmen of Lauwarghe's *wele* who on coming of age during his lifetime became *innate boneddigs* did not, however, become joint tenants with Lauwarghe, whether sons, grandsons, or great-grandsons. Their tribal rights were, not to a joint share in the land, but to that maintenance which was the common portion of every kinsman. They

CHAP. IV. claimed this maintenance, not by inheritance, but 'by kin and descent,' as members of the kindred and not as sons of their fathers, and the only doubt seems to be whether they claimed it from the head of the lesser or the greater kindred — whether from Lauwarghe ap Kendalyk as head of the *wele* in which they were born, or from the chief of the greater kindred to the ninth degree, or from the territorial lord of the district.

The *innate boneddig* claimed his maintenance from the kindred by 'kin and descent,' and not from his father.

Every *innate boneddig* on coming of age had, as we have seen, to become the *man* of a *lord* (*argluyd*) as well as *man* and *kin* to the chief of kindred. Till he was 14 his father was his lord (*argluyd*),[1] and maintained him at his own platter, but after that age his father was his lord no longer, and the lord (*argluyd*) whose man he had become had to give him his maintenance. If Lauwarghe ap Kendalyk was an *uchelwr* it seems probable that he may have had cast upon him as head of the *wele*, and *argluyd* of his man, the obligation of providing out of his tribal herds the necessary cattle for his maintenance as well as the *tyddyn* and the usufruct of the 'five free erws' which made up his *cyvarwys*.

Be this as it may, the new tribesman claimed his maintenance as a member of the kindred, 'by kin and descent,' and not by inheritance from his father.

There is a mysterious meaning hidden apparently in the word *tref*, which would help to clear our vision if it could be itself made transparent.

The phrase for inheritance is *tref y tat*, implying that what the son got in that case was from his

---

[1] i. pp. 203 205.

father's property and not from that of the kindred. CHAP. IV.
The word for kin is *car*, and the use of the word
cartref in the following passage seems to imply that
what the new tribesman got as his *cyvarwys* came
from his kindred.

> Three things without which there cannot be a home: a
> separate *cartrev*, privilege of country and kindred, and *cyvarws*
> secured by social compact (*cymmrawd*).[1]

All these three things the tribesman got by virtue
of his membership in the social organism of the
kindred and not by inheritance from his father.

But over and above these things that belonged
to every tribesman as an *innate boneddig* he had
prospective right of succession by inheritance to his
father's or his grandfather's position of privilege as
a landed person and the chief of his *wele*. When he
attained to this it was not by 'kin and descent' from
the kindred. In the words of the Venedotian Code
he had to 'ascend' to it, and he might live and die
without ever attaining it. The passage already
quoted from the Venedotian Code, which states that
the son at 14 who is an *innate boneddig* has no
privilege except his descent, as 'he ascends not to
the privilege of his father until his father's death,'
states further, 'and no one is a *marchog* [*i.e.* a horseman or knight] *until he shall ascend.*'[2]

What is the meaning of this addition? It gives
us incidentally another mark of the position of
the *uchelwr* or *breyr*, distinguishing him from
the subordinate tribesmen of his *wele*. His military dignity when the tribesmen go to battle is

Marginal notes:
He *ascends* to his father's privilege as a landed person on his father's death.

The *uchelwr* is a *horseman*; the *innate boneddig* only a foot-soldier.

---

marked by his fighting on horseback, whilst the subordinate tribesmen mostly fight on foot.

Giraldus Cambrensis describes the *nobiliores* as riding to battle on horseback, whilst the greater part of the people go to battle on foot.[1]

The *nobiliores* could hardly be other than the *uchelwrs* and *breyrs*, who are described in the Venedotian Code as *horsemen*, just as Cæsar describes the upper class of tribesmen in Gaul as *equites*.

So that it becomes clear, on the one hand, that the *innate boneddig* during the lifetime of the common ancestor of the *wele* to which he belonged remained in a subordinate position with rights of maintenance only, claimed ' by kin and descent,' like every other member of the kindred. On the other hand, his possible succession to the position of a landed *uchelwr* or *breyr* depended entirely on the rules of the *tir gueliawc*, so that when his turn came he claimed his succession by *dadenhudd*—i.e. by uncovering the family hearth and not by kin and descent.[2]

II. THE PROPERTY OF THE INDIVIDUAL TRIBESMAN UNDER THE CYMRIC TRIBAL SYSTEM.

In trying to realise a condition of things quite alien from anything within the experience of modern life it is always needful to guard against misconceptions arising from the ignorance of some material fact, perhaps too common to be mentioned, and only to be known by accident or inference.

An examination of the evidence of the Extents and the Codes has apparently shown that, setting

---

[1] *Descriptio Kambriæ,* I. cviii.

[2] ' A dadenhudd is not to be sued by kin and descent.' *Venedotian Code,* i. p. 171.

aside the possible introduction into the tribe from outside of ideas of private property in land which hardly belong to the tribal system, sufficient of purely tribal arrangements remained at the time of the Extents and the Codes to enable a fair judgment to be formed of the character and structure of tribal .society and its connection with the occupation of land.

So far as relates to the tribal occupation of land, the main facts elicited by the foregoing inquiry seem to be that the bundle of rights which approached most nearly to ownership were vested in the chiefs of kindreds and the heads of the family groups called *weles*, whilst the common herd of tribesmen were in the subordinate condition of possessing only the *cyrarwys* or right of maintenance.

The importance of this conclusion lies in the fact that it gives us a valuable economic point of comparison with other tribal systems, proving that the Cymric tribal system belonged to an early stage of economic development.

It can hardly be doubted that the Welsh *weles* resemble in their structure much more closely the ' patriarchal family ' under its *patria potestas* than what is known as the 'joint family' with its joint ownership under a chief who is only *primus inter pares*.

It seems to belong to the more archaic of the two systems.

Now, it has always been one of the mysteries even of the Roman *patria potestas* how the individuals under it, embracing all unemancipated sons, grandsons, and great-grandsons and their wives, were provided for.

CHAP. IV.

Mainte-
nance
under the
*patria
potestas.*
The
peculium
of its
subordi-
nate
members.

Sir Henry Maine, in his lectures on Ancient Law many years ago, suggested that the representative ownership of the head of the *patria potestas* ' must have been co-extensive with a liability to provide for all the members of the brotherhood out of the common fund.' [1] If in the case of slaves under the *patria potestas* there grew up by degrees the re-cognition of the *peculium*, how much more should not something like private property have become recognised in the sons and their descendants!

The
peculium
of the
Cymric
*innate
boneddig.*

It is worth while to examine further, in the light of this suggestion, into the question of the *da* or chattels of the individual tribesmen in Wales.

The fact that the payment of *galanas* was distributed amongst the kindred in stated proportions shows that they had individual property, probably mostly in cattle, wherewith to make payment.

The fact that in the Denbigh Extent the *tunc* payable by the Wele of Lauwarghe ap Kendalyk was distributed among the sub-*weles* and gavells composing it points in the same direction.

The fact that on the marriage of a daughter half a brother's share of the chattels was given with her *guaddol* confirms the same thing.

Let us follow these chattels given with the wife as her *guaddol*, and see in what it consisted.

> If a man take a wife by gift of kindred and leave her before the end of seven years, let him pay her *agweddi* to her.[2]
>
> . . . If she be left after the end of seven years, let there be an equal sharing between them, unless the privilege of the husband entitle him to more.

---

[1] *Ancient Law,* p. 145.
[2] That is, return to her the *agweddi* paid by her father to her husband on consummation of her marriage. *Venedotian Code,* i. p. 457.

If they be separated by death everything is to be equally
shared between them.[1]

In the Venedotian Code the property to be divided is defined as ' *everything belonging to them.*' [2]

The wife is to divide and the husband is to choose of the things which the law shall not share between them.

Certain things were specially named as to be given to the husband and certain other things to the wife.

The swine to the husband and the sheep to the wife, [or] if there be only one kind they are to be shared.

If there be sheep and goats, the sheep to the husband and the goats to the wife. . . .

Of the children, two shares to the father and one to the mother: the oldest and youngest to the father and the middlemost to the mother.

The household furniture is to be thus shared.

All the milking vessels except one pail go to the wife.

All the dishes except one dish go to the wife.

The wife is to have the car and the yoke to convey her furniture from the house.

The husband is to have all the drinking vessels.

The husband the riddle, the wife the small sieve.

The husband the upper stone of the quern, the wife the lower.

The clothes that are over them to the wife ; the clothes that are under them to the husband . . .

To the husband the kettle, the bed coverlet, the bolster of the dormitory, the coulter, the fuel axe, the auger, the settle, and all the hooks save one.

To the wife the pan, the trivet, the broad axe, the hedge bill, the ploughshare, all the flax, the linseed, the wool, the house bag with its contents except gold and silver (which are to be shared).

If there be webs, they are to be shared.

The yarn balls to the children (if any) ; if none, then shared.

The husband is to have the barn and all the corn aboveground and underground.

The husband the poultry and one of the cats, the rest to the wife.

The provisions are thus to be shared :

To the wife the meat in the brine and the cheese in the brine ; and after they are hung up to the husband.

---

[1] *Gwentian Code*, i. p. 747.   [2] *Venedotian Code*, i. p. 81.

> To the wife the vessels of butter in cut, the meat in cut, and the cheese in cut.
>
> To the wife as much of the meal as she can carry between her arms and knees from the storeroom into the house.[1]

That this description of the sharing belongs to the ordinary married tribesman seems to be clear, as the statement goes on to say :

> If the husband be privileged, let him show his privilege before the sharing, and after he shall have obtained his privilege let there be a sharing as we have said above.

This description of the chattels of husband and wife is graphic evidence of individual property in chattels on the part of the ordinary tribesman who has no privilege, *i.e. is not an uchelwr*, or a landed person.

It is strange that there is no mention of the cattle which presumably were the main part of the *da* of the tribesman. The omission of the *dog* also might lead to the suggestion that the cattle were part of the common herd of the kindred, and that in them the wife had no share. The same may be said of the mention of the ploughshare and omission of mention of the oxen wherewith the five free erws of the husband's *cyvarwys* must have been ploughed, and with which he joined with his fellows in coaration.

The reservation of the corn to the husband points in the same direction.

The *innate boneddig* is a dairy farmer.

But whatever may have been the rights in these respects of husband and wife, it is clear that the household of the married tribesman was that of a little dairy farmer with separate homestead, chiefly engaged in making butter and cheese ; but with a

---

[1] *Venedotian Code,* p. 83.

car and yoke of oxen for carrying and ploughing, with corn crops growing on his five free erws, as well as corn in the bin which, for household use, was ground by the quern, or at the chieftain's mill, into flour.

And thus his maintenance was not provided by his sharing in a common meal, or receiving doles in money or in kind from the common purse or produce of the kindred, but the result of his own labour and use of the cattle and *cyvarwys* which was received as his tribesman's right on his coming of age and assuming a tribesman's responsibilities.

It would seem, therefore, that his *da* and his *cyvarwys* were the nest-egg, as it were, of his *peculium*, and that he might become rich or poor by his good fortune and his thrift or the want of them.

His cyvarwys the nest-egg of his peculium.

Even, therefore, in the subordinate position of the ordinary tribesman there was individual property in chattels and consequent inequality of wealth, with the liability to that indebtedness to those above him which in Gaul, according to Cæsar, had become so prevalent and so ruinous.

Be this as it may, the lesson to be learned is, no doubt, that the possession of a *peculium* of private property in cattle and chattels was not inconsistent with the Welsh tribal system even in the archaic stage of the ' patriarchal family.'

The peculium not inconsistent with the patriarchal family.

There is an example of the same thing under the Hebrew patriarchal system so apt that it may well be used as an illustration.

It occurs in the story of Achan and his stolen wedge of gold, given in Joshua vii.

CHAP. IV.

Example
under the
Hebrew
patri-
archal

So Joshua rose up early in the morning, and brought Israel by their tribes; and the tribe of Judah was taken.

And he brought the families of Judah; and he took the family of the Zarhites.

And he brought the family of the Zarhites man by man; and Zabdi was taken.

Zabdi is the first individual named, and he thus was probably the oldest living ancestor and head of a household (LXX οἶκος)—*i.e.* he was the great-grandfather, head of his *wele*. What follows, therefore, reveals the interior of the Hebrew household or *wele*.

And he brought his household man by man; and Achan, the son of Carmi, the son of Zabdi, was taken.

Achan, therefore, was the grandson of Zabdi, the chief of the household or *wele*.

The guilt of Achan was acknowledged.

When I saw among the spoils a goodly Babylonish garment and two hundred shekels of silver, and a wedge of gold of fifty shekels weight [*i.e.* a Greek *maneh* in weight], then I coveted them, and took them; and behold they are hid in the earth in the midst of my tent, and the silver under it.

Achan, therefore, was a married tribesman with a tent of his own ; he was a little farmer with a family of sons and daughters who were great-grandchildren of Zabdi the chief of the household. He possessed also a *peculium* of cattle and chattels.

And Joshua, and all Israel with him, took Achan, and the silver, and the garment, and the wedge of gold, and his sons, and his daughters, and his oxen, and his asses, and his sheep, and his tent, and all that he had; and they brought them unto the valley of Achor. . . . And all Israel stoned him with stones, and burned them with fire, after they had stoned them with stones. And they raised over him a great heap of stones unto this day

III. THE APPLICATION OF THE GRADES OF KINDRED TO
MUTUAL RESPONSIBILITY FOR CRIME.

The organised kindreds under the chiefs of kindred and the *weles* occupying land forming groups round which metaphorically a ring fence might be drawn, containing respectively kindred to the ninth and to the fourth degree, must not be confounded with the grades of kindred to the fourth, the seventh and the ninth degree, which were liable for the *saraad* and *galanas*. No ring fence could be drawn round the kinsmen who were responsible for one another's crimes.

The grades of kindred liable in any given case did not correspond with any particular group surrounding a family hearth, or in joint occupation of a district, or under one chief of kindred.

A tribesman has committed a murder. For the purpose of the *galanas* he is the centre of the grades of kinsfolk on whom the liability for his crime is cast in recognised proportions. He is individually the centre of concentric rings of relationship extending to both paternal and maternal relatives within certain degrees, and as he lives and moves amongst his fellow tribesmen he carries, so to speak, around him a halo of responsibility, shading off as the degrees of relationship become more distant. Every tribesman is surrounded by others who are responsible for him in various degrees, and each of whom has his own particular halo of responsibility surrounding him. All within his particular halo are in different degrees liable for his frolics and his

Marginal note: CHAP. IV. Each tribesman surrounded by a halo of mutual responsibility for crime.

CHAP. IV. crimes, and he is reciprocally liable for each one
of theirs in settled proportions.

Thus the whole society is knit together by an
infinite number of crossing and intersecting threads of
mutual guarantee and liability, from the meshes of
which no tribesman can escape.

Even if the tribesman should emigrate beyond
the bounds of the district of the kindred or lordship
to which he belongs, he does not thereby cut the
thread of liability.

> Whoever shall pay *galanas*, if the whole of his kindred be in the
> same country (*gulat* [1]) with him, full payment is required of him by
> the end of a fortnight; if the kindred be scattered in several other
> countries a delay of a fortnight is right in respect to each country. [2]

This rule, however, does not seem to have prevailed as between the four greater divisions of
Wales.

> Should an innate *boneddig* of Powys be in Gwynedd, or one from
> Gwynedd be in Powys, and become subject to *galanas*, and his family
> kindred should not be in the country (*gulat*) with him, although many
> relations should, it is right for him to pay *galanas*, and to bring these
> along with him . . . and it shall be shared according to the number
> of his kindred that may be in the country. [3]

The
liability
extended
to
maternal
relations
and so
bound
kindreds
together.

The liability has already been mentioned, not
only of maternal relations, but also of sisters and
female cousins, to assist in the payment of *galanas*.
The result must have been to bind together, not only
individuals, but kindreds also, by the ties of a
common liability.

At first sight it may seem strange that females
should be liable at all, but a moment's consideration
will show that it was in harmony with the position of

---

[1] In the *Venedotian Code*
'lordship,' *arglvydiaeth*.

[2] *Gwentian Code*, p. 702.

[3] *Venedotian Code*, p. 232.

women in other respects under the tribal system.
We have seen that the daughter, no less than the son,
ceased to be supported by the father on attaining the
age of puberty. She, too, had her separate right of
maintenance under tribal arrangements, and if she
married she was entitled to her *gwaddol*. Rights and
obligations generally go together.

And if it be asked why had women this position
in the kindred, the answer is not far to seek. It is
found in an exceptional case, in which there was no
liability, viz. when it had ceased to be possible for a
woman to have children.

A woman does not pay spear-penny, for she has not a spear, but her
distaff only, neither do clerks pay it; and a woman does not pay
galanas if she make oath that she shall have no more children,
neither do clerks pay it: and it is not paid by a boy under fourteen
years of age.[1]

Another version has it thus:

And females and clerks shall pay it (*galanas*) unless they deny that
they shall ever have children, *for they shall pay for their children.*

Here, then, is the reason why women had their
place in the arrangements of the kindred. It was
in right of their children, and because they might
have children, that their place in the kindred was
reserved. So long as it was possible for them to
have children they were necessary links in the chain
of consanguinity. Without them the chain would
lose its continuity.

The mutual responsibility of kinsmen for *saraad*
and *galanas*, graduated according to nearness of kin
to the murdered man and the criminal, reveals more
clearly than anything else the extent to which the

---

[1] *Venedotian Code*, i. p. 227.

individual was bound by innumerable meshes to his fixed place in the tribal community—the extent to which, under the tribal system, individual freedom was sunk in the solidarity of the tribe.

That this solidarity had its origin in the necessities of defence from the wrongs of other and rival kindreds is strongly suggested by the fact that the payment of *galanas* did not apply within the kindred.

No *galanas* within the kindred.

The murderer of a kinsman had committed a wrong within his kindred. It was not a case for the payment of *galanas*. The passage from the Gwentian Code has already been quoted which states that the hate of the kindred will follow the murderer who cannot be slain. 'Since the living kin is not killed for the sake of the dead kin, everybody will hate to see him.'[1] As we have seen, he became a kin-wrecked man, and fled like an outlaw to seek safety and maintenance as a stranger and a suppliant wherever shelter could be found.

The murderer outlawed.

The payment of *galanas* was therefore a matter between two kindreds. It was accordingly exacted in solemn form, at the time of the Codes, through the territorial lords who were the representatives of civil authority.

> The period for *galanas* is a fortnight after being summoned for each lordship wherein they live, to apportion the payment, and twice that time for exacting the payment and to assemble them to pay it. And every lord is to have the exacting third in his own lordship. At three periods and in three thirds the *galanas* is to be paid: two periods for the kindred of the father and one for the kindred of the mother; because two thirds fall upon the kindred of the father, and therefore they are to have two periods. At the first period for the kindred of the father to pay one of their thirds, they are to have the oaths of one hundred of the best men of the other kindred, that their relation is forgiven. And at the second

---

[1] i. p. 791.

period, on their paying their second third, they are also to have the oaths of another hundred men of the other kindred that their relation is forgiven, and those of the best men of the tribe; and at the third period the kindred of the mother are to pay their third; and then they are to have the oaths of a hundred men of the other kindred, that their relation is forgiven; and everlasting concord is to be established on that day, and perpetual amnesty between them.[1]

Thus the *galanas* was a judicial arrangement of a *casus belli* between kindreds. At the time of the Codes it was no longer what it may have been at first, the subject of bargain between two kindreds. It had become a matter of tribal law. The amount was fixed, and the exaction was made by the higher judicial authority representing the tribe or nation of the *Cymry*. There was thus, so to speak, the intervention of a kind of international law and authority superseding the lynch law or blood feud between the kindreds. How early in tribal history this intervention may have existed cannot be known, but, whatever its origin, it added much, doubtless, to the solidarity of tribal society.

The galanas a judicial matter between kindreds.

IV. THE GRADES OF ARISTOCRACY IN THE KINDRED AS MARKED BY THE 'GALANAS.'

The rules of *saraad* and *galanas* not only bear witness to the solidarity of the tribe, they also bear witness to the existence of grades of aristocracy within the tribe, and even within the kindred itself.

They prove that under the tribal system the structure of society was rather that of aristocratic gradations of rank than of equality in the modern democratic sense. The Cymric tribes were conquering tribes, treating the conquered or alien races below

Tribal gradations of rank.

---

[1] *Venedotian Code*, i. p. 229.

CHAP. IV. them as strangers in blood and as belonging to a different race. And a conquering tribe is perhaps hardly likely to recognise equality, even in its own internal relations.

Men's lives of different grades of worth.

Accordingly, even within the tribe and the kindred the value of one man's life was greater than another's. The amount of payment of *galanas*, *i.e.* for killing a man, is sometimes spoken of in the Codes as his *worth* (*guerth*)—the same word being used for the worth of the *brenhin*, or head chieftain, as is used for the worth of a cow or a kettle.

The gradations in the *galanas* thus reveal the grades of worthiness of the several classes in the tribe.

The worth of the *brenhin.*

Thus, to begin with the *brenhin*, or king. The following is from the Venedotian Code :

The worth of the king is his *saraad* threefold. . . .
The *saraad* of the King of Aberffraw is to be paid thus :
A hundred cows from each *cantref* in his dominion and a white bull with red ears to every hundred cows, and a rod of gold equal in length to himself and as thick as his little finger, and a plate of gold as broad as his face and as thick as the nail of a ploughman who has been a ploughman for seven years. Gold is paid only to the King of Aberffraw.[1]

Of others of the royal family and household.

The *saraad* and *galanas* of the queen were one third that of the king.[2] The worth of the *edling*, or designated successor to the *brenhin*, was also one third of the worth of the *brenhin*.[3] The chief of the *brenhin's* household, being also a son of his, was likewise of one third the *brenhin's* worth. The worth of the king's steward was nine score and nine cows— *i.e.* 189 cows.[4] The worth of the other royal officers

---

[1] *Venedotian Code*, i. p. 7.　　[2] i. p. 7.
[3] p. 11.　　[4] p. 13.

was six score and six cows—*i.e.* 126 cows.[1] But the
worth of the baking woman and the laundress of the
court was only one half of the worth of their brothers.

These officers, even though originally strangers,
were free by reason of their office, and their worth
(126 cows) seems thus to be the normal worth of the
free tribesman.

But setting aside the official class and looking
within the kindreds, even the tribesmen were not all
of one worth.

According to the Venedotian Code, the following
were the grades of worthiness.[2]

The chief of kindred	. 189 cows.
The *uchelwr*	. 126 cows.
Man with a family without office	. 84 cows.
The innate *boneddig*	. 63 cows.
The *alltud* of the *brenhin*	. 63 cows.
The *alltud* of the *uchelwr*	. 31½ cows.
The bondman (*caeth*) of this island, one pound of silver, *i.e.*	. 4 cows.
The bondman from beyond sea, 1½ lb. *i.e.* . .	. 6 cows.

The *galanas* of a woman was half the *galanas* of
her brother,[3] just as her share in her father's goods
(*da*) was half a brother's share.[4]

According to the Gwentian Code the grades of
payment were virtually the same as those of North
Wales, except that the worth of the chief of kindred
was 567 cows and that of the members of his family
189 cows.

The Dimetian Code follows the Gwentian Code.

In both the latter Codes the *breyr* takes the place
of the *uchelwr* with the same worth, viz. 126 cows.

This worth of the *uchelwr* or *breyr* seems, there-

CHAP. IV   fore, to represent the worth of the full or typical free
tribesman, whilst that of the mere innate *boneddig*
was only one half of it, the same as that of the
stranger settled on the chieftain's land, and double
that of the stranger on the land of the *uchelwr* or
breyr.

Thus the youth born into the tribe, who was an
innate boneddig, notwithstanding that his blood was
pure to the ninth degree—that is to say, that he
was the ninth in the line of unbroken descent
from Cymric parents—on attaining fourteen, and
receiving his *cyvarwys,* did not jump all at once
into complete equality of communal value and
rights in a republic whose members were all ' free
and equal.' Provision was made, as we have seen,
for his maintenance as a member of the kindred, but
he was only a subordinate member. His worth was
only half that of the *uchelwr,* and the same as that of
the baking woman and laundress of the Court.

His worth was raised from 63 to 84 cows in North
Wales when he became a family man, but he might
live and die without becoming an *uchelwr.*

Hence the evidence of the rules relating to *saraad*
and *galanas,* like those of land-occupation, prove
that the structure of tribal society was patriarchal
and aristocratic and not republican.

The three
kinds of
men.

Thus several lines of evidence patiently followed
have led to the same conclusion. And now at last
it becomes easy to understand a statement of the
Dimetian Code,[1] which, though at first sight strange

---

[1] i. p. 351 and p. 469. See
also *Venedotian Code,* p. 91,
where, in reference to the *agweddi*
the three classes are the *brenhin,*
the *gwrda,* and the *aillt.*

and paradoxical, may now be recognised as summing
up the whole truth in a nutshell.

> There are three kinds of persons—a *brenhin*, a *breyr* [or
> *uchelwr*] and a *villein*, with their *aelodeu* (*i.e.* 'relatives,' literally
> 'members').

Under the tribal system the *wele* is the unit.
The *brenhin* and the members of his *wele* form the
royal and ruling class. The *breyrs* or *uchelwrs*, heads
of *weles* with the *innate boneddigs* under them, form
the second class of free tribesmen. The *villeins*, or
strangers in blood, form the third class; and beneath
all these were the *caeths*, or slaves, who could be
bought and sold.

The extraordinary solidarity of the kindreds and The
the tribe—a solidarity to which history bears ample solidarity
of tribal
testimony—was gained at the expense of the free- society.
dom and equality of the individual tribesmen. And
little as the Codes reveal to us of the actual condition
of the rank and file of Cymric tribesmen, it is impossible to shut our eyes to the easy possibility of
oppression on the part of the chieftains and *uchelwrs*.
It is easy to see how, if such was the structure of
the Gallic tribes described by Cæsar, his description
of tribal society might well be, in measure at least,
typical of tribal society generally in its early stages.
It might, under the pressure of want on the part of Liability
the tribesmen, or the unscrupulous use of power on sion.
to oppres-
the part of the *uchelwrs* or higher chieftains, easily
come to pass that the mass of tribesmen, with their
bare rights of maintenance and a *peculium* subject
to the vicissitudes of fortune, elsewhere than in the
Gaul of Cæsar's description might become almost
the serfs of the *uchelwrs*, or, as he describes them,
the *servi* of the *equites*.

V. CONFIRMATORY EVIDENCE OF THE DENBIGH EXTENT.

There is one other test to which may finally be put the correctness of the conclusion come to on the evidence of the Codes with reference to the subordinate position as regards rights in land and responsibility for crime of the ordinary tribesman in the *wele* to which he belonged.

The escheats in the Denbigh Extent.

The evidence of the escheats recorded in the Denbigh Extent has been adduced as proof that the landed rights of the *weles* were mainly undivided rights of occupation and grazing. The escheats in respect of members who died *contra pacem* were not of specific acres of land, but of fractions of undivided rights.

And, as we have seen, the surveyors could only arrive at the proportion of the lords in respect of these escheats by what was practically a rule-of-three sum. All the escheated fractions in a given villata added together amounted to such and such a proportion of the whole. The acreage of the whole villata was so many acres. The lord's proportion of those acres in respect of the escheats was so and so, and he could, by rough justice, seize upon an area so ascertained, inclose it, and let it out on the English fashion to his own tenants.

The lord claimed a proportion equal to the total of the escheated fractions in a district.

But, this being so, why may it not be said that the fact of a man dying *contra pacem*, followed by the escheat to the lord of a fractional share in the landed rights of the *wele*, proves that as a subordinate member of the *wele* to which he belongs he was already in possession of his proper share in those landed rights, instead of having only his right of maintenance as the Codes seem to imply? How otherwise can it be that a son or a grandson who has not yet ' ascended ' to the privilege of his father or grandfather has a share which could escheat? Does not this show that the patriarchal character of the Cymric *wele*, on which so much stress has been laid, had at least vanished from actual practice at the time of the Extent? And, if so, may it not fairly be doubted whether the system described in the Codes ever was more than an imaginary system, all very well on paper, but never in actual use?

These questions can only be met fairly by a further examination into the actual facts of the escheats as described in the Extent. This invaluable document will once more prove the safest guide to the true understanding of the Codes.

If, in the case of a death *contra pacem*, the escheat was of the particular fraction of rights belonging to the individual tribesman so dying, then the Extent must be admitted to be at variance with the Codes and Laws.

If, however, on close examination it should be found that the responsibility of the escheats was cast on the *wele* as a whole, then the evidence of the Extent must be allowed to confirm in a remarkable manner the patriarchal character of the *wele* as described in the Codes.

What are the facts?

Now, if the reader will refer to the summary given above of the *wele* of Lauwarghe ap Kendalyk, he will find that there had been two escheats, viz. :—

(1) $\frac{1}{4}$ of the gavell of Ken' ap Risshard ap Lauwarghe, *i.e.* $\frac{1}{36}$ of the original *wele* of Lauwarghe ap Kendalyk,

CHAP. IV.

If a tribesman had only a right of maintenance how could he have a share which could escheat?

Does the Extent show that he had a joint share in the land or rights of the *wele*?

One-sixth exactly of the *wele* of Lauwarghe ap Kendalyk was escheat,

CHAP. IV.
and (2) $\frac{5}{6}$ of the gavell of David ap Kendalo ap Lauwarghe, *i.e.* $\frac{5}{36}$ of the original *wele* of Lauwarghe ap Kendalyk.

Now, the two together make up $\frac{6}{36}$, so that exactly one-sixth of the original *wele* had escheated to the lord for deaths *contra pacem* of members of this *wele*.

and apportioned among the tribesmen of the *wele.*
The natural inference is that one-sixth of the original *wele* was adjudged after the war to be escheat, and that it was apportioned by arrangement within the kindred in the proportion of $\frac{1}{36}$ to the family of one of the grandsons, and $\frac{5}{36}$ to the family of one of the others ; the families of the other four grandsons being free from any part of it. This seems on the face of the figures more likely than that the rights of the individuals who had died *contra pacem* should have added up to an exact sixth of the whole right of the *wele*.

The case of the *wele* of Canon ap Lauwarghe,
Turning next to the summary of the villata of Prees, and taking first the escheats within the *progenies* or *wele* of Canon ap Lauwarghe, we have the following fractions :—

$$\frac{7}{16} \text{ of a gavell} \quad = \frac{14}{36} \text{ of a gavell.}$$
$$\frac{1}{4} \quad \text{,,} \quad \text{,,} \quad = \frac{9}{36} \text{ ,,} \quad \text{,,}$$
$$\frac{2}{3} \text{ of } \frac{1}{2} \text{ gavell} \quad = \frac{6}{36} \text{ ,,} \quad \text{,,}$$
$$\text{a whole } \frac{1}{2} \text{ gavell} = \frac{18}{36} \text{ ,,} \quad \text{,,}$$

Adding these fractions together, the total of the escheats equals $\frac{45}{36}$ of a gavell. Now, as there were $4\frac{1}{2}$ gavells belonging to the *progenies* of Canon ap Lauwarghe, $\frac{45}{162}$ or $\frac{10}{36}$ of his *wele* was escheat.

and the *wele* of Pythle ap Lauwarghe.
There were 8 *weles* embraced in the *wele* of Pythle ap Lauwarghe, of which one whole *wele* was escheat, and $\frac{3}{10}$ of all the other seven, making together $\frac{31}{10}$ of $\frac{1}{8}$, *i.e.* $\frac{31}{80}$ of the original *wele* of Pythle.

These cases do not seem at first sight to be evidence either way; but when it is considered that Canon ap Lauwarghe and Pythle ap Lauwarghe were brothers it becomes obvious that they were sharers in their father's original *wele*, so that if these fractions of $\frac{10}{36}$ and $\frac{31}{80}$—which in themselves suggest nothing —turn out to be divisions of an even fraction of the whole original *wele* of Lauwarghe, the father of Canon and Pythle, just as in the last case, the evidence will confirm the fact of the escheat having been thrown on the whole original *wele*.

CHAP. IV

These were parts of the original *wele* of their father, and the escheats from the two make one-third of the original *wele*.

Now, $\frac{10}{36}$ of Canon's *wele* and $\frac{31}{80}$ of Pythle's *wele* equal $\frac{5}{36}$ and $\frac{31}{160}$ of their father's *wele*; and, added together, these fractions amounted to $\frac{479}{1440}$—*i.e.* only $\frac{1}{1440}$ short of one even third of the original *wele*. The inference consequently must be that after the wars it had been adjudged that one-third of the original *wele* should be regarded as escheat, and, as a matter of fact, it was impossible to allot this one-third according to the tribal rules as to the responsibility of the families of tribesmen more exactly than was done in the fractions above-mentioned.

The same conclusion is arrived at when the internal division is considered. Take the case of the *progenies* of Pythle. Pythle was presumably dead at the date of the Extent, because his sons are recorded as the heads of *weles*. One of these sons is dead *contra pacem*, perhaps without sons, and the whole of his *wele* is escheat. There are seven other sons' *weles* to bear their share of the remainder of the escheat. They divide the rest of what falls to Pythle's share equally—*i.e.* $\frac{3}{10}$ of their rights are

I

CHAP. IV.

The
liability
for deaths
*contra
pacem* was
thus
charged
on the
original
wele as a
whole.

given up as escheat by each of the seven. How is it possible that exactly $\frac{3}{10}$ of the members of each of these *weles* had died *contra pacem*? They are evidently sharing a common liability which had fallen upon the original wele to which they belonged.

So far, therefore, from the evidence of the escheats of the Denbigh Extent clashing with that of the Codes as to the patriarchal character of the *weles*, it seems to confirm it in a remarkable manner, and to show that even so late as the conquest of North Wales the ordinary free tribesman of the Denbigh district was not treated as an individual owner of a fractional share in the landed rights of his family, but as a subordinate member of a *patria potestas*, whose head was responsible in his representative character, as head of the *wele*, for the misdeeds of all his descendants to the fourth degree of descent.

The
individual
tribesmen
were
therefore
treated as
members
of a *patria
potestas*
and not as
joint-
owners.

CHAPTER V.

THE RELATION TO THE TRIBE OF STRANGERS IN BLOOD.

I. THE VARIOUS CLASSES OF STRANGERS.

A GOOD deal has already been said with regard to the relations to the tribe of the strangers in blood.

If blood relationship was the tie which bound the kindreds of tribesmen together, and if the want of Cymric blood made the gulf between the tribesmen and strangers in blood, the refusal to recognise any efficient blood relationship as between strangers was the key to their legal condition under the tribal system. It was as though the tribesman was so conscious of the strength of the tie of his own blood relationship that he was blind to any other but his own. Or possibly his knowledge of the strength of that tie made him dread the growth of a similar tie amongst others of alien blood.

It is significant that the ties which were recognised, and even encouraged within cautious limits, were those which bound the stranger to the tribesman, and not those which would bind him to his fellow stranger. And no doubt from the point of view of the tribal system there was political wisdom in the instinct which set itself against what would help the non-

1 2

CHAP. V.

Each
stranger
under a
lord.

He was
not there-
fore a
serf.

Placed in a
maertref,
or *taeog-
tref*, in
'tref-
gevery,'
without
rights of
inherit-
ance;

tribesmen to organise themselves into a too powerful subject tribe.

Under the tribal system each stranger was individually subject to some Cymric superior and protector, who might, or might not, as we shall see, have proprietary rights over him. A tie of some kind always was formed between him and his Cymric superior, but, whatever it might be, it did not necessarily imply anything in the nature of bondage or serfdom, however easily it might grow into it.

Even if something like the relation of lordship and serfdom ultimately grew out of it, as the phraseology of the surveys would suggest had been the case, still, before we can understand its nature we must examine how it arose under the tribal system and by what tribal rules it was regulated. It is the more necessary to examine this point carefully, as it may possibly help to throw some light upon the origin and original nature of manorial serfdom.

The surveys have already made us familiar with the hamlets of so-called villein or bond tenants, holding under what the 'Record of Carnarvon' describes as a tenure of the nature of *trefgevery*.

These tenants are described in the Codes as *taeogs*, or *aillts*, or *alltuds*, and as sometimes located on the *maertref* of the Prince, and sometimes in *taeog-trefs*, *i.e.* in separate *trefs*, and not mixed up with the tribesmen.

Further, the description in the Codes of the nature of their tenure (which has already been quoted) was found to correspond with the description given in the 'Record of Carnarvon' of land held in *trefgevery*.

The peculiar point about these *taeog-trefs* was,

it will be remembered, the joint responsibility of the
taeogs in each *tref*, or hamlet, for the services, or
payments in lieu of them. In some cases on the
manor of Aberffraw they seemed to be arranged in
groups of nine, probably for this purpose.

The peculiar feature of the *taeog-tref* as described
in the Codes was the entire absence of any rights of
inheritance, all the *taeogs* sharing equally in the land,
sons having separate *tyddyns* during the lifetime of
their fathers, and sharing equally along with the rest,
excepting the youngest son, who remained with his
father and succeeded to his *tyddyn* on his death.

The equality was carried so far as to provide that
no one could commence the co-ploughing until every
taeog in the *tref* had found a place for his oxen in the
common ploughs.[1]

Recognising that this peculiar kind of tenure was
the natural result of carrying out the tribal principle that there was no true kinship and inheritance
among strangers in blood, it becomes obvious that it
was the typical kind of tenure for non-tribesmen,
and this was so whether they were settled in the
maertref of the *Brenhin*, or Prince, or in separate
taeog-trefs under the regulation of his *maer* and
canghellor, or scattered over the cantrefs and cymwds
under subordinate chieftains or *uchelwrs*. In all
cases, as a normal rule, non-tribesmen were placed
in regulated *trefs*, of *tir cyfrif*, held in *trefgevery*.

The ordinary class of *taeogs*, or *aillts*, born on
the land, whose ancestors had been on the land from
generation to generation, to whom the bridge of

---

[1] *Ancient Laws*, i. p. 772.

successive marriages with women of Cymric blood was shut out by the humility of their position, who were therefore in North Wales *taeogs* for ever, and in South Wales waiting for the ninth generation before there was any chance of rising into a higher status —these hereditary *taeogs*, or *aillts*, would naturally be described by the makers of the surveys as *nativi* and *bond tenants.*

And it was perfectly natural that new comers, strangers in blood, seeking protection and settlement, should, as a rule, be placed in such a *taeog-tref* and become *nativi* like the rest.

But further examination very soon makes it clear that all strangers and new comers were not treated alike.

Without entering into the question of terminology and the difference between an *alltud* and an *aillt* or *taeog*[1] (all being strangers in blood), it can readily be seen that the new comers might belong to different classes.

Take the case of the *car-shattered* or *kin-broken* tribesman. For some reason or other he had to leave his kindred. The cause of his leaving might well determine his position in the place where he sought his new home.

If driven by necessity like the ' Prodigal Son ' in the parable to take a menial position, to join himself to an *uchelwr*, he would naturally be placed to work in a *taeog-tref*. He might well be contented to perform the services of a *taeog* in return for

---

[1] Generally the *aillt* of the Venedotian Code seems to correspond with the *taeog* of the others, but not in every case.

protection and maintenance.   He would thus natu-   Chap. V.
rally drop into the position of an *aillt* or a *taeog*.

The word *aillt* is believed to mean 'a shaven or   easily be-
tonsured person.'[1]   The *tonsure* would be the Celtic   came an
aillt by
tonsure—from ear to ear—and his submission to it   tonsure,
would be the outward sign that he had become the
servant of his protector.

Such might well be the experience of any stranger
in humble or abject circumstances, driven by necessity to seek protection.   The following passage
couples with the '*kin-broken*' man, the illegitimate
son disowned by the kin, and the stranger seeking
a home in Cymru :—

> 'Strangers and their progeny are *adjudged to be aillts*, and
> also the reputed son, . . . and evil-doers, *till the end of the ninth
> descent*.
> 'And every aillt and taeog is required to be a sworn man,
> and appraised to the lord of the territory, and to his proprietary
> lord, *i.e.* the lord who shall take him under his protection, and grant
> him land in a taeog-trev. *And an aillt is to be at the will and
> pleasure of such until he shall attain the descent and privilege
> of an innate Cymro*, and that is to be attained *by the fourth
> descendant of his issue by legitimate marriages with innate
> Cymraeses*.'[2]

In this passage from the Triads, which obviously   and
refers to South Wales, the new comers are all de-   placed in a
taeog-tref.
scribed as located in *taeog-trefs*.   And if it stood
alone we might assume that admission into the *taeog-
tref* was the only recognised mode of dealing with
strangers in blood.

---

[1] *Aillt* means in old Welsh *shaven* or *tonsured*, the verb being in modern Welsh *eillio* (to shave), Irish *altan* (a razor). In Manx *inney-veayl* is a word for bond-woman (as in the case of *Hagar*, in the Biblical story), and it literally means the 'bald or cropped girl.' I am indebted to my friend Professor Rhys for this information.

[2] ii. p. 505.

CHAP. V.

Some favoured strangers placed on land and grow into tribesmen.

But from other passages it is clear that there were classes of strangers, probably in better circumstances, who were not thus placed once for all in a *taeog-tref* to take their chance as ordinary *taeogs.* These new comers were placed upon portions of the Brenhin's or *uchelwr's* waste to work themselves or their descendants in the fourth degree into the position of tenants *adscripti glebæ*, holding in kindreds and families, but still without the privilege of tribesmen. There is a passage which throws a flood of light into the question of the position, under the tribal system, of this class of strangers. Possibly it refers only to *alltuds* in the strict meaning of the term, but it shows how tribal principles and tribal analogies were applied to such cases.

> ‘ If an alltud [stranger] become a *man* to an uchelwr, and be with him until death ; and the son of the alltud be with the son of the uchelwr, and the grandson of the alltud with the grandson of the uchelwr, and the great grandson of the alltud with the great grandson of the uchelwr, that fourth uchelwr will be a *priodawr* over the great grandson of the alltud, and his heirs [will be] *priodorion* of the heirs of that grandson for ever, and, thenceforth, they are not to go to the country whence they are derived, away from their proprietary lords, on account of their having lost the time when they were to go if they willed to go.’ [1]

Remaining four generations, they become *adscripti glebæ*, and subject to family proprietorship.

This passage shows that the tribal rule that proprietorship in land was not attained till the occupation had continued till the fourth generation, was applied also to a lord's proprietorship of an *alltud.* If the *alltud* and his descendants remained on the land of the *uchelwr* for four generations, the great-grandchildren of the *alltud* became *adscripti glebæ* for ever after. And so complete was the

---

[1] *Ancient Laws*, ii. p. 87 (middle 14th century).

proprietorship thus established that it had become subject to the law of family possession under the further application of tribal rules; so that a father could not free the stranger for longer than his own life without his son's consent.

> ' No one can liberate an alltud, except during his own life, except by his departure to his own country, and although he may liberate him in his day, the claim will be fresh for the son, after his father, when he shall be minded to claim.' [1]

But there is another important inference to be drawn from the passage first quoted, viz. that any time before the fourth generation the *alltud* and his descendants could leave the *uchelwr's* service if they pleased.

Accordingly in another passage it is expressly stated that the *alltud* could avoid coming under permanent proprietorship by removal at intervals from one *uchelwr* to another.

> ' If an alltud when he comes from his country become a *man* to an uchelwr, and from him go to another, and he proceed, and his son after him, and his grandson, and his great-grandson, and his *goresgynydd*, from one uchelwr to another, without settling in any place more than another, let them be under the privilege of alltuds so long as they shall be thus without settling.' [2]

These passages make no special mention of any separate location on land. They may be of later date than the Codes. But the following passage from the Venedotian Code deals directly with the case of *alltuds* located on land, and it shows that they were dealt with on the same tribal principles.

It explains the acquisition by the *alltud* or his descendants of the privilege of permanent occupation

---

[1] ii. p. 77. [2] ii. p. 86 (middle 14th century).

CHAP. V.

of land, if they shall have occupied the same land under an *uchelwr* till the fourth generation. And it also explains that at the same moment in which the fourth man becomes a *priodawr*, he also becomes *subject to the proprietorship* of the *uchelwr*, and thenceforth practically *adscriptus glebæ*.

> 'And as the alltuds of the King become *priodorion* in the fourth man after they shall have been placed on the King's waste, so also the alltuds of the uchelwrs become *priodorion* in the fourth man if they have occupied the same land under them for so long a time, and from thenceforth they are not to go from the uchelwrs, for they are *priodorion* under them, and they are not to take their propriety, one from the land from whence they originate, and another here.
>
> 'After they are become *priodorion*, their tyddyns on the land, and land to them also they are to have, and their land, excepting such, to be arable among them.' [1]

It is further added :—

> 'If the alltuds will go away from their lords *before* they become *priodorion*, they are to leave half their goods to them.' [2]

thus confirming the point of their freedom to move as they pleased till the fourth generation.

These strangers acquire ultimately rights of inheritance.

Whether the first passage quoted might apply or not to strangers placed in *taeog-trefs* of 'register land,' it is clear that the last quoted passage deals with quite another class, *i.e.* with immigrants of a much higher position. These immigrants are strangers in blood. They are placed on the waste of a prince or an *uchelwr* apparently in groups, each with his separate *tyddyn*, and a few erws in croft around it occupied in severalty, and with other land held in common by the group which was to be arable among them cultivated by the co-aration of their common plough-teams. The great-grandchildren of

---

[1] *Venedotian Code*, i. p. 183.   [2] *Ibid.*

the original *aillts* become *priodorion*, and are distinguished from *taeogs* holding in *trefgevery.*

But it must not be imagined that in becoming
proprietors they also became Cymric tribesmen. Far
from it. It is true that the word *priodawr* is applied
to them as it is to tribesmen, but instead of being,
like the tribesmen, proprietors of tribal rights, they
become proprietors on what in the Extents is called
terra nativa. The fact seems to be that at the
moment when, from unbroken residence for four
generations, recognition of the rights of kindred was
at last conceded, instead of its establishing kinship
to the tribe and making them Cymry, it confirmed
their subordinate position and deprived them of their
freedom of departure from the land for ever.

This process of final recognition of kindred in
the families of strangers is thus strictly consistent
with tribal policy.

It must not be confused with the exceptional
bridges across the gulf between tribesmen and non-
tribesmen allowed in South Wales.

The families of these favoured strangers, whose
rights of kindred were recognised, remained permanently non-tribesmen, and it is interesting to
observe that notwithstanding this the tribal rules as
to grades of kinship were recognised as applying
to them. At the fourth generation the recognition
of kindred began, and the descendant of the original
alltud became an *alltud* of a kindred. But the
kindred was not a perfect one till the ' *alltud* of a
kindred ' had himself great-grandchildren.

' If there be an *alltud* of a kindred he is entitled to a *raith* as
upon a Cymro. An *alltud* of a kindred is an *alltud* whose parents

have been in Cymru until there have arisen brothers, cousins, second cousins and third cousins, and nephews to each of those.

'They are not thenceforth to go to the country from whence they originated, because they are a kindred; and there is no person of a kindred who is not entitled to have a *raith* adjudged to him, and that number of persons form a kindred; and there is no one who has not been primarily an advenient man; and all ultimately become proprietors and form kindreds if they continue in Cymru until the fourth descent.' [1]

This passage brings into view another consequence of the recognition of kindred in the case of *aillts*—another point in which the tribal system was consistent with itself.

One of the rights of the innate Cymro was protection by *raith* of his kindred—the right to call upon his kindred to protect him by their oath.

So long as the *aillt* was without recognition of kindred his oath was not recognised as of any value, because he had no kindred who could swear for him.

'Alltuds can be sold by their lord and given by law, and amends are not to be made for them if they be unlawfully killed, because they have no kindred who can demand it.' [2]

They had, indeed, a *worth* or *galanas,* but the lord alone could claim it. But so soon as they attained the privilege of kindred, their kindred could claim it, and the oaths or *raith* of a kindred had to be recognised.

There is a passage which seems to meet the difficulty of want of numbers in the *alltud's* newly-acquired kindred. He was still not a Cymro, and he had no right to call upon any but his kindred to be compurgators with him.

What, then, was he to do if in any case more

---

[1] ii. p. 95.   [2] ii. p. 403.

oaths were required than he had kinsmen to swear for him ? This was a difficulty which had to be met. And it seems to have been met by a kind of legal fiction.

> ' There is to be no rejection of the *raith* of an *alltud* when a *raith* of the country does not pertain to him, although persons shall not swear along with him ; for let him give his own oath repeatedly for so many persons as ought to swear along with him if he were of a kindred.' [1]

Thus it appears that the tribal law recognised not only kindred, but also the consequence of kindred, in the case of these *aillts* and *alltuds*, who, through residence for four generations on a lord's land, had become *adscripti glebæ*. But it also appears that the recognition of kindred among themselves, instead of making them Cymry, left them in such a legal position as to justify the Norman lawyers and surveyors calling them *nativi*, although, like the tribesmen, they were allowed to form *gwelys* instead of living under the normal tenure of the nature of *trefgevery*.

This explains how we come to find in the Extents of Anglesey, Carnarvon, Merioneth, and Denbigh, *nativi* living in *weles* like the free tribesmen. Occasionally in the Record of Carnarvon groups of *nativi*, instead of holding in *trefgevery*, are spoken of as holding by a tenure of the nature of *treveloge*—i.e. in *weles* with the rights of inheritance which follow the recognition of kindred.[2]

In the Denbigh Extent the prevalence of *weles* of *nativi* is very general. And this is entirely consistent with the Venedotian Code under which, whilst rights of kindred were recognised at the

---

[1] i. p. 513.

[2] Record of Carnarvon, p. 2. *Bodscathlan.* ' Eadem villa est de natura de Troweloge, et sunt in eadem villa duo Wele nativa, &c.'

CHAP. V.   fourth generation, no bridge was allowed across the gulf which separated the stranger from the Cymro, except in the case of officials of the Court who were enfranchised by reason of their office.

Enfranchisement of *weles* of *nativi* after the conquest.

It was not, apparently, till after the conquest that any general enfranchisement took place. And when it did take place the following example shows that it took the form of enfranchisement of the whole *wele* of *nativi*, and not of individuals only.

In the case of this example of a *gwely* of *nativi* it is curious to notice that they are still described as holding ' under the condition of trefgevery.' '

Example of the enfranchisement of a *wele.*

'This indenture, made between the venerable Father, Lord John, by grace of God, Bishop of St. Asaph, and the Dean and Chapter of St. Asaph, of the one part, and the *proprietarii et coheredes* of that *lectum* called *Gwely Gwarthhoet*, in the Villa of Bryngwyn, of the other part, *witnesseth* that whereas the aforesaid *proprietarii et coheredes* have ever before this time been called *nativi* and have held their lands and tenements there under the condition of *Trefgyfrif*, the aforesaid venerable Father, the Dean and Chapter, for themselves and their successors, at the entreaty of the aforesaid *proprietarii et coheredes*, have liberated both them and their heirs and their lands and tenements from that condition henceforth, and have exonerated them for ever, and have made them in all things of the same condition as the *proprietarii et coheredes* of that *lectum* called *Gwely Ithelwr* being in the same villa, so that the aforesaid *proprietarii et coheredes* of the aforesaid *lectum* called *Gwely Gwarthhoet*, and their heirs in future for ever shall pay to the lord . . . marks of annual rent on the Feast of the Apostles Philip and James for having this concession, whereas before they have been wont to pay five shillings of this rent on the feast aforesaid. In witness whereof the aforesaid parties have respectively placed their seals to this Indenture with these witnesses. Robert ap Gruffud, at that time Raglot of the Lord Bishop, Lewelyn ap Madoc Loyt, then steward of the same; Eden Moel ap Bleth Duy, then Ringildre at the same place; Eynon ap Ken ap Bleth . . . and many others.

'Given at St. Asaph on the Lord's Day next after the Feast of St. Michael the Archangel, A.D. 1355.' '

' For the Latin of this document, which is in the possession of Colonel Howard, of Wygfair, see Appendix E.

II. THE LINK OF FOSTERAGE BETWEEN TRIBESMEN AND
NON-TRIBESMEN.

That the custom of placing strangers upon the waste until their successors became proprietors in the fourth man was one common to all three of the Welsh divisions is clear from the following statements of the Codes. They are useful, also, in showing how the Venedotian *uchelwr* and his *aillt* corresponded with the Dimetian and Gwentian *breyr* and his *taeog*. They further show that not only was it a common thing for *aillts* and *taeogs* to be placed upon waste land, and to become proprietors, but also that where such was the case *uchelwrs* or *breyrs* placed their sons with them to foster.

CHAP. V.

The chiefs and *uchelwrs* place their sons with *aillts* to foster.

i. p. 195.	i. p. 543.	i. p. 767.
Venedotian Code.	*Dimetian.*	*Gwentian.*
If an uchelwr place his son to be reared with an aillt of a lord, by the permission or sufferance of the lord, for a year and a day, that son is to have a son's share of the aillt's land, and, ultimately, of his property.	If the taeog of the King take the son of a breyr to foster (*ar vaeth*), with the King's permission, such a foster son is to participate in the inheritance of the taeog, like one of his own sons. —Dewi of Brevi.	If a taeog take the son of a breyr to foster, with the permission of the lord, such a son is to participate in the patrimony of the taeog, like one of his own sons.

These facts, taken together, are additional proof of the anxiety to secure the loyalty of the best class of strangers in blood. In the case of these favoured strangers not only was intermarriage with innate *Cymraeses* allowed in South Wales with consent of the kindreds, and not only were they supplied with land from the waste, and allowed to become proprietors in the fourth man, but further the sons of their lords

Importance of fosterage under the tribal system.

were placed with them to be fostered, and thereby as foster-sons to share with their foster-brothers in the foster-father's inheritance if he had attained to the position of a proprietor.

Giraldus Cambrensis complains that the tie of friendship between foster-brothers was often stronger than the tie of natural kinship between brothers. It was thus that fosterage became so important an incident in the tribal system in Celtic as well as in other countries. It was one of the several means used under the tribal system for the purpose of tying strangers as tightly as possible to the tribe, quite consistently with the tribal policy of keeping the class of strangers in blood as loosely organised as possible *inter se*.

III. FURTHER EVIDENCE FROM ' CELTIC SCOTLAND.'

Various kinds of *nativi* in Scotland.

The resemblance between ancient Celtic custom in Wales and in Scotland, as regards strangers in blood and the stages and methods by which something like serfdom grew out of it, is too marked to be passed by without reference here.

In Celtic Scotland, as in Wales, there were so-called *nativi* or *bondmen* of various kinds and different origin.

There is a remarkable passage in the fragments of laws printed under the heading *Quoniam attachiamenta—De brevi de nativis*,[1] which may be translated as follows :—

'There are different kinds of nativi or bond-men.
'For some are *nativi. de avo et proavo*, which is vulgarly

---

[1] Acts of Parliament of Scotland, i. p. 655 (red paging), 291 (black do.).

called *de evo et trevo*, whom he (the lord) will claim to be his
nativi naturally, by beginning to narrate their ancestors, if their
names are known, to wit, of his *great-grandfather, grandfather,*
and *father*, who are convicted by his saying that they all are his
nativi in such and such a villa of his, and in a certain place
within the said villa on servile land, and that they rendered and
did to him and his ancestors servile service for many days and
years, and this " nativitas," or bondage, can be proved through the
parents of the convicted one, if they are alive, or *per bonam
assisam*.

' Likewise, there is another kind of bondage, similar to this,
where some stranger shall have taken some servile land from
some lord doing servile service for the same land, and if he die on
the same land, and his son likewise, and afterwards *his* son shall
have lived and died on the same land, then all his posterity
[*i.e.* his great-grandsons] shall be at the fourth grade altogether
in servile condition to his lord, and his whole posterity can be
proved in the same way.

' There is a third kind of *nativitas*, or bondage, where some
freeman, *pro dominio habendo vel manutencncia* [*i.e.* for protection or maintenance] from some magnate. gives himself up
to that lord as his *nativus* or *bondman* in his court by [the
tonsure of] the front hair of his head (*per crines anteriores
capitis sui*).'

СПАР. V.
——
Natiri
whose
great-
grand-
fathers
were so.

Settle-
ment on
servile
land for
four gene-
rations
makes
posterity
nativi.

Freemen
become
natiri by
tonsure.

It is not necessary to do more than point out
how remarkably this passage confirms the Welsh
evidence that under Celtic custom occupation
by strangers in blood of land under a lord for
four generations made the great-grandchildren of
strangers, who up to that time had been free to leave
as they liked, into a family whose posterity were ever
after *adscripti glebœ* ; and secondly, how the hereditary *taeog* or *nativus* is distinguished from the new
comer who by tonsure in open court became the
nativus of his lord, and so literally came within the
meaning of the Welsh word *aillt*, or ' tonsured person.'
It also is interesting to observe how this kind of
tonsure is clearly defined as the ancient Celtic
tonsure from ear to ear—*per crines anteriores capitis*

sui—and distinguished from the Roman ecclesiastical tonsure for which the Welsh Codes have another name, viz. *coron*, in allusion to the tonsure of the crown of the head.

These distinctions are of Celtic custom,

These Celtic and tribal touches in what otherwise might be regarded as feudal definitions of serfdom seem to suggest connecting links between tribal and feudal custom.

Mr. Skene, in his chapter on ' The Tribe in Scotland,' remarks with reference to the passages above quoted as follows :—

' These definitions of the different kinds of *nativi* or bondmen may, no doubt, apply to a later period, and be more or less connected with feudal forms, but we may notwithstanding infer that they preserve the characteristics of the servile class in Celtic times ; for although the upper classes may in the Lowland districts have been superseded by Saxon or Norman proprietors holding their lands in feudal tenure, the servile occupiers of the soil, of Celtic race, who were attached to the land, would remain and become the villeins of the feudal lord ; and so we find that wherever they appear in the Chartularies they possess Celtic names.' [1]

i.e. custom of ancient Cumbria.

Thus the evidence of the transition from tribal to feudal forms in this respect comes from the two extreme ends, as it were of the ancient *Cumbria*, and it is not the less interesting on that account.

---

[1] Skene's *Celtic Scotland*, vol. iii. pp. 221, 222.

IV. THE RECEPTION INTO THE TRIBE OF STRANGERS IN SOUTH WALES.

It has been shown that the recognition of kindred in the case of strangers in blood after residence for four generations on the land of a chieftain or *uchelwr*, so far from making them free tribesmen, tied them all the more permanently to the land, so that they became *adscripti glebæ*, or *nativi*.

CHAP. V.

Strangers in blood became *adscripti glebæ*.

This applied, according to the evidence of Codes and traditions, both in the northern Cumbria, from which Wales had long been severed, and in Wales itself.

In South Wales alone the rule was subject to carefully guarded exceptions.

Exception in South Wales.

The fact has several times been alluded to that in South Wales the attainment of the position of a free tribesman was possible by residence in Cymru for nine generations, and could be hastened by repeated intermarriages with ' innate Cymraeses.'

It may be worth while, before passing from the subject of strangers in blood, to quote one more passage from the Welsh Laws describing this process and having particular regard to the rights to which the stranger attained on becoming a tribesman.[1]

Where it was possible for strangers to become tribesmen.

'This is the mode of regulating those marriages—to wit, the son of an *aillt*, being a sworn man to the lord of the territory who shall marry an innate Cymraes with the consent of her kindred, is, by that marriage, in the privilege of the second degree of kin and descent; to their children attaches the privilege of the third degree; and one of those children, by intermarrying with a Cymraes of legitimate blood, assumes the fourth degree; a son by that marriage stands in the privilege of the fifth degree, and he is the grandchild of the original *aillt*[2]; and that son, by inter-

The process by intermarriages.

---

[1] *Welsh Laws*, ii. p. 505-6.
[2] *i.e.* the *aillt* who first marries a Cymraes.

marrying with an innate Cymraes, arises to the privilege of the sixth degree of kin, and a son by that marriage or a great-grandson of the original *aillt* is of the seventh degree, and by intermarrying with an innate Cymraes attains to the eighth degree under the privilege of his wife, for it is the privilege of every innate Cymraes to advance a degree for her *aillt* husband with whom she shall intermarry; and the son of this great-grandson by such marriage attains to the privilege of the ninth descent; and therefore he is called a seisor (*goresgynydd*).'

It is important to notice why he is so called, and what it is that he attains to :—

'For he seizes (*goresgyn*) his land (*tir*) or his fruition of five free *erws* and his *cyvarwys* and privilege of chief of kindred and every other social right due to an innate Cymro.'

That is to say, he becomes a *priodawr*, or tribesman, with right to location upon land and a *cyvarwys*. Further, as he begins a new kindred, so also he becomes its *Chief of Kindred*.

'And he becomes the stock of a kindred, or he stands in the privilege of chief of kindred to his progeny, and likewise to his seniors; for such of them as may be living, as father or grandfather or great-grandfather, and not further, obtain in their seisor the privilege of innate Cymry. And he is not in law called the son of his father in suits for land, but his seisor; and he is a seisor to his grandfather and also a seisor to his great-grandfather and a seisor to his uncles, and his cousins, and his second cousins, when they, one or other, shall descend from legitimate marriages.
'And the seisor becomes chief of kindred to them all after arriving at the full age of manhood; and every one of them is a man and kin (*gwr a char*) to him, and his word is paramount over them one and all . . .'

It would seem, however, that though in this sense the new tribesman ennobled his ancestors and relations so that their blood relationship to him could be recognised, yet they do not thereby all at once become tribesmen with a right to location on land and *cyvarwys* as he has done.

' Although they approach the kindred of the seisor and possess their privileges free under the protection and privilege of their chief of kindred, they obtain not their lands (*ni chafant eu tirodd*) except those who individually attain the degree or privilege of the ninth descent—that is, of seisor (*goresgynedd*).'

There seems to be in these statements confirmation of the facts before alluded to as characteristic of the structure of the Cymric tribal society, not only as regards the tenacity with which the tribal rules of kinship were carried out and applied to the entrance of strangers into the tribe, but also as regards the character of the normal right of the tribesman. The normal right, whether of the *innate boneddig* born into the tribe, or of the stranger in blood on becoming a tribesman, was not an equal share in certain tribe land, but the right of maintenance—the fruition of five free erws and whatever else was included in his *cyvarwys*.

CHAPTER VI.

CHIEFTAINSHIP IN THE TRIBE.

I. THE GRADES OF CHIEFTAINSHIP.

The fact that the tribe was complex, that it contained besides the kindreds of tribesmen various classes of strangers in blood, combined with the fact of the existence of territorial lordships, naturally gave a dual character to the matter of chieftainship.

From the strictly tribal point of view, the principle of blood relationship might work itself out simply enough.

Tribal gradations of chieftainship. Beginning with the chief of household, who was the head of a patriarchal family of kin within the fourth degree of descent, it was a perfectly natural tribal step upwards to the chief of kindred, under whose rule the many households included within the kinship to the ninth degree were bound together into an organised kindred. It was but another perfectly natural step to bind the several kindreds together under the higher chieftain of the larger kindred of the tribe.

But, side by side with this strictly tribal view of the gradations of chieftainship, the Welsh Codes show that there had grown up what, from another point

of view, look like similar gradations of territorial lordship. The tribal system had evidently found room
for the growing power and jurisdiction of a hierarchy
of territorial chieftains, very nearly resembling feudal
lords, holding courts with legal jurisdiction, and
possessed of landed estates in Norman eyes not to be
distinguished from manors, on which were settled
various classes of tenants which, to Norman eyes,
seemed more or less like the different grades of *villani*
on English manors. Some of them, as we have seen,
were *aillts* and *taeogs*, living in ' registered ' or *taeog
trefs*; whilst others were specially located on the
lord's waste and growing up into kindreds with or
without tribal rights.

Thus it would be easy, using words with a con-
ventional meaning, to describe the two principles or
influences working side by side in later tribal society
(and perhaps from the first) as *tribal* and *feudal*.

But by doing so some danger might be run of
falling into the error of begging the question at issue.
The real question is whether these so-called feudal
tendencies were the result of outside feudal influences
upon the tribal system, or whether what we call the
feudal system in Western Europe may not, itself, turn
out to have been in part the result of tendencies en-
grained in the very nature of tribal society and thus
underlying the conditions out of which feudalism
grew.

Recurring to the condition of things described in
the Codes, there seems in one sense to have been quite
a hierarchy of chieftains.

There was the *brenhin*, or King, of Aberffraw,
whose chieftainship extended over all Cymru. But,

CHAP. VI. under the Codes, Gwent and Dimetia each had its *brenhin*, subordinate, however, to the *brenhin* of Aberffraw. And each cantref or cymwd had also its chieftain who held courts and had legal jurisdiction of some kind among *uchelwrs* and *breyrs* who, themselves, were heads of kindreds or households, and in some sense petty chieftains with the privilege attached to proprietorship of land.

All this looks at first sight very territorial. And it also was ancient. For

> 'When Howel the Good, brenhin of Cymru, modified the laws of Cymru, he permitted various privileges to various persons in his kingdom, . . . and likewise he permitted every chief (*pennaeth*) to whom there might belong a cymwd, or cantref, or more, to hold a daily royal court of privileged officers, in number as he should deem proper, in a similar manner to himself, and privilege to hold a royal court of pleas in his country among his uchelwrs. . . . And he permitted every uchelwr to hold his own land according to its privilege, and to rule his bondmen according to conditional bondage in South Wales, and perpetual bondage in Gwynedd.' [1]

He reserved to himself, however, all suits pertaining to his crown as *brenhin* and to his relations (*aelodeu*)—*i.e.* members of his royal family.[2]

The words used in various passages in the Codes for the gradations of chieftainship are instructive and indicative of tribal origin.

Sometime *toisech* used for *brenhin*. In the preface to the Venedotian Code, Howel the Good is in some of the MSS. called the *tewysauc* (*i.e.* *toisech*) of all Cymru ; and it goes on to say that he summoned six men from each cymwd in his kingdom (*tehuysokaet*). Very shortly afterwards it is stated that ' the *saraad* of the King (*brenhin*) of Aberffraw is.

---

[1] *Ancient Laws of Wales*, ii. p. 365.   [2] *Id.* p. 365, d. 37.

'to be paid thus : a hundred cows for each cantref in his dominion (*argluydyaet*).'[1]

In the last passage the *brenhin* has authority over an *argluydyaet*, the words king and lord being practically interchanged. In the first passage the king or *tewysauc* (*toisech*) has authority over a *tehuysokaet*. These terms, in their Gaelic form, were used in Ireland and went back, according to the 'Annals of the Four Masters,' to early Irish tribal tradition ; for it was the mythic *Ollamh Fodla* (who flourished, it is said, twelve centuries B.C.) who appointed a *toisech* over every *tuath* in Ireland.[2]

In the preface to the Dimetian Code the word used for the prince is *brenhin*, and in one MS. *tywyssauc*, and his kingdom is called a *teyrnnas* (the same word as the Irish *tigernas*), the dominion of a *teyrn* or *tigerna*, or house-lord. In a further clause in the same Code, Howel is said to be accompanied by the *teyrnedd* or *tigerns* of Cymru in his visit to Rome, thus making a distinction between the *brenhin* or head king and the *tigerns* or subordinate kings.[3]

In another passage of less authority, dealing with the federate country of all Cymru, the same distinction is made between the head king or *brenhin penraith* of all Cymru and the subordinate *tywysawgs* or *toisechs* under him,[4] who, however, were themselves paramount in their own territories. And this *brenhin penraith* is said to be the *hynav* (eldest,[5] most ancient,

And sometimes argluyd,

and sometimes tigern.

---

[1] i. pp. 3-7.

[2] *Skene's Celtic Scotland*, iii. p. 156. The word *Toisech* occurs also in the entries in the margin of the 'Book of Deer,' and means 'first man,' or 'head man.' See *Windisch* '*Wörterbuch*,' *sub voce Tussech.*

[3] *Ancient Laws of Wales*, i. p. 338.

[4] ii. p. 502.

[5] Pugh.

CHAP. VI. or *ancestor*), *i.e.* the head of the royal or ruling family.

The distinction between the head chieftainship of Aberffraw and the sub-chieftains of the other divisions is maintained in the same way but with different words in another passage : [1]

'Three *mechdeyrn* rule all the *gwladychu* of Cymru, the *brenin* of Aberffraw, and the *arglwydd* of Dinefwr (in Dimetia), and the *arglwydd* of Mathrafal (in Powys).'

Here again the chief of Aberffraw alone is *brenhin.*

In the next sentence all these are called *teyrn*, and their *teyrnas* is said to be thus divided into three parts (*rhan*), but Aberffraw is said to have supremacy over the other two. 'And there are three *yeirll* (*iarlls*) [2] under it (Aberffraw), viz. of Caerllion (Gwent), of Dinefwr (Dimetia), and of Mathrafal (Powys).'

Here the distinction is between the *brenhin* and the subordinate *iarlls*. And there is another passage which states that when, according to the legend, *Maelgwn* became supreme king (*brenhin pennaf*) with Aberffraw for his principal court, the status of the lords of Powys, Dimetia, and Gwent became that of under-chieftains or *iarlls*. [3]

Why, then, it may be asked, are all the chieftains, including Aberffraw, called in the passage above quoted *mechdeyrn*? The word is translated *vicegerent*, and in its etymology it betrays again a tribal source. Like the Latin *dominus*, the word *tigerna* means the head of the house. And whether the word *mechdeyrn*

---

[1] *Ancient Laws of Wales*, ii. p. 583.

[2] See ii. p. 51.

[3] ii. p. 51.

originally meant the sons of the 'tigerna'[1] or whether the prefix had another derivation than son ; in either case the connection with the idea of the household is maintained. In Irish the word *octhigernd* means literally the *young tigerns*, but it is used also for a *sub-tigern*. Both words suggest that the sub-chieftains were the younger members of the ruling family, of which the head king was the *hynaf* or elder. As in older days the *brenhin* of Aberffraw was in a sense a subordinate king paying tribute to the king of *Lloegyr*, from this point of view he was a *mechdeyrn*.

Another passage states that :—

> ' Three *mechdeyrn* dues arise from all Cymry. To Aberffraw from the other two : (1) from Dinevwr four *tunell* of honey, each containing four *mu*, two *grenneit* in each *mu*, each *grenn* a load (llwyth) for two men on a pole ; flour from Gwynva (Powys) in the same manner.
>
> ' Three score and three pounds the King of Aberffraw should pay to the King (*brenhin*) of Lloegyr; then he was called King of London, for there were many kings (*brenhinedd*) formerly in Lloegyr.'[2]

All this may be confused tradition, but Cæsar himself testified to the number of kings in Britain, so that there is every reason to believe that the tradition of a head chieftain, of whom the Welsh chieftains were under-chieftains, may not be devoid of truth.

Were the *macti-gerns* younger sons of chieftains ?

---

[1] If Cymric, the prefix should be *map*. But the word *tigern* (*teyrn*) seems to be Goidelic as well as Cymric. See Gwentian Code, p. 626, *macuyeit* = youths ; Dimetian Code, p. 349, *maccuyeit* = youths ; Venedotian Code, p. 9, *macku-* *yuyet* = youths. And cf. *Vortigern* = *Gwr-theyrn*, which was both Goidelic and Cymric, and means probably the *supreme lord* = *Gor-tigern*.

[2] ii. p. 585.

II. THE TRIBAL CHIEFTAINSHIP THAT OF A FAMILY.

CHAP. VI.

In the Welsh Codes the tribal system of Wales is made throughout to turn upon the possession of Cymric blood, and Cymru in the time of the Codes had become to a great extent geographically identical with modern Wales.

Most of Wales originally *Goidelic.*

But Mr. Skene has shown that before the invasion of Cunedda and his sons the Cymric population was confined to the eastern part of Wales only. 'We find,' he writes, 'the seaboard of Wales on the west in the occupation of the Gwyddyl, or Gael, and the Cymry confined to the eastern part of Wales only and placed between them (*i.e.* the Gwyddyls) and the Saxons. A line drawn from Conway, on the north, to Swansea, on the south, would separate the two races of the Gwyddyl and the Cymry on the west and on the east. In North Wales the Cymry possessing Powys, with the Gwyddyl in Gwynedd, and Mona or Anglesey. In South Wales the Cymry possessing Gwent and Morganwg, with the Gwyddyl in Dyfed, and Brecknock occupied by the mysterious Brychan and his family.' [1]

The real Cumbria further North.

Mr. Skene shows, in fact, that, whilst Powys and the Severn Valley were ancient Cymric districts, the stronghold of the Cymry was the real Cumbria further north, viz. from the Dee and the Humber to the Firths of Forth and Clyde. [2]

Accordingly, when Cunedda and his sons in the

---

[1] *Four Ancient Books of Wales*, chap. iv.
[2] With the exception of Pictish Galloway. Skene's *Celtic Scotland*, vol. i. p. 238.

fifth century came from the north with their tribal
following of Cymry to drive out the Gwyddyls from
Wales, and only succeeded in doing it after two or
three generations of constant conflict, it does not
seem likely that they should recognise them as of
their own Cymric kindred just because both conquerors and conquered were Celtic in race. The
Cymry were new comers, and conquered North
Wales and Anglesey first, and it was not until the
time of Cunedda's great-grandson Maelgwn that
they became masters of South Wales also. Even
then, as regards the old inhabitants, they were still a
conquering tribe.

There is a curious passage in the Venedotian
Code which shows that the true Cymric land was in
the north, even after the time of Maelgwn. Under
the heading ' Privileges of Arvon ' the following story
is told :—

> ' Here *Elidyr* the Courteous, a man from the North, was
> slain, and after his death the men of the North came here to
> avenge him. The chiefs, their leaders, were Clydno Eiddin [of
> Edinburgh ?], Nudd the Generous, son of Senyllt, Mordav the
> Generous, son of Servari, and Rydderch, the Generous, son of
> Tudwal Tudglyd [of Strathclyde ?], and they came to Arvon, and
> because Elidyr was slain at Aber Mewydus, in Arvon, they burned
> Arvon as a further revenge. And then Run, son of Maelgwn,
> and the men of Gwynedd, assembled in arms, and proceeded to the
> banks of the Gweryd [Forth?] in the North, and there they were long
> disputing who should take the lead through the River Gweryd.
> Then Run sent a messenger to Gwynedd, to ascertain who were
> entitled to the lead, and some say that Maeldav the elder, the
> Lord of Penardd, adjudged it to the men of Arvon. Iorwerth, the
> son of Madog, on the authority of his own information, affirms
> that Idno the Aged assigned it to the men of the black-headed
> shafts. And thereupon the men of Arvon advanced in the van,
> and were valorous there, and Taliesin sang—
>
>> Behold from the ardency of their blades
>> With Run the reddener of armies,
>> The men of Arvon with their ruddy lances.

And then, on account of the length of time they remained in arms, their wives slept with their bond-servants, and on that account Run granted them fourteen privileges. . . . And if there be who shall doubt one of these privileges, the community at Bangor and that of Beuno shall uphold them.' [1]

There can be little doubt that this story is connected with a disputed succession on the death of Maelgwn. Possibly the question in dispute may have been what Cymric family had the right to the head-chieftainship, and the expedition of Elidyr from the north may have been to claim it. He is said to have married the daughter of Maelgwn. Be this as it may, the story shows that the traditional connection was not then broken between the Cymry of Wales and the old tribal home further north from whence they had sprung.

Cunedda's invasion a tribal migration.

Speaking broadly then, this invasion of Cunedda and his sons was one of those tribal movements of which history is so full, in which tribes allied in blood when conquered are as a matter of course treated as strangers and made what Bede calls ' tributary to the conquering tribe.' The Saxons reduced conquered Teutonic tribes into *gafolgelders*, and these *gafolgelders* were probably very much what the Welsh Codes call *aillts* and *taeogs*.

That Cunedda came from the north, that his court may have been at Carlisle, that he may possibly have held office in the Roman army, that his force on the Roman Wall was 900 horse (*i.e.* a Roman legion), that he wore the gold belt which was the badge of the Roman Dux, and that some of his ancestors' names were Roman—all this is not in

[1] *Ancient Laws of Wales*, i. p. 104-7.

the least inconsistent with his being the head-chieftain

of Northern Cymric tribes.[1] The great German Hermann was nearly all this, and, no doubt, his Roman training was one secret of his power. Roman forces withdrawn, tribal instincts would rise again into prominence, and conquests would be made on tribal lines.[2]

The very phrase ' Cunedda and his sons' suggests that his chieftainship was a tribal one, and it is perfectly consistent with tribal rules that it should be that of a royal family rather than a merely personal or individual thing.

It was also in accordance with tribal instincts that his sons should be sub-chieftains (*mechdeyrns*) and share in his kingdom, giving their names to the subordinate divisions of the conquered country ruled by them.

There are traces of this family or tribal character of the chieftainship as well in the legends of their history as in the succession to the head-chieftainship. Traces such as these are not without value where real history is wanting.

In the ' Life of St. Carannog,'[3] it is incidentally stated that Cunedda had several sons, that the first-born was *Tybiawn*, who died before Cunedda's raid into Wales. But it goes on to say that his brother *Meiriawn* divided the possessions of his father among his brethren.

---

[1] See Professor Rhys's *Celtic Britain*, p. 135.

[2] Nennius places the invasion of Cunedda 146 years before Mailcun (Maelgwn) reigned.

[3] *Lives of Cambro - British Saints* (Rees), pp. 100 and 400. The MS. from which it was transcribed is early 12th century.

So in the ' Life of St. Cadoc,' [1] the sons of *Glywys*, a so-called *regulus* of part of Glamorganshire and Gwent, *natalico more* divided their father's kingdom between them, every one taking his special province, whilst we learn from another legend that *Gwynllyw* the eldest ruled over the whole as *princeps dominator.* [2]

Thus chieftainship in a tribe seems to have been the family possession of a *gwely*, like the ' *tir gwely-awc* ' of the proprietary tribesmen.

So again in the succession to the head-chieftainship, it would almost seem as though there were traces of recurring periods in the royal family history when a new choice had to be made, and the headship became settled in a single family chosen out from the others. This choice obviously involved the subordination of the other families.

Thus from among the descendants of Cunedda *Maelgwn* was chosen, and the placing of him in the chair made of birds' wings on the sea-shore, according to the legend recorded in the Welsh Laws, may well have been the form taken by the ceremony on his election to the headship of all Cymru. [3]

Maelgwn's accession was evidently an epoch in Welsh tribal history. He took up his residence at Aberffraw as *brenhin* of Venedotia. There were other ruling families in different districts, but the headship of Cymru remained thenceforth in his family alone. [4]

---

[1] *Id.* pp. 22 and 310.
[2] *Id.* p. 146.
[3] *Ancient Laws of Wales*, ii.
p. 51.
[4] See Professor Rhys's *Celtic Britain*, p. 125 *et seq.*

He died, as already said, in the first visitation CHAP. VI.
of the 'Yellow Death,' about A.D. 547, and was
succeeded in the head-chieftainship ultimately by his
great-grandson *Iago*, who again was a great leader, Iago.
and fell in the Battle of Chester, A.D. 613.

Lastly, *Iago's* great-grandson, *Cadwaladr*, after Cad-
waladr.
raising the hopes of the Cymry by his leadership, died,
it is said, during the second visitation of the 'Yellow
Death,' about A.D. 664–683.[1]

So much for the traditional succession to the
chieftainship in the family of Cunedda.

But, side by side with the Aberffraw line of
Cymric chieftains, there seems to have been another
of the same kind in Powys.

As already said, Powys was seemingly Cymric Ruling
family of
Powys.
before the advent of Cunedda and his sons. And
the royal family of *Catel-Tigern-Lug*, according to
Nennius, dated back to the time of St. Germanus.[2]
He and his nine sons, according to Nennius, were
baptised by St. Germanus, and blessed in the words,
'A king shall not be wanting of thy seed for ever';
and Nennius adds, writing early in the eighth
century :—

> ' And, agreeably to the prediction of St. Germanus, he became
> a king, all his sons were kings, and from their offspring the
> whole country of Powys has been governed to this day.'

Thus legend and tradition alike testify to the tribal
character of Welsh chieftainship as that of a ruling
family, and not merely of a single person or leader.

---

[1] Professor Rhys's *Celtic
Britain*, p. 128.

[2] Whether Zimmer is right in
giving a late origin to this legend
or not does not much affect the
force of it in this connection.
Nennius Vindicatus, p. 72 *et
seq.*

CHAP. VI.

The chief's household under the Codes.

In the constitution of the *brenhin's* household, as described in the Codes, the tribal character of the royal family was in part at least sustained.

It had its *penteulu*, or chief of household, like any other family, and he must be of the royal blood—a son or nephew. A mere *uchelwr* could not occupy the position, because he was not of the chieftain's kindred. The *brenhin* himself could not be chief of the household because he had another office. Nor could the *edling*, or designated successor of the *brenhin*. He had another office and a higher privilege, equal to that of the *brenhin*.[1]

His family all edlings till settled on land.

The family of royal privilege is said in the Codes to consist of sons, nephews, and first cousins. In a sense they all were *edlings* ;[2] but they ceased to belong to it when they obtained separate possession of land for themselves. Their privilege became then that of their land.

' When the edling dies he is to leave his horses and his dogs to the brenhin, for that is the only ebediw he is to render, and the reason why he ought to render no other is because he is a near relation (*aylaut*) to the brenhin. The near relations (*aylodeu*) of the brenhin are his sons, his nephews, and his first cousins. Some say that every one of these is an edling ; others say that no one is an edling except that person to whom the brenhin shall give hope of succession and designation.

' The edling and those whom we have above mentioned shall possess that privilege until they obtain land ; after that, their privilege shall be identified with the privilege of the land they obtain, except they obtain land in villenage (*vyleyn dyr*, in another MS. *kaeth dir*). In that case the privilege of the land shall augment until it shall become free.'[3]

Hence the younger sons of the royal family, settled

---

[1] *Ancient Laws of Wales* i. p. 13.

[2] i. p. 8.

[3] i. p. 10. See also p. 351.

upon land, would become eventually *breyrs* and uchelwrs. But such a son, placed at the head of the *llys* of a *cantref* or *cymwd*, became in some sense a territorial chief. As such, he held a royal court of privileged officers among the *uchelwrs* of his district. So it was in Howel's time,[1] and his legislation, as already mentioned, recognised these sub-chieftains.

Hence it follows that the royal stock was from time to time, as it were, swarming off into new family stocks, or, to change the metaphor, overflowing into and swelling the number of Cymric proprietors of land. New kindreds, offshoots from the royal kindred, were from time to time taking their places side by side with the other kindreds of Cymru.

How many of the Cymric kindreds were descended from Cunedda and his sons, or others of his kindred who came with him to conquer Wales, or were sprung from the royal family of Powys, we cannot tell. But the centuries between Cunedda's chieftainship and Howel's afforded quite time enough for the Cymric stock in Wales to multiply without bringing into their tribe the conquered people of the land. A race which guarded its blood so keenly, which made the stranger family wait, unless hastened by intermarriage, till the ninth degree of kindred was reached before its members were sufficiently naturalised to be admitted into fellowship and freedom—allowed to bear arms and to share in responsibility for crimes—was not likely to have admitted the conquered races wholesale into tribal union. The two visitations of the 'Yellow Death' probably thinned the population

Descendants of chieftains become *uchelwrs* and merge in the tribe.

---

[1] ii. p. 365.

L 2

and prepared the way for the new comers, and whether the older races of the land were Goidelic or Brython, they were most likely regarded as strangers in blood to the conquering tribesmen, and as such treated as *taeogs* or *aillts*.

Thus whilst chieftainship in the tribe was the prerogative of a family rather than of a person, and the tie of blood-relationship bound together the head-chieftains and the sub-chieftains and the chiefs of kindreds and of households, and whilst the continuity of kindred so secured throughout the whole hierarchy of chieftains bound the whole body of tribesmen together by the tie of blood, the gulf remained as deep as ever between the tribesmen and the strangers in blood.

Lastly, if the Cymry came into Wales with Cunedda, or in the migration from the north connected by tradition with his name, then, unless it were in Powys, we must not look for evidence of the Cymric tribal system in Wales anywhere earlier than the coming of Cunedda, or in South Wales before Maelgwn's conquest, and the first visitation of the ' Yellow Death.'

It would be rash to regard this conclusion as other than provisional, till further light has been thrown upon the subject by Celtic scholars, but it has an important bearing upon the interpretation of the earlier evidence to which attention will hereafter be called, and which has to do with the contact in the sixth century between the Cymric conquerors of South Wales and the Christian Church.

III. THE CHIEFTAINSHIP IN ITS RELATION TO LAND.

The Extents of the so-called manor of Aberffraw have already familiarised the reader with the position, at the time of the conquest of North Wales, of the chieftain in relation, first to his so-called manor with its *maerdref*, its free officials of the court, and the hamlets of *nativi* holding in *trefgevery* and paying rents in produce, and, secondly, to the other hamlets of the *cantref*, whether occupied by *weles* of free tribesmen, paying food rents commuted into money, or by *nativi*, still for the most part paying rents in kind. But the family character of his land ownership was hidden, so to speak, under the shadow of the manorial aspect of his lordship.

The originally family character of the chieftain's ownership is, however, apparent enough in the charters of donations made by chieftains in the twelfth century, to say nothing of the earlier evidence hereafter to be examined.

There must always be some doubt how far under the tribal system the land which was set apart for the chieftainship in each *cantref* or *cymwd*, and the food rents from the tribesmen or strangers in blood, were at the chieftain's disposal, and how far his family (*aelodeu*) had rights of maintenance out of them.

It might well be that in newly conquered districts the chieftain's power of disposal was exceptionally great, not only because his own power would be greatest after victory, but also because there would be freshly conquered lands which could be

allotted or disposed of without displacing any tribesmen.

Moreover, if the inhabitants of conquered regions
were retained on the land as *aillts* and *taeogs*, and
made tributary (according to tribal custom), it would
be easy to transfer to a church or to a relative the
tribute of a holding or district without disturbing
anyone.

Further, even in ordinary times the chieftain's
power as head of the tribe over unoccupied waste
may always have been recognised. On the other
hand, what in modern phrase is meant by transfer of
the land itself, or transfer of the freehold, was probably an idea as foreign to the tribal system in its
early stages as individual contrasted with family
ownership. Transfer of the tribute and lordship of
a district was probably far more in accordance with
tribal conceptions. The tribal and family use of the
land upon payment of customary food rents or tribute was, perhaps, at first, the nearest approach to
ownership, and the transfer of the right to the
tribute the nearest approach to alienation.

In later times, as the lordship became more and
more manorial, modern ideas crept in together with
modern forms of conveyance. But even then there
is incidental evidence in the charters giving effect to
the grants to churches, made as late as the twelfth
century, that the subject of the donations was not
the individual and independent property of the chieftain making them. They show that his power of
making the donation was limited. To make it valid
his act required not, indeed, the consent and confirmation of any council or *witan*, but the consent

Consent
of the
chieftain's
family
needful
to the
validity
of his
donations.

and confirmation of his family, as in other cases of CHAP. VI.
' *tir gwelyawc.*'

Thus, in a charter of donation to the Abbey of The donation to the Abbey of Strata Florida. Strata Florida, in Cardiganshire, ' Resus, Prince of South Wales,' calls himself *proprietarius princeps*, and recites that he had built the abbey and made a donation of it and of land to its abbot in A.D. 1184, and yet it was necessary for his three sons to confirm the donation, thus, ' together with him establishing it before many of his army, in the Church of St. Brigid at Raiadr.' And further, ' he and his sons and all his posterity ' joined in giving it the usual immunities.[1]

So again, to take an example from another district, the necessity of the concurrence of heirs in the disposition of property belonging to the families of chieftains is very obvious in the following case, notwithstanding the lateness of date and the use of ordinary Norman forms of conveyancing.

A certain Gruffydd of Dinas Bran (son of Madoc, Donation by a chieftain to his wife for her life of the *cymwd* of Maelor Saesneg. the founder of the Abbey of *Valle Crucis*, and of Isota, daughter of Ithel, Prince of Gwent) had four sons, and died A.D. 1270.

After his death, in 5 Ed. I., an inquisition was held to inquire into the legality of the seizure by Prince Llewelyn of certain lands held in dower by his widow.[2]

From the finding of the jury, it appears that Gruffydd, on his marriage with Emma, gave to her

---

[1] See Dugdale's account of Strata Florida, *Monasticon*, v. p. 632.

[2] This inquisition and the charter cited in this case will be found in Appendix D. I am indebted for this instance to the Hon. Mrs. Bulkeley Owen, of Tedsmore Hall, Oswestry.

the whole *cymwd* (*patria*) of Maelor Saesneg (in Flintshire) for her life.   The charter by which he did this shows that he did it with the assent and consent of his heirs (*assensu et consensu heredum meorum*). The *cymwd* is described as '*totam patriam que vocatur Maylorseysnec,*' and it contained several *villæ* or *villatæ*, just as the Denbigh Extent might lead us to expect. The deed was witnessed by Anianus, the Bishop of St. Asaph, the Abbot of Valle Crucis, the donor's four sons, and others.

Then, by another charter, the same Gruffydd, again 'with the assent and consent of his heirs,' made a similar grant to Emma, of the property which came to him from his deceased brother Hywel, part of which had been purchased 'from all the heirs of Herbestoc' (*de omnibus heredibus de Herbestoc.*[1]) And, lastly, the four sons confirm to their mother, by a separate charter, all the above-mentioned property, also in addition that which their grandmother Isolda had purchased with their grandfather's

concurrence.   The Jury, on inquisition made into these circumstances, swore that this dower was given in due form by Gruffydd, with the confirmation of his *heredes* after his death, and with the confirmation of Llewelyn, then Prince of Wales, who confirmed all the donations.   And they said that the custom of Wales was that everyone at his own will could give to his wife his lands and tenements, before marriage or after, at his pleasure.   .

The prince, Llewelyn, had evicted the widow from this property, and the jury explained the reason of

---

[1] With regard to Erbistock see the interesting paper of Mr. A. N. | Palmer in the *Archæological Review*, March 1888.

his action, and stated that the custom of Wales was
such that as often as anyone from fear of war, or on
other occasion, leaves his land and retires from Wales
to other parts, the lord has a right to seize that land
as escheat to him, and deal with it at his pleasure.

Strictly speaking, this case must not be taken as
showing that under the tribal system dower was a
recognised incident, but rather that the practice was
sanctioned by later custom of a husband, with the
consent of his family, giving his wife a life interest
in some of his property.

Again, it shows, no doubt, that chieftains in later
times could and did purchase and dispose of property with family consent. The main provision made
in this case was, however, far more of the character
of a life interest in the tributes or dues of a lordship
than a life interest in a modern landed estate. The
grant embraced a whole *patria* or *cymwd*, and the
Denbigh Extent has made it clear that within the
cymwd there were under the tribal system numerous
weles of tribesmen and of so-called *nativi*. In the
case of Maelor Saesneg, it may not have been so, as
the district of which it was a part had been, for a
time at least, under Saxon rule, and during this period
it may well have lost some of its tribal characteristics.

On the whole, it must be recognised that even
under more strictly tribal conditions, with the consent of their family, chieftains could and did make
donations to churches, as well as to their wives,
and that these might be of two kinds :—

(1) The transfer of the tribute or food rent of land
from the chieftain, and the support of his establishment, to a church, or a monastery, without changing

CHAP. VI.   its amount, so constituting the occupiers of that land,
probably most often *aillts* or *taeogs*, thenceforth
tenants of a church, or monastery, instead of tenants
of the chieftain.

Of a
definite
area of
land.

(2) The donation of a certain area of land, on
which the church or monastery was built, freed from
all secular payments or dues, showing that there was
tribal land of some kind, cultivated or waste, allotted
under tribal conditions to the chieftain or his family,
or, possibly, *escheat* to him, which he, with the consent of his family, could dispose of to a church, or
otherwise.[1]

IV. THE CHIEFTAIN'S FOOD-RENTS FROM FREE TRIBESMEN.

The question of the transfer or donation of land
by chieftains is so closely connected with the food-
rents from the land that it will be convenient at this
stage of the inquiry to examine more closely into
their character.

Food-
rents com-
muted
into *tunc.*

In the Extents the food-rents of the free tribesmen were found to be commuted into definite money
payments made under the name of *tunc.*

Accordingly in the Codes the customary unit of

---

[1] This conclusion, drawn from
later charters, does not seem to be
inconsistent with the Codes.

It is true that the Triads represent that the right of co-
aration of the waste was a part of
the *cyvarwys* of every tribesman,
and that 'every wild and waste
belongs to the country and kindred in common ' (ii. p. 523). But
this is not inconsistent with the
full power of the *brenhin* to dispose of the special portion of the
waste in every *cymwd* allotted to
him. According to the Codes it
was the official duty of the *maer*
and *canghellor* ' to keep the waste
of the *brenhin* until he shall
dispose of it ' (i. pp. 490 and 673),
and, according to the *Venedotian
Code* (p. 190), these officers did
not lose their right of service upon
it even when it was disposed of.

gwestva is commuted into what is called the *tunc*
pound.

There are indications that originally, before the commutation, the payment of food-rents was arranged in such a way as to supply the customary provision for so many 'nights' entertainments,' a practice of which the *firma unius noctis* of the Domesday Survey and other mediæval documents, was probably a survival.

It is obvious that Cymric chieftains, when on progress from one place to another, whether on military or hunting and hawking expeditions, needed both shelter and also provision for the nightly entertainment of themselves and their company.

The onus of making provision for their shelter fell, under the Codes, upon the *aillts* or non-tribesmen.

The *brenhin's* hall consisted of six columns or poles, probably often newly felled trees, placed in parallel rows of three, and fastened together at the top to the roof-tree, thus forming a kind of nave. Then at some distance behind the poles low walls of stakes and wattle shut in the aisles. The roof was covered with branches and thatch, and there were wattle doors of entrance at the end. Along the aisles behind the poles were placed beds of rushes, called *gwelys*, and the footboards of the beds were used as seats in the daytime.[1] All houses put up in this way were alike, and each piece of timber had its customary value from the poles and the roof-tree down to the stakes and the wattle.[2]

---

[1] Giraldus Cambrensis, *Descr. Camb.* I. c. x.

[2] *Venedotian Code,* i. p. 293.

The fire was in the middle between the central posts, and divided the upper portion, where sat the chief, the *edling*, and principal officers, from the lower and humbler end of the hall. The silentiary stood by one of the central posts, and it was his duty to call attention by striking it with his staff.[1]

Such a hall as this was easily constructed and removed, and owed what fleeting grandeur it possessed to its curtains, and the weapons of the temporary inmates hung upon its sides.

At first sight the construction of buildings such as this for a few nights' shelter of the chieftain and his company might seem too onerous a customary obligation to be periodically imposed upon the chieftain's 'villeins.' But it is recorded in the Boldon Book that the *villani* of the Bishop of Durham had to furnish for his great hunts just such a hall in the forest, 60 feet long and 16 feet wide between the posts, together with a buttery, steward's room, chamber, privy, and chapel,[2] so that the following passage from the 'Venedotian Code' need not be surprising :—

> 'Nine houses which the villeins of the *brenhin* are to erect for him : a hall, a chamber, a buttery, a stable, a dog-house, a barn, an oven, a privy, and a dormitory.'[3]

Whether these buildings were put up afresh for every royal visit, or were only repaired on occasion, we are not told. Possibly the *brenhin* may have required such provision at frequent intervals, for besides his hunting and hawking he seems very often to have called out the tribesmen to join his host in the mili-

---

[1] i. p. 11, and pp. 848–851.
[2] *Boldon Book,* p. 575.
[3] *Venedotian Code,* i. p. 79, and see *Dimetian Code* p. 487.

tary exercises which perhaps had succeeded to more
strictly marauding expeditions of an earlier period.

> 'The king (*brenhin*) is not to go with his host out of the country
> except once a year, but they are to attend the king in his own
> dominion whenever he shall please. The king is to have from
> every *villein-tref* a man, a horse, and an axe to form encamp-
> ments, at his own cost.' [1]

According to Giraldus Cambrensis, Welsh tribesmen were eager to join in warlike expeditions—
gens armis dedita tota.[2] He represents not only the
uchelwrs (*nobiles*), but all the people as eager to
rush from the plough at the signal for war.

The tribesmen were free from having men or dogs
quartered upon them except during the great progress of the *brenhin's* household in winter.

> 'Neither *maer* nor *canghellor* is to be imposed upon a free
> *maenol*, nor progress, nor *dovraeth*, nor youths (*mackwyeit*), nor
> anything (except as above) except the great progress of the
> household in the winter.' [3]

What, then, was this great progress of the household to which the tribesmen were subject?

The
progress
of the
household
after
Christ-
mas.

> 'The chief of the [*brenhin's*] household is to have a progress
> assigned him by the king after separating from him at Christmas,
> himself and the household. The household is to consist of three
> parties: the elder party, the middle party, and the younger
> party; and alternately he is to be with each: and the party he is
> with is to choose its house. And so long as he shall be on that
> progress he is to have servants, a doorward and a cook, and ser-
> vants of the table, and these are to have the skins of the animals
> which are slaughtered, and the cooks are to have the tallow, the
> fragments, and the entrails.' [4]

The rough character of these progresses, though
restricted by the Codes, is apparent enough. The
slaughter of animals for the night's entertainment,

---

[1] i. p. 79. [2] *Desc. Camb.* c. viii. [4] *Venedotian Code*, i. pp. 16
[3] i. p. 191. and 190.

CHAP. VI. and the division among the followers of the skins, the tallow, and the entrails, are graphic features indeed. These progresses were, moreover, quite apart from the military and hunting or hawking expeditions of the *brenhin* himself, because when they were concluded the chief of the household was to return to him, and remain with him for the rest of the year.

The progress of the chieftain and his company.

The *brenhin's* own progress was of another kind. He and his company were not quartered on the tribesmen, but, whilst his *aillts* had to provide him with his necessary buildings for shelter, it was the duty of the free tribesmen to contribute the food and mead for his entertainment.

The *gwestva* of the free tribesmen for his 'night's entertainment.'

This they did by the payment of the *gwestva* or food-rent. And, as before said, there are incidental indications that it was provided originally on the system of the 'night's entertainment.'

Amongst the curious Welsh phrases into which the number nine entered, one is recorded in the 'Welsh Laws'[1] which is significant in this connection—*Nab nos gbesty*—'the nine nights of the guest-house.'[2] Further, in the 'Dimetian Code' each *tref* providing its *gwestva* to the chieftain is 'to light the fire three nights and three days for him,'[3] suggesting at least that the *gwestvas* were arranged so as to provide for periods of three nights at a time.

Again, the Venedotian food-rent, or *tunc* pound in lieu of it, was to be accompanied by the payment of 24*d.* of supper-silver for the 24 servants of 'every

---

[1] ii. p. 345.
[2] Translated in the Latin ver-

sion 'novem noctes hospitis,' ii. p. 874.
[3] i. p. 533.

feast at which mead was drunk,'[1] thus leading to the inference that the *tunc* pound of Venedotia was provision for one night's carousal of the *brenhin* and his company.

There is some obscurity in the Codes with regard to the method of clustering the households or homesteads of tribesmen into the groups from which the *gwestva*, or *tunc* pound in lieu of it, was due.

In the Venedotian Code[2] the *tyddyns* were grouped into *randirs*, the *randirs* into *gavaels*, the *gavaels* into *trefs*, and the *trefs* into *maenols*. And the *maenol* was the unit which paid the *gwestva*, or *tunc* pound. In South Wales the *gwestva*-paying group was the *tref*, and this was composed of four *randirs*, each of which contained 312 erws of 'arable, pasture, and wood, and space for buildings on the twelve erws.'[3]

Thus the *gwestva*-paying unit in North Wales seems at first sight to have been a certain number of *tyddyns*, whilst in South Wales it embraced a certain area of land. It is possible, however, that there may be some way of reconciling the two methods, for there are indications that in the description in the Venedotian Code the *tyddyn* is taken as a unit of land measurement. On the whole, however, it is better, perhaps, not to attempt at this point any further explanation than that the group of holdings called a *maenol* in Venedotia and a *tref* in South Wales was the *gwestva*-paying unit, bearing in mind also the fact, learned from the Denbigh Extent, that the *villatæ*, whatever they might be, were the fixed units, and that the *weles* of tribesmen were

---

[1] i. p. 23.   [2] i. p. 187.   [3] i. pp. 533 and 537.

easily moved, with their cattle and their internally complex tribal rights, from one district to another.

In what
the
gwestva
consisted.

In the
Venedo-
tian Code.
Passing, then, to the *gwestva*, or food-rent itself, in what did it consist?

In the Venedotian Code the '*tunc* of a free *maenol*' is thus described :—

> From every free *maenol* the *brenhin* is to have a vat (*keruÿn*) of *mead* nine handbreadths in length diagonally.
>
> If mead be not obtained, two of *bragot*; and if *bragot* be not obtained, four of ale (*gŏrÿw* = *cercvisia*).[1]

The vat of liquor was, therefore, a prominent feature in the *gwestva*, but other things also were included. A few clauses further on, the '*king's gwestva* from a free *maenol*' is more fully described, thus :—

> The measure of the *brenhin's gwestva* in winter from a free *maenol*: that is to say :—
>
> A horseload of the best flour that shall grow on the land.
>
> The carcase of a cow or an ox.
>
> A full vat (*keruÿn*) of mead 9 handbreadths in its depth diagonally and as much in breadth (*sic*).
>
> Seven thraves of oats of one band for provender.
>
> A three-year-old swine.
>
> A salted flitch of 3 fingerbreadths in thickness.
>
> A vessel of butter 3 handbreadths in depth, not heaped, and 3 in breadth.
>
> And if these cannot be obtained a pound is to be paid in lieu of them, and that is the *tunc* pound, and 24*d.* to the king's servants.

The statement is then repeated that if mead cannot be obtained two vats of *bragot* or four vats of ale are to be paid.

The *tunc* pound covered all, and it is further stated that it is to be reckoned as divided thus, viz. : 'Six score [pence] for bread, three score for liquor (*llyn*), and three score for *enllyn*.

---

[1] i. p. 197.

The *tunc* pound, therefore, contained twelve score,
or 240 pence. And as in the Latin version a
'score of silver' is rendered as '*uncia argenti*,' it is
clear that we have to deal with weights of silver
instead of coin, and with the Gallic pound of
20 pennyweights to the ounce and 12 ounces to the
pound. The equation, therefore, between the food-
rent and the pound of silver may, after all, be
founded on ancient custom.

In the Gwentian and Dimetian Codes the *tref* is
the unit for payment of the *tunc* pound, and the
gwestva, of which the latter was the equivalent, is
described almost in the same words as in the Venedotian Code, leaving out some of the smaller items.
It consisted of the horseload of wheat-flour, an ox,
7 thraves of oats, a vat (*gerbyn*) of honey, and 24 of
silver.[1]

When honey was wanting, two vats of *bragot* or
four of beer were to be paid instead. And the vat,
or *cerbyn*, is described in these words :—

'The height of the vat is to be nine handbreadths when
measured diagonally from the further bottom groove to the hither
rim. . . . And it ought to be sufficiently capacious for the *brenhin*
and his elder to bathe therein.'[2]

There was also a summer *gwestva*, which was to
consist of :—

a fat cow, a fat wether 3 years old, and a sow of 3 winters three
fingers thick, and [it is added] 'the *trev* is to bring all these to the
king, and to light a fire three nights and three days for him.'

In the Gwentian Code the summer *gwestva* is
only obscurely alluded to, but in other points the

[1] *Dimetian Code*, i. p. 533; | [2] i. p. 532.
Gwentian Code, i. p. 769. | [3] i. p. 533.

M

CHAP. VI. description in the Dimetian Code is closely followed, except that instead of the vat of honey the words used are ' what shall suffice for a vat of honey,' probably in both cases the meaning being as much honey as would brew into a vat of mead.

The *cervin* or vat of mead, *bragot*, or beer.

The vat (*keruyn* or *cerbyn*) of mead, or, if mead were wanting, to be filled four times with beer (*gbrÿw* or *cbrbf* = *cerevisia*), is of some interest. The word used throughout connects it not so much with mead as with the Gallic beverage beer. *Bragot* also seems to have been a Gallic drink. The word *bragot* (Irish, *brach*), in Latin *brace*, occurs constantly in connection with the food-rents of Brittany in the Redon Chartulary. It is mentioned by Pliny, and was used sometimes for malt and sometimes for the liquor brewed from it.[1]

This vat, by which all three beverages were measured for the *gwestva*, is always described in the Codes as nine handbreadths in its diagonal measure, following the traditional method of using the gauging-rod adopted by the professional gauger.

The method of measuring vessels in this way by their diagonal is a widely extended and ancient one. Thus, in the Icelandic *Gragas* the same method of measuring the size of a vessel is used.[2]

In the Latin version of the Dimetian Code the *dolium*, or vat, of mead is described as nine palms *in longo et in lato*,[3] but in the other Latin version the nine palms are to be *per obliquum a fundo usque ad*

---

[1] Cf. with the Greek χόρμα, and Irish *cuirm*, and Pliny's mention of the Spanish word *cerea*. And see Hehn's *Kulturpflanzen*, &c.

(Berlin, 1877), p. 132.

[2] *Gragas*, vol. i. p. 501; *Kaupa-balkr*. tit. lxxxv.

[3] ii. p. 788.

summum.[1] These may probably be taken as inexact translations from the Welsh, ' nine *handbreadths* diagonally measured.'

The handbreadth was a measure distinct from the palm, and, reckoning the width and height as equal, the contents of a round vessel with upright sides and with such a diagonal measurement would contain not much more or less than the Winchester quarter of 64 gallons (280 litres).

Thus, presumably, 64 gallons of mead or four times the amount of beer, together with the carcase of a cow or an ox, and a horseload of flour, with bacon and butter added, was the *gwestva* contributed by the *maenol* in Venedotia and the *tref* in South Wales towards the nightly carousals of the chieftain and his company.

The normal retinue or company of the *brenhin* is described in the Venedotian Code as consisting of thirty-six horsemen—equivalent to *uchelwrs* or *equites* —*i.e.* of the twenty-four officials of the king and queen, and twelve *gwestais*, possibly *uchelwrs*, bringing the *gwestvas* from the twelve *gwestva*-paying *maenols* in the cantref ; and there would be numerous hangers-on and dependents, including the twenty-four servants to whom supper silver was due.[2]

The normal retinue or company of the chieftain.

How many nights' carousal were provided for by the twelve *gwestvas* from the cantref in which the chieftain was making his progress remains undisclosed.

---

[1] ii. p. 827.　　　　[2] i. p 23.

V. THE CHIEFTAIN'S DUES FROM NON-TRIBESMEN.

CHAP. VI.

The main burden of the chieftain's progresses and maintenance was placed, no doubt, upon the shoulders of others than the free tribesmen.

The twelve *gwestvas* of free tribesmen from each cantref—six from each cymwd—were a substantial contribution to his maintenance, but it was supplemented by other provisions.

The *maertref* of the chief.

In the first place, according to the Venedotian Code, the *brenhin* is entitled in every cymwd to two *trefs*—one for his *maertref* and the other for his waste and summer pasture.[1]

These two *trefs* may be looked upon as constituting what in the Extents are described as the prince's manor in each cymwd. The obligations of the men of the *maertref* have already been alluded to in connection with the Manor of Aberffraw.[2]

Apart from this special provision for the chieftain, according to the Venedotian Code, the cymwd was to be arranged in twelve groups, or *maenols*.

Four *maenols* in each cymwd assigned to *aillts*. Their services.

Six of these, as we have seen, were *gwestva*-paying *maenols* of free tribesmen. Of the eight *maenols* left, two were set apart specially for the support of the *maer* and the *canghellor*. The remaining four were to be assigned to *aillts* to support dogs and horses and for the purposes of progress (*chylch*) and quarters (*dovraeth*).

The *maer* and *canghellor* were to make progress

---

[1] i. p. 187.
[2] The description in the Denbigh Extent of the manor and *maertref* of Dynrobyn in Ros Isdulas will be found in the Appendix.

in parties of four among the king's *aillts* twice in the
year. And besides this:—

> The *aillts* of the king (*brenhin*) are not to support him nor his
> household. . . . They are to furnish pack-horses to the king for
> the hosts, and they are to present the queen once every year with
> meat and drink, and they are to support the dogs, the huntsmen,
> the falconers, and the youths, all of them once every year.[1]

It has already been mentioned that the *aillts* had
to put up the chieftain's buildings, and furnish horses
and men, with hatchets, for making encampments on
his military expeditions.

In addition to these obligations, according to the
Venedotian Code, the bond *maenols* had to furnish
yearly two *dawn-bwyds*, or food-gifts.

In Winter.

A three-year-old swine.
A vessel of butter 3 handbreadths in depth and three in
breadth.
A vat full of bragot nine handbreadths in depth diagonally.
A thrave of oats of one band for provender.
26 loaves of the best bread grown on the land. . . .
A man to kindle the fire in the hall that night, or 1*d.*

In Summer.

A three-year-old wether.
A dish of butter.
26 loaves.
A cheese of one milking of all the cows in the *tref.*[2]

According to the Gwentian Code, the *dawn bwyds*
were as under :

Winter.

Vat of ale.
A sow 3 fingers thick.
A salted flitch.
60 loaves of bread. . . .
20 sheaves of oats.
1*d.* from every *randir* to the servants.

---

[1] *Ancient Laws of Wales*, i. p. 193.   [2] i. p. 199.

Summer.

Tub of butter 9 handbreadths in width and a handbreadth in thickness with the thumb standing.

Cheese of a meal's milk from all the *taeogs*, along with bread.[1]

According to the Dimetian Code, the amount of the *dawn-bwyds* was as under :

Winter.

A sow 3 fingers thick in her hams, &c. (or tub of butter).
A flitch of salted bacon.
60 loaves of wheaten bread (six of fine flour).
Vat full of bragot.
20 sheaves of oats and one band.
1*d.* for the servants.[2]

As to the summer *dawn-bwyd* there is some obscurity, but it did not differ much from that of the other Codes.

VI. CORROBORATION OF THE CODES BY THE EXTENTS.

Evidence of the Extents.

It will be convenient in concluding this chapter to return once more from the Codes to the Extents, in order to test the reality and authenticity of the customary law recorded in the former by comparison with the facts found by the surveyors actually existing at the date of the latter.

It refers back to the period before the conquest.

The earliest Extent of Aberffraw afforded evidence describing sufficiently clearly the money payments of the free tenants and the rents in kind of the hamlets of *nativi*. And the result of the petition of the tenants of Penros proved both that the description given was of the condition of things in the time of the princes before the conquest of North

---

[1] i. p. 771.   [2] i. p. 535.

Wales, and also that the greatest care was taken to
perpetuate the rents and services without alteration.

But we must go to the Denbigh Extent for an
example of a villata which was still the geographical
unit for payment of the food-rents of the free tribesmen commuted into the *tunc* pound.

If the reader will look back once again to the
analysis of the villata of Prees given above at p. 38,
he will see an example of a group of six so-called
progenies or *weles* located together in a single villata,
though by no means confined to that one locality.
The *progenies* of Canon and Pythle ap Lauwarghe
had several other locations. Their flocks and herds
and dwellings were scattered here and there in
places where they had rights of grazing. But at
Prees they each had rights to the occupation of an
undivided sixth part of the villata. And as this
villata was a geographical unit from which a *tunc*
pound was due, they had each to pay their sixth part
of the pound—*i.e.* 3s. 4d.

They were not paying the exact amount at the
date of the Extent because there had been escheats
and forfeitures. Instead of the full *tunc* pound the
tenants of Prees at the date of the Extent were
paying only 9s. 11¼d., but the entry of the surveyor
begins by saying that ' the villata of Prees with its
hamlets . . . . in the time of the Princes rendered of
tung 20s. 0½d. when it was entirely in the hands of
true heirs before forfeitures.'

Now the *progenies* of Pythle, under the name of
the grandsons of Pythle, also occupied the whole of
the villata of Tebrith, and paid, therefore, the whole
of the *tunc* pound of that villata.

CHAP. VI.

So also the villata of Tebrith was a *tunc*-paying unit.

It is only in a few cases like these that in the Denbigh Extent a single villata paid the full *tunc* pound, but there are a great many cases in which two or more clustered together would make up an even pound.

The unit for payment was a geographical area or district.

In the meantime the cases of Prees and Tebrith are sufficient to show that the unit of food-rent commuted into the *tunc* pound was payable from a geographical area or district, and not charged upon particular *weles* or even groups of *weles*. In a word, the tribute of the chieftain was thus territorial and not personal. The *weles* of free tribesmen could be shifted about from one villata to another, and the number of *weles* could increase or diminish without altering the payments of a particular area or the total of the chieftain's food-rents.

Possibly arranged so that the whole of Venedotia should provide for the year's entertainments.

If, for instance, the twelve free *maenols* of the Venedotian cantref each produced a vat of mead containing sixty-four gallons, the twelve vats from the whole cantref would produce 768 gallons; and if each vat contained the supply for three nights' carousal in the chieftain's hall the cantref would provide for thirty-six nights; and if at the time when the arrangement was made there were ten cantrefs in Venedotia, they might together provide for a year of 360 nights.

There is no evidence that this was the actual arrangement by which the year's supply of mead was provided—in fact, the number of cantrefs may have varied from time to time [1]—but it illustrates the possi-

---

[1] The authorities differ as to the number of cantrefs in North Wales, 10, 12, and 15 being mentioned. See under 'Cantrev' in the glossary to *Ancient Laws of Wales*, ii. p. 1111.

bility of dividing a chieftain's territory into fixed
geographical units, each of which should contribute
an aliquot part of the year's supply of mead, just as
King Solomon divided his tributary provinces so
that each should provide for a month's supply of the
wants of his luxurious court.

Besides the food-rents or *gwestva* payments of the
free tribesmen of the Codes, there was the burden
of the annual progress of the *brenhin's* household
at Christmas. And there were also various services
in connection with the furnishing of horses, the
support of dogs and youths, which in the Codes fell
upon the non-tribesmen in addition to their food
gifts. There are traces of these also in the Extent.

The *pastus* of the Denbigh Extent was in commutation of other services.

Besides the *tunc* of each cymwd, generally
divided into that from the free tribesmen and *nativi*
respectively, there is always mention of other payments, under the name of *pastus*, of various kinds—
*pastus principis, pastus familiæ principis, pastus
stalonis, pastus penmackew et wayssyon bagheyn,* &c.[1]

In the Latin version of the Dimetian Code the
brenhin's household is translated '*familia Regis*,' and
there can be little doubt that the *pastus* of the
Extent includes the payment in commutation of the
annual provision, not only for the progress of the
household, but also for other services connected
with the keeping of horses and dogs, the fosterage
of youths, &c.

Thus, in the Extent of the villata of Prees, immediately after mention of the *tunc*, is the entry : ' *De*

---

[1] *Pastus penmackew et wayssyon bagheyn* = *mackuyeit* and
gweisson bychen—i.e. fosterage
and young youths. See glossary,
Ancient Laws of Wales, ii., *sub*
' *Macwy*.'

pastu the prince had nothing, neither of the *pastus* of the family of the prince nor other kinds, because all the tenants of this *villa* do these services in other *villæ* as appears above in each place and *villata* respectively.'

The word *pastus* seems to be a word covering a variety of services, to some of which both classes of tenants were liable, nearly all of which at the time of the Extent had become commuted into money payments.

The evidence of the Extents strongly corroborates that of the Codes,

On the whole, as regards the relations of the chieftains to the tribesmen, the description contained in the Codes is corroborated by the facts recorded in the Extents. And, reviewing the evidence as a whole, as regards both the structure of the tribal society of the Cymry and its relation to the land, the

and the two together warrant belief in the reality of the tribal customs,

facts recorded by the surveyors in the Extents and the explanation of them in the rules of customary law contained in the Codes are sufficiently consistent to warrant belief in the reality of tribal customs which could produce such results.

and that in the main the principles of tribal custom have been correctly understood.

It would be presumptuous to suppose that in all cases the facts have been correctly grasped and the principles of tribal custom embodied in the Codes rightly understood. But the hope may, perhaps, be permitted that in the main, subject always to fresh evidence and constant reconsideration of what evidence already exists, a solid foundation has been laid for further historical and economic inquiry.

Importance of this to the understanding both of the

The almost unique advantage possessed by the Cymric tribal system in its survival into the period of Codes and Extents makes it a point of vantage for further research both backwards and forwards. Any understanding of the modern economic evolution of society in Wales must start from it. And it may be a stepping-stone also to a knowledge of the earlier past, not only as regards the tribal system in Wales, but also as regards other tribal systems, of which so little is known, but which have, nevertheless, made large contributions to the economic structure of modern European society.

CHAP. VI.

economic
evolution
of society
in Wales,
and also
of the
other
tribal
systems
of Europe.

CHAPTER VII.

THE TRIBAL SYSTEM AND THE CHURCH.

I. THE IMMUNITY OF THE CHURCH FROM THE EXACTIONS OF TRIBAL CHIEFTAINS.

WE have now to consider another element which strikes from outside like a wedge into the Welsh Tribal System.

It has already been noticed that the so-called Manor of Aberffraw was divided into two sections by the parish of Cadwaladr or Eglissel. This parish had two churches, one of which has perished. The surviving one contains the well-known stone with the inscription, supposed to be of the seventh century, in memory of St. Cadwaladr's grandfather, *Cadvan*, who reigned at Aberffraw about A.D. 616–630.

The Aberffraw chieftains made many donations to churches. Cadvan himself, according to the legends, had been converted by St. Beuno, and the church at Aberffraw—the church of the Palace—and the one at Trefdraeth, were both dedicated to that saint. St. Beuno's monastery at Clynnoc on the Carnarvonshire side of the Menai Straits was the gift of Cadvan's son Cadwallon.

The tradition of the gift of the site of this monastery is recorded shortly in the confirmatory charter of Edward I.[1] made after the conquest of North Wales on the evidence of the rector of the collegiate church of Clynnoc which had succeeded to the monastery.

'A certain *Gwithenit* gave his own villa of Clynnok Vawr to God and St. Beuno, then Abbot of Clynnok Vawr, for his soul and the soul of his *consobrinus* Catwalinus *sine censu Regali, et sine consule, sine proprietate alicui, quamdiu fuerit lapis in terra.*'

In the legendary life of St. Beuno the story of this gift is given more at length.

After the death of Cadvan (about A.D. 616) St. Beuno is said to have visited Aberffraw in order to purchase land from his son and successor, Cadwallon. In exchange for a golden rod (*guaell eur*) worth 60 cows,[2] which Conan (or Cynan)[3] son of Brochwel (Prince of Powys), had given to St. Beuno to be used as money, Cadwallon gave to the Saint a place called *Gwaredauc*, in Carnarvonshire. After he had built his church, and was walling in the boundaries, the title to the land was disputed by a woman to whom a child had been born, and who now claimed the land as the inheritance (*tref y tat*) of her child. She was probably the Cymric widow of an *aillt*, whose child had inheritance by maternity. Immediately St. Beuno went with the woman to Cadwallon, who, no doubt, had treated the land as escheat, and demanded either other land or return of the golden rod. The Prince,

---

[1] *Record of Carnarvon*, p. 257.

[2] It is clear that the golden rod was used as money, and equated with the cow, the usual unit of value.

[3] Cynan, son of Brochwel, invaded Glamorgan after Cadoc's death.—*Lives of Camb. Saints*, p. 375.

having refused his demand, was left by St. Beuno under a curse.   Whereupon his cousin Guidevit

> 'for the sake of his soul and of the soul of his cousin Cadwallon, gave to God and Beuno for ever his *tref* called *Kelynnawc* (Clynnoc) without tribute (*heb vab*), without service (*heb ardreth*), &c.'

The practical result of donations such as these to the saints and to the Church appears to have been to take the land so given once for all and absolutely from under the control of the chieftain of the district, and all tribal tribute and service to him.

Immuni-
ties of the
church of
Cad-
waladr.

Thus, in the 'Record of Carnarvon,' the land belonging to the church of St. Cadwaladr was described as follows :—

> 'EGHISSEL is a free villa and held of *St. Cadewaladre the King* and there are in this villa *two weles* (*wele* Ith ap Tanherñ and *wele* Welsonfraide ap Tanherñ) and the heirs are so and so. And nothing is thence rendered to the Prince per annum, nor do they make suit to either comot or hundred, nor pay reliefs nor amobr. And they say they are free to grind in their own houses; but they say that they owe appearance at two great turns of our lord Prince per annum for all other services. And in the second *wele* there are 3½ bovates escheated, which the *Communitas* of this villa now holds. *Summa per annum,* vii.*s.*[2]

Legen-
dary
miracles
in defence
of im-
munities.

It is important to observe further in how many cases the miraculous stories attributed to the Welsh saints in the legends turn upon the necessity of constantly guarding this freedom of Church lands from ordinary obligations to the tribal chieftains. Thus, to take another example from the life of St. Beuno, the same Cynan, Prince of Powys, who had given him the golden rod, had also granted to St. Beuno a place called Gwydelwerun in Merionethshire, on which he had erected a church. But it happened that Cynan's

---

[1] *Lives of Cambrian Saints,*
p. 16 and p. 304.

[2] *Record of Carnarvon,* p. 46.

nephews, in the ordinary course of a hunting expedition, came upon the land, and, according to tribal custom, claimed hospitality. St. Beuno acceded to their request and gave them a young ox for their meal ; but, by a miracle, prevented the fire from boiling the meat, and afterwards cursed them for ' demanding tribute and service (*mal ar dreth*) from what their fathers had given to God *free* (*yn ryd*).' [1]

Again, in the Life of St. Brynach,[2] a saint of South Wales, who lived before the first visitation of the Yellow Death, *i.e.* before a.d. 547, a somewhat similar story is told. A certain chieftain named *Clechro*, with the concurrence of his sons, granted his land to St. Brynach, the sons becoming disciples of the saint and he himself retiring to Cornwall. *Maelgwn*, coming that way with his retinue demanded entertainment (*cena*). The saint, to preserve his rights, declined. Whereupon the king's servants seized upon a cow. But with all their efforts the fire would not cook the meat, and seeing the miracle the king humbly submitted, and after having partaken of the hospitality now freely offered by the saint, confirmed his privileges, and made a further grant of land in the following words, which evidently followed the common form of a legal record, though by no means certainly of the sixth century :—

[3] ' In nomine Dei et Domini nostri Jesu Christi te [St. Brynach] et locum tuum totumque territorium ad locum tuum pertinens ; necnon omnes in eo commanentes, ab omni regia exactione in perpetuum libero ; insuper terram *Thelych* monachi ditioni tue liberam assigno : qui ergo contra hanc donationem meam de cetero venire presumserit Dei maledictionem omniumque fidelium Christi et meam celeriter incurrat.'

---

[1] *Camb. Saints*, pp. 15 and 302.

[2] *ib.* p. 10, from *Cotton MS.*

Vesp. xiv. fol. 77, B.M.

[3] *ib.* p. 12, from same MS. fol. 80.

CHAP.
VII.

The im-
munities
granted to
Llandaff.

Contemporary with St. Brynach was St. Teilo, the founder of the church of Llandaff, whose privileges are thus given in the 'Book of Llan Dav,' evidently following, in this case, an elaborately worded common form framed to withdraw the Church property absolutely from secular or tribal control. Whatever its date, it none the less testifies to the completeness of the immunity claimed by the Church, and the sort of exactions to which property was otherwise liable under the tribal system.[1]

ẏholl cẏfreith didi	To enjoy all its laws
hac dẏ thir, hac di dair	and its lands, and its territories
rẏd o pop guasannaith breennin bẏdaul,	free from all regal and secular service
heb mair, heb cẏghellaur,	without mair, without canchyllor,
heb cẏhoith, dadl ma y meun gulat	without attendance at public courts of litigation
hac nẏ dieithẏr,	either in the district or out of it,
heb luẏd	without going on expeditions
heb gavaẏl, heb guẏlma :	without arrest, without keeping watch and ward :
ẏ cẏfreith idi yn hollaul,	with complete legal cognizance,
o leitẏr, o latrat, o treis,	of thief, of theft, of violence,
o dynnyorn o cẏnluẏn	of slaying, of waylaying,
hac o losc, o amrẏson canguaẏt a heb guaẏt,	of incendiarism, and contention with blood and without it,
ẏ diruẏ hay cameul ẏndi didi ẏn hollaul,	with full right to fines and penalties for crimes,
o dorri nand ẏnnlann,	of violating the privilege of refuge,
hac ẏn dieẏthẏr lann,	either in or out of the precinct,
orachot ẏnn, luhẏn, hac dieithẏr luhẏn,	of attack, secret or open,
o cẏrch ẏpopmẏnnic ar tir Teliau	of assaults anywhere on the land of Teilo,
haẏ guir haẏ braut dẏ lẏtu ẏruluẏs ẏgundig Teliau ẏnn Lanntaff.	and with its right and jurisdiction over its dependents at the White House of Teilo at Llandaff.

---

[1] 'No one who has any know- | ment believe that Geoffrey, or any
ledge of Old Welsh will for a mo- | of his contemporaries could have

Now, whatever may be thought of the authenticity or antiquity of these legendary origins of
ecclesiastical property, and of its immunity from all
census terrenus or *census regalis, i.e.* from tribute or
food rents to secular chieftains, the contention that
it ought to be thus free was quite consistent with the
claims of the Gallic Church in the sixth and seventh
centuries.

Immunity
from all
*census
terrenus*
early
claimed
by the
Church.

Amongst the canons included in the collection of
so-called Irish canons, to which, however, Mr. Bradshaw assigned a Breton origin, is one headed ' *De
censu non dando super ecclesiam*,' and St. Augustine
is quoted : ' *si ipsi filii liberi sunt a censu in quolibet
regno terreno, quanto magis filii regni illius, sub quo
sunt omnia terrena regna.*' And St. Ambrose is
quoted as saying : ' *Ecclesia catholica libera est ab
omni censu.*' [1]

The phraseology of these passages coincides closely
with that of the legendary donations.

But it is possible that the grant to St. Teilo went
exceptionally far. It not only gave immunity from
all *census terrenus*, but transferred judicial jurisdiction from the *brenhin*, or king, to the bishop. The
general immunity according to the Codes did not
always go so far as this. Thus, in the Venedotian
Code is the following statement :—

> No land is to be without a *brenhin* (*dyurenhyn*). If it be
> abbey land he [the *brenhin*] is to have (if they be laics) dirwy and
> camlwrw and amobyr and ebediw and hosts (*llvyd*) and theft
> (*lledrat*). If it be bishop's land he is to have hosts and theft. If it
> be hospital land he is to have theft and fighting (*ymlad*), and
> therefore there is no land without him.[2]

written the Welsh of Teilo's
" Privilegium " or of the boundaries.' *Book of Llan Dav* (preface),

p. xxii and p. 120.
[1] *Wasserschleben*, p. 79.
[2] *Venedotian Code*, i. p. 171.

N

It may well be that the tribal chieftain of the
time of Howel had become jealous of ecclesiastical
encroachments, and did not willingly acquiesce in the
admission of the absolute immunity claimed by the

But ad-
mitted
com-
pletely on
the con-
quest of
N. Wales.

Church in the sixth century.   Certain it is, however,
that nothing could be more complete than the royal
admission of absolute immunity to the successors of
St. Beuno and the collegiate church of Clynnoc
immediately after the conquest.   No stronger words
could be used than those of the royal confirmatory
charter of Edward I. above alluded to.   It recited
and confirmed the royal gift to St. Beuno with
immunities as complete 'as though it were an
island in the midst of the sea' (*sicut insula in medio
maris*).

It is also a remarkable feature of the Denbigh
extent that among the names of the numerous *villatæ*
belonging to the honour or lordship there are
scarcely any with the common prefix *Llan*, the fact
being that the lordship was honeycombed with
ecclesiastical 'islands' of the kind mentioned, over
which the secular lordship had no jurisdiction.

In the same way the Extents comprised in the
'Record of Carnarvon' are full of *lacunæ*, to be filled
up only by adding the 'islands' of ecclesiastical
territory.

II. THE NATURE OF THE EARLY RECORDS OF DONATIONS TO THE CHURCH.

If the records of donations to the Church were of
only ecclesiastical interest, it might be left to the
ecclesiastical historian to examine them in detail.

But, as they contain the earliest evidence within

reach of the actions and habits and character of Cymric chieftains, they cannot be wholly ignored in an attempt to understand the Cymric tribal system.

Any real evidence dating back to the first contact of the successors of Cunedda with the saints of the sixth century, if contemporary, is certain to bristle with incidental details which cannot fail to be precious in the absence of more direct evidence.

Therefore, both as regards the relations between the tribal system and the Church, and as regards the tribal system itself, the attempt must be made to form a sound judgment upon the difficult question of their authenticity.

They suffer from their connection with the legends of the miraculous lives of the saints to whose churches they were made, and from the suspicion of interested motives in the scribes of the twelfth century, by whom they were collected and copied, and perhaps in some cases forged.

There is, no doubt, ground for suspicion and caution. But this is quite another thing from wholesale rejection.

Part of the difficulty disappears when the records are approached as they evidently ought to be, not as charters, but as simple notes or records of transactions. They seldom, if ever, profess to be documents made by and under the signature of the donors. They are mostly expressed in the third person, and profess to record solemn acts and to state who were the witnesses before whom they were transacted. When it is observed that the first of the witnesses may be ' *Deus omnipotens*,' or the saint, long at rest, at whose altar the transaction took

First contact of Cymric chieftains with the churches.

Nature of the early records of donations; not charters but notes of transactions.

Some-
times
written
in the
margin of
Gospels,

place, the character of the record becomes at once apparent.

When the record was written in the margin of a richly illuminated copy of the 'Gospels,' as was often the case, it becomes all the more obvious that we are not dealing with charters in the ordinary sense, but with acts done under solemn religious sanctions and placed under the protection of the altar at which the transaction took place.

and, as in
the ' Book
of Deer,'
copied
from one
book to
another.

Several such records were recorded, for instance, in the 'Book of Deer' in the vernacular Gaelic of Scotland, in the eleventh and twelfth centuries. This copy of the Gospels does not claim to have been itself written before the ninth century, but the first of the entries, probably made in the eleventh century, is the record of the original foundation of the monastery in the sixth century.

Thus it appears that if a sacred copy of the Gospel came into the possession of an abbey at a certain date there would be no inconsistency in the records originally made in a copy earlier in use being transferred to it by a copyist. So in the ' Book of Deer' the initial entry and the records of several of the earlier grants are all in one handwriting, and were written probably at the same time.[1]

And thus
may be
modified
without
fraud.

Obviously, therefore, it is by no means certain that there is fraud wherever the language or hand-writing of an entry betrays that it is not contempo-rary. And, further, it was obviously so much easier a thing to modify an existing entry for a purpose in transcribing it than to forge an entirely new docu-

---

[1] *Book of Deer*, Mr. Stuart's preface, p. xxv.

ment that there might be fraudulent alteration without material departure from the original form of the record.

There is another point of negative evidence in favour of the substantial correctness of the records of donations in the margins of Gospels, or presumably copied from them.

In the legendary lives of Welsh saints it often happens, as in the two cases above alluded to, that a miraculous story is the prelude to a record of donation which follows a legal formula, and makes no mention of the miracle. When this is the case the inference is natural that the formal record gave rise to the legend rather than the legend to the record.

As we proceed to examine some of these records, it will be recognised that, while they are full of little archaic touches, belonging to a very early period, they are almost entirely free from the miraculous elements which are rampant in the twelfth century legendary lives of the saints to whose monasteries the donations were made.

III. THE MS. ENTRIES IN THE 'BOOK OF ST. CHAD.'

The illuminated Gospel, called the 'Book of St. Chad,' was, according to Mr. Bradshaw, transferred to St. Chad's Church, at Lichfield, before 964–973, because it bears the signature of Wynsige, Bishop of Lichfield, whose episcopacy covered those years.[1]

The earliest entry was evidently made whilst the book itself was in possession of St. Teilo's Church, at Llandaff. The handwriting of the entry was con-

---

[1] *Collected Papers*, p. 459.

sidered by Mr. Bradshaw to belong to the early part of the ninth century. It is as follows :—

' Ostenditur hic quod emit + gelhi + filius ariht iud hoc evangelium de cingal et dedit illi pro illo equum optimum et dedit pro anima sua istum evangelium deo et sancto teliaui super altare. + Gelhi + filius aryht iud ... et + cincenn + filius gripiud.[1] '	' Here is shown that Gelhi the son of Ariht iud bought this gospel from Cingal and gave to him for it a "best horse," and gave for his soul this gospel to God and St. Teilo upon the altar. + Gelhi, son of Aryht iud . . . et Cincenn the son of Gripiud.'

Further entry.

The next entry carries us a step further, in that it shows that Elcu, the son of Gelhi, was in possession of a property called the land of Telih.

' Surexit tutbulc filius liuit ha gener tutri dierchim *Tir Telih* haioid ilau elcu filius gelhig haluidt juguret amgucant pel amtanndi ho diued diprotant gener *tutri* o guir inguodant ir degion guragun tage rodesit *elcu* guetig equs tres uache, tres uache nouidligi namin ir ni be câs igridu dimedichat guetig bit did braut grefiat guetig nis minn tutbulc hai cenetl in ois oisoud. ' + *teliau* testis *gurgint* testis *cynhilinn* testis *sp's* testis tota familia teliaui. De laicis *numin map aidan* testis, *signou map jacou* testis *berthutis* testis *cinda* testis. ' Quicunque custodierit benedictus erit, quicunque frangerit maledictus erit.'[2]	' *Tutbulc*, the son of *Liuit*, and son in law of *Tudri*, arose to claim the land of TELIH which was in the possession of *Elcu* the son of *Gelhi* and the tribe of *Juguret*: he complained long about it: at last they dispossess the son-in-law of *Tudri* of his right. The nobles said to one another, ' Let us make peace ': *Elcu* gave afterwards a horse, three cows, three newly calved cows, provided only there be no hostility between them from this reconciliation thenceforward to the day of doom. *Tutbulc* and his people will require afterwards no title for ever and ever. . . . 'Whoever shall keep this shall be blessed, whoever shall break it shall be cursed.'

---

[1] *Book of Llan Dav*, preface p. xliii.

[2] *Ibid.* p. xliii, where also the accompanying somewhat tentative translation is given. Mr. Bradshaw considered the hand-writing tenth century. The two Gelhis may nevertheless be the same person, as the second record may have been written after the transaction.

This record connects the family of Elcu, son of Gelhi, who bought the Gospel from Cyngal (?), with the family of Tutbulc, the son of Liuit, and the dispute between the two families related to the land of Telih; but there is nothing to show that the land of Telih belonged to Llandaff.

Now, in the 'Book of Llan Dav'[1] there is a record confirming to Llandaff the ownership of the *Cella Cyngualan*, in Gower, which it states had belonged to St. Dubricius and St. Oudoceus, but had been lost in the first visitation of the 'Yellow Death.'

And there is also another record of about A.D. 929,[2] which states that *grifud rex, filius ijugein*, to make amends, *inter alia*, for a violation of the refuge of the monastery of St. Cingual, granted to Llandaff, *Penn ibei in Rosulgen* (*i.e.* Rosilli in Gower). And in the boundaries appended to the donation, the land thus granted is described as touching in one place ' *usque ad agrum cinguali*,' and in another a modius of land ' *juxta telich*.' [3]

This tenth-century record of the boundaries thus shows that the monastery or cell of St. Cingual was adjoining to *Telich*, and that both were in the peninsula of Gower, adjoining Rossilli. This proximity suggests that Gelhi may have bought the Gospel from the monastery of St. Cingual, and given it to St. Teilo, at Llandaff, as it was afterwards transferred from Llandaff to St. Chad, at Lichfield.

In the very next record in the 'Book of Llan Dav,'[4] probably of between A.D. 961 and 967 (in the reign of King Edgar), Morgan Hen, King of Glamorgan,

CHAP.
VII.

Coincidences
with the
'Book of
Llan Dav.'

---

[1] *Book of Llan Dav*, p. 144.   [3] P. 240.
[2] *Ib.* p. 239.   [4] P. 240.

described as 'Morcant, son of ẏugein,' is said to restore and confirm to Llandaff all the territories which had belonged to it in the time of St. Dubricius, St. Teilo, and St. Oudoceus, naming certain churches and their territories. Amongst these is 'Machumur, *i.e.* Lann Liuit,' and in its boundaries occur the words ' across to Is Guaissaf, of liquallaun, the son of Tutbulch.'

These boundaries connect the land of *Lann Liuit* with *Tutbulc.* This, again, is an incidental corroboration of the entries in the 'Book of St. Chad,' where Tutbulc is said to be the son of Liuit.

Record of an emancipation by four brothers

The next three records, written in the 'Book of St. Chad,' are of more direct interest. They are roughly dated by the mention of Nobis,[1] Bishop of Llandaff, who was translated to St. David's, A.D. 840. The first is a manumission by four brothers of one Blethiud, the son of Sulgen, *et semini suo in sempiternum*, on payment of four pounds (or, possibly, four cows), and eight ounces, presumably, of silver.[2]

This is interesting, as a ninth-century example of a case resembling that of St. Patrick, viz. of the family ownership of slaves, or of *aillts*, or *taeogs*, and of the emancipation of a whole stock or family, like that already quoted, of a *gwely* of *nativi* by the Bishop of St. Asaph.

It is imperfect, but it is supposed to read thus :—

Nobis . necesse est scribere literas quod IIII filii bledri gu[or ti]girnn [cim]ulch et . . . arthuis dederunt libertatem bleidiud filio

---

[1] Mr. Bradshaw's *Collected Papers*, p. 460. Nobis is described by Asser, in his *Life of Alfred*, as his *propinquus*.

[2] Four cows = one pound of silver, and the worth of a bondman was one pound in the Codes. The final letters, ' as,' are the only letters remaining, the margin of the record being injured.

sulgen et semini suo in sempiternum pro precio . atque hoc est [con-
firmatio] quod dedit pro libertate ejus quatuor [libr]as [or vaccas]
et oc[to u]ncias. Coram idoneis [his t]estibus:

De laicis Riguo[llau]n filius [coff]ro guen . . . filius . . . r
gnoluic filius . . . dan Ov . . . filius guur [cinn] im . mer[chgu]inn
filius salus arthan filius cimulch judri filius judnerth.

De clericis vero Nobis episcopus teiliav saturnguid sacerdos
teiliav. Dubrino et cuhelin filius episcopis, saturnbiu cam ibiav
et sulgen scholasticus qui hec fideliter scripsit . . . Qui custodierit,
etc.

The other two are records of ninth-century dona- Two dona-
tions of
tions, of a *tref* with a *census* or food-rent. ninth cen-

The items of this census were :—In the first tury with
food-
case, two score loaves and a wether in the summer rents.
and two score loaves and a sow and two score sucking pigs in winter ; in the second case, three
score loaves and a wether and a vessel of butter—
thus resembling the summer and winter *dawn-
bwyds* of the *taeog trefs* of the Codes, though not
absolutely identical in all the details, and taking back
the system of food-rents a century earlier than the
Codes.

The records are difficult, both in the reading of
the manuscript entries, and in translation ; but, as in-
terpreted in Mr. Evans's edition of the ' Book of
Llan Dav,' sufficiently intelligible for the present
purpose.[1]

Ostendit ista scriptio quod dederunt ris et luith grethi treb
guidauc imalitiduch cimarguith-
[i]eit, hic est census ejus . douceint
torth ha maharuin . in irham . ha
douceint torth in irgaem . ha huch
. ha [do]uceint mannuclenn . deo
et saucto eliudo . deus testis .

This writing shows that Ris
and Luith Grethi gave Tref-
guidauc. As story tellers say, this
is its census, two score loaves and
a wether in the summer, and two
score loaves in the winter, and a
sow and two score sucking pigs, to
God and St. Eliud. God witness,

---

[1] *Book of Llan Dav*, preface, p. xlv.

saturnnguid testis . nobis testis .
guurci testis cutulf testis . de
laicis cinguernn testis . collbiu
testis . cohorget testis . ermin testis
. . . hourod testis . quicunque custodierit benedictus erit et qui
franxerit maledictus erit a deo.

Saturnguid witness, Nobis witness, Guurci witness, Cutulf witness. Of the laity, Cinguernn
witness, Collbiu witness, Cohorget
Ermin witness, Hourod witness,
Whoever shall keep this shall bo
blessed and whoever shall break
it shall be cursed of God.

Osdendit ista conscriptio quod
dederunt *ris* hahir . . . . ha . . rdid
ha *gurci* . r . . . . . g . . . . . . g . . . . cibrac-
ma . behet hirmain guidauc . ofoid
celli irlath . behet cam dubr . isem
hichet triuceint torth . h[a maha]
ruin . ha guorthoneir emeninn . .
deus omnipotens testis . saturnnguid sacerdos testis . nobis testis .
gurci testis . cutulf testis . de laicis .
cinguern testis . [collbiu] testis . cohorget [testis] . ermin testis . [qui-
cunque custo]dierit [bene]dictu[s
erit . et] qui fra[nxer]it . m[ale-
dic]tus . er[it . a deo].

This writing shows that Ris
&c. . . . gave . . . Guidauc . . .
as far as . . . its tribute three
score loaves and a wether and . . .
butter. God Almighty witness,
Saturnguid priest witness, Nobis
witness, Gurci witness, Cutulf witness. Of the laity : Cinquern witness, [Collbiu] witness, Cohorget
[witness], Ermin witness. Whosoever shall keep this shall be
blessed, and whoever breaks it
shall be cursed by God.

There can be no reason to doubt for one moment
the authenticity of these records written on the
margins of the Gospel of St. Chad, and they are
important not only in their subject-matter but also
as a link in the chain of evidence as regards the
practical authenticity of the records of earlier
donations.

IV. THE EVIDENCE OF GILDAS.

Maelgwn's
conquest
of S.
Wales.

None of the records in the 'Book of St. Chad' are
of very early date; but they clear the ground for the
consideration of the many donations to churches in
South Wales, which so far as the transactions recorded
are concerned, date back to the period immediately

succeeding the Cymric conquest of South Wales by CHAP. VII. Maelgwn.

Maelgwn is said to have died in the first visita- Yellow Death, A.D. 547. tion of the Yellow Death, *i.e.* about A.D. 547. This date is approximately fixed by the mention of its ravages, both in Irish and Welsh records.[1]

Many of the early donations to churches in South Wales are recorded in the 'Book of Llan Dav,' St. Dubricius and St. Teilo being the reputed founders of that see. The witnesses to many of these records are the abbots, or heads, as well as members of the three monasteries of St. Cadoc, St. Illtud, and St. Monas-teries of St. Cadoc, St. Illtud, and St. Dogwin. Dogwin, who appear thus to be in close connection, both geographically and spiritually, with the Church or Bishopric of Llandaff.

Besides the records of donations in the 'Book of Llan Dav' are others still more remarkable appended to the legendary life of St. Cadoc, in a twelfth-century MS. in the British Museum,[2] printed, though very incorrectly, in Rees's 'Lives of Cambro-British Saints.'

Whether the records were contemporary or not, Donations to St. Cadoc. all the donations to St. Cadoc belong, so far as the subject-matter is concerned, to the time preceding and following the first occurrence of the Yellow Death (A.D. 547).

This is precisely the period as regards which Contem-porary with Gildas. there exists the contemporary evidence of Gildas. Whatever facts, therefore, can be extracted from

---

[1] See Zimmer's *Nennius Vindicatus*, p. 101, quoting from the *Ulster Annals*, A.D. 545-548 for the appearance of the '*mortalitas magna*' in Ireland. The *Annales Cambriæ* give the date A.D. 547.

[2] *Cotton MS.*, Vesp. A. xiv. Brit. Mus.

his 'turgid rhetoric' ought to throw light on these donations.

That Christianity had been introduced from Gaul during the Roman period there can be no doubt. And the lamentations of Gildas, for what they are worth, are evidence of the condition of things during the century following the Roman withdrawal from Britain and the struggle with the Saxon invaders.

Coincident with the Roman withdrawal was the coming of Cunedda and his sons in North Wales, and Gildas wrote during the Cymric conquest of South Wales under Maelgwn. The decay of the Roman peace in Britain, succeeded by the breaking up of the united action of British chieftains when the stress of resistance to the Saxons was over, had resulted, according to Gildas, in civil wars. These wars were, moreover, quarrels between nominally Christian rulers.

That Gildas wrote his lamentations like a Hebrew prophet in declamatory and stilted language may be granted, but in the main he doubtless 'did well to be angry,' and it is impossible to believe that, writing in this spirit, he should not have alluded to the coming of the Yellow Death as a scourge from

heaven if it were either past or present when he wrote. Further than this, his direct diatribe against Maelgwn himself, who died of that plague, proves that Gildas wrote before its ominous date.

In an undoubtedly confused passage Gildas speaks of the battle of *Mons Badonis* as having occurred in the first month of the forty-fourth year [of his own age], and as marking the close of the struggle against the invading Saxons. A considerable time must have elapsed since that date to account for his adding—

> 'And yet not even now are the cities reinhabited, but, deserted and destroyed, they lie waste to this day, an end having come to external wars, but not indeed to civil wars.' [1]

Evidently the writer was now an old man, for he speaks of the generation which had experienced the 'terrible desolation' as having departed, and of a new generation as having risen up. Again, in his preface, he speaks of having delayed his epistle ten years or more, and describes himself as now at last discharging his debt long ago due,[2] constrained by the entreaties of his brethren, in a style which he admits to be severe against evil-doers, but, nevertheless, 'faithful and friendly to all young soldiers of Christ' (*Christi tyronibus*).

These phrases are those of an old man patronising a younger generation of Christian workers. And if 43 in A.D. 516 (the date of the battle of Badon Hill according to the *Annales Cambriæ*), Gildas, having previously written his work, would be 74 at the time of the Yellow Death (A.D. 547). And having survived its visitation he may well have lived to attain his ninety-eighth year at his retreat in the bay of Morbihan, where he is said to have died, A.D. 570, according to the *Annales Cambriæ*.[3]

An old man when he wrote.

Died A.D. 570.

---

[1] *Hist. Gildæ*, c. xxvi.

[2] 'Debitum multo tempore antea exactum.'

[3] It is quite true that Bede read the passage referring to the battle on *Mons Badonis* as stating that it occurred in the forty-fourth year from the arrival of the Saxons, but the event last mentioned by Gildas was the leadership of Ambrosius, to which his '*Ex eo tempore*' may refer and from which his forty-three years may have run, thus making

CHAP.
VII.
___

The main point is that the evidence of Gildas was contemporary with the sixth-century donations, and its value consists in the light it throws upon the contact of the tribal chieftains with the Church in the most Romanised part of Britain still left to the Britons.

Roman
names of
British
chieftains.

That the British chieftains of the older (probably Goidelic [1]) race had acquired, to say the least, a Roman varnish which still lingered in their names, is shown in the mention by Gildas of Constantine of Dumnonia and Aurelius Conanus (probably of Powys).

Many
over-
thrown by
Maelgwn.

That even Cunedda himself was to some extent Romanised may well be believed, but that Cunedda's invasion was a Cymric tribal migration seems equally clear. The conquest of Maelgwn in the south, depriving many of the older chieftains, as Gildas puts it, ' of their kingdoms and their lives,'

---

the date of his birth A.D. 473. Bede may have put a wrong construction on the passage as we have it. Recent writers have indeed assumed that he did so, but to fall themselves, as it would seem, into a greater difficulty, by reading the passage as meaning that Gildas was writing in the forty-fourth year of his age, having been born in the year of the battle. This can hardly be a correct reading, for in the first place if only forty-four when he wrote, he could hardly have assumed so completely the tone of an old man, and in the next place forty-four years from the

battle (516 + 44) would make the date of his writing A.D. 560, which is an impossible date, as it would be after the Yellow Death, and Maelgwn would by that time have been ten years in his grave. It seems best, therefore, to adhere to the dates of the *Annales Cambriæ* after all, as most consistent with the facts.

[1] The inscriptions of the Roman and post-Roman period, both Latin and bilingual, in Roman letters and in Oghams, are, according to Professor Rhys, mainly Goidelic, if the test word *mac* instead of *map* may be trusted.

was an extension of the same tribal invasion. Roman civilisation, we may believe, no longer softened the character of the great-grandsons of Cunedda. The crimes which Gildas deplored were the crimes of the old tribal nature cropping up again—gross crimes of murder and incest—deepened in his view by the fact that they were the crimes of chieftains who, in childish superstition and the blind impulse of remorse, had professed Christian conversion and become children of the Church.

Gildas represents these chieftains and their relations as entering the monasteries and submitting to penances and penalties, and then breaking out again into crime.

The sister of the wife of Cuneglasse, according to Gildas, had taken the vow of holy virginity. And Maelgwn himself not only had been under Christian training, but also, in a moment of remorse after crime, had taken the monastic vow before he committed the fresh crimes of murder and incest of which Gildas accused him.

The Church had evidently set itself to convert these tribal chieftains, and they or members of their families rushed into her offices and assumed her dignities. This is contemporary evidence, and at least lends some colour to the genealogies which make the chief saints of South Wales—St. David, St. Teilo, and St. Dubricius—closely allied in blood with the royal family of Cunedda and his descendants.

Nor is Gildas silent on the ecclesiastical side of these transactions.

When he feels himself bound to speak of the ' *malitiæ episcoporum vel cæterorum sacerdotum aut clericorum in nostro quoque ordine,'* and accuses Constantine, King of the Dumnonii, of the murder of royal youths with sword and javelin at the very altar under shadow of the abbot's cloak, his evidence is good that there were bishops and abbots, as well as priests and monks of his own order, in the monasteries and churches of South Wales and Britain.

Ecclesiastical abuses blamed by Gildas.

Nor can it be possible to disregard the nature of the ecclesiastical sins deplored, however much his language may bear the impress of exaggeration. The worldliness and sensuality of clerks neglecting spiritual duties; the simony of both priests and bishops buying their ecclesiastical dignities from tyrannical princes, or crossing the seas and travelling far to obtain them, and returning with foolish ostentation and pomp; the apathy and want of courage in the better class of clergy in standing out against the evil of others and imposing the proper penances on them for their sins—all this is the evidence of an eyewitness, and helpful in judging of the records of transactions belonging to the same period.

V. THE FORM OF CONTEMPORARY CONTINENTAL RECORDS OF DONATIONS TO THE CHURCH.

Form of sixth-century Continental records.

The direct and contemporary evidence of Gildas has brought us into the atmosphere in which the transactions recorded in the records of sixth-century donations, if authentic, took place.

The question of the authenticity of the records themselves may be approached from another point of view, viz. that of a comparison of their form as documents, and the formalities by which the donations were accompanied with the forms and formalities in use during the same period on the Continent.

The Cymric tribal system was not the only one with which, on the break up of the Roman Government, the ecclesiastical system had to deal.

Romanised as the Church itself was, its influences must needs have been to a large extent Roman, and in the Roman provinces of Gaul it evidently continued to follow and to represent Roman legal forms and principles in its action under Merovingian and even later rulers. And this was so in a modified sense even in its contact with the less Romanised tribes which fell under its influence—tribes who still adhered more or less to tribal custom. It is quite obvious that in the formation of the Alamannic and Bavarian Codes of the seventh century ecclesiastical influence was a strong factor. Not only had local custom to be codified, as in the case of the Welsh Codes, but a *modus vivendi* had to be found for the Church. The Codes, therefore, disclose the methods adopted by the ecclesiastics under Merovingian rule in securing the interests and property of the Church in districts newly conquered by the Franks.

Donations
to the
Church
under
Merovin-
gian rule.

These districts on the borders of Gaul had more or less, like Britain, been under the provincial rule of Rome. They therefore present many analogies with the most Romanised portions of South Wales. Hence there is at least some probability that the Church would use the same legal forms and methods in the one district as in the other. Why not? Especially in the case of donations to churches and monasteries, the monks were as likely to impose their own technical methods and legal formulæ in

o

South Wales as in Gaul, and in the Alamannic and Bavarian districts. Happily the Cadoc and Llandaff records of donations can be compared with the Continental methods, and the comparison is the best direct test to which their genuineness can be put.

What, then, were the methods described in the Alamannic and Bavarian codes as regards these donations?

The *Leges Alamannorum Illotharii* are considered to belong to the reign of the second prince of that name, A.D. 613–622.

The first clause is as follows [1] :—

The Alamannic Laws allow donations and fix their forms.

Ut si quis liber res suas vel semetipsum ad ecclesiam tradere voluerit, nullus habeat licentiam contradicere ei, non dux non comes nec ulla persona sed spontanea voluntate liceat christiano homini Deo servire et de proprias res suas semetipsum redemere. Et qui voluerit hoc facere per cartam de rebus suis ad ecclesiam, ubi dare voluerit, firmitatem faciat, et testes sex vel septem adhibeat, et nomina eorum ipsa carta contineat, et coram sacerdote qui ad ecclesiam deservit *super altare* ponat, et proprietas de ipsas res ad illam ecclesiam in perpetuo permaneat.

That if any freeman wishes to hand over his property or his own person to the Church, no one shall have license to thwart him, neither duke nor count nor any person, but of his own free will it shall be lawful for a Christian man to serve God and to redeem himself with his own property. And whoever wishes to do this shall confirm by charter what he wishes to give of his property to the Church, and shall produce six or seven witnesses, and the charter shall contain their names, and in the presence of the priest who serves at the church he shall place it upon the altar, and the property in those things shall remain for ever to that church.

The point of this enactment is to allow freemen, subject to Roman law, to make donations to the Church, and it prescribes the form in which it is to be done by charter, naming the witnesses, the donor in presence of the priest placing the charter on the altar.

---

[1] Pertz, *Legum* iii. p. 45; and Mon. Germ. Hist. *Leges Alamannorum*, p. 63.

The Bavarian laws have the same provision, but also define what the donor may give, viz. *de portione sua postquam cum filiis suis partivit*—his own portion after division with his sons—according to the provisions of the Roman law. The outward formality is required that the witnesses should place their hands upon the *epistola*, which is then to be placed on the altar. The subject of the donation was thenceforth to remain the absolute property of the Church, and neither the donor nor his sons could disturb it unless the representative of the Church should choose to allow the donor to hold it as a benefice.[1]

Also the Bavarian Laws.

This last clause brings before us another very common feature of early donations, which is more fully described in the following passage from the Alamannic laws, viz. the custom to allow the donor to retain the use of the property granted to the Church by way of usufruct, paying the *census* of the land in the meantime to the Church.

Retention by the donor of the usufruct as a benefice paying a census.

Si quis liber qui res suas ad ecclesiam dederit et per cartam firmitatem fecerit sicut superius dictum est, et post hæc a pastore ecclesiæ per beneficium susceperit ad victualem necessitatem conquirendam diebus vitæ suæ : et quod spondit persolvat ad ecclesiam *censum* de illa terra, et hoc per epistulam firmitatis fiat, ut post ejus discessum nullus de heredibus non contradicat.[2]	If any freeman who shall have given his property to the Church and confirmed it by charter as before said, and afterwards shall have received it as a benefice from the pastor of the Church as a provision for his bodily needs for the days of his life, let him pay what he has promised to the Church as *census* from that land, and let this be done by a letter of confirmation, in order that after his decease none of his heirs shall gainsay it.

[1] 'Nisi defensor ecclesiæ ipsius beneficium præstare voluerit ei.' Title 1, c. 1, Pertz, *Legum* iii. p. 270.

[2] Pertz, *Legum* iii. p. 45 ; and Mon. Germ. Hist. *Leges Alamannorum*, p. 66. E, Cod. B.

CHAP.
VII.

Donations of this kind, reserving the usufruct to the donor as a *beneficium* or *precaria*, are of very common occurrence among those made to the Abbot of St. Gall in the eighth century.[1]

Roman law also permitted a donation with a simple reservation of the usufruct.[2] And that in the sixth century it was a common thing for a donor to make a donation retaining the usufruct is shown by the mention of it in the Rules of St. Benedict :—

Sanctioned by the Rules of St. Benedict.

> If they wish to offer something to the monastery for their salvation, they shall make a donation of the things which they wish to give to the monastery: *retaining the usufruct for themselves, if they wish.*[3]

Hence there were donations of two kinds : (1) those in which the property given was occupied by tenants paying a *census* and transferred to the Church, in which case the Church obtained the property and received the *census*; (2) those in which the donor, who might be also the occupant, retained the usufruct and paid the *census* to the Church. And instances of both kinds occur among the Cadoc donations.

The census fixed by custom.

Moreover, the *census* seems to have been in these cases a fixed customary food-rent. Whether on the *terra regis* or on the land of the Church there were two classes of tenants paying their legitimate *census* or *tributum* to the king or to the Church— *liberi* and *servi*.

---

[1] *Urkundenbuch der Abtei St. Gallen* (Wartmann), Theil i., Nos. 3, 10, 17, 18, &c.

[2] *Dig. Just.* vii. 1; and *Codex,* viii. 53, *De Donationibus*; and *Cod. Theod.* viii. 12; and *Gaius,* ii. 33.

[3] Rule 59, '*reservato sibi, si ita voluerint usufructuario.*'

Thus, in the Alamannic laws it is enacted as follows :—

Liberi autem ecclesiastici, quos colonos vocant, omnes, sicut et coloni Regis, ita reddant ad ecclesiam.[1]	Freemen of the Church, who are called *coloni*, all shall render to the Church just as *coloni* of the king do.
XXII	XXII
Servi enim ecclesiæ tributa sua legitime reddant, quindecim siclas de cervisa, porcum valentem tremisse uno, panem modia duo, pullos quinque, ova viginti.	Let the servi of the Church render their tribute according to law, fifteen siclæ of beer, a pig worth a tremissis, two modii of bread, five hens and twenty eggs.

So that the law laid down actually what the legitimate or normal tribute or *census* of the unfree class of tenants, called *servi*, consisted of—viz. fifteen siclæ of beer, a pig worth a tremissis,[2] two modii of bread, five hens, and twenty eggs.

The normal census of servus 15 siclæ of beer, &c.

That this *census* of the typical servile holding was adhered to in the Alamannic district in the eighth century is proved by the very frequent occurrence of it and its double in the donations to St. Gall.[3] And it seems to have extended down the Rhine valley as a common usage.[4]

It was natural that the ecclesiastics should introduce their own Continental methods into the Romanised districts of South Wales. The Church was already more or less established in these districts, even in Roman times, and when it first came into contact with the conquering Cymric chieftains tribal and ecclesiastical methods must have come to some compromise.

---

[1] Tit. xxiii.

[2] The *tremissis* = 32 wheat grains weight of gold.

[3] *Urkundenbuch der Abtei St. Gallen*, Nos. 17, 18, 24, 33, &c.

[4] See *Codex Laureshamensis Diplomaticus*, iii. pp. 177 *et seq.*, where there are numerous cases of *hubæ servíles*, with a *census* of 'situlæ xv de cervisa, &c.'

CHAP.
VII.
———
Com-
promise in
Wales
between
tribal
rules and
the legal
methods
of the
ecclesias-
tics.

The donations in Wales were made, for the most part, by tribal chieftains, whose possessions were subject to the tribal custom of *tir gweliawc.* On the donor's side, therefore, tribal custom and habits, and not Roman law, must needs rule the form of the donation. Even a chieftain could not alienate family property without the consent of other members of his family. But, on the side of the Church, the recipients of the donation—the ecclesiastics—would bring their own forms and formulæ with them. They would insist that there must be the written charter with its witnesses. They would introduce the formal act of delivery by placing the writing on the altar or on the Gospels. If the transaction did not take place in a church, some other formality would be required. The placing of the writing upon the hand of the recipient, as we shall see, was the actual form most often adopted.

The transfer of a property, the food-rent or *census* of which had hitherto been paid to the donor or the chieftain, must here as elsewhere have meant the transfer to the donee of the right to receive the settled food-rent of that holding. The donation of a holding by the occupant, who desired still to retain the occupation, would here as elsewhere mean his payment of his food-rent to the Church instead of to his chieftain, and therefore would require his chieftain's consent. Such transactions would be certain to be mixed up with little archaic points of detail fitted to the time and locality; and, lastly, authentic records of donations would be hardly likely to make mention of miracles!

If on examination these various conditions are

found to be complied with, the reader will be able CHAP.
to judge how far it is possible for the records to VII.
which attention will now be turned, whether contemporary with the donations or not, to be the
forgeries of a later hand, however cunningly desirous
to aggrandise the episcopal see to which he might
belong. And, at the same time, if substantially
authentic, the reader will not fail to appreciate the
value of the light they throw on the earlier conditions of tribal life.

VI. THE EARLY RECORDS OF DONATIONS IN THE 'BOOK OF LLAN DAV.'

Returning, then, to the 'Book of Llan Dav,'
St. Dubricius and his companions may well have
been among the 'youthful soldiers of Christ' to
whom Gildas alluded.

The legend describes Dubricius as embracing   Disciples
among his disciples the following, viz. :—Teilo,   of St.
Samson, Ubeluius, Merchguinus, Elguoredus,   Dubricius
Gunuinus, Congual, Arthbodu, Congur, Arguistil,   charge of
Junabui, Conbran, Guoruan, Elheharn, Judnou,   churches
Guordocui, Guernabui, Louan, Aidan, Cinuarch.[1]   as founded.

These, with many others, are represented as
living together in a kind of college, and afterwards
as located in smaller groups in charge of churches
as they were founded. The smaller groups formed
thus little collegiate and missionary centres, whilst
remaining in close communion and intercourse.[2]

Now, there are in the 'Book of Llan Dav' records
of nine donations made to St. Dubricius during his

---

[1] *Book of Llan Dav*, p. 80.   [2] P. 81.

lifetime, the witnesses to which generally include some of the above-mentioned disciples.

The first of these donations is as follows :—

Donation
of son-in-
law of
Constan-
tine.

Lann Custenhinn garth benni in Ercicg.

Sciendum est nobis quod Peipiau, rex filius erb . largitus est *mainaur garth benni* usque ad paludem nigrum inter siluam et campum et aqnam et jaculum Constantini regis socri sui trans Guý amnem deo et Dubricio archiepiscopo sedis landauie . et junapeio consobrino suo pro anima sua et proscriptione nominis sui in libro uite cum omni sua libertate sine ullo sensu terreno et principatu paruo et modico nisi deo et sancto Dubricio seruientibns ecclesie Landauie in perpetuo tenuitque peipiau gra- fium super manum Dnbricii sancti ut domus orationis et peni- tentie atque episcopalis locus in eternum fieret episcopis landauie et in testimonio . relictis ibi tribus discipulis suis ecclesiam illam consecrauit . De clericis testes sunt in primo Dubricins, Arguistil, Vbeluin, Jouann, Junapius, Conuran, goruan. De laicis uero Peipiau rex testis, Custenhin, Guourir, dihiruc, Condiuill, guid- gol, clem. Quicunque custodierit hanc elemosinam deo datam . custodiat illum deus . qui autem non seruauerit . destruat illum deus.[1]

The Church of Garth benni of Constantine in Erging.

Be it known to us that Peipiau, king, son of Erb, bestowed *Mainaur Garth benni*, up to the black marsh with wood, field, and water, and the casting-net of King Constantine, his father-in-law, across the River Wye, to God and Dubricius, Archbishop of Llandaff, and to Junapeius his own cousin, for his soul, and for the writing of his name in the Book of Life, with all its liberty without any earthly census and sovereignty smaller or greater except God and St. Dubricius, and the servants of the Church at Llandaff for ever. And Peipiau held the writing upon the hand of St. Dubricius in order that it might be for ever a house of prayer and penitence, and bishop's place for the Bishops of Llandaff. And in testimony leav- ing three of his disciples there, he consecrated that church. Of the clergy are witnesses, first Dubricius, Arguistil, Ubelniu, Jonaun, Junapius, Conuran, Goruan. And of the laity Peipiau, king, is witness, Custenhin, Guourir, Dihiruc, Condiuill, Guid- gol, Clem. Whosoever shall guard this alms given to God, God guard him. Whoso however shall not keep it, may God destroy him.

Now this is the record of a donation by Peipiau, son of Erb, king of Gwent and Erging, and son-in- law (*socer*) of Constantine, of a *mainaur* called the⸳

---

[1] *id.* p. 72.

Garthbenni of *Custenhin*—*i.e.* of Constantine. The
donation is made to St. Dubricius and his cousin
and disciple *Junapeius*, for the good of the donor's
soul, and that his name might be written in the
Book of Life, and it was to be held free from all
secular tribute (*census terrenus*) for ever.

Perhaps it would be going too far to connect this
King Custenhin with the Constantine, king of the
Dumnonii, who, as already mentioned, was reproved
by Gildas for having slain at the altar two royal
youths in the very year in which he was writing.
At all events, this would be consistent with the entry
in the *Annales Cambriæ*, A.D. 589, ' *Conversio Constantini ad Dominum,*' and the tradition that he
became a saint.

Recurring to the phraseology of the record, the
peculiarity in the form of delivery is worth notice,
as the only case in which, in the ' Book of Llan Dav,'
the writing is held by the donor upon the hand (*super
manum*) of the ecclesiastical recipient.

Had the ceremony of delivery been completed in
the church after the consecration, it would probably
have been performed at the altar ; but it could not be
so in this case, as it preceded the consecration.

In another case Erb, the father of the last-mentioned donor, makes a donation of *unam tellurem de
propria sua hereditate*, and in confirmation *misit
manum super quattuor evangelia tenente beato Dubricio
cum predicta tellure.*[1]

In another case two donors, before all the witnesses, *posuerunt hanc dotem super quattuor evangelia
in perpetuo*, &c.[2]

---

[1] *Book of Llan Dav*, p. 75.   [2] P. 75.

Another record testifies that, *in primo tempore,*
Noe,[1] the son of Arthur, gave to God and St. Dubricius *Pennalum, Lann Maur* on the Tyvi, and another
site on the river Tam—*mittens*[2] *noe manum super
quatuor evangelia et commendans in manu archiepiscopi
Dubricii hanc elemosinam in perpetuo, &c.*—the witnesses again being his companions Arguistil, Ubelbiu,
Jouann, Junabui, Conbran, Guoruan, Elhearn,
Judnou, Gurdocui, Guernabui.

The last-mentioned donation was of the three
places in which churches dedicated to St. Teilo exist,
each of which, according to the legend, laid claim to
his body, the first on the ground that at Pennally
his ancestors were buried, the second because it was
a place where he had dwelt with his disciples, the
third, on the coast at the mouth of the Tam, because
it was the place where he died. The donation contains
no mention of the miracle vouched for by the legend
whereby a body was provided for each of the three.

If this record be genuine, it refers to the original
donation to St. Teilo in his lifetime of the three
places where he made settlements and built churches,
and which were therefore most closely identified
with his name ; and it does not profess to be a
record contemporary with the grant. It distinctly
states that the donation was made ' *in primo tempore,*'
the disciples of St. Dubricius being witnesses to the
transaction, and not to the present record.

There is yet another of these records in the
' Book of Llan Dav ' requiring particular notice.

---

[1] P. 77.

[2] *Leges Alamannorum,* ii. 2.
Cf. ' *qui manus suas in cartam
miserunt* '; and see Brunner's

*Zur Rechtsgeschichte der
Römischen et Germanischen
Urkunde,* p. 230.

One of the disciples of St. Dubricius was Merch-guinus. He is called in the record *Merchguinus Rex, filius gliuis*—*i.e.* he was one of the *sub reguli* of the family to which St. Cadoc belonged—and it states that under his rule a person named Guordoc (also one of the disciples of St. Dubricius) devoted (*immolavit*) his virgin daughter Dulon to the Church of Llandaff along with four modii of land, in Gower, *et communione tota regionis Guhiri in campo in aqua et in pascuis.'* [1]

Now it must be clearly understood that there is nothing to show that these records were contemporary records. They do not claim to be such. In one case a distinct disclaimer has been alluded to, the record speaking of the donation as having been made *in primo tempore*, which suggests a considerable interval.

The donations themselves are recorded to have been made in all cases in the lifetime and presence of St. Dubricius and some of his disciples. In no case yet are the witnesses, as so often afterwards in the records in the 'Book of Llan Dav,' the abbots and members of the three little monasteries of St. Cadoc, St. Illtud, and St. Dogwin. The inference is that they were made before these monasteries had been founded, *i.e.* in the first half of the sixth century.

There are, moreover, some geographical points connected with these early ecclesiastical settlements which should not be overlooked.

In the first place they are not in a Cymric district, but in a Goidelic district (Guir et Cetgueli,

Marginalia:

CHAP. VII.

A royal relative of St. Cadoc 'immolates' his virgin daughter.

The records do not claim to be contemporary. They record past events.

---

[1] *Book of Llan Dav.* p. 76.

CHAP.
VII.

i.e. Gower and Kidwelli), the chieftains of which had not long surrendered to the conquests of Maelgwn.[1]

The three settlements of St. Teilo were in Pembrokeshire and Carmarthenshire, and in what became the diocese of St. David.

Allusion has already been made to the dispute between Llandaff and St. Illtud, and ultimate confirmation to Llandaff of the cells of Cyngualan, Arthruodu, and Congur, and Pencreic, which had been lost to St. Dubricius in the Yellow Death. All these cells were in close neighbourhood in Gower, or adjacent parts of Glamorganshire.

Lastly, the three monasteries of St. Cadoc, St. Illtud, and St. Dogwin were in close proximity to Llandaff.

Episco-
pacy not
yet terri-
torial.

When, therefore, the episcopacy became or was becoming territorial in South Wales, difficulties arose naturally out of the geographical position of St. Teilo's settlements, which, though in the territory of St. David's, naturally belonged to Llandaff, of which St. Teilo was the saint.

But at the time of these donations there was no ground for such difficulties. What bishops there were were not territorial. The Church in South Wales was monastic rather than episcopal. Or more correctly the missionary work of the Church was carried on by the foundation of little monastic churches or colleges of monks, some of whose members were bishops, but whose heads were the abbots.

And both the historical importance of these monastic churches and the time of their prevalence are

---

[1] *Historia Brittonum,* s. 14, and see Zimmer's *Nennius Vindicatus,* p. 84-91.

marked by the fact that the system which had originally spread from Gaul, through Brittany, into Wales,
was carried over by the Irishman Finian, who was a
disciple of St. David, St. Gildas, and St. Cadoc, into
Ireland, becoming there the second of ' the three
orders of Saints ; ' viz. that immediately following
the order of St. Patrick.[1]

VII. THE DONATIONS TO THE MONASTERY OF ST. CADOC.

We may now proceed to examine the records[2] of
donations to St. Cadoc. They divide themselves into
three groups when placed as far as possible in
chronological order.

The first group is that of records of donations
made in the lifetime of St. Cadoc ; and of these, two
relate to the founding of monastic churches—one by
a favourite disciple and the other by St. Cadoc himself.

[3] Notū sit oīnib3 p mutabili-
tate tēpo꒳ ꝉ successib3 hui°
mundi regū . q̄d Elli allūpn°
beati Cadoci . ab ipso diligenꝷ
a p̄meua etate educat° . ac sac̄s
apicib3 ap̄me institut° illiꝗ
cuncto꒳ disciꝓlo꒳ suo꒳ ca-
rissim° . Et asseruit Elli dicens .
Ecce ego construxi ecc̄am ꝉ
domos in nŏe Dni . ꝉ ipse
cunctiꝗ successores mei . familie Cadoci erim° obedientes
subiecti . atꝗ beniuoli . familie
Cadoci. Dedit etiā Elli ꝓsc̄pte

Be it known to all, on
account of the mutability of
times and of the successions
of the kings of this world,
that Elli, the pupil of the
blessed Cadoc, having been by
him educated lovingly from
tenderest age and well established in sacred learning and
being the dearest to him of
all his disciples, made decla-
ration saying : ' Lo, I have
built a church and houses in
the name of the Lord, and I

---

[1] Skene's *Celtic Scotland*, ii.
c. ii.
   [2] The Latin of these records
has been copied from the Cotton

MS., Vesp. A. xiv., B.M., and I
have to thank Mr. W. K. Boyd
for the care bestowed upon them.
   [3] Fol. 39 old ref., 40 new.

CHAP.
VII.

Founda-
tion of a
monastic
church.
Food-
rents of
'three
nights'
summer
and
winter.

familie ppetua pensione sinḡlis
annis cibaria p tres noctes in
estate ac totidē in hieme cū
gīarū actione ʇ leticia . oīonibȝ
ʇ hymnis sp̄ualibȝ uerū etiā
in substituendo administᵃtore
eiˢdē eccƚe ꞉ abbas cenobii
Catocj p̄ses semp erit ʇ auctor.
Ceteꝛ si contiḡit q̄d Catocˢ
atꝗ successores illiˢ cū illoȝ cli-
entela minime veน̂int꞉ dentʳ illis
duo boues ad recognitionē
subiectionis ʇ societatis. Vn̄
cōuenientes ad monasฺiū elli
pactionē hāc cū pacis osᶻlo
c̄firmaueꝛt in conspectu elli
iuxta crucē q̄ . ē . in uia multis
nota.

Huiˢ rei s̄t testes . Catoc .
Elli. Cleophas. Samson . Jacob .
Boduan . Conocan . Mach .
Ierunt un̄q'sꝗ ad loē suū de
bn̄dictiōe in bn̄dictione Am̄.

myself and all my successors
shall be obedient, subject, and
well disposed to the family of
Cadoc.' Moreover, Elli gave to
the aforesaid family in perpetual yearly payment provisions for three nights in
summer and as many in winter, with giving of thanks
and joy, prayers and spiritual
hymns. Moreover, in changing
the administrator of the same
church the abbot of the community of Cadoc shall have
the chief power and authority
for ever. But if it shall happen that Cadoc and his successors with their followers
shall diminish, then shall be
given unto them two oxen as
recognition of subjection and
alliance. Whereupon coming
together to the monastery of
Elli they confirmed this agreement with the kiss of peace
in the sight of Elli hard by
the cross which is on the road
known to many.

Of this thing are witnesses
Catoc, Elli, Cleophas, Samson, Jacob, Boduan, Conocan,
Mach. They departed each to
his own place blessing and
blest. Amen.

Sciendū . ē . noƀ q̄d Cadoc
construx̄ eccƚam Mach moilo
discip̄lo eiˢ eāꝗ munimine
uallauit ac in ende altare
composuit . qᵃtinˢ illo hospita-
retʳ qᵃndo iret ad Guent ac in̄
rediret . dimisitꝗ Mac moilū
in ea p'orē atꝗ ad ministᵃtionis

Be it known to us that
Cadoc built a church for Mach
Moilus, his disciple, and walled
it securely, and constructed an
altar therein, to the end that
therein he should be enter-
tained when he should go to
Gwent and return thence, and

toti⁹ ꝓcuratorē . Pollicit⁹ . ē .
q̄, Cadoc⁹ regni p̄mia celoꝫ
cunctis q¹ ei⁹dē eccl̄e posses-
siones ag¹s seu pecuniis aut
elemosinis auxerint : Testes s̄t .
sup hoc . Cadoc ꞇ cl̄ici ei⁹ .
Pachan . Detiu . Boduan .
Quicq̄, custodierit b̄nd̄ . e . a
Ꝺo . ꞇ q¹cq̄, frangit maledict⁹
erit a d̄no Am̄.[1]

he ordained Mac Moilus as
prior therein, and to be procurator of the whole of its administration. Moreover, Cadoc
promised the rewards of the
kingdom of heaven to all who
should increase the possessions
of the said church by land or
moneys or alms.

The witnesses thereof are
Cadoc and his clergy, Pachan,
Detiu, Boduan.

Whosoever shall keep [this]
shall be blessed by God ; whosoever shall break it shall be
cursed by God. Amen.

Donations very similar to these, of churches built
or founded by the donors, occur in Continental car-
tularies.[2] In the donation by Elli, the companion of
Cadoc, of his church—' Llanelli '—there is an interesting variation in the description of the annual
' pensio,' or ' census.' It is described, not as a food-
rent of so many measures of beer, with bread, flesh,
and honey, as in most cases, but as *three nights'*
cibaria, i.e. *gwestva,* payable in summer and winter
respectively, the equivalent details of which are
taken as well known, and not needing definition.
This is an early illustration of the adaptation of the
food-rent or *gwestva* to the nightly supply of the
wants of the *familia* of the monastery to whom the
donation was made. Instances will follow of the
transfer of food-rents from a chieftain to a monastery
without alteration. It will be noticed that, as in
this case of the nights' entertainments, so also in
other cases, the numbers are reckoned in *threes.*

The three
nights'
gwestva.

---

[1] Fol. 88 d. old ref., 39 d. new.
[2] *Cart. de St. Bertin,* pp. 28. 29 (A.D. 677).

The next record is of a different character :—

CHAP.
VII.

A chieftain murders two nephews, and, in redemption of the crime, he and another make donations of land with its food-rents of beer, bread, flesh, and honey.

Post inꝖuallū temporis occidit Euan Buurꝛ duos uiros filios sororis ei⁹ . Atgan scił ꝛ Aidnerth . Quā ob rē uenit Cadoc ꝛ Eltuth . ꝛ maledixeīt Euan . Vñ coact⁹ uenit Euan ꝛ Reges cū eo ad ꝑsentiā Codoci atꝗ Eltuti ꞉ confessusꝗ ē eis sceła sua . At illi dixeꝛt ei . Redime culpā homicidij . Respondit Catlon dicens . Dabo agrū nõe Lan Hoitlon Cadoco . Pensio ei⁹ . ij . vasa sex modioȝ ceruise cum pane ꝛ carne ꝛt melle . Ꝣcꝺm solitā debitā debiti mensurā . Merchiaun uᵒ dedit villā uidelicet Conhil Eltuto . atꝗ . iii . uasa ꝗ sex modios ꝣuise continebāt unū quodꝗ uas cū agꞌs consecᵃntes ꞉ ꝑfatis scīs in ppetuā elemosinā ꝯtuleꝛt . At illi satisfactionē Euan suscipientes . xiiii . annos penitencie iniunxerūt ei.

Cui⁹ facti testes fueꝛt . Catlon . Merchiaun . Euan . Cethij . Sꞓs Catman . Hoitlon . Virgo Cadoc . Finiau scott⁹ . Eutegrȳn lector . Familia ꝗ Cadoci . atꝗ Cadoci . atꝗ Eltuti ꞉ testes Ꝣt . Quicꝗ custodierit ꞉ benedict⁹ erit a Do . ꝛ qꞁcunꝗ frangꞁt maledict⁹ erit.[1]

After an interval of time Evan Buurr killed two men, sons of his sister, to wit Atgan and Aidnerth. Whereupon came Cadoc and Illtud and cursed Evan. Whereby constrained came Evan and the kings with him to the presence of Cadoc and Illtud, and confessed to them his crimes. And they said to him, ' Redeem the crime of homicide.' Catlon replied saying, ' I will give land called Lan Hoitlan to Cadoc ; the *pensio* thereof is two vessels each of six modii of beer, with bread and flesh and honey, according to the due and accustomed measure.' Moreover, Merchiaun gave a villa, *i.e.* Conhil, to Illtud, and three vessels which contain six modii of beer, consecrating each vessel with the land. They conferred them on the aforesaid saints in everlasting alms. Moreover, they receiving satisfaction from Evan enjoined upon him fourteen years of penitence. Of which fact the witnesses were Catlon, Merchiaun, Evan, Cethii, St. Catman, Hoitlon, Virgo Cadoc, Finiau Scottus, Eutegyrn the reader. Also the family of Cadoc, and of Cadoc and Illtud, are witnesses. Whoever shall keep this shall be blessed of God, and whoever shall break it shall be cursed.

---

[1] Fol. 38 d. old ref., 39 d. new.

This record is interesting in several ways. A chieftain has murdered two sons of his sister. St. Cadoc and St. Illtud are courageous enough to charge him with the crime. He brings two other chieftains with him (probably members of his family), and makes confession, whereupon the two abbots require him, according to Church law, to redeem the crime of homicide. There is no *galanas* within the kindred, but the Church must have her due. The two chieftains comply with the demand, and respectively make to the monasteries of the two abbots donations of properties, and these, according to custom, are described by the amount of the annual payments or food-rents due from them, viz. in one case two vessels, each of six *modii* of beer, with bread, flesh, and honey, according to customary amount and measure ; in the other case, three such vessels, each of six *modii* of beer, and bread, flesh, and honey, in addition.

But this is not all. Having received these dona- tions, the two abbots impose upon the murderer fourteen years' penance, *i.e.* seven years' penance for each of the two murders, according to the rules laid down in contemporary Penitentials.[1]

What could Gildas ask more from the abbots than this ? The witnesses comprise amongst others the two chieftains who make the donations. One of them, Merchiaun, as we shall find from another record, was afterwards murdered by his relative, Guoidnerth. Gildas did not, it seems, overrate the crimes of chief-

---

[1] ' Hibernensis sinodus dicit : Omnes homicidæ si toto corde conversi fuerint, VII annorum penitentiam districte sub regula monasterii peniteant.' *Die Irische Kanonensammlung,*Wasserschleben, p. 96. Lib. xxviii. c. 10.

CHAP.
VII.

The Irish
monk
Finian as
witness.

tains. Another witness was *Finiau Scottus.* This can hardly be other than the Irish monk Finian,[1] already alluded to, who, according to Irish authorities, came over when thirty years old into Wales, to be the disciple, as already mentioned, of the Welsh saints David, Cadoc, and Gildas, and, after remaining thirty years in Britain, returned to Ireland to found the 'second order' of monasteries. He died, like so many others, of the Yellow Death, according to the annals of Ulster, in A.D. 548.[2] The appearance of Finian as a witness to this record puts back the date of the transaction, if authentic, some years, at least, before the Yellow Death.

VIII. THE DONATIONS TO THE MONASTERY OF ST. CADOC (*continued*).

Donations
whilst
Conige
was
abbot of
Llan-
carvon.
Donation
of land
with re-
servation
of occupa-
tion and
payment
of food-
rent of
beer, &c.

The next three donations are linked together by the fact that they were made in the time of Conige, the abbot of St. Cadoc's monastery, and that some of the witnesses were common to them all.

Sciendū . ē . q̄d Theudor fili⁹ Mourici dedit gladiū vestiñtūq, Catoco ꝶ familie ei⁹ q̄ᵃtin⁹ iñ emerēt ꝉrā in sustentatione ei⁹dē . Conige u° abbas altaris sc̄i Cadoci tribuit gladiū illū uestiñtūq, Spois ꝶ Rodrico ꝓ uilla cui noñ Conguoret in Pencenli . qⁱ concesseꝶt hanc Cadoco ꝶ eiusdē eccle possidendā iure ꝓpetuo . q̄ annua pensione psolů)et ꝑmisso Coniḡ

Be it known that Theudor son of Mouricus gave a sword and garment to Cadoc and his *familia* to the end that therewith they should buy land for the sustentation of the same. Moreover, Conige abbot of the altar of St. Cadoc, assigned that sword and garment to Spois and Rodricus for the villa named Conguoret in Pencenli, who granted it to

---

[1] Rees misread the manuscript as 'Finian Seoctus,' and so failed to recognise the name of the Irish monk.

[2] Reeve's *Life of St. Columba,* lxxiii., n. ; Skene's *Celtic Scotland,* ii. p. 50.

ac ꝑlibate familie . ꝑ manū Spois ⁊ filioꝝ ei⁹ in eťnū . nouē modios ceruise panē q̃ carnē ac mel . Et ut ista possessio liƀa ⁊ qͥeta foret ab om̄ibꝫ seruitiis ⁊ exactionibꝫ ťrenoꝝ regū :/ isdē Spois fili⁹ Gurhur smptit⁹ . ē . iii . uaccas Guornemet . uñ ꝑfat⁹ Rodri tenuit cartā siue gᵃphiū sup manū Conige abbatis Nantcarbanan in confirmatiōem hui⁹ donationis. Postea u° conueneŕt Rodri ⁊ Spois ac filii ei⁹ . Conige etiā ⁊ clerici ei⁹ attuleŕt crucē sc̄i Cadoci ⁊ humū ei⁹ ⁊ circueundo ꝑdictū agrū congueret . illudq; uendicaueŕt ⁊ ꝑscͥpti sc̄i humū in signū ꝓpͥe possessionis sup illū corā idoneis testibꝫ conspseŕt.

De laicis, testes . Rodri . Guornemet . Guoguoret . Hoilbin . Honhoer . Colbin. De clericis . Samson . abbas altaris sc̄i Eltuti . Conige abƀ altaris sc̄i Cadoci . Plossan . Ætern . Iouan . Minnocioi . Brenic . ⁊ familia sc̄i Cadoci . testis ē . Qui conseruauͧit conseruet illū Ds . ⁊ qͥ fregerit maledict⁹ erit a Dno am̄.[1]

Cadoc and his church in possession by perpetual right so that in annual *pensio* it should pay to the said Conige and his *familia* aforesaid by the hand of Spois and his sons for ever nine *modii* of beer, also bread, flesh, and honey, and that this possession should be free and quit of all services and exactions of earthly kings the said Spois son of Gurhur bestowed three cows on Guornemet. Whereupon the said Rodricus held the charter or writing upon the hand of Conige the abbot of Nantcarvon in confirmation of this donation. Afterwards, moreover, came together Rodricus and Spois and his sons, also Conige and his clergy brought the cross of St. Cadoc and his earth, and by going round the said land Congueret both sold it and scattered on it the earth of the saint aforesaid as a sign of proper possession before fit witnesses. Of laity, witnesses: Rodricus, Guornemet, Guoguoret, Hoilbin, Honhoer, Colbin. Of clergy: Samson abbot of the altar of Illtud, Conige abbot of the Altar of St. Cadoc, Plossan, Ætern, Iouan, Minnocioi, Brenic, and the family of St. Cadoc is witness. Who shall have kept this God keep him. Who shall have broken it shall be accursed by God. Amen.

[1] Fol. 38 old ref., 39 new.

Sword
and vest-
ment
used as
money.

This record presents many points of interest.

Theudor, the son of Mouric, gives a sword and a vestment to the monastery of St. Cadoc to be used as money to purchase land for its maintenance.

Conige, the abbot, buys with them a villa named Conguoret, in Pencenli, from Spois and Rodric. They, however, retain possession. The food-rent of nine *modii* of beer, with bread, flesh, and honey, is to be paid by them and their sons for ever. And, that it might be freed from all secular services, Spois, the son of Gurhur, gives three cows to Guornemet. Rodri holds the charter or writing upon the hand of Conige, the abbot, in confirmation of the gift, and then, lastly, Rodri and Spois with his sons, and the abbot with his clergy, carry the cross of St. Cadoc and earth from his altar or sepulchre round the newly purchased land in the presence of witnesses.[1] Cadoc is now evidently dead.

The next record is as follows :—

Donation
of land by
a father
and three
sons, re-
serving
occupa-
tion under
food-rent.

Sciendū ē q̃d Bronnoguid fili⁹ Febric dedit dimidiā partē agri Idraclis p̄ aīa sua 't ut nom̄ ei⁹ in libro Catoci ap̄ Nantcarban sc̄ibet^r . Đo 't monas͡tio sc̄i Cadoci . Et ip̄e q̄dē Bronnoguid 't tres filii ei⁹ Guedan . 't Guobrir . 't Meue . tenuert sc̄iptū g^aphii sup̄ manū Conige p̄ncipis altaris Cadoci in sempit͡no donationis iure Đo 't sc̄o Cadoco . Ann⁹ 't eni illi⁹ aḡ census p̄petuus ē ⫶ tres modii ceruise . 't panes 't carnes 't mina mellis . Hec eni Bronnotguid 't tres filii ei⁹	Be it known that Bronnoguid, son of Febric, gave a half share of the land Idraclis for his soul, and that his name might be written in the book of Cadoc at Nantcarvan, to God and the monastery of St. Cadoc. And he, to wit Bronnoguid, and his three sons, Guedan and Guobrir and Meue, held the writing of the document upon the hand of Conige, chief of the altar of Cadoc, in everlasting right of donation to God and St. Cadoc. Moreover, the annual

---

[1] See *Book of Llan Dav*, pp. 71, 121, 161, 162, for other examples of this kind of ceremony.

꒒ gñatio illoӡ annuati debeut psoluere familie Cadoci usꝗ ad diē iudicii . Hui⁹ puctiōis testes ŝt . Bronnotguid dñs fundi ꒒ filii ipsi⁹ . Guoidan . Marcant . Iunemet . Conige abʦ . Elionoẏ . Brenic . Mannocoi . Beduan . Plosan . Qui hāc donationē seruauit : custodiat illū Đs . Et qⁱ fregit : maledict⁹ erit a Đo . Am̃.[1]

permanent *census* of that land is three *modii* of beer, and bread, and flesh, and a *mina* of honey. For Bronnoguid and his three sons and their offspring ought to pay these annually to the family of Cadoc until the day of judgment. Of this agreement are witnesses, Bronnoguid, *dominus fundi*, and his sons Guoidan, Marcant, Junemet, Conige abbot, Elionoy, Brenic, Mannocoi, Beduan, Plosan. Who shall keep this donation God guard him, and who shall break it shall be cursed by God.

In this case the donor and his three sons hold the writing, as in other instances, upon the hand of the abbot. They, however, retain the occupation of the land, and the father, who is the *dominus fundi*, and the three sons and their kindred, are henceforth to pay to the abbey the *census* of three *modii* of beer and bread and flesh, and a *mina* of honey yearly, till the day of judgment.

The next record is of the same kind. Possession is retained and the *census* payable to the abbot is exactly double that of the last case.

Sciendū . ē . ꝗd dedit Conbelin agrū Lisdin borrion uocat⁹ ꝑ cōmercio regni celestis cū corpore suo Đo ꒒ s̄co Cadoco ꝗd ei annuati psolűet sex modios ċuise . cū pane ꒒ carne ꒒ melle . Testis . ē . Conige qⁱ sup manū suā sc̄ⁱpsit [? sumpsit] concuū . i . Cyrogᵃphum.[2]

Be it known that Coubelin gave land called Lisdin borrion for purchase of the kingdom of heaven with his own body to God and St. Cadoc so that he should pay to him (Cadoc) annually six *modii* of beer with bread and flesh and honey. The witness is Conige, who, upon his own hand, [took (?)] . . . chirograph.

[1] Fol. 38 old ref., 39 new.   [2] Fol. 40 old ref., 41 new.

IX. DONATIONS TO THE MONASTERY OF ST. CADOC

(*continued*).

The next record is that of a donation to God and St. Cadoc by a father, who commended a villa to his son so that the latter should serve the abbey and pay out of the surplus produce the food-rent of nine *modii* of beer with bread and flesh and honey to St. Cadoc.

Donation by a father, reserving occupation to his son, with food-rent to St. Cadoc.

Sciendū . ē . sane q̃d Gualluiur donauit Đo ꝼ Sc̄o Cadoco agrū Pencarnov . ꝑ aīa sua in sempiꞇnū :ʹ usꝗ ad diē iudicii . Guallunir aū hanc uillā comm̄dauit Iudnou filio suo . qᵃtin⁹ ipse ꝼ heredes ipsi⁹ seruirēt familie Cadoci ex sūptibȝ hui⁹ agⁱ p̄ꞇ ipsos. Cens⁹ hui⁹ agⁱ . ē . nouē modii ceruise . panes ꝼ carnes c̄ melle . Quinimmo :ʹ qᵒc̄ꝗ clerici Cadoci uoluerint manducare ꞇ biꝛe :ʹ uidelicet in Basseleg . seu in Pencarnov :ʹ p̄fat⁹ Iudnou cibaria ꝼ potiōem q̃ p̄libauim⁹ afferet ad illos.

Hui⁹ pactionis testes ŝt Paulus abbas Nantcarban . Guenlioui f̄r ei⁹ . Tunic . Canapoi . Tanet . Hierbrith . Merhitr. Concū . Quic̄ꝗ custodierit . custodiȝ illū Đs . ꝼ qⁱ freḡit maleꞇ . e. a Đno . am̄.[1]

Be it well known that Gualluiur gave to God and St. Cadoc the land Pencarnov for his soul for ever till the day of judgment, Guallunir, moreover, ' commendavit' this villa to Judnou, his son, to the end that he himself and his heirs should serve the family of Cadoc out of the produce of this land beyond their own needs.[1] The *census* of this land is nine *modii* of beer, bread and flesh and honey. But nevertheless, that whenever the clergy of Cadoc wish to eat or drink, namely, in Basseleg or in Pencarnov, the said Judnou shall supply them with food and drink as aforesaid. Of this agreement are witnesses: Paulus, Abbot of Nantcarban, Gwenlioui his brother, Tunic, Canapoi, Tanet, Hierbrith, Merhitr, Concum. Whoever shall keep this, God keep him; and who shall break it shall be cursed by God.

[1] Fol. 38d old ref., 39d new.

The following is a simple one :—

Sciendū ē . q̄d Temit dedit agrū . id est de Ag° Crucin . altari sc̄i Cadoci in ppetuā possessionē cū filiis suis . in tempore Pauli abb̄is de Nant-caruan . q̄d annuati .vj. modios ceruise c̄ panib₃ ꝉ carnib₃ familie sc̄i Cadoci . iugit̄ psolūet.

Testes ŝt . De clicis . Gnouan . Matganoj . Son . Brenic . Elionoe . Pill lector . De laicis u° :ꞌ Cungrat . Guedhoc . Eliunui . Rimogeat . Branoc . Cunhape . Quicq̄ seruauit hāc obtonē :ꞌ conseruet illū Ðs . ꝉ qⁱ abstutit :ꞌ confringet illū Ðs.[1]

Be it known that Temit gave land, *i.e.* of Ager Crucin, to the altar of St. Cadoc in perpetual possession, with his (Temit's) sons, in the time of Paul, Abbot of Nantcarban, so that he should pay annually six *modii* of beer, with bread and flesh, to the family of St. Cadoc for ever.

Witnesses are, of the clergy : Gnouan, Matganoi, Son, Brenic, Elionoe, Pill the reader. Of the laity, Cungrat, Guedhoc, Eliunui, Rimogeat, Branoc, Cunhape. Whoever shall keep this, God keep him ; and who withdraws it, God will break him in pieces.

Similar donation by a father and his sons.

Here again the donor and his sons retain possession on payment of the *census* of six *modii* of beer with bread and flesh.

The rest of these remarkable records are proved by numerous coincidences in the witnesses to be contemporary with those in the 'Book of Llan Dav,' which belong to the time of the Bishop Oudoceus. This bishop succeeded St. Teilo, it is supposed, about A.D. 574, and, according to the 'Book of Llan Dav,' he received donations from three chieftains in succes-

---

[1] Compare this with the following passage in Gregory of Tours, *De Virtutibus S. Martini,* lib. iv., s. 11 : ' Tradidit ei omnem possessionem suam dicens : " Sint

hæc omnia penes Sancti Martini ditionem quæ habere videor et hoc tantum exinde utar, ut de his dum vixero, alar.'

[2] Fol. 39 old ref., 40 new.

sion—viz. Meurig, who is said to have died A.D. 575 ;[1] his son Athrwys, and his grandson Morcant.

The first three donations now to be considered were made whilst Jacob was Abbot of St. Cadoc, and the next two during the abbacy of Sulien. The first two were made during the lifetime of Meurig, and the rest in the time of his grandson Morcant. In the meantime, it was under Meurig's son, Athrwys, that the dispute arose between St. Oudoceus and Biuon, Abbot of St. Illtud, which gave rise to the charter in the 'Book of Llan Dav,' whereby the cells of the disciples of St. Dubricius—Cyngualan, Arthruodu, and Congur—which had been lost in the Yellow Death, were confirmed to the see of Llandaff. The correspondence between the witnesses to this confirmatory charter and those of the following records of donations to the monastery of St. Cadoc, so far as it goes, is confirmatory evidence of the substantial genuineness of both. And the date of the donations is fixed within the limits of the episcopacy of Oudoceus, roughly embracing the closing decades of the sixth century.

Purchase from a chieftain and his family of land, thereupon given to St. Cadoc.

Notū sit omib3 q̄d Guorcinnim emit uillā Reathr a Mourico in p̄iā hereditatē p̄ gladio cui⁹ capulū extitit deauratū p̄ciū . xxv . uaccarū app̄ciatū . Imptit⁹ . c̄ . q̄ Concennio Pauli filio equū in p̄cio . iiijᵒʳ . uaccař . Preciař etiā triū unciař uestim̄ti .

Be it known to all that Guorcinnim bought the villa Reathr from Mouricus for his own inheritance for a sword whose hilt was gilded and valued at the price of twenty-five cows. He bestowed also on Concennius, son of Paulus, a horse of the value of four cows, also of

---

[1] Rees' *Lives of Cambro-British Saints*, supplementary notes, p. 6.

Cōmoro aū q̄ndā equū optimū
Concenni filio . S₃ ꝗ Andreso
Morcanti filio gladiū ī p̄cio .
iiijᵒʳ . uaccaꝝ . Itē idē largitꝰ .
ē . p̄ciū . iiijᵒʳ uaccaꝝ . Iudnertho
Mourici filio unāꝗ bouē Cor-
nouano nutⁱtori suo ꝗ aliā
uaccā ꝑcuratori regis Guengartho . Pᵘ hāc gᵒ emptionē
tenueꝛt Mouric ꝗ Concen
gᵃphiā carte sup manū Guorcum in sēpitna hereditatē sibi
ꝗ eiꝰ ꝑgeniei . Ip̄e uᵒ Guorcum
dedit hac uillā ecclesie sc̄i
Cadoci in ppetuā possessionē .
usꝗ in diē iudicii . tenuitꝗ
cyrogᵃphū donationis sup manū
Iacobi abb̄is Carbani uallis ꝑ
cōmemoꝛone huiꝰ elemosine
corā idoneis testib; . qᵒ₃ nōa
subscⁱbuntʳ . Eudoce ep̄s . ꝗ
Cethig p̄positꝰ altaris sc̄i
Docgwini . Iacob; p̄positꝰ siue
abb̄s altaris sc̄i Cadoci . ꝗ
familia eiꝰ secū . De familia
Eltuti : Testes ꝫt Conmoe
ps̄br . Comnil Magisꝶ . ꝗ
Ioseph ps̄br . Biuone . Catgen .
De laicis uᵒ : Mouricꝰ ꝗ filii
eiꝰ . Andrus . Guedgen . Bramail . Concit filiꝰ Ermit .
Guorbes filiꝰ Berran . Geintoc .
Assail . Arcon . Guallimir .
Iudhol . Matton . Eliudꝰ .
Hilon . Om̄s testes sup hanc
donationis conscⁱptionē . Predicta nāꝗ uilla Reathr . Cōpe-
tebat Mesioco hereditario iure .
cui Guorcinnī . equū p̄stitit ut
huic concessioni adqⁱescet ha-
beutē p̄ciū triū uaccarū . Qui

garments of the worth of three
ounces [of silver ?]. Moreover,
to Commor, the son of Concennius, a certain 'best horse';
also to Andresus, son of Morcant, a sword of the value of
four cows. Item, the same
[donor] granted the price of
four cows to Judnerth, son of
Mouricus, together with an ox
to Cornovanus, his foster-father,
and another cow to Guengarth,
the procurator of the king.
Therefore, on account of this
purchase, Mouric and Concen
held the writing of the charter
upon the hand of Guorcinn for
everlasting inheritance for himself and his offspring. Moreover, Guorcinn himself gave
this villa to the church of St.
Cadoc in everlasting possession
till the day of judgment, and
he held the chirograph of donation upon the hand of Jacob,
the abbot of Carban valley, in
commemoration of this alms,
before fit witnesses whose
names are subscribed. Eudoce,
bishop, and Cethig, prepositus
of the altar of St. Docgwin,
Jacob, prepositus or abbot of
the altar of St. Cadoc, and
his family with him. Of the
family of Illtud are witnesses :
Conmoe priest, Comnil magister,
and Joseph priest, Biuone, Catgen. Of the laity Mouric and his
sons Andrus, Gwedgen, Bramail,
Concit son of Ermit, Gurbes son
of Berran, Geintoc, Assail, Ar-

hoc temerauit ꞏ maledict⁹ erit a Deo.[1]

con, Gwallimir, Judhol, Matton, Eliudus, Hilon, all witnesses of this conscription of donation. For the aforesaid villa of Reathr belonged to Messiocus by right of inheritance, to whom Guorcinn gave a horse worth three cows that he should assent to this grant. Who shall violate this shall be accursed by God.

Gold-hilted sword, &c., used as money.

This record represents Guorcinnim as buying a certain villa from Meuric the king with a gold-hilted sword worth twenty-five cows. A horse worth four cows is also paid to Concenn. Vestments worth three ounces [of silver] are paid to Conmor, and a 'best horse' to the son of Concenn. A sword worth four cows is given to the son of Morcant, and another worth four cows to the son of Meuric, and an ox is given to his foster-father. Lastly, a cow is paid to Guengarth, procurator of the King Meuric. This done, and the consent of all these having been thus obtained, Meuric and Concenn hold the written charter, according to the prevalent form of delivery, on the hand of Guorcinnim, the purchaser, in token of eternal inheritance to him and his descendants. Then the purchaser gives the villa so bought to the church of St. Cadoc, and holds the chirograph of the donation upon the hand of Jacob the abbot in the presence of Bishop Oudoceus and others. But even now all has not yet been done. Another person claims hereditary rights in the land, and Guor-

---

[1] Fol. 39d old ref., 40d new.

cinnim has to give him a horse worth three cows to get quit of his claim. Surely we have in this, as in some other cases, an example of a sale of land belonging to a chieftain's *gwely.*

Ostendendū . ē . futuris p temporū mutacionib; et regū successib; . q̄d Mouric⁵ Rex dedit partē agri ꝑ aīa sua qⁱ uocat͛ Insule Tuican . ac due partes agⁱ q̄ ꝑpⁱᵉ fueṝt Gorbrith ꝉ Gassoc . necñ ꝉ sororis sue pariꝉ Sule . sup q̄ ēb; Mouric⁵ rex gᵃphiā consc͛ptionis tenuit sup manū Iacob abb̄is Cathedre sc̄i Cadoci . ut ip̄e lib̄as ꝉ qⁱetas faꝛet ab om̄i censu ꝉ ab om̄i calūpnia . ꝉ ab om̄ib; ꝉ seruitiis excepto famulitio sc̄i Cadoci . Qua ꝑpꝉ p° hec dedit Iacob equū Mourico regi . at ille largit⁵ . ē . illū Guodgen filio Brocmaili . Huⁱ⁵ rei testes s̄t . Iacob abb̄s . Rumceneu . Catthig . ꝉ p̄res eoꝫ Cōmogoe . Conmil . Guorgeneu . Beuonoe . Catgen . Hearngen . Crasgell . Outegurn . Guitlon . Sulien . Clerici. De laicis Mouric⁵ sup ipsū solū . ꝉ sup filios suos . a gñ̄ratiōe in gñ̄ratiōē . Guetlgen filiᵒ Brocmail . Guallunir . Guorcinnim . Guorbes . Mor-cenev . Morhoen . Hii s̄t testes sup hoc pactū : ut . ñ . soluat͛ in eꝷnū . Deiñ Mouric⁵ rex confirm̄auit hāc donatiōē sup altare sc̄i Cadoci corā senioriḃ; suis . Quicꝗ conseruauit b̄udict⁵

Be it declared to posterity, because of the changes of times and the successions of kings, that King Mouric gave for his soul a part of the land called Insula Tuican and two parts of the land which belonged to Gorbrith and Gassoc as well as their sister Sula, equally, with respect to which King Mouric held the written document upon the hand of Jacob abbot of the chair of St. Cadoc, so that he himself might make them free and quit from all *census,* and all claims, and all services except the service of the family of St. Cadoc. Wherefore in this behalf Jacob gave a horse to King Mouric and he bestowed it upon Guodgen son of Brocmail. Of this thing are witnesses : Jacob abbot, Rumceneu, Catthig, and their fathers Comogoe, Conmil, Guorgeneu, Beuonoe, Catgen, Hearngen, Crasgell, Outegurn, Guitlon, Sulien, clergy. Of the laity : Mouric on behalf of himself alone and his sons, from generation to generation. Guetlgen son of Brocmail, Guallunir, Guorcinnim, Guorbes, Morceneb, Morhoen. These ·

Donation by a chieftain confirmed on the altar before his elders.

erit . ꝯ qᵢ dissoluit maledict⁹
erit a Deo.[1]

are witness over this agreement that it be not loosed for ever. Then King Mouric confirmed this donation upon the altar of St. Cadoc before his own elders. Whoever shall keep this shall be blessed, and whoever dissolves it shall be cursed by God.

This record is very similar to the last, except that the donation, after the usual formalities of delivery, is confirmed upon the altar of St. Cadoc by Meuric the king in the presence of his elders. Nor is it needful to dwell upon the next.

Donation of land with usual food-rent.

Sciendū ē q̄d Terengual dedit agrū Letguoidel Đo ꝯ Cadoco qᵢ annuati psoluet Cadoco ꝯ familie ei⁹ tres modios ceruise ꝯ panes ꝯ carnes ꝯ si forte ceruisa caruerit :′ reddet . iiiiᵒʳ . modios tᵢtici ūl clamidē albū . Hāc elemosinā dedit Terengual Đo ꝯ sc̄o Cadoco liƀam ꝯ qᵢetā ab om̄i regali ꝯ ꞇreno seruitio . ꝑ aīa sua ꝯ ꝑ aīa Morcāt.

Inde testes s̄t Iacob p̄posit⁹ altaris Cadoci ꝯ familia ei⁹ . Conmogoi . Connul . Ioseph . Biuuonoi . Catgen . De famili Eltuti . testes . Marcant . Gualunir . Guedgen . Guengarth.

Finis h⁹ agᵢ . ē . a Pull tenbuib :′ usꝗ Dirprise . Quicꝗ seruauit bn̄dict⁹ sit . ꝯ qᵢ uiolauit maledict⁹ erit a Đo.[2]

Be it known that Terengual gave the land Letguoidel to God and Cadoc, which annually shall pay to Cadoc and his *familia* three *modii* of beer, and bread and flesh, and if by chance beer shall be lacking, it shall give four *modii* of wheat or a white cloak. This alms gave Terengual to God and St. Cadoc free and quit from all regal and earthly service for his soul and the soul of Morcant. Witness thereof are Jacob prepositus of the altar of Cadoc and his *familia*, Conmogoi, Connual, Joseph, Biuuoni, Catgen. Of the *familia* of Illtud are witnesses : Marcant, Guallunir, Guedgen, Guengarth. The boundary of this land is from Pulltenbuib as far as Dirprise. Whoso shall keep this be blessed, and whoso shall violate it shall be cursed by God.

[1] Fol. 40 old ref., 41 new.

[2] Fol. 39d old ref., 40d new.

The following record refers to the fratricide already mentioned of *Merchiun*, and the donation to St. Cadoc of Lann Catgualader, with its *census* of three *modii* of beer, by way of redemption of the crime.

A very similar record of donation is contained in the 'Book of Llan Dav,' but making Berthguin, Bishop of Llandaff, the recipient of the gift.

Notíficandū . ē . posͭis q̄d dedit Guoidnerth Lann Catgualader Ɖo ꝛ scͦ Cadoco qᵃtinᵒ qᵒt annis uas . iii . modiorū ꝯuise illi psolueretʳ cū om̄ibȝ debitis ꝑpͭ frͥicidiū germani sui Merchiun . atqͭ tandem reddit⁹ dedit Docgwinno . Sup hoc testes fuerͭt Berthgwinᵒ epͨ . Conmil . Terchan ꝛ Congregatio ei⁹ . Sulien abͭbs . Nant carban . Lumbiu psͭbr . Biuoni . Iouab . ꝛ Congregatio sͨi Cadoci . Saturn pⁱnces altaris Docgwinni . Marcant . Guoidnerth . Quírͨqͭ seruauͭit : benedict⁹ erit . Et qⁱ temerauͭit : maledict⁹ erit a Deo.[1]

Be it made known to posterity that Guoidnerth gave Lann Catgualader to God and St. Cadoc to the end that each year should be paid to him (Cadoc) a vessel of three *modii* of beer with all dues, on account of the fratricide of his own brother Merchiun, and after that he gave the rents to Dogwin. Concerning this the witnesses were Berthgwin bishop, Conmil, Terchan and his congregation, Sulien abbot of Nantcarban, Lumbiu priest, Biuoni, Saturn chief of the altar of Dogwin, Marcant, Guoidnerth. Whoever shall keep this shall be blessed, and whoever shall violate it shall be cursed by God.

Donation in redemption of fratricide.

The following record is perhaps the most graphic and interesting of all :—

Sciendū . ē . q̄d Morcant Rex uenando uenit usqͭ ad ripā fluminis Nadhauon ꝛ iecit accipitrē sup anatē . ꝛ ambo simul accipiͭt ꝛ anas flum̄ uolatu tᵃnsmeauerͭt . Et subito ueniebat aqⁱla de ripa maris ut rapet

Be it known that Morcant, king, came a-hunting to the bank of the river Nadhauon, and threw his hawk upon a duck, and both at once hawk and duck crossed the river in their flight. And suddenly

Donation by a chief and his *procurator* of a *villa* and its *census*.

accipitrē . Qđ ut uidit Marcant
rex :′ ualde c̄t¹stat⁹ . ē . Ast
concite alūpn⁹ regis ueniens
nōe Guengarth . eques c̄ scuto
꒻ gladio ac lancea se in fluᷝ
ꝓripuit . ꒻ accipitrē a raptu
aq¹le n̄ modico uiritr eripuit :′
uer̄ etiā lepori꒜ accipitrē cū
anate ad manū Morcant Regis
attulit . illūq̊ tali facinore n̄
minimū letificauit . Quo c¹ca
dix̄ Morcant Guengartho . Ecce
t¹buo t¹ uillā Cadroc in ius
hereditariū habentē longitudinē
ab urbe Trotguid :′ usq̊ ad fluᷝ
Nadauan . ꒻ latitudinē a fonte
Guengarth :′ usq̊ ad aliū fontē
Guengarth . Eodē die Morcāt ꒻
Guengarth prexer̄t ad q⁰ddā
꒜ritoriū Cadocj . ꒻ t¹buit Guengarth Đo ꒻ sc̄o Cadoco censū
ꝓsc¹pte uille Cadroc ꝑ aīa sua ꒻
ꝑ aīa Morcanti regis . scit
sinḡlis annis . xii . modios꒜uise
꒻ sextariū mellis . debitū q̊
panē ꒻ carnē . Insup etiā idē
Guengarth dedit Conmogoẏ
Hipiclaur gladiū suū deauratū
ꝑ aīa sua q̄d habuit ꝑciū . lxxᵗᵃ .
uaccar̄ . Quare consuluit Cōmo-
goẏ Guengardo q⁰ gladiū illū
Morcanto ꝑstaret . ut ille donationē Guengardi c̄firmaret sup
pago Catroc:′ q̄d ꒻ fec̄ . Qua de
re Morcant ꝑlibatā donationē
ratā habuit atq̊ sc¹pto corro-
borauit sup manū Sulien illa
illinc fore litā ꒻ q¹etā ab oᷝi
꒜reno seruitio . uerū fundit⁹
obscq¹o Đi ꒻ sc̄i Cadoci obnoxia.

Hui⁹ rei testes s̄t . Morcāt .
sup sc ipsū . ut nullus hui⁹

there came an eagle from the
sea shore to seize the hawk.
Which when King Morcant
saw he was exceeding sorrow-
ful, but in a moment a foster
son of the king, named Guengarth, coming up on horseback
with shield and sword and
lance, hurled himself into the
river, and with no little bravery
snatched the hawk from the
grip of the eagle. And, moreover, lightly brought the hawk
with the duck to the hand of
Morcant the king, and by such
achievement delighted him not
a little. Whereupon Morcant
said to Guengarth : ' Behold, I
grant to thee the villa Cadroc
as an inheritance stretching
from the city Trotguid as far
as the river Nadavan, and in
breadth from the spring Guengarth as far as another spring
Guengarth.' On the same day
Morcant and Guengarth reached
a certain territory of Cadoc,
and Guengarth consigned to
God and St. Cadoc the *census*
of the aforesaid villa Cadroc
for his soul and the soul of
Morcant the king, to wit every
year twelve *modii* of beer and
a sextar of honey, and the
bread and flesh due therewith.
Over and above this the same
Guengarth gave to Conmogoy
for his soul his gilded sword
' Hipiclaur,' which was of the
value of seventy cows. Wherefore, Conmogoy concurred with
Guengarth when he bestowed

ꝑritorii pcurator extat nᶦ Guengarth ꞇ heredes illi⁹ . De Clicis . Sulien . Cōmogoi . Danoc . Guorguethen . Legan . Elgnou . De laicis uᵒ Guingueri . Iacob . Boduan . Elguan . Gurhitr . Cuncuan . Quicꝙ cᵒtodierit ᵫnꝺ erit . ꞇ qⁱ ꝺꝼregit maleꝺ a ꝥo ꞇ a Cadoco . Aᵯ.[1]

that sword on Morcant, that he should confirm the donation of Guengarth with regard to the 'pagus' Catroc, which also he did. Concerning which thing Morcant aforesaid ratified the donation, and corroborated it by a writing upon the hand of Sulien, thenceforth to be free and quit from all earthly service, but completely subject to the service of God and St. Cadoc. Of this thing are the witnesses Morcant on behalf of himself that no one should be procurator of this territory except Guengarth and his heirs. Of the clergy : Sulien, Conmogoi, Danoc, Guorguethen, Legan, Elgnou. Of the laity : Guingueri, Jacob, Boduan, Elguan, Gurhitr, Cuncuan. Whoever shall guard this shall be blessed, and whoever shall break it shall be cursed by God and St. Cadoc.

Morcant, the grandson of Meuric, is hawking with Guengarth, his *procurator*, and, as a reward for saving his hawk, the impulsive king gives him on the spot a villa, apparently, according to the boundaries, adjoining that occupied by Guengarth. Then the two together, on the same day, go to a certain territory of St. Cadoc, and there Guengarth gives to St. Cadoc the *census* of the villa so lately given to him by Morcant for the souls of himself and King Morcant—namely, twelve *modii* of beer and a sextar of honey, and the usual bread and flesh. Thereupon Guengarth gives to Conmogoy, a cleric, his gilded

---

[1] Fol. 39 old ref., 40 new.

A gilded
sword
named
' Hipi-
claur,'
worth
seventy
cows, and
used as
money.

sword named ' Hipiclaur,' worth seventy cows, for his soul. And the reason why Guengarth has to give him the sword turns out to be that the confirmation of Conmogoy is needful to the donation. Lastly, the king Morcant confirms it by a writing placed on the hand of Sulien, the abbot of St. Cadoc, and witnesses that no one shall be *procurator* of that territory except Guengarth and his heirs.[1]

We have now arrived at the last of these records.

Donation
of land at
Caerleon.

Significandū . ē q̄d Retone dimidiā partē ag^i iuxta Ciuitatē Legionis Ɖo atq̨ Sc̄o Cadoco ppetuo iure possidendā q̄ illū ħeditario iure contīgebat . ĩn qz ĩc ad Herbic deuoluta fuerat eandē ab illo emit . ꝶ Ɖo ꝶ sc̄o Cadoco t^lbuit.

Cui^9 rei ỿ s̄t testes . Herbic . Curnet . Congale clerī . De laicis . Guornet . Guedguon . Guedgui . Son^9 . Atderreg . Qui c^9todierit . sit bn̄dict^9 . q^l uiolaủit sit maledict^9 . Am̃.[2]

Be it signified that Retone [gave] the half share of land near Caerleon to God and to St. Cadoc in perpetual right of possession which concerned him by right of inheritance, and after had devolved upon Herbic, bought the same from him and gave it to God and St. Cadoc. Of which thing are witnesses : Herbic, Curnet, Congale, of the clergy. Of the laity : Guornet, Guedguon, Guedgui, Sonus, Atderreg. Who shall keep this shall be blessed, who shall violate it shall be cursed. Amen.

X. AUTHENTICITY OF THE EARLY EVIDENCE.

These
early re-
cords in
keeping
with tribal
rules as to
the family
character
of owner-
ship.

The reader will now be able to judge for himself how far in these remarkable records we seem more or less to breathe the air of the sixth century, into which the lamentations of Gildas introduced us.

On the one hand, comparing the character of the transactions recorded with what has been already

---

[1] See supra, p. 154, n.　　　　[2] Fol. 88d old ref., 89d new.

learned from the Codes and surveys of the tribal
system, surely the habits and actions of the donors of
the donations are in close keeping with the customary
rules of tribal chieftainship.

In the family character of their ownership and
the necessity for the concurrence of relations, both
as regards the redemption of their crimes and the
validity of their grants, there is strong incidental
evidence both of the mutual responsibility for crime
and of the land ownership in *gwelys* under the rules
of *tir gweliawc.*

At the same time, the use of gold-hilted swords,
and vestments, and ' best horses,' instead of money—
nearly all of them equated with cows—belongs to
that earlier stage of tribal life to which the Codes look
back as the period when ' all payments were made in
cattle,' a period of which the reckoning of the gradations in the *galanas* in cows was a survival.

The moral atmosphere of these transactions clearly
belongs to a lower and an earlier stratum of tribal
life than that of the Codes. The impulsive passions
of the chieftains, leading to so many murders of
members of their own family, naturally belong to
the uncurbed, childish stage of human life, which is
prone to superstition, and succumbs so easily to
spiritual terrors. It is in this early stage that pride
and passion so soon are succeeded by temporary
remorse and submission. At no other time than in
the first moment of contact with the Church would
the chieftains of conquering tribes be likely to
succumb so submissively to the purely moral and
spiritual power of the saints and the monks.

Moral at-
mosphere
under
early
tribal
system.

Nor at any other period than this of first contact .

Mutual
influence
of the
Church
and tribal
system.

would conquering chieftains follow tribal instincts
so impulsively as not only to endow with donations
the conquering spiritual power, but also themselves
to rush into its communion, claiming chieftainship
in it by themselves becoming monks and saints, so
giving rise to saintly families of royal or chieftain
blood, as in the case of St. Cadoc himself, St.
Dubricius, and others.

The tribal system to a certain extent absorbed
into itself the spiritual power to which the successors
of Cunedda had to yield.   And how naturally and
inevitably this process of mutual absorption of one
another by the tribal and spiritual powers produced
or promoted in South Wales precisely those scandals,
both in churchmen and chieftains, to which the
lamentations of Gildas so loudly bore contemporary
witness!

Formali-
ties and
forms of
delivery.

Finally recurring to the technical side of these
donations, and comparing the picturesque formalities
used in making them with contemporary Continental
forms, there is close resemblance without servile
imitation.   Perhaps nowhere else do we find exactly
the formality of placing the writing upon the hand
(*super manum*) of the recipient in the presence of
witnesses.   There is an out-of-doors air about this
form which seems to show that the transactions did
not always take place in a church.   Where the
transaction took place in a church, the writings, as
on the Continent, were laid upon the altar, or upon
the copy of the Gospels which lay upon the altar.
These Gospels naturally became, as in the case of
the copy which Gelhi purchased from Cingual, and
placed on the altar of St. Teilo, the recipients of

memoranda of similar donations, but there is no mention in the Cadoc records of this practice having yet commenced.

All this is in keeping with the methods described in the Alamannic and Bavarian laws of the early seventh century.

There is the same correspondence in the process by which an absolute donation is made to the Church to last for all eternity, or 'till the day of judgment,' whilst at the same time continued usufruct of the property is permitted to the donor or his family on payment of the customary food-rent. Where else can be found among British records anything like the habitual use of what quotations from the Alamannic and Bavarian laws and from the Rules of St. Benedict prove to have been common forms in use on the Continent in the sixth and seventh centuries?

The origin of these forms of donation in the development of Roman law has been clearly described at length by the late M. Fustel de Coulanges.[1] There was first the simple donation with a reservation of the usufruct. The Roman law allowed even the devise by the testator of the property to one person without the usufruct, which went in that case to his heir.

But there was also the other method by which, having made a donation, the donor received back the usufruct as a benefice or as a *precaria*. M. de Coulanges pointed out that originally the transaction in such cases was a triple one. First came the absolute *donatio*. Secondly came the *petitio* for continued

---

[1] *Les Origines du Système Féodal*, c. iv. and c. v.

user. Thirdly, the transaction was completed by the *præstatio* on the part of the new owner, by which the donor received permission to continue the occupation as a *precaria*. But ultimately the processes were more or less united in one transaction, and recorded in a single document.

Thus both methods resulted practically in very much the same thing. The St. Gall charters sometimes take one form and sometimes the other. They both were connected with the practice of *commendation* which had grown into importance under the peculiar circumstances described by Salvian—the Gildas of Gaul—and both were probably equally familiar to the ecclesiastics of Brittany and South Wales.

To which of the two classes the Cadoc donations belong it is not perhaps easy to determine.

In the meantime it is enough for this inquiry, if, without claiming that the records were strictly contemporary with the donations, the facts they record may be taken as substantially authentic. We are not dealing with them here as title-deeds to properties, but as evidence of tribal habits and customs at the time of the first contact between the chieftains and the Church. And surely, all things taken

together, it can hardly be considered likely, or even possible, that any monastic scribe of a later century could so far anticipate modern historical methods as to acquire the knowledge and the skill whereby he could put himself so completely into the atmosphere of the sixth century as to be able to forge records such as these of St. Cadoc and Llan Dav without at least a basis of contemporary authority.

XI. VALUE OF THE EARLY EVIDENCE.

If, in conclusion, we may fairly regard these records, whether themselves strictly contemporary or not, as, in the main, describing with substantial correctness sixth-century transactions between tribal chieftains and the abbots of monastic churches, they have a value for the purpose of this inquiry which will justify the amount of attention bestowed upon them.

Without entering into questions reserved for an other volume, there are two points to which special reference may be made.

First as to the food-rents. Passing by, for the present, the remarkable resemblance between the food-rents of the Cadoc records and those of the servile and other holdings described in the Alamannic and Bavarian laws, it will be seen, upon closer examination, that the food-rents of the Cadoc records are arranged upon a system which, in principle, corresponds remarkably with that of the Welsh Codes.

The one case in which the food-rent was described as the *cibaria* for three nights in summer and three nights in winter illustrates the mention in the Dimetian Code of the obligation connected with the payment of the *gwestva* to light the chieftain's fire for three nights.

But apart from this direct allusion to the 'nights' entertainment' there is a system incidentally running through the records which shows that, as in the Codes, the holdings were arranged in multiples of a certain unit of possession or area from which the unit of food-rent was due.

The donations are of larger or smaller areas of

CHAP. VII.

Value of the early evidence.

The food-rents of the Cadoc records.

The provision for three nights.

The connection of the food-rents with the land.

The food-
rents
graduated
in multi-
ples of
three
modii of
beer.

land, varying from the *lann* and half-*ager*, up to the *villa* or *pagus*, and the food-rents rise accordingly. There are two cases each of a half-*ager* and one of a *lann*, and these each pay three *modii* of beer. There are two cases of the full *ager* with a food-rent of six *modii* of beer. There are two cases of *villæ* paying nine *modii* of beer, three cases of *villæ* (one of them also called a *pagus*) and another of an *ager*, paying twelve *modii* of beer, and lastly one *villa* paying eighteen *modii* of beer. The food-rents embraced bread, flesh, and honey in addition; but it is obvious that the size of the donation was measured by its food-rent in multiples of the unit of three *modii* of beer.

There are no data affording ground even for a guess as to which of the multiples of the unit of three *modii* corresponded with the 'three nights' entertainment,' and even if there were such data it would be too much to expect exact correspondence between the food-rents of the Cadoc donations and those of the Codes. It is enough if the correspondence in principle between the food-rents of the Codes, of the entries in the margin of the 'Book of St. Chad,' and of the Cadoc records is close enough to warrant the inference that the system of food-rents with local or temporal differences was substantially the same throughout, and that it formed an essential element in the arrangements of tribal society in Wales from the time of the Cymric invasion or a still earlier period to the final conquest of North Wales.

Corre-
spondence
in princi-
ple with
St. Chad
food-rents
and those
of the
Codes.

The other point referred to as relevant to this part of the inquiry relates to the tenacity with which the tribal instinct of patriarchal and family, rather than individual, possession was maintained throughout.

Perhaps it would be difficult to find a stronger proof of this than the fact that it was applied to what, at first sight, would not seem to lend itself readily to such application. The Cadoc records, as already pointed out, are full of incidental evidence that even a chieftain could not make a donation without the concurrence of other members of his family. Even the chieftainship seems from the first to have been a family privilege and, in a way, shared by brothers or sons as though it were a family possession.

Allusion has already been made to the harmony in this particular between the Codes and the Cadoc records as *pro tanto* evidence in support of the authenticity of the latter. But, conversely, the authenticity of the Cadoc records being granted, their evidence that this trait of the tribal system was in force from the first Cymric conquest of Wales becomes important.

When it is considered that in no fewer than seven of these records the donations are family donations, in the sense that the consent of others of the family of the chieftain making the donation was necessary to its validity, the evidence is very strong in confirmation of that of the Codes as to the family character of the chieftainship.

Again, the stipulation in the last record but one, that, after the donation to the monastery of St. Cadoc by the King Morcant and his foster-son and *procurator* Guengarth of a *villa* or *pagus*, ' no one should be *procurator* of this territory except Guengarth and his heirs,' is incidental evidence how early even tribal offices under the chieftain tended to become hereditary in a family.

This is in complete harmony with the fact revealed by later evidence that even when a chieftain founded a church the same instinct resulted in the benefice being held as a family possession.

The evidence of Giraldus Cambrensis.

Giraldus Cambrensis was not slandering the Church, but giving unwilling testimony to the tenacity of a tribal instinct, when he complained that nearly all the Welsh churches had as many parsons and coparceners as there had been families of chief men (*uchelwrs*) in the parish.[1] He also complained that sons obtained the benefices by succession from their fathers, not by election but by inheritance, and that the institution of any other person would lead to acts of revenge on the part of the kin. He adds that these two abuses were evidently inherently British, inasmuch as they prevailed in Brittany also.

Example in the case of Caergybi.

The existence of portionary or tribal churches in Wales appears also in the 'Taxatio' of St. Nicholas in A.D. 1291, and as an actual instance of the application of tribal rules to ecclesiastical patronage it is only necessary to refer to the case of Caergybi in Anglesey, to which Mr. A. Neobard Palmer called attention, and the facts of which he was able to trace with remarkable success in the Record of Carnarvon.[2]

In this case two chieftains seem in the twelfth century to have joined in restoring the ruined church

---

[1] 'Ecclesiæ vero istorum omnes fere tot personas et participes habent, quot capitalium virorum in parochia genera fuerint.'— *Desc. Camb.* lib. ii. c. vi.

[2] *Portionary Churches of Mediæval North Wales*, annexed to Mr. Palmer's 'History of the Parish Church of Wrexham.'

or monastery of Caergybi, and in the record of Carnarvon and another document of the fourteenth century the *weles* sprung from these two chieftains are still found to possess fractional rights of patronage to the canonries—rights which had descended to them according to the rules of *tir gweliawc.*

CHAP.
VII.

The rights
of patron-
age be-
came
subject to
the rules
of the
*tir
gweliawc.*

This is a late illustration of the extent to which the tribal system in Wales, as in Ireland, forced even ecclesiastical arrangements into its mould. And it adds interest to the earlier evidence of the same tendency already visible in the Cadoc records. In spite of the Continental form of the records on the ecclesiastical side, the recorded transactions themselves are distinctly those of tribal chieftains acting under tribal custom already formed and in force.

It was not without great hesitation that the substantial authenticity of these records was admitted, but, once admitted, the importance of their evidence made it necessary to give to them due place in this volume.[1]

---

[1] I am indebted to Mr. M. R. James, of King's College, Cambridge, for the suggestion that the Cadoc records may have been copied out of a Gospel book of Cadoc's Church, such a one being mentioned as 'yet remaining in the Church of St. Cadoc covered with gold and silver,' and as used by the Welsh for taking oaths upon, in *Caradoc of Lancarvon's Life of Gildas* (Usher's Works, v. 585).

CHAPTER VIII.

CONCLUSION.

THROUGHOUT this volume attention has been purposely confined almost exclusively to the strictly Welsh evidence.

Further light may undoubtedly be thrown upon the Cymric tribal system by extension of the inquiry to other tribal systems, and by a careful use of the comparative method. But in this volume the object has been to obtain a solid and independent foundation to be used as a stepping-stone to further research. And it seemed best to do this by the examination of the Cymric tribal system on its own evidence.

The reader will be able to judge how far this object has been substantially attained.

If, on the one hand, the facts recorded in the Denbigh and other Extents by the surveyors have been found to be the natural results of the long-continued use of the rules of customary tribal law collected and recorded in the Codes and other legal treatises, and if, on the other hand, the authenticity of their description of tribal custom has been in some main points corroborated by the records of sixth-century donations to the monasteries, then it may fairly be said that the picture of tribal society derived from the Codes has received confirmation from two opposite poles.

In both cases, too, the evidence comes from outside of the tribal system itself, and from disinterested, legally trained, and independent witnesses.

On the one hand, Norman surveyors, coming upon the tribal system full of manorial theories and used to manorial phraseology, found themselves compelled against their own instincts to describe large districts as still occupied by *weles* of tribesmen embracing descendants down to great-grandchildren and paying from time immemorial their *quota* of commuted food-rents. And again Norman lawyers, putting into their own legal language the donations of half-Anglicised tribal chieftains, found it needful to make the kinsmen and families of the chieftains join in the grants. Norman evidence on these points was reluctant and convincing.

In the same way, on the other hand, Gallic ecclesiastics of the sixth century or later, accustomed to Roman law and to the use of Merovingian formulæ, found themselves under a similar necessity. Their incidental description of the habits of tribal chieftains, the family character of their tribal donations of land, and the prevalence of food-rents in the sixth as in the thirteenth century, when admitted as substantially authentic, was as impartial and convincing in its way as that of the later Norman surveyors.

Thus supported by extrinsic evidence from two quarters, before and after an interval of six centuries, the description of the tribal system in Wales contained in the Codes and legal treatises can no longer:

it is submitted, be regarded with the same suspicion as may have been heretofore justified.

The existence of a body of tribal custom extending over so many centuries being now proved on independent and outside evidence, the character of the documents themselves becomes more easily understood. It becomes natural that at various times and in various localities collections of tribal rules and customs should be made, such as those which have come down to us of more or less merit and authority. The fact that some of them are modern, and yet contain ancient traditions of tribal rules in the form of Triads on the one hand and adaptations of modern forms of pleadings to Welsh customs on the other hand, no longer need raise suspicion of invention and literary dishonesty. For the tribal system was not a system coined by one brain and enacted by one lawgiver at a particular date. Its customary rules had grown up with the Cymric tribe in Northern Cumbrian lands as well as in the old Cymric district of Powys. Subject more or less to modification and growth, the structure of tribal society in its main features had existed in Wales from the first coming of Cunedda and his sons to the conquest of Edward I. It had lingered on, suffering, no doubt, partial disintegration, till the substitution of English for Welsh law under Henry VIII.

The Venedotian, Dimetian, and Gwentian Codes, traditionally dating back to the time of the first attempt to commit tribal customs to writing under Howell the Good, contain undisguised additions of later date. These additions imply the previous existence of the main body of custom, and in no way suggest its modern origin. The more private and recent treatises, written after the conquest, add greatly to our knowledge of ancient custom, without professing to add anything to its authority.

The conquest itself, and the necessary inquiries of Norman lawyers into the mysteries of tribal law, may well have been the direct cause of the making of some of these collections; and the fact that Welsh law was not abolished till the statute of Henry VIII., and not forgotten till the Crown lawyers of Queen Elizabeth brought the various classes of tenants—free tribesmen and non-tribesmen—under some category of English law, explains the possibility of even very late versions of old tribal custom. But the later the version and the farther it was removed from the time when ancient tribal custom existed in its full force, the more difficult would it be for its author to invent a body of custom from which it would be possible to arrive at the principles and details of the structure of a tribal society such as that examined in the foregoing pages.

The strongest possible proof that such a tribal society as is described in the Codes and treatises once existed in Wales must after all be found in the fact that, so far from its being isolated in its character, it is so full of analogies, and bears in its structure marks of such close relationship to other tribal systems, that it is quite impossible to believe it could have been the result of later invention or imposture. This intrinsic evidence, after all, is the strongest proof of its substantial authenticity.

On the whole, therefore, recurring to the object of this volume and its place in the wider economic inquiry of which it forms only a part, it is with some confidence that the tribal system in Wales is placed before economic students as worthy of careful study.

No attempt has been made to forestall the results of further critical examination of Celtic manuscripts by competent Celtic scholars, or to exhaust the rich materials for Welsh history which lie all but unused in the Public Record Office.

The real knowledge of one tribal system the best stepping-stone to a knowledge of others.

New material will be discovered, and that imperfectly made use of in this volume will require repeated reconsideration. Some of the inferences drawn from it will, no doubt, need correction. But in so far as the attempt has been approximately successful to place the knowledge of the main features of one single tribal system upon a solid foundation of evidence, a step at least will have been gained towards a knowledge of other tribal systems and of their place in economic history.

The further pursuance of the inquiry, with reference chiefly to the methods of tribal societies, must be left to another volume.

APPENDICES.

CONTENTS OF THE APPENDICES.

APPENDIX A.

DOCUMENTS RELATING TO ABERFFRAW.

APPENDIX B.

EXTRACTS FROM EXTENT OF THE CASTLE AND HONOR OF DENBIGH, 8 EDW. III., A.D. 1335.

R   1

Contents of the Appendices.

APPENDIX C.

APPENDIX D.

APPENDIX E.

APPENDICES.

APPENDIX A a.

EXTENT OF ANGLESEY, 22 EDW. I., 13 MARCH, A.D. 1294.

Rentals and Surveys Roll 768, *Public Record Office.*[1]

ANGLESEYA.

Extenta facta de villa de Lammas die Lune in c^a^stino sc̃i Gregor̃ Anno Regni Regis Edwardi vicesimo sc̃do. APP. A a. — A.D. 1294.

De Redđ Burgagioꝝ viłł de Lammas ꝑ annū—viij. lĩ .viij. s̃ .v. đ . õ q^a^.

s̃s Sm^a^—viij. lĩ .viij. s̃ .v. đ . ob̃ q^a^.

De xiij carucat̃ terr̃ que sunt in đnico Maner̃ de Lammas videłt de q^a^libꝫ carucat̃ xxx. s̃.

s̃s Sm^a^—xx. lĩ .x. s̃.

De quodam p^a^to ibiđ ꝑ annū .xxx. s̃.

De gardiñ Mañii ꝑ annū—vj. s̃ .viij. đ.

De q^o^dam molenđ aq^a^tico .C. s̃. Et aliud Molenđ in eođ Mañio obrutū de quo nicħ.

s̃s Sm^a^—vj. lĩ .xvj. s̃ . viij. đ.

De passag̃ eiusđm ꝑ annū—xij. lĩ. De quolꝫ doleo vini ⁊ ꝯuis venientis ad portum ⁊ cariag̃ de portu usq₃ ad villam sumptibꝫ Reg̃ .x. đ. De custum̃ Mesyaꝝ allec̃ vendit̃ vidꝫ ꝑ .v. Meys̃ .j. đ . que valet .x. s̃. De quolibꝫ batello Exitꝰ portꝰ

[1] The 'copy' herein referred to is Rentals and Surveys Roll 769, P.R.O.

APP. A a. — A.D. 1294.

piscant̃ allec̃ exeunte ṽl ingrediente portum .j. Meis̃ Regi p̧ .ij. s̃ . que custumma val; p̧ annū xvij. s̄. De custūma cui⁹libet nauis applicant̃ ad portū . iiij. đ . que valet .xxvj. s̃ .viij. đ. Đ custuma batellož quož quilib; semel in annū cariare deƀ victual đni Reg̃ .xvj. s̄. Đ .v. passagiariis port⁹ que deƀnt sumptib; p̧p^lis in batello Reg̃ fac̃e passagiū p̧ una caruc̃ ⁊ duab; bouat̃ terr̃ quas tenēt .xv. s̃ .viij. đ. Đ Theoloneo Carrož carianciū corea lanas ⁊ alias M'candis̃ nūdinar̃ pan̄ ɔuis̃ Medon̄ carnificū pistož sutož p̧ annū .viij. lī .viij. s̄. Đ furno Reg̃ .xl. s̄. Đ quol; bracineo ɔuis̄ .xxx. lag̃ p̧ .vij. đ . oƀ . de quo .lx. s̃. Đ opac̃ ville de Lammas . vid; . Metenđ cariand ⁊ ƀciand .xxvj. s̃ .viij. đ. De am̃c̃ Cur̃ releuiis ⁊ aliis p̧quis̃ .xij. lī .x. s̃.

s̃s Sm^a—xliij. lī .x. s̃ .x. đ.

s̃s Sm^a to^l. vill de Lammas—Lxxviij. lī .v. s̃ .xj. đ . oƀ q^a.

Commot⁹ de Dyndaythow.

De Redđ ass̃ . vill de Thlandeuenay .Lvj. s̃ ij. đ.

Iт̃m de potur̃ .xxiiij. s̃.

s̃s Sm^a—iiij. lī .ij. đ.

De Redđ ass̃ vill de Batha̋neneytha .Lxvij. s̃ .vj. đ.

Đ potur̃ ei⁹sđ .xxx. s̃.

s̃s Sm^a .iiij. lī .xvij. s̃ .vj. đ.

De redđ ass̃ vill de Bathaȗwyon cū potura .Lxxviij. s̃ .viij. đ.

s̃s Sm^a—Lxxviij. s̃ .viij. đ.

De redđ ass̃ vill de Pentreyth .Lxxiiij. s̃ .iiij. đ . ō.

Đ potur̃ ei⁹đ ville .xxx. s̃.

s̃s Sm^a .Ciiij. s̃ .iiij. đ . oƀ.

De redđ ass̃ vill de Castilheuthlaur .viij. s̃ .x. đ . ō.

Đ potur̃ ei⁹đ .iiij. s̃.

s̃s Sm^a .xij. s̄ .x. đ . oƀ.

De redđ ass̄ vill de Dynthylow ⁊ de ɔuic̃ hoīm ei⁹đ .xxij. s̃ .iiij. đ.

Đ pot^ra ei⁹đ—.xlvj. s̃ .iiij. đ.

ẜs   Smͣ—Lxviij. ẜ .viij. đ.

De redđ asẜ de Bodeueneu .xxvj. ẜ .viij. đ.

Ð Ðnico ei⁹đm .vj. ẜ.

Ð potuꝛ ei⁹đ .xlvj. ẜ .iiij. đ.

De consuetudine ⁊ ẛuic̄ hoīm ei⁹đm .xiij. ẜ .x. đ.

ẜs   Smͣ .iiij. lī .xij. ẜ .x. đ.

Ð redđ asẜ vilt de Chstelbulhen .xviij. ẜ .iij. đ.

ẜs Smͣ .xviij. ẜ .iij. đ.

Ð redđ asẜ vilt de Perkyr .v. ẜ.

Ð potuꝛ ei⁹đ .iij. ẜ.

ẜs   Smͣ—viij. ẜ.

Ð redđ asẜ vilt de Portaythowe Cons̄ ⁊ ẛuic̄ .x. ẜ.

Ð passaḡ ei⁹đ .Liij. ẜ .iiij. đ.

ẜs   Smͣ .Lxiij. ẜ .iiij. đ.

Ð redđ asẜ cons̄ ⁊ ẛuic̄ ville de Garytegwain vj. ẜ .j. đ.

ẜs   Smͣ—vj. ẜ .j. đ.

Ð redđ asẜ ville de Trefforbolch .iij. ẜ .iiij. đ.

ẜs   Smͣ—iij. ẜ .iiij. đ.

Ð redđ asẜ ville de Cremelynhelyn .iij. ẜ .iiij. đ.

De potuꝛ ei⁹d—xiij. ẜ .ix. đ.

ẜs   Smͣ—xvij. ẜ .j. đ.

Ð aduocaꝛ toci⁹ cōmoti p̄đc̄i .xvij. ẜ .ij. đ.

ẜs   Smͣ—xvij. ẜ .ij. đ.

ẜs   Smͣ . tot . hui⁹ Cōmoꝛ—xxxiij. lī .viij. ẜ .iiij. đ.   pᵬ.

Extenta Manͥii de Abberfray.

Primo . dicunt q̃d in Manͥio de Abberfrau sunt .v. carucaꝛ ꞇre ⁊ vat carucaꝛ p annū .xxx. ẜ.

ẜs   Smͣ—vij. lī .x. ẜ.

Item sunt ibi .iij. Molenđ . que Reddit [1] p annū lx crannoc̄
blađ ⁊ vat cᵃnnoc .ij. ẜ.

ẜs   Smͣ—vj. lī.

Iꞇm de duobꝫ pᵃꞇ q̃ vat p annū .xiij. ẜ .iiij. đ.

---

[1] So in the Record.

ẜ   5

APP. A a.

A.D.
1294.

Redđ
liƀoʒ teñ
ei⁹đ
Maŀŀii.

Iꝉ de qᵃđ piscaꝛ q̃ vaꝉ p annū .ij. ꝥ.

ꝥꜱ Smᵃ .xv. ꝥ .iiij. đ.

De redđ liƀoʒ teñ ei⁹đ ville .xxix. ꝥ .viij. đ.

Iꝉ de Hameletto de Bodeueurykę de redđ asꝥ .xv. ꝥ .xj. đ.

Iꞇm de Hameletto de Trefwaspatrykę de redđ asꝥ liƀe teñ .x. ꝥ.

Ð villañ ei⁹đ ville de Tunkę .v. ꝥ .vj. đ.

Ð eisđm villañ in farina butiꝛ ꝉ lacte ꝉ opaꝋ .xiij. ꝥ .vij. đ . oƀ.

Ð Hameleto de Trefberewet de redđ .ix. villañ .ix. ꝥ .viij. đ.

Ð iiijᵒʳ cᵃnoꞇ faꝛ ordei .v. ꝥ .iiij. đ.

Ð .ix. Multoñ .iiij. ꝥ .vj. đ.

Ð ix agnis xviij. đ . de eisđm villañ de butiro .ij. ꝥ .iij. đ.

Ð . C .iiij. oū .vij. đ.

Ð . ix. galliñ ix. đ.

Ð dĕis ix hŏibʒ xxxvj. ꝥ .ij. đ . ŏ p opaꝋ . Clxj. diei.

ꝥꜱ Smᵃ—vj. lī .xv. ꝥ .vj. đ.

Ð Hameleto de Dyncloydan de redđ uni⁹ villañ .ij. ꝥ. vidʒ de Ðd Hiƀnico ꝟl medieꝋ blađ ꝉ lacꝋ q̃d vocatʳ Mꝉionuth. -

Ð filiis Grigori ab Lewelyn de una cᵃnnoꞇ fꝛi ꝉ iiijᵒʳ Cᵃnnoꞇ aueñ viij. ꝥ .vj. đ.

Ð eisđm de duobʒ Multoñ xij. đ.

De duobʒ agnis iiij. đ.

Ð eisđm de butiꝛ vj đ.

Ð eisđ de .xl. ouis j. đ . ŏ.

Ð eisđm de vj galliñ vj. đ.

Ð eisđ de oꝓ xxx. dieʒ .iij. ꝥ .ix. đ.

Ð Pellipaꝛ de dimiđ cᵃnnoꞇ faꝛ ordei de Međ uni⁹ Multoñ de Međ uni⁹ agni . Ð .x. cunis de butiꝛ de Međ uni⁹ galline xiij. đ . ŏ . Ð opaꞇ ei⁹đ vij. dieʒ .xj. đ . qᵃ.

Smᵃ—xviij. ꝥ .ix. đ . qᵃ.

De Hameleto de Weuentefrau de redđ villanoʒ ei⁹đ .iij. ꝥ .iiij. đ.

Ð eisđ de uno angno ꝉ dimiđ Angū de butiꝛ de xxx cunis
de .v. galliñ ꝉ dimiđ ꝉ de uno istor bladi de opac t¹um dieƺ
.xviij. đ . õ . ꝉ Responđ de Mꝛ)yonnyth cū villañ de Trefberewet.

Ð villañ de Aberfraw de redđ asꝫ dc̃oƺ villanoƺ .viij. ꝫ
.viij. đ.

Ð eisđ de .x. c·nnoc̃ ꝉ dimiđ fr̄i.

Ð .vij. c·nc̃ far̄ aueñ.

Ð .iiij·ᵒʳ. c·nnoc̃ far̄ ordei .xlviij. ꝫ .vij. đ.

Ð .ix. villañ ei°đ ville de lacꝉ t¹um vaccaƺ . de iiij·ᵒʳ Multoñ
dimiđ.

Ð .ix. angnis . de butir̄.

Ð .CL. oū.

De xxvij galliñ—xvj. ꝫ .iij. đ.

Ð .vj. tenem̃ vastis . de t¹bꝫ Multoñ . Ð .vj. angnis . de
.ix. galliñ de butiro.

De C. oū .v. ꝫ .j. đ.

Iꞇm sunt in dc̃a villa .ix. villani de q¹bꝫ xxvij galliñ .ij. ꝫ
.iij. đ.

Ð quolꝫ eoƺ opac̃ t¹um dieƺ ad sercland blađ ꝉ vaꞇ opac̃o
eoƺ .ij. ꝫ .iij. đ . q̖ quilibꝫ eoƺ recipit unū panem p̱ diem.

Ð eisđ villañ ꝑ igne ꝉ st·mine in Cur̄ đni Reg̃ .xxx. ꝫ.

Iꞇm de opac̃ in Autūpno de CCC hoïbꝫ quos .xv. villani
de Mañˣˣio inuenient . ꝉ de iiij hõibꝫ quos villani forinsec̃ de
Cantređ inueniet̃ .Lxvj. ꝫ .ix. đ.

Iꞇm de . DC . hoïbꝫ ꝉ equis ad ħiciand p̱ unū diē Lxxv. ꝫ .
p̱ diem j. đ . õ.

Iꞇm de ꝑquiꞅ Cur̄ . de Aberfraw .xl. ꝫ.

Ð pastur̄ .xx. ꝫ

Itm de dc̃is villañ de Aberfraw .x. c·nnoc̃ aueñ ad ꝑ̃bend
.vj. ꝫ .viij. đ.

ꝫꞅ Smᵃ .xvj. lĩ .vj. ꝫ .iiij. đ . oᵬ.

ꝫꞅ Smᵃ toᷠ—xxxviij. lĩ .v. ꝫ .xj. đ . õ . qᵃ.

Extenta de Cantređ de Aberfrau.

Aᴘᴘ. Λ a.

A.D.
1294.

Ð redđ asš de Tounsokę ꝗ aliis Hameleẗ de ꝑgēie Hɔna .viij. lī .v. š.

Iẗm de eisđ vilẗ .xl. cᵃnnoc̄ farīe aueñ ꝑ̃ .iiij. lī.

Iẗm .x. cᵃnnoc̄ frī p̄c̄ .xx. š.

šʙ   Smᵃ .xiij. lī .v. š.

Ð vilẗ de Trefoweyn de redđ . liƀe tenenc̄ .xxxiij. š .xj. đ . õ.

šs   Smᵃ—xxxiij. š .xj. đ . õ.

Ð vilẗ de Kelemokę de redđ asš liƀe teñ .xvj. š . de villa de Bodelowe . de redđ asꝫ liƀe teñ .ıj. š .vj. đ.

Ð vilẗ de Thwayn de redđ asꝫ liƀe tenenẗ .xxxvij. š.

Iẗm de eađ vilẗ de teñ Map̄ Ađ Goch xl š.

šs   Smᵃ—iiij. lī .xv. š .vj. đ.

Ð vilẗ de Drianuylch ꝗ Trefichod de redđ asꝫ liƀoꝫ hõum .Liiij. š .ix. đ.

šs   Smᵃ .Liiij. š .ix. d.

Ð . vilẗ de Bodarchewrau de redđ asꝫ liƀe teñ .v. š.

Iẗm de iij cᵃnnoc̄ ꝗ dī faꝛ aueñ .vij. š.

šs   Smᵃ .xij. š.

Ð vilẗ de Crucanel de redđ asꝫ liƀe teñ .vij. š .xj. đ.   Iẗ de .iij. cᵃnnoc̄ faꝛ .vj. š.

šs   Smᵃ .xiij. š .xj. đ.

Ð vilẗ de [1] Griffry de redđ asꝫ liƀe teñ .x. š.

Iẗ de vilẗ de Bochornach de redđ asꝫ liƀe teñ .xxiij. s .v. đ . õ.

Ð vilẗ filioꝫ Meurikę de redđ villanoꝫ .xix. š .iiij. đ . õ ꝗ Iacent in vasto .iij. bouaẗ terꝛ.

Iẗ de frīo uniᵒ cᵃnnoc̄ dimiđ ꝗ j. buselẗ p̄c̄ iiij. š .iiij. đ . õ.

Iẗ iiijᵒʳ. cᵃnnoc̄ faꝛ aueñ p̄c̄ viij. š.

Iẗm de potuꝛ .Dxx. hoïm ꝑ unū diē .xliij. š .iiij. đ . vidꝫ ꝑ hoïe ꝑ unū diē .j. đ.

Itm de iiij equis q̃ valent .x. s̃ . vid; p equo .j. d̃ . ō.

Itm de quol; villañ unus porcᵘ . si ħuerint porc̃ . p̃c̃ xx. d̃.

De qᵃlib; domo una gallina de p̃c̃ .j. d̃ ⁊ val; .ix. d̃.

s̃s Smᵃ .vj. lĩ .xj. d̃ . ō.

Đ vilł de Bodenaylwẏn de redđ villanoₓ .v. s̃.

It̃ de fr̃o .ij. cᵃnnoc̃ . p̃c̃ .v. s̃.

It̃ . iiij.ᵒʳ cᵃnnoc̃ far̃ aueñ ⁊ iij. buss p̃c̃ .ix. s̃ .vj. d̃.

Itm in potur̃ .CCClx. hoĩm p unū diē xxx. s̃.

It̃ de potur̃ .Cxx. eqⁱs .xv. s̃.

It̃ de qᵒl; villano j. porc̃ de p̃c̃ .xx. d̃.

It̃ de qᵒl; villañ [j galliñ ⁊] sunt viij vilł ⁊ vał . viij d̃.

s̃s Smᵃ .Lxvj. s̃ .x. d̃.

Đ vilł de Trefolyn de redđ as̃s̃ . cons̃ ⁊ aliis s̃uic̃ .x. s̃ .x. d̃.

s̃s Smᵃ .x. s̃ .x. d̃.

Đ vilł de [Thledwygant]hles de redđ as̃s̃ liƀoₓ hoĩm .xxiiij. s̃ .ix. d̃.

Đ .j. cᵃnnoc̃ far̃ aũe ij. s̃.

s̃s Smᵃ .xxvj. s̃ .ix. d̃.

Đ vilł de [Bodbetwyn] de[redđ as̃s̃] liƀoₓ hoĩm .xxj. s̃ .iij. d̃.

Smᵃ .xxj s̃ .iij d̃.

Đ vilł de [Trefdrefvastrondeon] de redđ as̃s̃ liƀe teñ Lxiij. s̃.

It̃ de iiijᵒʳ. cᵃnnoc̃ far̃ . aũe . dimiđ ⁊ .ij. ptib; .j. buss̃ ix. s̃ .iij. d̃.

It̃ de d[uob; lageñ butir̃] x. d̃.

s̃s Smᵃ .Lxxiij. s̃ .ij. d̃.

Đ vilł de Trefdrefdysteyn de redđ as̃s̃ iiij lƀ xvj. s̃ .x. d̃.

ō qᵃ . de una cᵃnnoc̃ fr̃i . Đ una cᵃnnoc̃ aueñ ⁊ dimiđ ⁊ de xij [ferr̃] equoₓ vj s̃ vj. d̃.

s̃s Smᵃ .C .iij. s̃ .iiij. d̃ . ō . qᵃ.

Đ vilł de Badaon ¹ de redđ as̃s̃ .xxij. s̃ .iiij. d̃.

---

¹ Bodaon in the copy.

Ŝs   Smᵃ . xxij ꝩ . iiij đ.

Đ vilł de Dorodeweyt de redđ asꝩ . viij ꝩ viij đ.

Ŝs   Smᵃ . viij ꝩ viij đ.

Đ vilł de Trefwalkemay de redđ asꝩ .xviij. ꝩ .ij. đ . de duobꝫ cᵃnnoĉ faꝛ aũe ꝉ ij . ꝑtibꝫ uni⁹ cᵃnnoĉ v. ꝩ .iiij. đ.

ꝩs   Smᵃ . xxiij ꝩ vj. đ.

Đ vilł de [Trygor] de redđ asꝩ .xij. ꝩ .iiij. đ.

ꝩs   Smᵃ .xij. ꝩ .iiij. đ.

Đ vilł de [Dryndrovelł] de redđ asꝩ [xxxviij ꝩ . iiij đ oƀ].

[Đ iiij] cᵃnnoĉ fꝛi .x. ꝩ.

Đ [vij] cᵃnnoĉ faꝛ aueñ xiiij ꝩ.

Đ iij vaꝩ [but]uꝛ . [xij ꝩ de eađm vilł cum duobꝫ villanis de Trefdraes de potuꝛ].

De potuꝛ .Lxxij. eꝗ [ix ꝩ . De] potuꝛ CCxl. hoĩm ꝉ caniũ xx. ꝩ.

[ꝩs   Smᵃ] .Ciij. ꝩ .iiij. đ . ổ.

Đ vilł de Rosm[awr de Redđ asꝩ .xx. ꝩ].

Đ potuꝛ [l]j eꝗ .xviij. ꝩ .x. đ . ổ.

Đ potuꝛ [de .D. hoĩm] ꝑ unũ diē .L. ꝩ.

Ŝs   Smᵃ iiij lĩ viij ꝩ x đ ổ.

Đ vilł de [Keuentrefraw] de redđ asꝩ iij ꝩ iiij đ . de
potuꝛ . iiij equoꝫ ˣˣ x ꝩ . de potuꝛ . CCxl hoĩm ꝉ caniũ xx. ꝩ.

ꝩs   Smᵃ .xxxiij. ꝩ .iiij. đ.

Đ oīibꝫ villañ de dĉa Cantreda de vj cᵃnnoĉ fꝛi . xv ꝩ.

Đ .xix. cᵃnnoĉ faꝛ aueñ xxxviij. ꝩ.

Đ viij cᵃnnoĉ aueñ ad pƀ .v. ꝩ .iiij. đ.

De xxvij galliñ .ij. ꝩ .ij. đ.

Đ quolꝫ unũ porcũ si ħuerint de p̃cio .xx. đ.

Iꞇ qˡlꝫ eoꝫ debet arrare ꝩemel in annũ ꝗ valꝫ . xxiiij ꝩ viij đ.

Ŝs   Smᵃ .iiij. lĩ .vj. ꝩ .xj. đ.

Đ placiꞇ ꝉ ꝑquiꝩ Cantrede de Aberfraw .xl. ꝩ.

Ŝs   Smᵃ .xl. ꝩ.

ꝝs   Smᵃ toᵗ Cantrede de Aberfrau—Lxv. lĩ .xvìj. ꝫ .vij. đ .
ŏ . q̃.

Extenta Manꝺii de Kemmeys.

Primo dicūt q̃d sūt in Manꝺio de Kemmeys .iiijᵒʳ. carucaꞇ
terr̃ p̃c caruc̃ .xxx. ꝫ . p annū.
ꝝs   Smᵃ vj. lĩ.
Ð iiijᵒʳ . pᵃtis . ibiđ que valent p annū xx. ꝫ.
De gardino ibiđ .xl. đ.

xx
Ð tⁱbꝫ . Molenđ . iiij crannoc̃ farine aueñ viij. lĩ p̃c crannoc̃
ij. ꝫ.
De piscar̃ ibiđ .iij. ꝫ . iiij đ.
ꝝs   Smᵃ .ix. lĩ .vj. ꝫ .viij. đ.
Ð redđ asꝫ liƀe teñ ville de Kemmeys .Cvj. ꝫ .xj. đ.
ꝝs   Smᵃ .Cvj. ꝫ .xj. đ.
Ð villañ . eiᵒđ ville de aliis consꝫ . ꞇ ꝫuic̃ . p annū .xiij. lĩ.
.xiiij ꝫ.
ꝝs   Smᵃ xiij lĩ xiiij ꝫ.
Ð placïꞇ ꞇ pquiꝫ Cur̃ .xl ꝫ.
ꝝs   Smᵃ xl. ꝫ.
ꝝs   Smᵃ toᵗ Manꝺii de Kemmeys .xxxvj. lĩ .vij. ꝫ .vij. đ. p̃ᵇ.

Extenta Cōmoꞇ de. Talboleon.

Ð redđ asꝫ vilꞇ de Trefnedeuent de liƀo teñ xxxvij. ꝫ .ij. đ
ꝝs   Smᵃ xxxxij. ꝫ .ij. đ.
Ð vilꞇ de Thlanvugel Thledwyghan ¹ de redđ asꝫ .xj. ꝫ.
ꝝs   Smᵃ .xj. ꝫ.
Ð vilꞇ de Threfchlawrcħ . de redđ asꝫ liƀoꝛ teñ . eiᵒđ ville
xlviij. ꝫ.
ꝝs   Smᵃ .xlviij. ꝫ.
Ð vilꞇ de Codanewe de redđ asꝫ vij. ꝫ vij. đ . ŏ.
ꝝs   Smᵃ .vij. ꝫ vij. đ . ŏ.

---

¹ Thledwygan only in the copy.

11

Ð vilt de Bodaokɩ de reddꝭ ass̃ .xj. s̃.

s̃s Smᵃ .xj. s̃.

Ð vilt de Carnethour̃ de villanis eiꝰdꝭ de Tunkɩ xiiij s̃ iiij dꝭ.

De eisdm villañ ꝑ potur̃ ⁊ cons̃ Lxij s̃ v. dꝭ.

De terra Yarward fit Maddocy viij s̃ iij. dꝭ.

Ð terris vastis eiꝰdꝭ ville xj. s̃.

s̃s Smᵃ .iiij. lĩ .xvj. s̃.

Ð reddꝭ ass̃ . ville de Trefwadokɩ .xlix. s̃ .viij. dꝭ.

s̃s Smᵃ .xlix. s̃ .viij. dꝭ.

Ð reddꝭ ass̃ liboꝫ vilt de Kemelyn .xix. s̃ .xj. dꝭ.

De villañ eiꝰdꝭ ville ꝑ potur̃ ⁊ aliis ꝰuic̃ .xxxiij. s̃. viij. dꝭ.

s̃s Smᵃ .Liij. s̃ .vij dꝭ.

Ð vilt de Kardekande de reddꝭ ass̃ liboꝫ hoĩm Lxxvj. s̃.

s̃s Smᵃ .Lxxvj. s̃.

Ð vilt de Thlegarn de reddꝭ ass̃ liboꝫ hoĩm Lix s̃ .v. dꝭ.

s̃s Smᵃ .Lix. s̃ .v. dꝭ.

Ð vilt de Bronewey ⁊ Conternowe de reddꝭ ass̃ . liboꝫ hoĩm .xxix. s̃ .xj. dꝭ.

s̃s Smᵃ xxix s̃ xj. dꝭ.

Ð villa de Aberhalowe de reddꝭ ass̃ liboꝫ hoĩm v. s̃.

De villanis eiꝰdꝭ ville de Tungɩ .xvij. s̃ vj. dꝭ.

de eisdm villanis ꝑ potur̃ ⁊ aliis ꝰuic̃ .xxiij. s̃ .v. dꝭ.

de t̃ra Adꝭ Ruffy dĩ m̃.

Ð t̃ra Map Porth vj. s̃.

de t̃ra Hona fit Keñ .v s̃.

de t̃ra ꝰui garcilis ij. s̃ .v. dꝭ.

s̃s Smᵃ .Lxvj. s̃.

Ð vilt de Bodewygan de reddꝭ ass̃ .xiij dꝭ.

s̃s Smᵃ .xiij dꝭ.

Ð villa de Thalanuoyl de potur̃ ⁊ opac̃ villanoꝫ eiꝰdꝭ ville—iiij. lĩ .xvij. s̃ . ob̃.

s̃s Smᵃ iiij lĩ xvij s̃ ob̃.

Ð vilt de Carnethur de Tung̃ .v. s̃ . de potur̃ ⁊ aliis cons̃ .xj. s̃ .iiij. dꝭ.

Ᵹs Smᵃ .xvj. ꝫ .iiij đ.

Ð vilł de Thlandogewel de Tung̃ .xx. đ. de potʳra ⁊ aliis conꝫ .viij ꝫ iiij đ.

Ᵹs Smᵃ .x ꝫ.

Ð vilł de Bodewarnan de redđ villanoꝫ x ꝫ.

Ᵹs Smᵃ .x ꝫ.

Ð vilł de Boderonyn de redđ ⁊ conꝫ villanoꝫ xxvj. ꝫ .vj. đ.

Ᵹs Smᵃ xxvj ꝫ vj đ.

Ð vilł de Meriogan de conꝫ villanoꝫ .xxiiij ꝫ.

Ᵹs Smᵃ xxiiij ꝫ.

Ð vilł de Trefnegoch de redđ potuꝛ̃ ⁊ conꝫ villanoꝫ xxiiij ꝫ ix đ ō qᵃ.

Ᵹs Smᵃ .xxiiij ꝫ ix đ ō qᵃ.

Ð pteẍionibꝫ eiusđm Commoti viij ꝫ j đ.

Ᵹs Smᵃ viij ꝫ j đ.

Ð pquiꝫ eiᵖđ Commoti xl. ꝫ.

Ᵹs Smᵃ xl. ꝫ.

Ᵹs Smᵃ toˡ huiᵖ Cōmoti .xl. lĩ .iij ꝫ .ij đ ō qᵃ pƀ.

Extenta Maꝛꝺii de Penros.

Ð redđ asꝫ eiᵖđ Maꝛꝺii . Lviij ꝫ iiijđ.

Iłm de eođ p p̃sentacōm iuratoꝫ . xxiij ꝫ xj đ.

vj. lĩ
Ð dnico . iiijᵒʳ carucaꝛ̃ terĩ ⁊ vał caruc̃ .xxx. ꝫ.

Iłm de tˡbꝫ Molenđ iiij. lĩ .vj. ꝫ .viij. đ . de potuꝛ̃ CC .x.

hoĩm . CCCC . ij . eqᵒꝫ . Cix ꝫ ō qᵃ.

de redđ blađ iiij lĩ xiiij ꝫ j. đ.

Iꝉ de Mꝺꝛyonnith lactis cuiᵖđ Rustici viij. ꝫ .ix. đ.

Ð redđ butiꝛ̃ xj. ꝫ .vij. đ.

Ð blado ad p̃benđ Palefriđ đni ij ꝫ.

Ð angñ . ⁊ gallinis vj ꝫ viij đ.

Ð redđ ferꝛ̃ fabꝛ̃ . iij ꝫ.

... error
.. ex-
tenta ...
a ... e ...
original
...

13

APP. A a.

A.D.
1294.

Opa ꝓ
conꝯ vilł
de
Penros.

de ouis ꝉ butiꝛ vj đ.

De cariaḡ turbaꝣ ꝉ tᵣbis x ꝭ.

 Đ literꝛ dĩ mᵃꝛ.

ꝭs Smᵃ .xxvij lĩ xiiij đ . ŏ . qᵃ.

Đ villa͠n . eiusđm ꝑ ꝰuicio in Autūpno . Scꝣ ꝑ .iij. Menꝭ .
singłm . Menꝭ . ꝑ viij dies . s . sinḡlo . dieꝣ ꝑ xxxvj hoïes.
ꝙd ꝰuiꝫ valet ꝑ diē singulo j. đ . ŏ—C . viij ꝭ . De xiij.
Cołelł ꝑ opibꝣ xiij hoïm ꝑ iij dies in autūpno ꝙd ꝰuiꝫ valet
iiij ꝭ x đ ŏ . de opibꝣ .xx. equoꝣ sine garcioͫ ad ħcianđ tēpe
yemali . ꝑ unū diē ꝙd valet xx. đ . De opibꝣ .vj. equoꝣ
ˣˣ
v. garꝫ ad ħcianđ tēpe qᵃdraḡ . ꝑ unū diē ꝙd valet xl. ꝭ.
ˣˣ   +

Đ opibꝣ . xviij gaueloꝣ quoꝣ quilꝣ debꝣ ħciaꝛ ꝑ .iij. Menꝭ .
         ˣˣ   +
vidꝣ ꝑ iiij .x. dies cū uno equo ꝉ uno garcõe . ꝙd´val . xiij lĩ .
x ꝭ.

Đ eisđm de opibꝣ extᵃhenciū fimū cū xx . equis ꝉ garcõem
ꝑ unū diē .xl. đ.

Smᵃ—xxj. lĩ .vij. ꝭ .x. đ . oƀ.

Smᵃ Man͠ii de Penros .xlvij. lĩ .ix. ꝭ .j. đ . qᵃ.

[On a small parchment schedule sewed on to the Roll the
following appears.]

Videtꝛ ꝙd sit error in extenta Manerii de Penros in
ptiꞇlis ꝭbscᶦpꝉ . Videłt ꞏꞏ de redđ eiusđm Man͠ii . Potura
hoïm ꝉ eqᵒꝣ . Et redđ bladi . que iđo sunt cruce signati in
extenta.

Smᵃ .xiiij. lĩ .v. ꝭ .iiij. đ . oƀ qᵃ . Qui respᶜtuantꝛ ꝑ errore
usꝗ sup compꝑ Camͫarii . corã consilio Pᶦnꝫ ꝑ peticõnem
villanoꝣ de Penros ad pliamentū t͠mīo sꝛei Hillarii . Anno
Regni Reḡ Edwardi Tricesimo tercio.

Commotꝰ de Turkelyn.

Đ redđ assꝭ ville de Henescot vj. ꝭ .viij. đ.

ꝭs Smᵃ .vj. ꝭ .viij. đ.

14

Slagoruc¹ ꝛ Sleckou cū ptiñ de redđ asꝛ j mᵃc̃.

Đ potuꝝ eoꝫđ xxij ꝛ iiij đ.

Đ ꝉra Gꞌꝉuasii fiꝉ Phi que nūc est in manu Reḡ xxiij ꝛ x đ.

ꝛꝛ Smᵃ . Lix ꝛ .vj. đ.

Sistulas cū ptiñ de villa ꝑdc̃a cū villis sꞇ respondentibꝫ viij lī vij ꝛ vj. đ.

ꝛs Smᵃ . viij lī vij ꝛ vj. đ.

Đ hõibꝫ de Curchlayt Manentibꝫ ꝛr teñ de Sistulas . ꝑ potuꝝ . Lxviij hoīm . Lxviij canū ꝛ iiijᵒʳ eꝗ xj. ꝛ .x đ.

ꝛs Smᵃ .xj. ꝛ x đ.

Đ redđ asꝛ ville de Reccow . xlviij ꝛ viij đ.

ꝛs Smᵃ . xlviij ꝛ viij đ.

Bodaneu ꝛ Bodenawyn cū ptiñ de eisd de redđ asꝛ vj. lī .xvij ꝛ iiij đ.

ꝛs Smᵃ .vj. lī .xvij ꝛ iiij đ.

Đ potuꝝ eiꝰđ ꝑ CCCL . hõibꝫ . ꝛ Lxxv . canū ꝛ Lxxv . eꝗ ꝑ unū diē ꝗd vaꝉ xl ꝛ vij đ õ.

Codanou ꝛ Both-unokꝑ.

Đ opibꝫ ꝑ tres dies in Autumpno siñḡlo die ꝑ xvj hoïes ꝗd vaꝉ xvj. ꝛ . siñḡlo ꝑc̃ ꝑ diē j. đ õ.

de Lx . galꝉ ꝛ iiijᵒʳ angnis eoꝫđ v. ꝛ .vj. đ.

Đ Mꞌꝉionith eiꝰđ cū viꝉꝉ adiac̃ . ꝛ . Rosmanach Bodeueney ꝛ Derẏ iiij lī vij ꝛ j đ õ.

de eisđm vj cᵃnnoc̃ aueñ que vaꝉ iiij ꝛ.

Iꝛ de eisđ ꝑ auꞋagiis . xj ꝛ iiij đ.

ꝛs Smᵃ—vij lī xiiij ꝛ vij đ.

Đ redđ asꝛ teñ eiꝰđ x ꝛ.

Bodeueneu.

Đ opibꝫ xv hoīm in eađ villa ad metenđ ꝑ unū diē ꝗd vaꝉ xxij. đ . oꝺ.

Iꝛ de xv. galꝉ ꝛ uno anguo .xvj. đ.

Iꝛ de tꞁbꝫ crannoc̃ fꝛi de redđ vij ꝛ vj đ.

ꝛs Ṡmᵃ xx ꝛ ix đ õ.

---

¹ Tlagoruc in the copy.

App. A a. — A.D. 1294.

Rosmangħ. Ð reddꝺ ei⁹dm . iij s iiij ꝺ . de opibȝ xxvij hoı̄m ad metenꝺ ꝑ unū diem . iij s iiij ꝺ ob.

Itm de xxvij galt ⁊ uno angñ de reddꝺ ij s v ꝺ.

Itm de uno teñ ei⁹ꝺ j cannoc̄ fri q̄d valȝ .ij. s vj ꝺ.

ss Smᵃ xj s vij ꝺ ō.

Dery. De opibȝ .xxiiij. hoı̄m ad metenꝺ ꝑ j . diem . iij s.

It . de xxiiij galt ⁊ angñ ⁊ dı̄ ij s iij ꝺ de iiijᵒʳ villanis supᵃdc̄is . s . Boteynokꝭ Bodeueneu Rosmangħ ⁊ Dery . ꝑ potur̄ CCCC . hoı̄m .CC. canū .CC. eq̄ ꝑ unū diē .Lxxv. s.

ss Smᵃ .iiij. lı̄ .iij. ꝺ.

Bodewryt. Ð reddꝺ ij s vj. ꝺ.

Itm ꝑ potur̄ . xlix hoı̄m . xlviij canū ⁊ iij eq̄ ꝑ unū diem viij s v ꝺ ō.

It de uno cᵃnnoc̄ far̄ aueñ .ij. s.

ss Smᵃ . xij s xj. ꝺ ō.

Slorathenryet. Ð reddꝺ ei⁹ꝺ dı̄ m̄.

Troscloyndysteynet de reddꝺ dı̄ m̄.

Ð Bedelt tot̄ cōmot̄ de reddꝺ ij s vj ꝺ.

It ꝑ eisdm ij cᵃnnoc̄ fri v s.

It ꝑ viij cᵃnnoc̄ ⁊ t̄cia ꝑte j . cᵃnnoc̄ far̄ aueñ xvj s viij ꝺ.

Ð aduocar̄ v. s x ꝺ.

Ð batelt de portu de Dulas .xx. ꝺ.

ss Smᵃ xlv. s.

Nanmaur̄ Sudon Vachᵃn ꝑ Regē. Ð reddꝺ ass̄ ei⁹ꝺ . Lx s ij ꝺ.

It de vij cᵃnnoc̄ ⁊ dı̄ fri de reddꝺ xviij. s . ix ꝺ.

It de xxviij cᵃnnoc̄ dimiꝺ iij buss̄ farñ auē . Liij s vj ꝺ.

ss Smᵃ .vj. lı̄ .xij. s .v. ꝺ.

ss Smᵃ totᵗ hui⁹ Cōmot̄ . xliiij lı̄ ix s .j. ꝺ . ō.

Extent of Anglesey, 1294.

Extenta Cōmoť de Mene.

Primo R̃endunt [1] de ďnico pp̔lo Reg̃ q̃d sunt in Mañ̃io de

Rofeyr̃ .x. car̃ terr̃ de q̔lbʒ . vj caruč sūt de ďnico ꝉ iiij^{or} de

excaeť ꝉ vať . quelʒ . caruč .xxx. s̃.

ss Sm^a . xv lĩ.

Iťm de Gardino ďni Reg̃ . iij s̃.

Iť de iijᵇ³ . p^atis v. s̃.

Iť de pastur̃ . xx s̃.

Iť de t^ıbʒ Molenď que R̃endunt [1] de iiij c^annoč far̃ ꝉ vať

Cvj s̃ viij ď p̃c c^annoč .xvj. ď.

Iť de firmar̃ ꝉ villanis de redď ass̃ xxx s̃ xj. ď.

Iť de Albo ꝉ M^rʼionitħ vj s̃ iij ď.

Iť de eoď vj c^annoč fr̃i ꝉ vať xv. s̃.

Iť de eoď iij c^annoč far̃ ordei ꝉ val iiij s̃.

Iť de villañ de xxij c^annoč iij bʒ far̃ ordei ꝉ vať xxx s̃

iiij ď.

Iť de xij villañ q̃ tenet xij gauelť una teñ ꝉ rendunt [1] xij

c^annoč ꝉ dĩ far̃ aueñ ꝉ val . xvj s̃ viij ď.

Iť de Fabris iiij^{or} c^annoč far̃ ordei vať .v. s̃ iiij ď.

Iť de eisď villañ iij c^annoč aueñ . ad p̃ƀ . palefr̃ Reg̃ xij ď .

p̃c c^annoč iiij ď.

Iť de Liiij^{or} galť de quibʒ xviij falcoñ ꝉ vať . iiij s̃ vj ď p̃c

galť j ď.

Iť de exeuñ villanoʒ . iij s̃ iiij ď.

Iť p̃dc̃i villani debẽt inueniř . CC .xl. eq^os cū tot hõibʒ

ad ħcianď ꝉ vať xxx. s̃ p̃c opis equi j ď ꝉ hõis oƀ.

Iť debẽt Mer̃e cū CCCC . hõibʒ p unū diẽ ꝉ vať op̃ .

xxxiij s̃ iiij ď . Vidʒ quilʒ p diẽ .j. ď.

Iť deƀ cariar̃ . blaď cū Lxxij hõibʒ ꝉ Lxxij eq^ıs p unū

diẽ ꝉ vať . ix s̃ vidʒ p hoĩe . oƀ . ꝉ equo j ď.

Iťm deƀnt ext^aere fimū cū xiiij eq^ıs ꝉ vať op̃ . xiiij ď.

Iť deƀ inueniř ďno Ignem vel xx s̃.

APP. Λ a.

——

A.D.
1294.

Concesse
Regine
p Regem

---

[1] So in the Record.

App. A a.

A.D.
1294.

Iᵗ de stᵃmine x ꝫ.

Iᵗ de eisđm de quolꝫ . ħnte pĩes agnos qᵃ .v. dabunt unū .
꒓ vaᶩ iij ꝫ iiij đ.

Iᵗm de p̃đc̆is villañ de quolꝫ ħente galliñ .xx. oua .xx. đ.

Iᵗm de p̃titis ꒓ pquiꝫ Cuꝛ̃ xl . ꝫ.

ꝫs   Smᵃ . xx lĩ .vj. đ.

ꝫs   Smᵃ toᶩ istius Maꝫii .xxxv. lĩ . vj đ.

Porthamal
Geythrem[1]

Ð eađ vilᶠ de redđ asꝫ . iiij lĩ . xviij ꝫ iij đ qᵃ.

ꝫs   Smᵃ . iiij lĩ xviij ꝫ iij đ q̃.

Sode-
wyndrū.

Ð eađ vilᶠ de redđ asꝫ Lxix ꝫ vj đ ŏ.

ꝫs   Smᵃ Lxix ꝫ vj đ ŏ.

Srefarthen

De eađ vilᶠ de redđ asꝫ xxvij ꝫ viij đ.

Igaerwen.

De eađ vilᶠ de redđ asꝫ . xij ꝫ viij đ.

Ᵽan-
dygadou.

De eađ vilᶠ de redđ asꝫ . vij ꝫ iiij đ.

Kaeruan.

De eađ vilᶠ de redđ asꝫ .xj. ꝫ.

Ternocet.

De eađ vilᶠ de redđ asꝫ . xxiij ꝫ iij đ ŏ.

Trefolwyn

De eađ vilᶠ de redđ asꝫ . vj ꝫ v đ.

Grukdowy

De eađ vilᶠ de redđ asꝫ . xxiiij ꝫ iiij đ.

Myssoglen

De [firmaꝛ̃] eiᵖđ vilᶠ iiij ꝫ vj đ.

Iᵗ de potuꝛ̃ Clxxij . hoĩm Lvij equoꝫ p unū diē ab eisđ
firmaꝛ̃ xxj ꝫ v đ oᵬ . Vidꝫ p hoĩe j đ ꒓ p equo j đ ŏ.

Smᵃ xxv. ꝫ xj. đ ŏ.

Boteurydɑ

Ð redđ asꝫ .x. đ.

Iᵗ de eađ vilᶠ .viij. galliñ viij đ.

Smᵃ viij đ.

Denan.

Ð eađ vilᶠ p potura .CCC. xxix hoĩm ꒓ C. ix eq̃ xlj ꝫ oᵬ.

Iᵗ de eađ villa xiiij galᶠ ꒓ vaᶠ xiiij ꝫ.

Smᵃ xlij ꝫ ij đ ŏ.

Heyrdes-
weyth.

Ð eađ vilᶠ p potuꝛ̃ de CLiiij hoĩm .CC. xviij. eq̃ . iiij lĩ
xx đ.

Ð eađ vilᶠ xxx. galᶠ ꒓ vaᶠ xxx. đ.

Iᵗ p arratuꝛ̃ eiᵖđ vilᶠ ꝗ multū remota a Cuꝛ̃ ij ꝫ vj đ.

---

[1] Not in the copy.

It p aūag̃ istius ville cū vilł p̃cedente iij ꝶ iiij đ.

Smᵃ iiij lī x ꝶ.

De redđ asꝶ ei°đ ville iij ꝶ iiij đ.

It p potura . CClxxvij hoīm ⁊ canū xxiij ꝶ j đ.

Smᵃ . xxvj ꝶ v đ.

Đ redđ asꝶ ei°đ viij ꝶ vj đ.

It p potuꝛ de D ⁊ iiij hoīm ⁊ C. lxviij eꝗ . Lxiij ꝶ.

It de xiiij galliñ xiiij đ.

Iŧm de istis vj. vilł p M')ionitħ xiij ꝶ iiij đ.

It de teñ de Skyuiokę de redđ asꝶ . vij đ.

It .ij. cᵃnnoꝼ̃ fr̃i . ij cᵃnnoꝼ̃ faꝛ̃ aueñ ij cᵃnnoꝼ̃ faꝛ̃ ordei ⁊ vał xj. ꝶ viij đ.

It de terra Madyn ab Ađ de redđ vj. đ.

Smᵃ . iiij lī xviij ꝶ ix đ.

Đ eađ villa de redđ asꝶ .xl. ꝶ viij đ.

Đ tⁱb; hõib; eiᶜđ ville de redđ asꝶ . ij ꝶ vj đ.

Đ eađ vilł vj cᵃnnoꝼ̃ fr̃i . ⁊ vał xv. ꝶ.

It xij cᵃnnoꝼ̃ braꝶ aueñ .xij. ꝶ . p̃ᷓ cᵃnnoꝼ̃ xij đ.

It de uno Menꝶ butiꝛ̃ ꝗ valet iij ꝶ iiij đ.

It .ij. cᵃnnoꝼ̃ faꝛ̃ ordei ꝗ vał ij ꝶ viij đ.

It .ij cᵃnnoꝼ̃ aueñ xvj. đ.

It .ij. Multoñ ⁊ vał xvj. đ.

It xvj galł xvj đ.

It de exheuñ tam de butiꝛ̃ qᵃ ouis xvj đ.

It de Đd Gotħ de Trefynan j buꝶ fr̃i ⁊ vał vij đ õ ⁊ uno buꝶꝶ faꝛ̃ ordei ⁊ vał iiij đ.

It p pte dc̃i Đd . exheuñ iij đ.

It de eođ de M')ionnitħ .ij. đ.

It de quol; ħente płes agnos qᵃ .v. unū agnū ⁊ estimantʳ xx agni de quib; . iij ꝶ iiij đ.

Smᵃ . xliij ꝶ.

Đ eađ vilł de fr̃o . iiijᵒʳ cᵃnnoꝼ̃ ⁊ iij buꝶꝶ .xj. ꝶ .x đ õ.

---

[1] Trefscaweyn in the copy.

App. A a.

A.D.
1294.

Iͭ de braꝫ aueñ .ix. cᵃnnoꝁ . ꝛ dī ꝛ valꝫ ix ꝫ vj đ.

Iͭm de farina ordei una cᵃnnoc̄ ꝛ dī ꝛ valꝫ ij ꝫ.

Iͭ de duabꝫ ptibꝫ uni⁹ vaꝫ butiꝛ̄ ꝛ ꝉcia pte unius ptis uni⁹ vaꝫ butiꝛ̄ ꝛ vaꝉ ij ꝫ vj đ ō qᵃ.

Iͭ de Multoñ xij đ ō qᵃ.

Iͭm de exheuñ ei⁹đ ville xvj. đ.

Iͭ de aꭒag̃ istius vilꝉ ꝛ p̄cedenc̄ xx đ.

Iͭ de quolꝫ ħente pꝉes agnos qᵃ .v. unū agnū de quibꝫ iij ꝫ iiij đ.

Iͭ de M᷑ionnitħ duaꝛ đc̄aꝛ vilꝉ .iij. cᵃnnoc̄ fꝛ̄i . iiijᵒʳ cᵃnnoc̄ faꝛ̄ ordei iiijᵒʳ crannoc̄ faꝛ̄ aueñ ꝛ valent xxiij ꝫ iiij đ.

Iͭm de Albo vj ꝫ viij đ.

Iͭ de Lalwarchvoyl .v. ꝫ.

Iͭ de eađ vilꝉ j Crannoc̄ aueñ ad p̊ƀ . ꝛ valꝫ viij đ.

Iͭm de ptectionibꝫ Rꝑ xix ꝫ iiij đ.

Iͭm de pquiꝫ Cuꝛ̄ xl. ꝫ.

Smᵃ .vj. lī .viij. ꝫ .iiij đ.

Smᵃ toꝉ istius Cōmoti p̃ꝉ maneꝛ̄ .xxxix. lī .xj. đ.

Tᷤ.ra Ep̄i
in Can-
trede.

Đ vilꝉ de Bodeyhan de redđ asꝫ xiiij ꝫ iiij đ.

ꝫs Smᵃ . xiiij ꝫ iiij đ.

Đ vilꝉ Ioħ Maphython de redđ asꝫ conꝫ ꝛ aliis ꝫuic̃ xxxix ꝫ . ix đ ō.

ꝫs Smᵃ xxxix ꝫ . ix đ ō.

ꝫs Smᵃ totaꝉ terꝛ̄ Ep̄i . Liiij ꝫ j. đ oƀ.

De quibꝫ allocantʳ vic̃ .L. ꝫ . p cartā Reg̃ qᵃm Ep̄s ostendit.

Tᷤ)ra
Aƀƀ de
Cone-
wey.

De iiijᵒʳ carucac̄ terꝛ̄ in Manꝫio de Cornuchles p̃c̄ caruc̄ xxvj ꝫ viij đ.

ꝫs Smᵃ Cvj ꝫ viij đ.

Đ uno Molenđ fracto de quo nͭ . de pastʳa xx ꝫ . de redđ asꝫ liƀoꝛ ꞇeñ iiij lī . x ꝫ . viij đ . de villañ ei⁹đ ville de redđ v. ꝫ.

Iͭ p potuꝛ̄ ꝛ aliis conꝫ ꝛ ꝫuic̃ . Liiij ꝫ iiij đ.

ꝫs Smᵃ viij lī x ꝫ.

20

Tursemon q̃ est hamelett⁹ ptinens ad Gerneweles cū hameleť de Westdrewy de redđ ass̃ istoꝛ hameleť Cxvj s̃ ix đ.

  s̃s Smᵃ C .xvj. s̃ .ix. đ.

Đ T⁾bonmaylokꝑ de Ꞽra Abƀ . de redđ ass̃ ꝛ aliis consꝛ ꝛ ꝭuic̃ . ei⁹đ .xxxv. s̃.

  s̃s Smᵃ .xxxv. s̃.

  s̃s Smᵃ toᵗ terꝛ Abƀ .xxj. lĩ .viij s̃ v. đ.

  s̃s Smᵃ totaɫ dc̃e extente .CCCC iiij .iij. lĩ .x. s̃ .xj. đ . qᵃ. ˣˣ

Terre contente in extenta collate diꞹsis hoïbꝫ p Cartas Rꝑ . post confeccõem extente p̃dc̃e . De quibꝫ vic̃ nô debet oꞹari in comp̃ suo sup contentis in eađm extenta.　Videlt.

Đ villaꝛ de Bodeyhan ꝛ Joħ Maphython que extenduntʳ ad . Liiij s̃ .j. đ . oƀ quas Ep̄s̃ Bangoꝛ tenet p cartâ . Rꝑ . L. s̃ imppᵖm.

Đ Maꞹio de Cornuthles cū Hameleť de Tursemon ꝛ Westdrewy ꝛ T⁾lonmaylokꝑ que Abbas ꝛ cõuent⁹ de Conewey tenent p cartam Rꝑ .xxj. lĩ .viij. s̃ .v. đ . imppeꝛm.

Smᵃ toᵗ .xxiij lĩ xviij s̃ v đ.

Đ villa de Nantmauꝛ qᵃm Tudeꝛ Vāchᵃn tenet p cartani Rꝑ ad Ꞽninū vite ip̄i⁹ Tuderi ꝛ Resi filii sui .vj. lĩ .xij s̃ v đ. —ad Ꞽim vite . Et meᵈ q̃d ista sūma px̃ p̃cedēs alloc̃ vic̃ in decasu ꞉ꞏ ut pꝫ in dorso roᵗ ꝯpoꝛ vic̃.

Smᵃ xxiij. lĩ .xviij. s̃ .v. đ.　Qui deƀnt s̃btᵃhi de Smᵃ toɫ extēte qᵒad vic̃.

Et eciam .xxiiij. lĩ .x s̃ de pɫit ꝛ pquis̃ que continentʳ in eađm extenta in diꞹsis cõmotꝑ p eo q̃d iđm vic̃ respond iude siꝳl cū increꝳto in pɫit ꝛ pquis̃ toci⁹ Com̃ p diꞹsas pticulas extᵃ extentam.*

  * Et sic dꝫ vic̃ oꞹaꝛ de cõtentꝑ in exꝛ de claꝛ de . CCCC . xxx . v. lĩ .ij. s̃ .vj. đ qᵃ . pƀ . Eo q̃d Smᵃ subseꝗns de pɫis ꝛ pquis̃ subtᵃhitur sicut Ꞽre collaꝛ ut supᵃ.¹

---

¹ Not in the copy.

[On the dorse of the Roll.]

Escaete In Cantreᵭ de Aƀfrau temp͂ ᵭni Edwardi P¹nciᵽ Walᵵ.

. Escaeta.

Wilᵵs ap Daniel qui tenuit .xxx. acras ᶵre cū ptinenc̃ in Aƀfrau ad ᶵminū vite sue de ᵭno Leweliñ qᵒndā P¹nc̃ Walᵵ obiit ᶵꞟo sc̃i Mich̃ anno P¹nc̃ P¹nc̃ . Eℓ . ij° . Per cuiˢ mortē Henꞃ̄ de Dynintoñ tūc vic̃ seisiuit ᶵrā ꝑdc̃am in manū ᵭni P¹nc̃ tanqᵃ escaetā . ᴸ ꝑdca escaeta valet ꝑ annū ꝑ extentā fc̃am ꝑ iꝑm vic̃ . xl ᵭ. Unde vic̃ eiusᵭm Com̃ debet respondere annuatī sup compͦ suū ad Scᵃcm ap Caerñ.

Smᵃ .xl. ᵭ.

Escaeta.

Dauid ap Llewelin qui tenuit víllam de Tƀlallybion cū ptiñ in Cantꞃ̄ de Aberfrau ad voluntatē ᵭni Reg̃ ꝑ liƀac̃oem ᵭni . I . de Haꞟinggℓ post ꝗguerram Maddoci ap Lewelyn obiit mense Augusti Anno P¹ncipatˢ . Eℓ . P¹nc̃ sc̃do . Post cuiˢ mortē Wenthliana ux̃ eiusᵭm Ðd ᴸ Lewelinˢ filius eoꝛ iniuste occupauerūt ꝑdc̃am villā usꝗ mensem Septembꞃ̄ anno P¹ncipatˢ Eℓ P¹nc̃ iij quo mense ꝑdc̃us Lewelinˢ obiit tempe Walᶠi de Wyntoñ vic̃ Angleꝡ que debuit fuisse escaeta ᵭni P¹nc̃ post mortē dc̃i Ðd . Et hoc pcepto ꞉ Henꞃ̄ de Dynigtoñ vic̃ qui recepit ꝑdc̃am villam in manū P¹nc̃ tanqᵃꞟn escaetā suam . Et valet ꝑdc̃a villa ꝑ annū in õibꞝ exitibꞝ .vij. lꞟ .xj. ꝥ .iiij. ᵭ. Unde vic̃ eiusᵭ Com̃ debet respondͤ annuatī sup compͦ suū ad Scᵃcm apᵭ Caerñ.

Smᵃ .vij. lꞟ .xj. ꝥ .iiij. ᵭ.

Escaeta.

Lewelinˢ Voyl ap Griff ap Gogan qui tenuit villā de Kenleuyokℓ cū Hamelettis de [Keyru]¹ ᴸ Kilgwyn ad ᶵꞟm vite sue de dono ᵭni Eℓ . illustᶥs Reg̃ Angᵵ filio per Cartā iꝑius Reg̃ . obiit . iiij° die Apᶥᵵ anno P¹nc̃ P¹nc̃ . Eℓ . v° . ꝑ cuiˢ mortē Henꞃ̄ de Dyninton tūc vic̃ seisiuit ꝑdc̃am villā cū Hamelettis in manū ᵭni P¹nc̃ tanqᵃ escaetā . Et ꝑdc̃a villa cū Hamelettis valet ꝑ annū ꝑ extentā fc̃am per iꝑm vic̃ .xij. lꞟ .xviij. ꝥ .xj. ᵭ.

Smᵃ xij. lĩ .xviij. ʂ .xj. đ.[1]

Ð ᶠra Ioჳ Duy ap Dauid in villa de Trebaddokℓ qui intᶠfecit Dauid p̄rem suũ Mense Maii aᵒ Pⁱncip̄ đni E . Pⁱnc̄ quarto que extenditʳ p vic̄ ad tres soliđ . Unde vic̄ debet respondeᶠ annuatī ʂr ꝯp̄.

Smᵃ . iij ʂ.

Ð Candalo ap Thom̃ ꝉ Keñ ap Thomas de quodam annuo redditu aduocarie concelato ꝉ recupato coram W . đe de Suttoñ Iustic̄ in anno Pⁱncipatꝰ đni Eℓ Pⁱnc̄ iiijᵗᵒ . unde vic̄ . deƀ oñari ꝉ c̄ . đĩ qᵃrᶠ frm̃i . p̄c̄ ij. ʂ .vj. đ.

Smᵃ .ij. ʂ .vj. đ.

Ð Madđ Vaghan . de Rosmanakℓ p quod añuo redđ concelato ꝉ recupato coram p̄fato Iustic̄ in anno iiijᵗᵒ p̄dc̄o unde vic̄ deᵇ oñari ꝉ c̄—xvj. đ . oƀ.

Smᵃ xvj. đ . oƀ.

Ð xiiij bouatis ᶠre arrabiꞇ una domo . uno pᵃto . una pꞇe tʳbarie dc̄o teñ spectante que fueᶠt . Madđ ap Idewal in Pentraytʰ et que ʂt in manu Pⁱnc̄ p excaꞙtam . et que extenduntʳ p H . de Dynyntoñ vic̄ ad xvj. ʂ .iiij. đ in anno ꝉ c̄ qⁱnto . de quibჳ debᶜt ʂbtrai .v. ʂ . pro redđ annuo eiusđm teñ contenꞇ in extenta Com̃ . et deƀ vic̄ oñari in compoto suo de xj. ʂ .iiij. đ . de residuo dc̄e extente una cũ appꞷwamc̄to.

Smᵃ—xj. ʂ .iiij. đ.

Smᵃ toꞎ—xxj. lĩ .xj. ʂ .ix. đ . oƀ.

[2] Hee sunt pcuracōnes ꝉ ʂuicia hĩm Manerii de Penros in Cōmoto de Tʳkeꞇ ubi inuenti fũnt .xij. Gauelli cũ dimiđ ꞇpe qᵒ villa extentata fuit.

Et de dc̄a ᶠra . gauellus soluebat . xxᵗⁱ . qⁱnჳ hoïes p unũ diem ad secanđ blada p sex septimanas ꞇpe autũpnali.

Et de qⁱnჳ aliis acris .vꝺ . hoïes p unũ diõ ut supᵃ.

Iꞇ de om̃ibჳ ilꞇ Gauellis soluebant qⁱnqᵃginta eqᵒs cũ tot garcōibჳ ad carianđ blada eođm ꞇpe p unũ diem.

---

[1] The copy ends here.

[2] On a parchment schedule sewed on to the end of the Roll.

Iŧ .lx. eq°s p unū diem ad hercianđ ŧras Pˡncip̄ cū' tot garcōibȝ ŧpe v̄nali.

Iŧ .x. eq°s sine garcōibȝ ad fimanđ ŧras cˡca Pascha.

Iŧ .xx. eq°s ad hercianđ frum̃ta ordea fabas et pisa ac siligines sine garcōibȝ ᴸ hoc p unū diem.

Iŧ p pcʳacōe uni⁹ eqˡ ī hyeme ᴸ vere unā c̃nocā Lewelini qªlibȝ septimana cum straminibȝ ᴸ victualibus p Garc̃one.

Iŧ in autūpno victualia p Garc̃one sine eq° . ī estate niĉh.

vij
Iŧ pcʳac̃ōes .xx. eq°ȝ et tot equ°ȝ p unū diē ᴸ noctē ŧpe hyemali . Et . xxᵗˡ . melioribȝ eqˡs de illis p sex ī die unam c̃nocā Lewelini ᴸ ōibȝ . viij . de illis aliis palefredis unam c̃nocā.

Iŧ in vere p octuagīta eqˡs pcuracōnes ut supra p aliis.

Iŧ in estatē p .lx. valetis pcʳacōes sine eqˡs ᴸ totidē in autūpno.

Iŧ p igne ad op⁹ đni Pˡncip̄ de glebario suo soluebant p tres vices ī aduētu ipi⁹ videlicȝ autūpno Hyeme ᴸ v̄e p unªȝ vice cētū tªssas de glebis ᴸ tūc isti hoīes habebant unū glebariū liƀe ᴸ iāduđ exªctū est ab eis ilŧd.

Iŧ p q°libȝ Gauello q°libȝ ŧpe anni duas tªssas stªminum ad opus bettoȝ.

Iŧ de unoqȝ° gauello .xiiij. đ p annū.

Iŧ de ōibȝ gauellis .xv. galones butiri p annū.

Iŧ extra gauellos ȿt .vj. acre ᴸ p qªlibȝ illaȝ solūnt p annū .xij. đ.

Iŧ de ōibȝ gauellis .xxviij. galīas.

Iŧ ī eađm villa ȿt .vj. gauelli de qˡbȝ đn̄s haƀet reddit⁹ pᶜunarios cū frum̃to . videlicȝ de Gauello Bledyn Grachais.

Iŧ de Gauello Ade ap Madauc .vij. soŧ .viij. đ.

Iŧ de dimiđ gauelli Madoci Capellani .xl. đ.

Iŧ de gauello Philip Sayr .vij. soliđ.

Iŧ de ŧra Gemllin Portarii .ij. ȿ .vj. đ.

Iŧ de gauello fabªȝ .vj. c̃nocas frum̃ti de cªnoca Lewelini.

Extent of Anglesey, 1294.

Iŧ de Gauello Philippi Capellani .iij. c̓noc̄ cū dimiđa de
eađ m̄sura.

Iŧ de eođ .xx^{ti}. đ .vj. galones butiri . duos . agnos .lx. oua
⁊ hoc p̄ ānū.

Iŧ de dimiđ gauelli Adam ap Byndelw .v. ꙅ .iij. đ.

Iŧ cŏitas toti⁹ ville soluet p̄ annū . xxx c̓nocas de c̓nocis
Lewelini ad plus . videlicet ꝑciā p̄tē frum̄ti ⁊ aliam ꝑciā farine
auenaꞇ ⁊ ꝑciā p̄tē fariñ ordeacee ⁊ aliqᵃndo dñs faċet eis
gᵃciam q̃d nō peꝑet ab iꝑis nisi .xx. cᵃnoc̄.

Iŧ ꝑ maronia lactis p̓dc̄e ville ī estate ⁊ autūpno dimiđ
toti⁹ lactis dicioris hŏis de villa ⁊ ilŧd aliqᵃndo c̄et frucꞇ .iiij.
vacca⅌ ⁊ aliqᵃndo dua⅌ iŧle vacce ī festo oĩm sc̄o⅌ redirēt ađ
suū possessorē.

25

SHERIFF'S ACCOUNT OF ABERFFRAW AND PENROS, 30 EDW. I., A.D. 1302.

Chapter House Miscellanea ₂ᵃ₃ᵃ, Public Record Office.[1]

PP. A o.

A.D. 1302.

Compot⁹ Walteri de Wyntoñ Viꝯ Angleꝰ a festo sancti Micħis anno regni Regis Edwardi vicesimo nono usꝗ festum sꝯi Micħis anno regni Regis predꝯi tⁱcesimo.

. . . .

Aber-frau.

ꝰs Maneriū de Aberfrau.

Idem respondet de firᵃ ꝺnicoꝫ eiusꝺm Maneꝛ
   Corsodelen ꞇ Tᵉfcastel p anñ   .   . vij. lĭ .x. ꝛ

Ꝺnicꝑ.

Ꝺ redꝺ asꝛ liꝛe tenꝯ eiusdem Maneꝛ p idem
   temp⁹   .   .   .   .   . xxxij. ꝛ x. ꝺ.

Ꝺ redꝺ asꝛ villanoꝫ Mꝯ)dredi eiusdem Maneꝛ
   . p idem temp⁹   .   .   .   . xx. lĭ .iij. ꝛ . ꝺ qᵃ.

Molenꝺ. Ꝺ firᵃ .iij. Molendīoꝫ ibidem p idem temp⁹ viij. lĭ.

Portaꝛ. Ꝺ firᵃ Portaꝛ eiusdem Maneꝛ p idem temp⁹ xiij. ꝛ .iiij. ꝺ
   Smᵃ totał dꝯi Maneꝛ .xxxvij. lĭ .xix. ꝛ ·ij. ꝺ . ꝺ . qᵃ.

. . . .

Tur-kelyn.

ꝰs Maneꝛ de Penros.

Idem respondet de redꝺ villanoꝫ Mꝯ)dredi de
   Penros . per anñ   .   .   .   . xvj. lĭ .xxiij. ꝺ.

Ꝺ firᵃ .iiij. Carucaꝉ terꝛ ꝺnicoꝫ eiusdem
   Maneꝛ p idem temp⁹   .   .   . C. ꝛ.

Ꝺ firᵃ .iiij. Molendīoꝫ eiusdem Maneꝛ p idem
   temp⁹   .   .   .   . x. lĭ.

Ꝺ firᵃ Portaꝛ eiusdem Maneꝛ . per idem
   temp⁹.   .   .   .   . xiij. ꝛ .iiij. ꝺ.
   Smᵃ totał istius Maneꝛ .xxxj. lĭ .xv. ꝛ .iij. ꝺ.

---

[1] Now Ministers' Accounts, Bundle 1227, No. 3.

APPENDIX A c.

PETITION OF THE VILLANI OF PENROS AND INQUISITIONS AS TO THEIR CUSTOMS AND SERVICES, 16 EDW. II., A.D. 1322.

Inquisition Ad Quod Damnum, 16 *Edw. II.*, *No.* 40,
Public Record Office.

A ñre seignʳ le Roi ⁊ a son counseil monstrent ses poures vileins de son Maner de Penros en le Countee Dangleseye en Northgales q̃ come eaux par errou del estente du dit Maner ᵛ soient nounduement chargez p an de .xxj. lī .vj. đ. ultre leur due rente ⁊ acostumee auxi come de rente assese des queux deñs unq̃s le dit seignʳ ne nul seignʳ de celes pties auaunt le conqueste ne peus nestoit ne ne deuoit p resoun estre ŝuy, ⁊ mesmes ceaux vileins a leur peticioun nadguers sʳ ceo baille en plement p auisement ñre dit seignʳ ⁊ son counseil eussent briefꝑ de la Chauncelerie a monŝ Esmon Counte Darundel Iustice de Gales a enquerre de cel errour :ᵛ ⁊ li ⁊ son dit counseil sʳ ceo c̃tifier p ses tres :ᵛ ⁊ puis aꝑs pᶦse sʳ ceo p la dite Iustice diligente enqueste en forme de lei ⁊ retʳne duement en la dite Chauncelerie p la quele piert pleinement qil sunt de les ditz deñs p an chargez countre resoun :ᵛ eaux p enchesoun de la morrẏne le leur bestes ⁊ de leur aler nadguers peus la prise de cele enqueste en .e ŝuiz ñre dit Seignʳ countre ses enemẏs ⁊ rebeaux en diners liens ount taunt este empoueriz qil ne ount mẏe este de poair de trouer les coustages a seure sʳ ceo remedie, dount le Chaumbrelein de Caernaruan ⁊ le Viscounte Dangleseẏe leur fount pʳ ceaux deñs destreindre greuosement pʳ tut leurs temps, issint q̃ si ñre dit seignʳ ⁊ son counseil ne voillent a ceste foiz sʳ ceo

ordener remedie ꞉́ il leur couient lesser leurs ꞓres ꞏꞏ tenementz ꞉·
ꞏꞏ aler mendinauntz pᴿ toutz iours saunz releuer . Ᵽ quoi il
prient au dit seignᴿ ꞏꞏ a son conseil pᴿ Dieu q̃ eaux quise la
dite enqueste ꞏꞏ examiuee ꞉́ voillent ordener qil soient
deschargez de ceaux deꞃls ꝑ an pᴿ le temps passe ꞏꞏ a venir ꞉́
ou qil leur plaise comaunder brief de la Chauncelerie a la
dite Iustice ou a son lieu tenaunt en Northgales a estendre
le dit Maner oue les appᴿtenaunces de nouel ꞉́ issint qil
peussent sᴿ ceo estre mẏs a leur c̃tein des ore en auaunt ꞉́ ꞏꞏ q̃
eaux ne soient mais eu tiele maꞃle greuez ne tᵃuaillez ꞉́ ꞏꞏ q̃ leur
destresces soient pᴿ le ꝑfit du dit seignᴿ relessez ꞉́ q̃ leur
gaignerẏe ꞏꞏ leur viure ne soient arerẏz ou desaitz ꞉́ ꝑ defaute
de succour.

Il semble a Counseil sil plest a Roi q̃ bon ꝫreit q̃ le Maner ,
sut de nouel estendu ꝑ bones ꞏꞏ suffisauntz gentz, issint q̃ ñre
seignᴿ le Roi pusse sauer la v̈ite del extente ꞏꞏ comaunder
outre sa volunte.

Corā Rege.

Veniat Inquiꞩ cū peticõe coram Rege.

Edwardus Dei gr̃a Rex Angꞏ Dñs Hibñ ꞏꞏ Dux Aquiꞇ
dilc̃o ꞏꞏ fideli suo Ed̃o Comiti Arundelꞇ Iustic̃ suo Walꞇ vel
eius locū tenenti in ptibᴣ Northwalꞇ salꞇm. Ex parte villanoᴣ
ñroᴣ de Maꞃlio ñro de Penros in Cõm Angleꞩ noꞓ est ostensum
q̃d cū antecessores sui villani de eodem Maꞃlio temporibᴣ
Principis Walꞇ ꝑ ꞓris ꞏꞏ teñ que iꝓi villani nunc tenent eisdem
Principibᴣ viginti ꞏꞏ unam libras ꞏꞏ sex denaꞃ ꝑ om̃imodis
consuetudinibᴣ ꞏꞏ ꝫuiciis ꞇm soluere consueuissent ac post
conquestū ꞓre Walꞇ consuetudines ꞏꞏ ꝫuicia ꝑdc̃a ad quadraginta
ꞏꞏ duas libꞃ ꞏꞏ duodecim denarios ꝑ Ministros d̃ni Ē quondā
Regis Angꞏ patris [ñri] erronice extensa fuissent ac etiam
supoꞃlata . ꞏꞏ licet ad ꝑsecuc̃oem villanoᴣ ꝑdc̃oᴣ idem pater ñr
nuꝑ Iustic̃ suo ꞏꞏre ꝑdc̃e ꝑ bꞃe s̨uū mandasset q̃d de errore ꞃito

28

in faciendo extentam p̄dc̄am inquisiuisset pleni⁹ veritatem
ip̄mq̟ p̄rem nr̄m inde c̄tificasset ut idem pater n̄r dc̄is villanis
iusticiam fieri fecisset in hac pte ꞓ p̄dc̄us tamen Iustic̄ p̄missa
fac̄e non curauit, p quod dc̄i villani de viginti ꞇ una libr̄ ꞇ sex
denar̄ ult* rectam ꞇ antiquā extentam annuatim a tempore
extente p̄dc̄e sic erronice fc̄e ad sc*cm nr̄m de Kaernaruan
indebite onerant^r, ꞇ p eisdem viginti ꞇ una libr̄ ꞇ sex denar̄
nob ad idem sc*cm reddend g*uil̄ distringunt^r ꞇ ea occōne
inquietant^r min⁹ iuste in ip̄oꝫ villanoꝫ dispendiū non modicū
ꞇ iacturam . Nolentes q̄d ip̄i villani indebite p̄grauent^r in hac
parte . Vob mandam⁹ q̄d p inquisicōem p vos si necesse fuit
inde faciend ꞇ aliis viis ꞇ modis quibꞩ potitis vos pleni⁹ in-
formetis quantū videlicet antecessores villanoꝫ p̄dc̄oꝫ p consuetudinibꞩ ꞇ s̄uiciis suis ante conquestū p̄dc̄m dederint ꞇ
quo tempore extenta p̄dc̄a fc̄a fuit ꞇ p quos ꞇ qualil̄ ꞇ quo
modo, ꞇ utrū erronice fc̄a fuit ut p̄dc̄m est ꞓ p quod ip̄i villani
de p̄dc̄is viginti ꞇ una libr̄ ꞇ sex denar̄ exon̄ari debeant nec-
ne . Et cū sup p̄missis eritis pleni⁹ informati nos de in-
formacōe illa sub sigillo v̄ro distincte ꞇ apte sine dilone
reddatis c̄tiores hoc br̄e nob remittentes ut ultius p̄fatis
villanis sup p̄missis fieri faciam⁹ quod de consilio n̄ro fore
viderim⁹ faciend . T̄ me ip̄o apud Eboꝫ . xviij die Maii anno
1322.

P peticōem de consilio.

Inquisicio facta coram Thoma de Wynnesbur̄y tenente
locū d̄ni Edmundi Comitis Arundell̄ Iusticiar̄ Wall̄ in North
Wall̄ apud Penros die Iouis px̄ post fm sc̄i Iacobi Ap̄li anno
regni Reḡ . E . filii Regis . E . sextodecimo, q*ntum videll̄
antecessores villanoꝫ d̄ni Reḡ de Manerio suo de Penros in
Com̄ Angleseye dederūt p consuetudinibꞩ ꞇ seruiciis suis ante
conquestū l̄re Wall̄, ꞇ quo tempe facta fuit extenta eiusdem
Manerii in qua consuetudines ꞇ seruicia eoꝫdem villanoꝫ
post dc̄m conqūestū ad quadraginta ꞇ duas libras ꞇ duo-

App. A c.

A.D.
1322.

decim denarios sterlingoӡ extendebant͞r, ꝉ p quos qualiꞇ ꝉ
quo modo, ꝉ utrum eadem extenta erronice facta fuerit p
quod iꝑi villani de viginti ꝉ una libꝛ̄ ꝉ sex denariis . videꞇt
de medietate quadraginta ꝉ duaӡ libᵃӡ ꝉ duodecim denarioӡ
in bꝛ̄i content͞ exoꝥari debeant nec ne ꞉ʾ p hos iur̄ . Howel
Whẏtꞑ, Tuꝺ ap Leweꝉ, Howel Lippa, Leweꝉ ap Howel,
Eignon ap Ioӡ, Madoc ap Eignon, Edeneuet ap Eignon, Ioӡ
Widel, M̊ꝇdutꞑ Duẏ, Eignon Vaghᵃn, Ioӡ ap Philip ꝉ
Madoc Vaghᵃn. Qui dicūt sup sacr̄m suū q̄d antecessores
dc̄oӡ villanoӡ ꝺni Reḡ de Manerio suo de Penros tempibӡ
Principū Walꝉ ante conquestum eiusdem ꝉre soluerūt
eisdem Principibӡ annatim de redditu assīo p sex gaueꝉ
ꝉ dī ꝉre ibidem ꞉ʾ qᵃtuor libras, nouem solidos ꝉ qᵃtuor
denarios preter Ꝭuicia ꝉ consuetudines eoӡdem que iꝑi
fecerūt p residuo ꝉraӡ suaӡ ibidem ꝉ qᵃtuor carucatis ꝉre
ꝺnice predc̄i Manerii eisdem villanis dudū liberaꞇ . Et dicūt q̄d
predicta seruicia ꝉ consuetudines post predc̄m conquestū ex-
tendebant͞r ad decem ꝉ octo libras, qꞁnqᷓ solidos, duos denarios,
obolū ꝉ qᵃdrantem, ꝉ q̄d Magister Ric̄us de Abyngdoñ clericus
ꝺni Reḡ fecit extentam predc̄oӡ seruicioӡ ꝉ consuetudinū p
duodecī hoīeӡ iur̄ de Coꝳ Angleseẏe, que quidem extenta ita
gᵃuis ꝉ suponerosa facta fuit q̄d nūqᵃm aliquis denarios
sūme in eadem extenta contente leuare potuit hucusqᷣ nec
sūmam illam attingꞋ)e, p viginti solidos ꝉ sex denarios
annuatim . Et q̄d post extentā illam sic fc̄am ꞉ʾ frater
Lewelinus tunc Prior fr̄um Predicatoӡ Bangoꝛ̄ qui associatus
fuit predc̄o Maḡro Ric̄o p dc̄m dꝴm Regem ad extentam
predc̄am faciendam qᷓ iꝑe Magister Ric̄us eundem fr̄em
Lewelinū ad extentam illam facienꝺ non expectauit ꞉ʾ accessit
ad Manerıū de Penros ꝉ fecit unam nouam extentam ꝉ illam
tunc irrotulari fecit simul cū pꞁma extenta in rotulo extente
totiᵖ Coꝳ Angleꝭ . Ita q̄d p errorem extente p prefatū
Lewelinū ꝉ gᵃuitatem ꝉ suponeracōem extente p predc̄nı

30

Petition of the Villani of Penros, 1322.

Magr̄m Ric̄m fact ꞉ʼ supᵃdc̄i villani indebite onerati sunt de App. A c.

A.D.
1322. viginti ꝉ una libra ꝉ sex denariis sterlingoꝗ annuatim.

In cuius rei testimoniū predc̄i Howel, Tuđ, Howel, Leweꝉ, Eignon, Madoc, Edeneuet, Ioꝗ, Mᵓeduth, Eignon, Ioꝗ ꝉ Madoc sigilla sua p̄sentibꝛ apposuerūt, loco die ꝉ anno supradictis.

Cancellaꝛ̄ đni Regis Angꝉ p Iustic̄ Walꝉ. [En-

dorsed.]

Scribatʳ Cam̄aꝛ̄ de Kaernaꝛ̄ q̄d pᵃᵗ . p̄dict demandam quā fac̄ villani Regis de Penros de xxj. lī .vj. đ ultᵃ antiquā extentā . . . . . oꝗ usꝗ in crastino Purificacōis ᵬe Marie . Et inꝑim scrutat extentas de qᶦbꝛ inquisicio facit mencōem ꝉ inde ꝛtificet Thes̄ ꝉ Baroñ de Scᵃcio ad diē p̄dc̄m.

COURT ROLL OF ABERFFRAW, 20 EDW. III., A.D. 1346.

APP. A d.

[20 Edw.
III. A.D.
1346.]

Court Rolls, Bundle 215, No. 13, Public Record Office.

Magnus Turnus Cōmoti de Malt^ith tenͭ apͦd Crucanel die Venͥis pͯ post fm Decolacōis sͨi Ioͪis Baͬte . anno . rͬ . Ē . xx°.

Aͭfrau.

       nicͪ
Atha Loit q̗ . ve . loco q^nq̗ iuͬ.

    +   v. š
Villata q̗ nō . ve . ad iuͬ . Et postea ve . ad pͦš q̃d Rees ap Madyn Esspyn qui attacͪ fuit q̗ fregit pacem in Nunͩ ꝗ t^xit sang̃ de Laurence fregit p^sonā ꝗ euasit a custoͩ portaͬ ꝗ fugit.

   +   +
Rag̃ ꝗ Portaͬ q̗ . nō ͪueͬ attacͪ . Iō in m̃a.
  + vj ͩ + vj. ͩ   xij ͩ   vj. ͩ
Ioꝝ . Eign̄ filii Meur^c ap Iockꝑ Ieu^n ap Teg̃ . Ieu^n ap Teg̃ ap Itͪ vocati nō ve . ad t^rnū.

   iiij. š
Villata p .iiij. conceͭ in m^a.

[12 Sept.
A.D.
1346.]

Magn^o t^n^o Cōmoti de Turkelyn tenͭ apͦd Lanuol die Martis pͯ ante fm Naͭ ͭe Maͬ anno rͬ . xx°.

Penros.

   +
De villata q̗ pt^rbat Cuͬ.

      ij. š
Pͦ)š q̃d Ðd ap Itͪ t^xit sang̃ de Lowargͪ Duy.

32

ca⸱ in carcere

Et q̃d Eigñ Gogh Soykę feloñ fur̃ fuit unū rete p̃cii iiij. đ

de Ieu⸱n ap Deykę.

Cōptū est q̃d villata fr̃ defeñ eo q̃d nō soł ꝑpartē p̃cii

equoȝ cariaḡ exc̃cit⁹.

ij. s̃

Villata ꝑ conceł.

Cōptū est q̃d Atha Ioȝ ꝶ Ðd filii Eigñ Gogh Crethe

deḃent esse aduoc̃ Princ̃ et . r̃ . se ꝶ sedent suꝑ r̃am Eꝑi

aꝑd Thlanderadokę.

APPENDIX A e.

EXTENT OF ABERFFRAW WITH ITS HAMLETS, 13 EDW. III., A.D. 1339.

Chancery Inquisition Post Mortem, 13 Edward III. (2nd nrs.)
No. 58, Public Record Office.

APP. A e.

A.D.
1339.

Edwardus Dei gr̄a Rex Angł Dn̄s Hibn̄ ꝉ Dux Aquiꝉ Iustic̄ suo Northwalł vel eius locū tenenti ibidem . salꞇm . Quia quibusdam c̃tis de causis c̃tiorari volumus sup vero valore Mañii de Aberfrawe cum ptiñ in Northwalł . exceptis una carucata ꞇre ꞇ dimiđ in eodem Mañio que dilc̄us noꝉ Magr̄ Rog̃us de Heytoñ Surigicus ñr tenet ad ꞇminū vite sue ex concessione ñra . quantum videꞇt valeat p annū una cū đnicis . homagiis . ꝰuiciis . redditibƷ . ac aliis exitibƷ ꞇre iuxta verum valorem eiusdem . Voꝉ mandamus q̃d p sacr̄m pboƷ et leg̃ hoīm de balliua v̄ra p quos rei v̄itas melius sciri poꞇit mañium p̃dc̄m . exceptis dc̄is carucata ꞇre ꞇ dimiđ . in forma p̃dc̄a diligenꞇ extendi fac̄ et extentam illam distincte ꞇ apte fc̄am noꝉ in Cancellar̄ ñram sub sigillo v̄ro ꞇ sigillis eoƷ p quos fc̄a fuꝉit sine dilōne mittatis ꞇ hoc br̄e . T̄ . Edwardo Duce Cornuꝉ ꞇ Comite Cestr̄ fił ñro carissimo . Custode Angł apud Kenyngtoñ .xx. die Febr̄ . anno . r̄ . ñ . ꞇciodecimo.

P br̄e de priuaꞇ sigilł.

[En-
dorsed.]

Execuc̄o istius br̄[is] patet in extenta huic br̄i cōsuta.

Extenta Manerii de Aberfrau in Northwalł, facta apud Caerñ die Sabꝉti p̃x post festum sc̄i Gregorii anno . r̄ . Rꝑ Ē . ꝉcii post conquestum ꞇciodecimo coram Wilꞇmo de Shaldc-forde locum tenente đni Ric̄i Comitis Arundelꞇ Iustic̄ đni

34

Regis in Northwalł . virtute cuiusdam br̄is eisdem ¹ Iustic̃ v̄l
eius locū tenenti de Cancellar̄ Angł directi :′ p̄ sacr̄m Kenewric
ap Griffutħ . Ienaf ap Yereward . Griffutħ ap Dauid Vagh*n .
Howeli ap Leweł, Griffutħ ap Dauid Gethyn . Ieuan ap Howel .
Eignon Terrioc . Edeneuet Gogh . Howel ap Dauid ap Roppert .
Ieuan ap Phelip . Blethyn ap Madoc . ꝉ Kenewric ap Eignon
de Coñ Angleꝫ—Qui dicunt sup sacr̄m suū q̃d sunt in
Manerio de Aberfrau sunt qⁱnꝙ carucate terre . De quibꝫ
Magisł Roꝗꝰus de Heytone tenet unam carucatam ꝑre ꝉ
dimiđ . et s . . . . ꝑre ꝉ dī . que valent p̄ annū
.Cv. ꝫ . videłt quełt carucata .xxx. ꝫ—Item dic̃ q̃d sunt
ibidem . iij . Molenđ que valent p̄ annū .ix. lī—Item . . . .
p̄ annū .xiij. ꝫ .iiij. đ . It̄ .j. piscaria que valet .ij. ꝫ.—Item
de redditu libere tenentiū ibidem xxix. ꝫ .viij. đ—It̄ de
redditu tenentiū de Bodeueur̄ ptiñ eidem Manerio .xv. ꝫ .xj. đ.
—Item de redditu liꝭe tenentiū de Hameletto de Trewaspatⁱkꝑ
.x. ꝫ.—Item de villanis eiusdem ville de Tunkꝑ v. ꝫ .vj. đ—
Item de eisdem villanis p̄ farina, butiro, lacte ꝉ opac̃onibꝫ
xiij. ꝫ .vij. đ . oꝭ—Item de Hameletto de Trefberwytħ huic
Manerio annexo de redditu assiso ij villanoꝫ .ix. ꝫ .viij. đ.
Item de . iiijᵒʳ cronocis farine ordei .v. ꝫ .iiij. d.—It̄ de
ñltonibꝫ .iiij. ꝫ .vj. đ.—Item de .ix. agnis xviij. đ—It̄ de
eisdem villanis p̄ butiro .ij. ꝫ .iiij. đ.—Item de C̄iiij. ͯͯ ouis
.vij. đ.—It̄ de .ix. gallinis .ix. đ.—It̄ de dc̃is .ix. hoñibꝫ p̄
opac̃onibꝫ de .Clxj. diei .xxxvj. ꝫ .ij. đ . oꝭ.

Smᵃ .xxj. lī .xv. ꝫ .xj. đ.

Hamelettum de Dynthlodan eidem Manerio de Aberfrau
annexū . Ð redditu assiso .j. villani ibidem .ij. ꝫ. Videłt de
Dauid de Hiꝭnico p̄ medietate blađ ꝉ lac̄ quod . . . .
Mꝰaonnytħ—Item de filiis Gregorii ap Lewelyn p̄ .j. cronoko
fr̄i ꝉ . iiijᵒʳ cronocis farine aueñ :′ viij. ꝫ .vj. đ. De eisdem p̄ .iij.
multonibꝫ .xij. đ. De eisdem . . . De eisdem p̄ Butiro .vj. đ.—

---

¹ So in the Record.

App. A e.

A.D.
1339.

APP. A e.

A.D.
1339.

De eisdem p̄ .xl. ouis .j. đ .‚oƀ—De eisdem p̄. vj. gallinis .vj. đ.
De eisdem p̄ opaconibȝ .xxx. dierū .iij. ꝟ .ix. đ . De Pelipaɼ
p̄ dĩ . . . cronoci farine ordei . medietate .j. m̃ltonis . medieꞇ .j.
agñi ˙. p̄ .x Cunnis butiɼ ꝉ p̄ medietaꞇ .j. galline .xiij. đ . oƀ.
De opaconibȝ eoȝdem vij dieȝ .xj. đ qᵃ.

Smᵃ—xviij. ꝟ .ix. đ qᵃ.

Hameletꞇ de Keuyntreffrau eidem Manerio annexū . De
redditu villanoȝ eiusdem ville .iij. ꝟ .iiij. đ . De eisdem p̄ .j.
agno ꝉ dĩ . p̄ butiɼ . De . . . . . . gallinis ꝉ dĩ . p̄ Estor
blađ . de opaconibȝ .iij. dieȝ xviij. đ . oƀ . Et respondent de
M꙰ionytħ cum villanis de Trefberwytħ.

Smᵃ—iiij. ꝟ .x. đ . oƀ.

Villani de Aberfrau . De redditu assiso d̄c̄oȝ villanoȝ
.viij. ꝟ .viij. đ . De eisdem de .x. cronoc̄ ꝉ dĩ frĩ . De .vij.
cronoc̄ farine aueñ, et de . . . . . . xlviij. ꝟ .vij. đ . De .ix.
villanis eiusdem ville p̄ lacte .iiijᵒʳ. vacc̄ .iiijᵒʳ m̃ltoñ ꝉ dĩ .ix.
agñ . Butiɼ .Cxl. ouis ꝉ .xxvij. gallinis .xvj. ꝟ . . . . . . tribȝ
m̃ltonibȝ .vj. agnis . ix. gallinis . butiɼ ꝉ .C. ouis v. ꝟ .j. đ—
Item sunt in d̄c̄a villa .ix. villani . De quibȝ .xxvij. gallinis
.ij. ꝟ . . . đ . . . . . . iij. dieȝ ad serclanđ blađ .ij. ꝟ .iiij. đ .
q̣ quiꞇt eoȝ recepit p̄ diem .j. prandium—De eisdem villanis
p̄ igne ꝉ stramie in Cuɼ đni . . . . . . in autumpno de .CCC.
hom̃ibȝ . quos xvj. villani de Manerio de Aberfrau inuenient .

Etde.iiij.hom̃ibȝ quos villani forinceci de Cantredo [invenient.]
De hom̃ibȝ ꝉ equis ad hercianđ p̄ .j. diem .Lxxv. ꝟ . caꝑ p̄ diem
.j. đ . oƀ.—Item de d̄c̄is villanis de Aberfrau p̄ .x. cronocis
. . . . . De pastʳa .xx. ꝟ . De p̄quisiꞇ Cuɼ .xl. ꝟ.

Smᵃ .xvj. lĩ .xviij. đ.

Smᵃ toˡ .xxxix. ħ .xij. đ . oƀ . qᵃ.

In cuiꝰ rei testimoniū p̃d̄c̄i Iuɼ huic [ext]en[te] sigilla sua
apposuerunt.

Daꞇ apud Caerñ die ꝉ anno supᵃd̄c̄is.

36

APPENDIX A f.

ASSESSMENT TO A FIFTEENTH OF ABERFFRAW WITH ITS HAMLETS [A.D. 1320-1340].

Treasury of Receipt, Miscell. $\frac{QR}{4}$, *Public Record Office.*[1]

Rotul⁹ taxacōnis oīum bono₃ mobiliū īpraliū çmoti
Maltraeth ad . xvᵃᵐ . ptē p taxatoř videl₃ . p Tuderū Gam ꝗ
Dđ Gethyn.

Iᵉ rotul⁹ exʳ cū nouo ꝗ noïa cōcordant.

*   *   *

Villa Aƀfrau cū suis Hamletɇ.

Io₃ Voel ħt in bōis taxatɇ vid₃—xx. boū . ꝓ c⁹l₃ v. ꝑ—
xvj. vac̃ . ꝓ . c⁹l₃ iij. ꝑ .iiij đ .—v. eq⁰s ꝓ . c⁹l₃ .v. ꝑ .—iiij.
aůia .iij. āno₃ . ꝓ . c⁹l₃ ij. ꝑ .vj. đ . iiij aůia .ij. āno₃ . ꝓ .
c⁹l₃ .ij. ꝑ .xx. oues . ꝓ .ij. vac̃ . ꝑ .vj. ꝑ .viij. đ—xx. Cř . fru .
ꝓ . c⁹l₃ ij. ꝑ .vj. đ .xl. Cř . fař . aue . ꝓ c⁹l₃ .ij. ꝑ .—vj. Cř .
piꝑ ꝗ orđ . ꝓ cui⁹b₃—xvj. đ.

Dđ ap Ẏkeneẏn ħt in bo . tax .iiij. bou . ꝓ . c⁹l₃ .v. ꝑ .ix.
vac̃ . ꝓ . c⁹l₃ iij. ꝑ .iij. đ—vj. eq⁰s . ꝓ . c⁹l₃ .v. ꝑ .—ij. aůia
.iij. āno₃ . ꝓ . c⁹l₃ .ij. ꝑ .vj. đ .—iij. aůia .ij. āno₃ . ꝓ . c⁹l₃
.ij. ꝑ .—xxiij oues . ꝓ . c⁹l₃ .vj. đ—iij. Cř . fru . ꝓ . c⁹l₃
ij. ꝑ .vj. đ—iiij. Cř . orđ . ꝓ c⁹l₃ xvj. đ .—xiiij. Cř . fař .
aue . ꝓ . c⁹l₃ .ij. ꝑ.

Mađ ap Dđ ħt in bo . tax̃ .iij. vac̃ . ꝓ . c⁹l₃ .iij. ꝑ .iiij. đ .
—j. aůiū .iij. āno₃ . ꝓ ij. ꝑ .vj. đ—j. aůiū .ij. āno₃ . ꝓ .ij. ꝑ—
j. Cř . fař . ꝓ .ij. ꝑ.

Eẏnō ap G̃g̃ ħt in bo . tax̃ .iij. boū ꝓ . c⁹l₃ .v: ꝑ .—j.
eqū . ꝓ .v. ꝑ—iiij. vac̃ . ꝓ . c⁹l₃ .iij. ꝑ .iiij. đ .—j. Cř . fru .
ꝓ .ij. ꝑ .vj. đ .—ij. Cř . fař . aue . ꝓ c⁹l₃ .ij. ꝑ.

---

[1] Now Lay Subsidy 242¹⁄₄².

Sᵃ .iiij. š .v. đ. ob. — Iož Goch ħt in bo . tax̃ .iij. boũ . ꝑ cᵒlȝ .v. s .—iij eqᵒs ꝑ cᵒlȝ .v. s̃ .—iij. vac̃ ꝑ cᵒlȝ .iij. s̃ .iiij. đ .—xij. oues . ꝑ . cᵒlȝ vj. đ .—ij. Cr̃ . fru . ꝑ . cᵒlȝ .ij. s̃ .vj. đ .—vj. Cr̃ . far̃ . aue . ꝑ . cᵒlȝ .ij. s̃ .—ij. aũia .ij. ãnož ꝑ cᵒlȝ .ij. s̃.

Sᵃ—ij. s̃. — Ux̃ G̃g̃ ap Kyff ħt in bo . tax̃ .j. bou . ꝑ .v. s̃.—j. iumẽtũ . ꝑ .v. s̃ .—j. aũiũ .iij. ãnož . ꝑ .ij. s̃. vj. đ .—j. aũiũ .ij. ãnož . ꝑ .ij. s̃ .—ij. vac . ꝑ . cᵒlȝ .iij. s̃ .iiij. đ .—j. Cr̃ fru . ꝑ .ij. s̃ .vj. đ .—iij. Cr̃ . far̃ . aue . ꝑ . cᵒlȝ . ij. s̃.

Sᵃ .ij. s̃. — Dđ Voel ħt ĩ bo . tax̃ .ij. boũ ꝑ . cᵒlȝ .v. s̃—j. eqũ . ꝑ .v. s̃ .—ij. vac̃ . ꝑ cᵒlȝ .iij. s̃ .iiij. đ . Diᵐ . Cr̃ . fru . ꝑ .xv. đ —iij. Cr̃ . far̃ . aue . ꝑ . cᵒlȝ .ij. s̃.

Sᵃ .xvj. đ. — Mađ ap Ẏgwascric ħt in bo . tax̃ .ij. eqᵒs . ꝑ . cᵒlȝ .v. s̃ . —j. boũ . ꝑ .v. s̃ .—Diᵐ . Cr̃ . fru . ꝑ .xv. đ—ij. Cr̃ far̃ . aue . ꝑ . cᵒlȝ .ij. s̃.

Sᵃ .xxij. s̃ .j. đ. — Eẏnõ ap Ioke ħt in boñ tax̃ . vidȝ .xvj. boũ . ꝑ cᵒlȝ .v. s̃ .viij. đ .—vj. eqᵒs ꝑ . cᵒlȝ .v. s̃ .—xv. vac̃ ꝑ . cᵒlȝ .iij. s̃ .iiij. đ .—xij. aũia .iij. ãnož . ꝑ , cᵒlȝ .ij. s̃ .vj. đ .—xv. oues ꝑ cᵒlȝ . ꝑ .v. s̃ .—xij. Cr̃ fru . ꝑ . cᵒlȝ .ij. s̃ .vj. đ .—xl. Cr̃ . far̃ . aue . ꝑ cᵒlȝ .ij. s̃—xij. Cr̃ . pis̃ . ⁊ orđ . ꝑ . cᵒlȝ .xvj. đ.

Sᵃ iij. s̃. ob. — Ymetyr̃ ħt in bo . tax̃ .iij. boũ . ꝑ cᵒlȝ—v. s̃ .—j. iumẽtũ . ꝑ .v. s̃—.iiij. vac̃ . ꝑ . cᵒlȝ .iij. s̃ .iiij. đ—.j. aũiũ .ij. ãnož . ꝑ .ij. s̃—v. oues ꝑ—xx. đ—j. Cr̃ . fru . ꝑ .ij. s̃ .vj. đ .—iij. Cr̃ far̃ ꝑ cᵒlȝ .ij. s̃.

Sᵃ .xviij. đ. — Gwenlł f Ađ ħt in bo . tax .j. boũ . ꝑ .v. s̃—j. iumẽtũ ꝑ .v. s̃ .—ij. vac̃ ꝑ cᵒlȝ .iij. s̃ .iiij. đ .—ij. aũia .ij. ãnož . ꝑ . cᵒlȝ—ij. s̃—.j. Cr̃ . far̃ . ꝑ .ij. s̃.

Sᵃ .iiij. s̃. — Dđ ap Ioke ħt in bo . tax .ij. boũ . ꝑ . cᵒlȝ .v. s̃—iij. eqᵒs ꝑ cᵒlȝ .v. s̃ .—v. vac̃ . ꝑ cᵒlȝ iij. s̃ .iiij. đ —.ij. Cr̃ . fru . ꝑ cᵒlȝ .ij. s̃ .vj. đ—.vj. Cr̃ far̃ aue . ꝑ cᵒlȝ .ij. s̃ —.j. Cr̃ orđ . ꝑ .xvj. đ.

Sᵃ .xxij. đ. — Mađ ap Ioke ħt in bo . tax̃ .j. bou . ꝑ .v. s̃—.j. iumẽtũ ꝑ .v. s̃ iij vac̃ ꝑ cᵒlȝ iij. s̃ .iiij. đ . Diᵐ Cr̃ . fru . ꝑ .xv. đ—iij. Cr̃ far̃ aue . ꝑ cᵒlȝ ij. s̃.

Pħ Amluch ħt in bo . tax .j boũ . ꝑ .v. s̃—.j. iumẽtũ ꝑ .v. s̃

—iiij. vaꝯ . p̄ . cᵒlƷ iij: ꝝ .iiij. đ—iij. aủia .ij. ānoƷ . p̄ . cᵒlƷ App. A f.

.ij. ꝝ—ix. oues . p̄ . cᵒlƷ .vj. đ—j. Cr̄ . fru . p̄ .ij. ꝝ .vj. đ— Sᵃ .ij. ꝝ

iij. Cr̄ . far . aue . p̄ cᵒlƷ .ij. ꝝ. .x. đ.

Dđ ap M̄led ħt in bo . taꝓ .j. eqũ . p̄ .v. ꝝ—ij. boũ . p̄ .

cᵒlƷ .v. ꝝ—iiij. vaꝯ p̄ . cᵒlƷ .iij. ꝝ. iiij. đ—ij. Cr̄ . fru . p̄ cᵒlƷ Sᵃ iij. ꝝ

.ij. ꝝ .vj. đ—.vj. Cr̄ . far̄ aue . p̄ . cᵒlƷ .ij. ꝝ—.vj. oues p̄ . cᵒlƷ .iij. đ.

.vj. đ.

Sussanaf ħt in bōis taꝓ .v. vaꝯ . p̄ . cᵒlƷ .iij. ꝝ .iiij. đ. Sᵃ xiij.

Dđ ap Gwasbeuno ħt in bo . taꝓ .vj. boũ . p̄ cᵒlƷ .v. ꝝ.— đ. oꝫ.

ij. eqᵒs . p̄ . cᵒlƷ .v. ꝝ.—v. vaꝯ . p̄ . cᵒlƷ .iij. ꝝ .iiij. đ—ij. aủia Sᵃ viij. ꝝ.

.iij. ānoƷ . p̄ cᵒlƷ .ij. ꝝ .vj. đ.—j. aủiũ .ij. ānoƷ . p̄ .ij. ꝝ.—xiiij. oꝫ.

oues . p̄ . cᵒlƷ .vj. đ.—vj. Cr̄ . fru . p̄ . cᵒlƷ .ij. ꝝ .vj. đ—xvj.

Cr̄ far̄ aue . p̄ . cᵒlƷ .ij. ꝝ.—vj. Cr̄ far̄ orđ p̄ cᵒlƷ .xvj. đ.

Matħu ap Dđ ħt in bo . taꝓ .ij. boũ . p̄ cᵒlƷ .v. ꝝ.—j. Sᵃ .xxj.

ium̄tũ . p̄ .v. ꝝ—ij. vaꝯ . p̄ cᵒlƷ .iij. ꝝ .iiij. đ.—diᵐ . Cr̄ . fru . đ. oꝫ.

p̄ .xv. đ—ij. Cr̄ . far̄ . aue . p̄ . cᵒlƷ .ij. ꝝ.

Robẏn ħt in bo . taꝓ .j. boũ . p̄ .v. ꝝ—j. eqũ . p̄ .v. ꝝ.—j.

vaꝯ . p̄ .iij. ꝝ .iiij. đ/—ij. aủia .ij. ānoƷ . p̄ . cᵒlƷ .ij. ꝝ/—j. Cr̄ . Sᵃ .xix.

fru . p̄ .ij. ꝝ .vj. đ/—ij. Cr̄ far̄ . aue . p̄ . clᵒƷ .ij. ꝝ. đ. qᵃđ.

Eẏnō ap Dđ ħt in bo . taꝓ .iiij. bou . p̄ . cᵒlƷ .v. ꝝ—ij. eqᵒs .

p̄ . cᵒlƷ .v. ꝝ—iiij. vaꝯ . p̄ .j. aủiũ .iij. ānoƷ . p̄ .ij. ꝝ .vj. đ.— Sᵃ .v. ꝝ

ij. aủia .ij. ānoƷ . p̄ .ij. ꝝ.—vij. oues . p̄ cᵒlƷ .vj. đ.—iij. Cr̄ . .xj. đ.

fru . p̄ cᵒlƷ .ij. ꝝ .vj. đ—xij. Cr̄ . far̄ . aue . p̄ . cᵒlƷ—ij. ꝝ—.iij.

Cr̄ . orđ p̄ . cᵒlƷ .xvj. đ.

Eẏnō ap Ẏdrẏn ħt in bo . taꝓ .iiij. vaꝯ . p̄ cᵒlƷ .iij. ꝝ .iiij. đ/

j. aủiũ .iij. ānoƷ p̄ .ij. ꝝ .vj. đ .ij. aủia .ij. anoƷ .ij. ꝝ j. Cr̄ . Sᵃ .xxj.

fru . p̄ .ij. ꝝ .vj. đ/ij. Cr̄ . far̄ . aue . p̄ . cᵒlƷ . ij. ꝝ. đ.

IoƷ ap Pħ ħt ı . bo . taꝓ .j. eqũ . p̄ .v. ꝝ/.ij. vaꝯ . p̄ . cᵒlƷ

.iij. ꝝ .iiij. đ/ij. aủia .ij. ānoƷ . p̄ cᵒlƷ .ij. ꝝ. j. Cr̄ . fru . p̄ Sᵃ .xvij.

.ij. ꝝ—j. Cr̄ far̄ aue . ꝯ . diᵒ . p̄ .iij. ꝝ. đ.

Pħ ap Ađ ħt ı bo . taꝓ .j. eqũ . p̄ .v. ꝝ .iiij. vaꝯ . p̄ cᵒlƷ

.iij. ꝝ .iiij. đ—.j. bou . p̄ .v. ꝝ.—xij. oues p̄ cᵒlƷ .vj. đ .j. Cr̄ . Sᵃ .ij. ꝝ

frũ . p̄ .ij. ꝝ .vj. đ./ij. Cr̄ . far̄ . aue . p̄ cᵒlƷ .ij. ꝝ. .iiij. đ. õ.

qᵃ.

Gwtanes ħt in bo . taꝓ .iiij. vaꝯ . p̄ .cᵒlƷ .iij. ꝝ .iiij. đ. / ij. Sᵃxxiij.đ.

Assessment to a Fifteenth of Aberffraw, 1320-40.

[A.D.
1320–
1340.]

Sᵃ .ij. ꝥ
.iiij. đ.

Sᵃ .iij. ꝥ
.vij. đ.

Sᵃ .ij. ꝥ
.v. đ. õ.

Sᵃ .xxij.
đ.

Sᵃ .iiij. ꝥ
.vij. đ.

Smᵃ .iiij.
ꝥ.

Sᵃ.xvj. đ.

Sᵃ .xij. đ.

Sᵃ iiij. ꝥ
.ij. đ.

Sᵃ .iiij. ꝥ
.iij. đ. õ.

iuñta . ꝥ . cᵒlȝ .v. ꝥ .j. auiu .ij. ānoȝ . ꝥ .ij. ꝥ.—j. Cř fař . c̃ diᵒ . ꝥ .iij. ꝥ.

Ykedẏn ħt in bo . tax̃ .j. boũ . ꝥ .v. ꝥ .j. iuñtũ . ꝥ .v. ꝥ / iiij. vac̃ . ꝥ .iij. ꝥ .iiij. đ. xiiij. oues ꝥ cᵒlȝ .vj. đ .j. Cř fru ꝥ .ij. ꝥ .vj. đ / j. Cř . fař . ꝥ .ij. ꝥ.

Kediuoř ħt ī bo . tax .j. boũ . ꝥ .v. ꝥ. / iiij. eqᵒs . ꝥ .v. ꝥ.— ij. vac̃ . ꝥ . cᵒlȝ .iij. ꝥ .iiij. đ . ij auiu .ij. ānoȝ . ꝥ . cᵒlȝ . ij. ꝥ. —xiij. oues ꝥ cᵒlȝ .vj. đ. / dimᵐ. Cř fru . ꝥ .xv. đ. / .iiij. Cř fař aue . ꝥ. .ij. ꝥ.

Yfromarth ħt ī bo . tax̃ .ij. iuñta . ꝥ . cᵒlȝ .v. ꝥ. / iij. vac̃ ꝥ . cᵒlȝ .iij. ꝥ .iiij. đ / ij. auia .ij. āñoȝ . ꝥ . cᵒlȝ .ij. ꝥ./ ij. auĩa .iiij. āno̊ȝ . ꝥ cᵒlȝ .ij. ꝥ .vj. đ. j Cř . fru . c̃ diᵒ . ꝥ .iij. ꝥ .ix. đ. / j. Cř . c̃ diᵒ fař . ꝥ .iij. ꝥ. / ij. oues . ꝥ .xij. đ.

Ienᵃ ap Mađ Vichᵃn ħt ī . bo . tax .j. iuñtũ . ꝥ .v. ꝥ j. boũ ꝥ .v. ꝥ. / iiij. auia .ij. āñoȝ . ꝥ . cᵒlȝ .ij. ꝥ. / iiij. oues ꝥ cᵒlȝ .vj. đ. j. Cř . fru . ꝥ .ij. ꝥ vj. đ. / iiij. fař . aue . ꝥ . cᵒlȝ .ij. ꝥ.

Ioř ap Iok� ħt ī bo . tax̃ .j. boũ . ꝥ .v. ꝥ / ij. eqᵒs . ꝥ . cᵒlȝ .v. ꝥ./v. vac̃ . ꝥ . cᵒlȝ .iij. ꝥ .iiij. đ. iij. auĩa .ij. āno̊ȝ . ꝥ . cᵒlȝ .ij. ꝥ / xv. oues ꝥ . cᵒlȝ .vj. đ. j. Cř fru . ꝥ .ij. ꝥ .vj. đ. iij. Cř fař aue ꝥ . cᵒlȝ .ij. ꝥ.

Feydath ħt in bo . tax̃ .j. iuñtũ . ꝥ .v. ꝥ / j. boũ . ꝥ .v. ꝥ. v. vac̃ . ꝥ cᵒlȝ .iij. ꝥ .iiij. đ. / iij. auĩa .ij. āno̊ȝ . ꝥ . cᵒlȝ .ij. ꝥ .xxiij. oues . ꝥ . cᵒlȝ .vj. đ. iij. Cř . fru . ꝥ cᵒlȝ .ij. ꝥ .vj. đ. / iiij. Cř fař aue . ꝥ cᵒlȝ .ij. ꝥ.

Ioȝ ap Blеđ ħt in bo . tax̃ .j. iuñtũ ꝥ .v. ꝥ. ij. vac̃ . ꝥ . cᵒlȝ .iij. ꝥ .iiij. đ .iij. auĩa .ij. āno̊ȝ ꝥ cᵒlȝ .ij. ꝥ. j. Cř . fru . ꝥ .ij. ꝥ .vj. đ.

Mađ ap Bleđ ħt ī bo . tax̃ .j. iuñtũ ꝥ .v. ꝥ. / ij. vac̃ . ꝥ . cᵒlȝ .iij. ꝥ .iiij. đ . j. auĩu .ij. āno̊ȝ . ꝥ .ij. ꝥ. dimᵐ. Cř fru . ꝥ .xv. đ.

Ykest ħt Ī . bo . tax .ij. boũ . ꝥ .v. ꝥ. / ij. iuñta ꝥ .v. ꝥ. / iij. vac̃ ꝥ . cᵒlȝ .iij. ꝥ .iiij. đ auĩa .ij. āno̊ȝ ꝥ cᵒlȝ .ij. ꝥ. / xxiiij. oues . ꝥ cᵒlȝ .vj. đ. j. Cř fru . ꝥ .ij. ꝥ .vj. đ. / v. Cř fař aue . ꝥ cᵒlȝ .ij. ꝥ.

Dđ ap Iokᵨ lȝ ī bo . tax .ij. eqᵒs . ꝥ .v. ꝥ. / ij. boũ . ꝥ .v. ꝥ /

App. A f.

[A.D.
1320–
1340.]

v. vaē . p̄ . cᵒlȝ .iij. ȝ .iiij. đ.   xxx. oues p̄ cᵒlȝ .vj. đ.   j. Cr̄

fru . p̄ .ij. ȝ .vj. đ. / v. Cr̄ far̄ aue . p̄ cᵒlȝ .ij. ȝ.

Ioȝ ap Elidyr̄ h̄t in bo . tax .iiij. boū . p̄ . cᵒlȝ .ᴠ. ȝ. / iij.

eqᵒs . p̄ . cᵒlȝ .v. ȝ. / ij. aûia .ij. ānoȥ . p̄ . cᵒlȝ .ij. ȝ.—x. oues .   Sᵃ vij. ȝ

p̄ . cᵒlȝ .vj. đ. / vj. Cr̄ . fru . p̄ . cᵒlȝ .ij. ȝ .vj. đ. / .ix. Cr̄ ʹfar̄   j. đ.

aue . p̄ . cᵒlȝ .ij. ȝ. / vj. vaē p̄ . cᵒlȝ .iiij. ȝ .iiij. đ. / ij. Cr̄ piȝ

ꝧ orđ . p̄ cᵒlȝ .xvj. đ. / uteñ . p̄ .vj. ȝ .viij. đ.

Dđ Du h̄t ī bo . taẍ .j. ium̄tū . p̄ .v. ȝ / .ij. vaē . p̄ . cᵒlȝ   Sᵃ ij. ȝ

.iiij. ȝ .iiij. đ. / ij. boū . p̄ cᵒlȝ .v. ȝ. / iiij. aûia .ij. ānoȥ . p̄ .   .vj đ.

cᵒlȝ .ij. ȝ. / x. oues . p̄ . cᵒlȝ .vj. đ. / ij. Cr̄ far̄ aue . p̄ cᵒlȝ .ij. ȝ.

Utē . p̄ .xij. đ.

Mađ ap Yriskynit hȝ ī bôis taẍ .j. eqū . p̄ .v. ȝ. / iij. vaē .   Sᵃ .xvij.

p̄ cᵒlȝ .iij. ȝ .iiij. đ / .iiij. Cr̄ far̄ . aue . p̄ cᵒlȝ .ij. ȝ.   Uteñ p̄   đ. oᵬ.

.xij. đ.

Gyllabrýdi h̄t in bo . taẍ .ij. boū . p̄ cᵒlȝ .v. ȝ. / j. ium̄tū   Sᵃ iiij. ȝ .j.

p̄ .v. ȝ / v. vaē . p̄ . cᵒlȝ .iij. ȝ .iiij. đ.   v. oues . p̄ . cᵒlȝ .vj. đ.   đ. ŏ.

j. Cr̄ . fru . p̄ . ij. ȝ .vj. đ.   j. Cr̄ . orđ . p̄.xv. đ. / iiij. Cr̄ far̄

aue . p̄ cᵒlȝ .ij. ȝ.   Uteñ . p̄ .xij. đ.

Ioȥ ap Deikҽ h̄t ī bo . taẍ .ij. bou . p̄ . cᵒlȝ .v. ȝ. / iij.

ium̄ta . p̄ . cᵒlȝ .v. ȝ. / viij. vaē . p̄ cᵒlȝ .iij. ȝ .iiij. đ.   j. aûiū   Sᵃ .v. ȝ.

.iij. ānoȥ . p̄ .ij. ȝ .vj. đ. / ix. oues . p̄ . cᵒlȝ .vj. đ. / ij. Cr̄ . fru .

p̄ . cᵒlȝ .ij. ȝ. vj. đ. / v. Cr̄ far̄ aue . p̄ . cᵒlȝ .ij. ȝ. / j. Cr̄ orđ .

p̄ .xvj. đ.

Ieⁿ Du h̄t ī bo . tax .ij. vaē . p̄ . cᵒlȝ .iij. ȝ .iiij. đ / iij.   Sᵃ .xiij.

aûia .ij. ānoȥ . p̄ cᵒlȝ .ij. ȝ   .v. oues . p̄ cᵒlȝ .vj. đ. / j Cr̄ c̃   đ. oᵬ.

diᵒ. far̄ . p̄ .iij. ȝ.

Eynō ap Deikҽ h̄t in bo . taẍ .j. boū . p̄ .v. ȝ. / ij. ium̄ta .

p̄ . cᵒlȝ .v. ȝ. / v. vaē . p̄ cᵒlȝ .iij. ȝ .iiij. đ.   j. aûiū .iij. ānoȥ   Sᵃ .iiij. ȝ

p̄ .ij. ȝ / xlvj. oues . p̄ cᵒlȝ .vj. đ.   Uteñ .iij. ȝ .iiij. đ / iij. Cr̄   .xj. đ. oᵬ.

fru . p̄ cᵒlȝ .ij. ȝ .vj. đ. / iij. Cr̄ . far̄ aue . p̄ cᵒlȝ .ij. ȝ.   j. Cr̄ .

orđ p̄ .xvj. đ.

Ađ ap Eynō h̄t ī bo . tax .j. boū . p̄ .v. ȝ. / ij. eqᵒs p̄ . cᵒlȝ   Sᵃ .v. ȝ

.v. ȝ / viij. vaē p̄ cᵒlȝ .iij. ȝ .iiij. đ.   L . oues . p̄ . cᵒlȝ .vj. đ.   vj. đ

App. A f.

Sᵃ .iiij. š
.iiij. đ.
oᵬ.

Uteñ . ꝓ .iij. š. / j. Cr̃ . frn . c̃ diᵒ. ꝓ iij. š .ix. đ / iij. Cr̃ far̃
aue . ꝓ cᵒlȝ .ij. š. ij. Cr̃ . orđ . ꝓ .xvj. đ.

Dđ ap Ađ ħt in bo . tax̃ .iij. boũ . ꝓ . cᵒlȝ .v. š. j. eqũ .
ꝓ .v. š / iiij. vac̃ . ꝓ cᵒlȝ .iij. š .iiij. đ. ij. aũia .iij. ãnoȝ . ꝓ
cᵒlȝ .ij. š .vj. đ / xx. oues . ꝓ .cᵒlȝ .vj. đ ' Uteñ . ꝓ .xij. đ / ij.
Cr̃ fru . ꝓ . cᵒlȝ .ij. š .vj. đ / v. Cr̃ far̃ aue . ꝓ cᵒlȝ ij. š. / orđ
ꝓ xvj. [đ].

Sᵃ vj. š
.iij. đ.

Mađ Cor ħt ĩ bo . tax̃ .ij. boũ . ꝓ . cᵒlȝ .v. š / iiij. iuñita . ꝓ
cᵒlȝ .v. š. / viij. vac̃ . ꝓ cᵒlȝ .iij. š .iiij. đ. / iij. aũia .ij. ãnoȝ .
ꝓ . cᵒlȝ .ij. š. / xliiij. oues . ꝓ . cᵒlȝ .vj. đ. / Uteñ . ꝓ .ij. š. j.
Cr̃ fru . ꝓ .ij. š .vj. đ. / j. Cr̃ . orđ ꝓ .xvj. [đ] / iiij. Cr̃ far̃ aue .
ꝓ cᵒlȝ .ij. š.

Sᵃ iij. š
.v. đ.

Filii Ieᶜn Gam ħt in bo . tax̃ .ij. boũ . ꝓ .v. š. j. iuñtũ
ꝓ .v. š / v. vac̃ . ꝓ . cᵒlȝ . iij. š .iiij. đ. xx. oues ꝓ cᵒlȝ .vj. đ/.
.iiij. Cr̃ . far̃ aue . ꝓ . cᵒlȝ .ij. š. diᵐ. Cr̃ . fru . ꝓ .xv. đ.

Sᵃ xiiij.
đ. qᵃ.

Eynõ ap Ađ ħt in bo . tax̃ .ij. vac̃ . ꝓ . cᵒlȝ .iij. š .iiij. đ.
j. aũiũ .ij. ãnoȝ ꝓ ij. š. vij. oues . ꝓ cᵒlȝ .vj. đ. diᵐ. Cr̃ .
fru . ꝓ .xv. đ. j. Cr̃ . orđ . ꝓ .xv. đ. j. Cr̃ far̃ . c̃ diᵒ . ꝓ
.iij. š.

Sᵃ .ij. š
.x. đ.

Elydir ħt in bo . tax̃ .j. boũ . ꝓ .v. š / iiij. vac̃ . ꝓ . cᵒlȝ
.iij. š .iiij. đ / ij. aũia ij. ãnoȝ ꝓ cᵒlȝ .ij. š / xx. oues ꝓ cᵒlȝ
.vj. đ. / Uteñ . ꝓ .xij. đ / j. Cr̃ . frũ . ꝓ .ij. š .vj. đ / iij. Cr̃ .
far̃ . aue . ꝓ .cᵒlȝ .ij. š.

Sᵃ .iij. š
.ij. đ.

Mađ ap Eynõ ħt in bo . tax̃ .j. boũ . ꝓ v. š .iiij. vac̃ . ꝓ
cᵒlȝ .iij. š .iiij. đ / .j. iuñtũ . ꝓ .v. š .ij. aũia .ij. ãnoȝ . ꝓ cᵒlȝ
.ij. š. / xl. oues . ꝓ cᵒlȝ .vj. đ . / v. Cr̃ far̃ . aue . ꝓ cᵒlȝ .ij. s .
/ iiij. Cr̃ . orđ . ꝓ cᵒlȝ .xvj. đ.

Sᵃ j. š .x.
đ.

Mađ ap Ioȝ ħt in bo . tax̃ .j. iuñtũ . ꝓ v. š / .iiij. vac̃ . ꝓ
cᵒlȝ .iij. š .iiij. đ / iij. aũia .ij. ãnoȝ ꝓ cᵒlȝ .ij. š . / xx. oues .
ꝓ cᵒlȝ .vj. đ . / j. Cr̃ . orđ . ꝓ .xvj. đ / .iiij. Cr̃ . far̃ . ꝓ cᵒlȝ
.ij. š.

Sᵃ iiij. š
.vij. đ.

Dđ ap Teg̃ ħt in bo . tax̃ .ij. boũ . ꝓ cᵒlȝ .v. š . / j. eqᵒs
ꝓ cᵒlȝ .v. š. / ij. vac̃ . ꝓ cᵒlȝ .iij. š .iiij. đ .iij. aũia .ij. ãnoȝ .
ꝓ . cᵒlȝ .ij. š. / xx. oues . ꝓ cᵒlȝ .vj. đ / .iij. Cr̃ . fru . c̃ diᵒ . ꝓ

.ij. s̃ .vj. đ .vj. Cr̃ . far̃ aue . p̃ . c°lȝ .ij. s̃ .j. Cr̃ orđ . c̃ diᵒ .
p̃ .ij. s̃.

Ioȝ ap G̃g̃ h̃t in bo . tax̃ .ij. vac̃ . p̃ c°lȝ .iij. s̃ .iiij. đ / .j.
ium̃tū . p̃ .v. s̃ / iiij. auĩa . p̃ . c°lȝ .ij. s̃ .iiij. oues . p̃ c°lȝ Sᵃ .ij. s̃.
.vj. đ / j. Cr̃ fru . p̃ .ij. s̃ .vj. đ .j. Cr̃ orđ c̃ diᵒ . p̃ .ij. s̃ / ij.
Cr̃ . far̃ c̃ . diᵒ . p̃ . c°lȝ .ij. s̃.

Guff ap Ioȝ h̃t in bo . tax̃ / ij. boũ . p̃ . c°lȝ .v. s̃ / j. eqũ Sᵃ .iij. s̃.
p̃ .v. s̃ / j. vac̃ . p̃ .iij. s̃ .iiij. đ.

Gwenlt f. Ygof h̃t in bo . tax̃ / v. vac̃ . p̃ . c°lȝ .iij. s̃ Sᵃ .xxij.
.iiij. đ / ij. auĩa .ij. ānoȝ . p̃ . c°lȝ .ij. s̃ .viij. oues . p̃ . c°lȝ đ.
.vj. đ . / j. Cr̃ . fru . p̃ .ij. s̃ .vj. đ.

Ieᵃn Ameth h̃t in bo . tax̃ .ij. boũ . p̃ . c°lȝ .v. s̃ . / j.
ium̃tū p̃ .v. s̃ / ij. vac̃ . p̃ . c°lȝ .iij. s̃ .iiij. đ .v. oues . p̃ . c°lȝ Sᵃ .ij. s̃
.vj. đ .j. Cr̃ . frɔ . p̃ .ij. s̃ .vj. đ . / iiij. Cr̃ . orđ . p̃ . c°lȝ iij. đ. ob.
.xvj. đ . / ij. Cr̃ . far̃ . p̃ . c°lȝ .ij. s̃.

Dđ ap Melŷr h̃t in bo . tax̃ .j. boũ . p̃ .v. s̃ / iiij vac̃ . p̃ .
c°lȝ .iij. s̃ .iiij. đ / ij. auĩa .ij. ānoȝ p̃ . c°lȝ .ij. s̃ / viij. oues . Sᵃ .xxiij.
p̃ . c°lȝ .vj. đ / j. Cr̃ . fru p̃ .ij. s̃ .vj. đ / j. Cr̃ . far̃ . p̃ .ij. s̃ / đ.
j. Cr̃ . orđ . p̃ .xvj. đ.

Ieᵃn ap Teg̃ h̃t in bo . tax̃ .j. ium̃tū . p̃ .v. s̃ / iiij. vac̃ .
p̃ . c°lȝ .iij. s̃ .iiij. đ / xxv. oues . p̃ . c°lȝ .vj. đ .iij. auĩa .ij. Sᵃ ij. s̃
ānoȝ . p̃ c°lȝ .ij. s̃ / j. Cr̃ . fru . p̃ .ij. s̃ .vj. đ. .vij. đ.ob.

Ith Hacarn h̃t in bo . tax̃ .iij. boũ . p̃ . c°lȝ .v. s̃ / iiij.
eq°s . p̃ . c°lȝ .v. s̃ / iiij. vac̃ . p̃ . c°lȝ .iij. s̃ .iiij. đ / iij. auĩa Sᵃ .ij. s̃
.iij. ānoȝ . p̃ c°lȝ .ij. s̃ .vj. đ . / xl. oues . p̃ . c°lȝ .vj. đ . / ij. .vj. đ. ob.
Cr̃ fru . p̃ c°lȝ .ij. s̃ .vj. đ .viij. Cr̃ . far̃ aue . p̃ c°lȝ .ij. s̃ / ij.
Cr̃ orđ . p̃ . c°lȝ .xvj. đ.

Ior̃ Du h̃t in bo . tax̃ .j. boũ . p̃ .v. s̃ . / j. eqũ . p̃ .v. s̃
.ij. vac̃ . p̃ . c°lȝ .iij. s̃ .iiij. đ . Uteñ . p̃ .xij. đ / ij. Cr̃ . fru . Sᵃ ij. s̃
p̃ c°lȝ .ij. s̃ .vj. đ / v. Cr̃ far̃ aũ . p̃ . c°lȝ .ij. s̃ . / j. Cr̃ . orđ .v. đ.
p̃ xvj. đ .iiij. oues . p̃ . c°lȝ .vj. đ.

Teg̃ Goch h̃t in bo . tax̃ .v. boũ . p̃ . c°lȝ .v. s̃ / iij. eq°s .
p̃ c°lȝ .v. s̃ / iiij. vac̃ . p̃ . c°lȝ .iij. s̃ .iiij. đ / ij. auĩa .iij. ānoȝ . Sᵃ .v. s̃
p̃ . c°lȝ .ij. s̃ .vj. đ / ix. oues . p̃ c°lȝ .vj. đ . / Uteñ p̃ .xij. đ / .vij. đ.

43

App. A f.

[A.D.
1320–
1340.]

ij. Cr̄ . fru . ꝑ . cᵒlꝫ .ij. ꝫ .vj. đ . / vj. Cr̄ . far̄ aue . ꝑ . cᵒlꝫ
ij. ꝫ / ij. Cr̄ . orđ ꝑ cᵒlꝫ .xvj. đ.

Sᵃ iij. ꝫ.
oꝺ. miᵒ.

Ieᵃn ap Maꝺ ħt in bo . tax .ij. ium̃ta . ꝑ . cᵒlꝫ .v. ꝫ / iij.
boũ . ꝑ .cᵒlꝫ .v. ꝫ / ij. vac̃ . ꝑ . cᵒlꝫ .iij. ꝫ .iiij. đ . Uteñ .xij. đ
/ ij. Cr̄ fru . ꝑ cᵒlꝫ .ij. ꝫ .vj. đ / ij. Cr̄ . far̄ aue . ꝑ cᵒlꝫ .ij. ꝫ /
ij. Cr̄ . orđ . ꝑ cᵒlꝫ .xvj. đ.

Teg̃ ap Ieᵃn ħt in bo . tax̃ .j. boũ . ꝑ .v. ꝫ / iiij. eqᵒs ꝑ

Sᵃ .v. ꝫ
iij. đ. oꝺ.

cᵒlꝫ .v. ꝫ / iiij. vac̃ . ꝑ cᵒlꝫ .iij. ꝫ .iiij. đ .iij. aꝺia .ij.
ānoꝫ . ꝑ cᵒlꝫ .ij. ꝫ . / xl. oues ꝑ cᵒlꝫ .vj. đ . / j. Cr̄ fru . ꝑ
.ij. ꝫ .vj. đ / .v. Cr̄ far̄ . ꝑ . cᵒlꝫ .ij. ꝫ / ij. Cr̄ orđ . ꝑ cᵒlꝫ
.xvj. đ.

Sᵃ xiij. đ.
qᵃ.

Aꝺ ap Teg̃ ħt in bo . tax̃ . ij. eqᵒs . ꝑ . cᵒlꝫ .v. ꝫ / ij. vac̃ .
ꝑ cᵒlꝫ .iij. ꝫ .iiij. đ.

Sᵃ iiij. ꝫ
.ij. đ. ŏ.

Filii Maꝺ Du . ħnt in bo . tax̃ .iij. boũ . ꝑ . cᵒlꝫ .v. ꝫ / j.
eqũ . ꝑ .v. ꝫ / ij. vac̃ . ꝑ . cᵒlꝫ .iij. ꝫ .iiij. đ .iij. aꝺia .iij.
ānoꝫ . ꝑ . cᵒlꝫ .ij. ꝫ .vj. đ . / vj. oues . ꝑ cᵒlꝫ .vj. đ . Uteñ
.xij. đ .iij. Cr̄ . fr̄u . ꝑ cᵒlꝫ .ij. ꝫ .vj. đ / vj. Cr̄ far̄ ꝑ cᵒlꝫ .ij. ꝫ
/ ij Cr̄ orđ ꝑ cᵒlꝫ xvj. đ. [đ].

Hynaf ap Melyr ꞇ Maꝺ ap Iokᵽ ħnt in bõis tax̃ .vj. boũ .

Sᵃ vj. ꝫ
.vj. đ. oꝺ.

ꝑ cᵒlꝫ .v. ꝫ .iiij. eqᵒs ꝑ cᵒlꝫ .v. ꝫ / vij. vac̃ . ꝑ . cᵒlꝫ . iij. ꝫ
.iiij. đ .iiij. aꝺia .ij. ānoꝫ . ꝑ cᵒlꝫ .ij. ꝫ / v. oues ꝑ cᵒlꝫ .vj. đ /
Uteñ .xij. đ .ij. Cr̄ . fru . ꝑ cᵒlꝫ .ij. ꝫ .vj. đ .viij. Cr̄ far̄ ꝑ
cᵒlꝫ .ij. ꝫ / iiijᵒʳ Cr̄ orđ . ꝑ cᵒlꝫ .xvj. đ.

Sᵃ xv. đ.

Tuꝺ ap Hynaf ħt in bo . tax̃ .j. boũ . ꝑ .v. ꝫ / j. eqũ . ꝑ
.v. ꝫ / ij. vac̃ . ꝑ cᵒlꝫ .iij. ꝫ .iiij. đ / j. Cr̄ far̄ . ꝑ .ij. ꝫ.

Meric ap Iokᵽ ꞇ m̃r sua ħnt in bo . tax̃ .iij. boũ . ꝑ cᵒlꝫ

Sᵃ iij. ꝫ
.ix. đ.

.v. ꝫ / iiij. vac̃ . ꝑ . cᵒlꝫ .iij. ꝫ .iiij. đ. / ij. eqᵒs ꝑ cᵒlꝫ .v. ꝫ. j.
aꝺiũ .ij. ānoꝫ . ꝑ .ij. ꝫ / x. oues ꝑ cᵒlꝫ .vj. đ / iij. Cr̄ fru . ꝑ cᵒlꝫ
.ij. ꝫ .vj. đ / ij. Cr̄ . far̄ . ꝑ .ij. ꝫ / ij. Cr̄ orđ ꝑ . cᵒlꝫ .xvj. đ. .

Eẏnõ ap Brygkẏ ħt in ī bo . tax̃ .iij. vac̃ . ꝑ .cᵒlꝫ .iij. ꝫ .iiij. đ

Sᵃ xiiij.
đ. qᵃ.

.j. aꝺiũ . ꝑ .ij. ꝫ.—x. oues . ꝑ .iij. ꝫ .iiij. đ / j Cr̄ . fru . ꝑ .ij. ꝫ
.vj. đ.

Ieᵃn Vichᵃn ħt in bo . tax̃ .j. iumtū . ꝑ .v. ꝫ / ij. vac̃ . ꝑ .

Sᵃ xiiij.
đ.

cᵒlꝫ .iij. ꝫ .iiij. đ / ij. aꝺia ꝑ .ij. ꝫ—j. Cr̄ . far̄ . ꝑ .ij. ꝫ.

Assessment to a Fifteenth of Aberffraw, 1320–40.

Sm^a . ville . in p̄tē regē—xij. lib̄ .xij. ꝣ .vij. d̄.

p̄b.

Malt^aht.

exa^r.

xv^a. Cōmoti de Maltraetĥ—L . iij. lī .v. ꝣ .j. d̄ . q^a.

p̄b.

De Comitatu Angleꝣ.

Maltraĥ.

Sm^a exaīata de toto Cōmoto—Liij. lī .v. ꝣ .j. d̄ . q^a.

45

APPENDIX A g.

ACCOUNT OF THE ISSUES OF ABERFFRAW, 25 EDW. III., A.D. 1351.

Ministers' Accounts, Bundle 1149, No. 1, Public Record Office.

Aberfrau.

Compot⁹ . Thoṁ de Harbergh ꝉ Wilłi de Waltoñ firmaꝛ Maneꝛ de Aberfrau . de exitibus eiusđm a fo sc̄i Michis anno regni Regis Eꝑ ꞇcii post conquestū xxiiij⁽ᵘ⁾. ꝉ Principat⁹ đni Eꝑ Princip̄ Walt Duc̄ Cornuꞇ ꝉ Comitis Cestꝛ viij°. usꝗ iđm fm pxiṁ seqñ anno dc̄i Rege xxvᵗᵒ Principat⁹ đni Princ̄ ix°.

Ꝺ exitibӡ .iiij. caruc̄ ꞇre iꞇm que ad vj. łi ext̄ p anū sicut cont̄ in extent̄ facta . tempe Reḡ aui Rꝑ nūc . Quint̄ caruc̄ ꞇre iꞇm que dimitteꞇ diusꝑ tenent̄ de Trefcastel p .lx. ӡ p anū . uni⁹ pᵃti ꝗd ad vj. ӡ .viij. đ ext̄ p eand extent̄ ꝉ redđ anno p̄ceđ xv. ӡ . aꞇ pᵃto quod sitił extʳ ad vj. ӡ .viij. đ. Piscaꝛ eiusđm Maneꝛ que ad ij. ӡ . ext̄ .j Molenđ de Dyndryn ꝗd ad xl. ӡ ext̄ ꝉ r̄ soꞇ x. ӡ .j. đ ultᵃ extent̄ . ałł molenđ iꞇm ꝗd ad xl. ӡ [ext̄] ꝉ r̄ soꞇ x. ӡ .j. đ ultᵃ eanđm extent̄ . Tᵗⁱcii moꞇ voc̄ Mullebunt ꝗd sïlił ad xl. ӡ ext̄ p anū . ꝉ r̄ . soꞇ x. ӡ j. đ ultᵃ eanđm extent̄ . xxx acꝛ ꞇre in viłt de Aꞇfrau que fueꝛ Wilꞇ Daniel . exist̄ in mañ đni ut escaeꞇ p morꞇ eiusđm Wilꞇi que soꞇ dimitti ad iij. ӡ .vj. đ extᵃ extent̄ seu cui⁹đm pastuꝛ iufra dc̄m Maneꝛ que ad xx. ӡ extend p annū . Nec de .lx. ӡ tenent̄ de Trefcastel tenent̄ inł se j. caruc̄ ꞇre duđ de đnico đui sic̄ arrent̄ post confec̄t extent̄ p anñ ad iiijᵒʳ ꞇmïos videꞇt Oïu sc̄oӡ . Puꝛ ꞇe Marie Ap̄loӡ Ph̄ ꝉ Jacoꞇ ꝉ Guꞇ Augusti .xxix. ӡ .viij. đ . De redđ asӡ lib tenenc̄ ville de Aꞇfrau sicut conꞇ in extent̄ ad p̄dc̄os iiij. ꞇmïos .xv. ӡ .xj. đ . De redđ asӡ

46

Hameletti de Bodeueryk ad p̄dc̄os .iiij. t̃mīos x. s̃ . de redd
ass̃ lib̃ teñ de Trewaspatrikę ad p̄dc̄os .iiij. t̃mīos .v. s̃ vj. d̃ .
De redd villañ eiusd̃m ville de Trūc ad eosd̃m t̃mīos xiij. s̃
vij. d̃ . de eisd̃m villañ p firma butir̃ . lact̄ ꝉ opac̄ arrent̄ ad
eosd̃ . t̃m̃os ix. s̃ .viij. d̃ . de redd ix villañ hameletti de Tref-
berwetę ad eosd̃m t̃m̃os v. s̃ .iiij. d̃ de eisd̃m p iiij. cᵃnnoc̄ fariñ
ordi ad eosd̃m t̃m̃os iiij. s̃ .vj. d̃ . de eisd̃m p ix m̃ltoñ arr̃ ad
eosd̃m t̃m̃os xviij. d̃ . p ix agñ arr̃ ad .ij. s̃ iij. d̃ . de eisdem p

butur̃ arr̃ ad eosdem t̃mīos vij. d̃ . de eisd̃m p Ciiij^{xx} ouis
galliñ arrent̄ ad eosd̃m t̃mīos .ix. d̃ . de redd .ix. galliñ de
eisd̃ ad eosd̃m t̃m̃os .xxxvj. s̃ .ij. d̃ ob̃ de eisd̃m p Clxj. opibus
j. die ad eosd̃m t̃mīos . ij s̃ de redd j. villñ qui quond̃m voc̄
Dd de Hib̃nico . Hameletti de Dynthladau loc̄ med̃ blo꜀ suo꜀
ꝉ lact̄ q̃d voc̄ M')yonith ad eosd̃m t̃m̃os viij. s̃ .vj. d̃ . De fit
Gregor̃ ap . Lt . p j. cᵃnnoc̄ fr̃i ꝉ iiij cᵃnnoc̄ aueñ ad eosd̃m
t̃mīos xvj. d̃ . de eisd̃m p ij m̃ltoñ ꝉ ij. agñ ad eosd̃m t̃m̃os
vj. d̃ . de eisd̃m p butir̃ ad eosd̃m t̃mīos .j. d̃ . ob̃ de eisd̃m p
xl. oū galliñ ad eosd̃m tñ̃os .vj. d̃, de eisd̃m p vj. galliñ ad
eosd̃m t̃m̃os .iij. s̃ .ix. d̃ de eisd̃m p opib꜀ xxx dierū ad eosd̃m
t̃m̃os xiij d̃ ob̃ . de Pellipar̃ p dï cᵃnnoc̄ farine ordi mediet̄ j.
m̃ltoñ .j. agñ .j. gallñ ꝉ .x. cunis butir̃ ad eosd̃m t̃mīos xj. d̃
qᵃ, de eod̃m p opib꜀ vij. die꜀ . ad eosd̃m t̃m̃os iij. s̃ .iiij. d̃ de
redd villañ hameletti de Keuentrefau ad eosd̃m t̃mīos xviij d̃ .
ob̃ de eisd̃m p j. agñ ꝉ dï xxx. Cuñ butir̃ v. gallñ dï .j. Histo꜀
blad̃ de opac̄ iij. die꜀ . ad eosd̃m t̃mīos seu de M')ionnyth .
seu viij s̃ viij d̃ de redd villañ de Ab̃frau p anñ ad eosd̃m
t̃mīos xlviij. s̃ vij. d̃ de eisd̃m p x. cᵃnnoc̄ dï fr̃i . vij cᵃnnoc̄
fariñ aueñ iiij cᵃnnoc̄ fariñ ordi ad eosd̃m t̃mīos ṽj. s̃ .viij. d̃ de
eisd̃m p x. cᵃnnoc̄ aueñ ad p̊bnd̃ ad eosd̃m t̃m̃os .xvj. s̃ .iij d̃
de ix villañ eiusd̃m ville p lact̃ iij. vacc̄ iiij m̃ltoñ dï .ix. angñ
xxvij gallñ .Cl. oū ꝉ butir̃ ad eosd̃m t̃m̃os v. s̃ .j. d̃ dè vj.
tenent̄ vast̃ p iij m̃ltoñ vj. agñ . ix gallñ .C. oū ꝉ butir̃ ad
eosd̃m t̃m̃os ij. s̃ .iij. d̃ de ix villañ dc̄e ville p xxvij galliñ ad

47

App. A g.

[A.D. 1351.]

eosđm P̃m̃os ij ꝰ .iij. đ de eisđm p opibꝫ iij dierū ad blađ đni sarclanđ ad eosđm P̃m̃ios xxx. ꝰ de eisđm villañ ꝑ igne ᒄ stram̃ne in Cur̃ đni Reg̃ ad eosđm P̃ .lxvj. ꝰ .ix. đ de opibꝫ

autupī CCC hoīm quos xv villñ Maner̃ inuēient ᒄ iiij ^{xx} hoīm quos villañ forinc̃ inuenient ađ eosđm P̃m̃os .lxxv. ꝰ de DC hoībꝫ ᒄ eq̄ ad ħeam ꝑ j. diem ad eosđm P̃m̃os . Seu de p̃titis ᒄ pquiꝰ Cur̃ eiusđm Maner̃ ꝑ temp꙯ comp̃ releū ᒄ Gobr̃ tolñ Nunđ ibm pquiꝰ Cur̃ Nunđ eaꝫđm seu xx. ꝰ . de firma portar̃ ibm n¹ r̃ hic eo q̃d đc̃m Maner̃ de Abfrau una cū om̃ibꝫ exitibꝫ ᒄ pfic̃ p̃dc̃is eiđm Maner̃ ꝑtiñ seu inde quouismodo ꝓueñ conc̃ p̃dc̃is Thom̃ ᒄ Willtmo ex dimiꝰꝰ Joħnis Delues locū teñ Iustic̃ Northwalt ᒄ Camer̃ ibm ꝑ temp꙯ hui꙯ comp̃i . Redđ inde đno .xx. lī.

r̃ Esc̃.

De quibꝫ xx. lī iiđm Thom̃ ᒄ Willm̃s r̃ inferius . Đ boñ intestat̃ defunctoꝛ escaet̃ n¹ r̃ . qᵭ Willm̃s de Ellertoñ firmar̃ escaetrie ħt h꙯i pfic̃ ad firm̃ ꝑ tot̃ Com̃ Angleꝰ ut sup^a . Đ am̃c̃ tenenc̃ Maner̃ in Tᵣno vic̃ seu de Wrecco mar̃ nõ atting̃

r̃ Vic̃.

valorem xl. ꝰ n¹ r̃ qᵭ đc̃us Willm̃s de Alertoñ firmar̃ vic̃ Angleꝰ ħt eađm pfic̃ ult^a firm̃ suam . Nec de wrecco mar̃

r̃ Vic̃.

đc̃m valorem xl. ꝰ exceđ n¹ qꝫ iđm Wilt de Allertoñ deb̃ inde comput̃ ᒄ r̃ in comp̃ suo de hoc anno.

* * *

Đ xij. đ de inc̃ro firme xxx. acr̃ t̃re in Maner̃ de Abfrau exist̃ in mañ đni a diu p reũ)c̃ post mort̃ Wilti Daniet qui eas teñ ad t̃im vite de doñ .Lt. Princip ult^a iij ꝰ vj. đ ad quos p¹us dimitt̃ dimiꝰꝰ anno ultīo p̃tito Howel Tew ꝑ Thom̃ le Tᵣnour Esc̃ sic̃ cont̃ in comp̃ eiusđ Thom̃ de eođm anno n¹ qᵬ firmar̃ ħnt eađm pfic̃ infr^a firm̃ suam ut s^a.

APPENDIX B a.

EXTRACTS FROM EXTENT OF THE CASTLE AND HONOR OF DENBIGH, 8 EDW. III., A.D. 1335.

Extent of the Villata of Astret Canon. Progenies of Canon ap Lauwargh located there.

ꝭ Villata de Astretꝑ Canoñ.

Villata de Astret Canon que dum fuit integᵃ in manibꝫ ꝑgeïj Canon ap Lauwargh in .iiij. gauellis quaꝫ quełt gauella reddit de Tungꝑ tempe Princiꝓ .ij. ꝭ .vj. đ . de quibꝫ patebit statim inposteꝫ Et sunt om̄es tenentes libi . ꝺ c̃ . videłt.

hꝫ domū   hꝫ domū
Ithel Loyd ap Cadugan Lewelyn Vaghᵃn ap Lł ꝺ

hꝫ domū
Ithel ap Ioꝫ Duy ap Lł tenent dī gauełt integr̃ que fuit Lauwargh Vaghᵃn reddendo de Tungꝑ inꝓ se xv. đ ꝼmᶦo Oïm Sc̃oꝫ Et ꝑ pastu Princiꝓ ad Natał Dni .xxij. đ . ꝺ quołt alio ꝼmino de iijbꝫ ꝼm̄is supᵃdc̃is .xv. đ . ꝺ ceła ꝯuic̃ cum aliis in cõi ut pꝫ inferius et ħent excamꝥ in Wyckewere ꝺ alibi ꝑ eoꝫ heredił in Astret . Ita q̃d tota eoꝫ ħedił in Astret est in mañ dni ꝺ arenʳ inferiᵒ uᵗ patebᵗ.

Gauella Lauwargh Vaghᵃn

hꝫ domū   hꝫ domū
Cadugan Bottum ap Edeñ . Lewel Duy ap Eignon .

hꝫ domū   hꝫ dom̃   non hꝫ dom̃
Edeñ ap Tuder ap Eden Keñ ap Heillyn ap Mađ ꝺ Madokꝑ frał eius tenēt dī gauełt integr̃ que fuit Ioꝫ ap Canon . Reddendo de Tungꝑ ꝑ aᵐ . ꝼm̄is ꝑdc̃is xv. đ Et ceła ꝯuicia in oīnibꝫ ut dī gauełt ꝑcedens . et om̄es ħent excamꝥ in aliis villis ut ceꞁi supius Ita q̃d illa dī gauella integr̃ remaneꝫ đno in Astret ꝺ appᵘatʳ ut patebit inferius.

Dī gañ Ioꝫ ap Canon.

App. B a.

A.D. 1335.

h; domū h; domū
Keñ ap Routħ ap Ienafꝭ ap Ririd Heilyn ap Grono ap
h; domū h; domū
Ririđ Edeñ Loyđ ap Ken . ap Grono . Griff ap Lł Eigñ
h; domū habet domū h; domū
Gaū Ienaf ap Canoñ. Ken . fraꝰ eius Guyn ap Madokꝭ Gogħ Cadug̃ ap Ririd ap
h; domū ħet domū
Eignon Bletħ ap Ienafꝭ ap Cadug̃ ⁊ Ioꝫ ap Cadug̃ ap Yeuᵃ
[p. 76.] teñ ꝉciam ptem ⁊ deciam ptem gauelł Ienafꝭ ap Canon . reddendo de Tungꝭ intꝰ se .xij. đ qᵃ . et ꝑ pastu Princip̃ ad Natał Ðni Ðni .ij s̃ .ij. đ ob̃ qᵃ ⁊ quołt alio ẗmīo de iijᵇ; ẗm̃is p̃dictis xviij. đ ⁊ ceẗa ẛuicia in cōi ut patebit inferius Et ħent excamƀ in aliis villis Ita q̃d tota gauella ista in Astret integr̃ remaneat đno ⁊ appᵘatʳ cum aliis ⁊ c̃.

habet domū non h; domū ħ dom̃
Yeuan Loyd ap Grono ap Cadug̃ . Keñ ⁊ Dauiđ
non h; domū h; domū
fr̃es eius Eden Loyd ap Mađ ap Grono . Madokꝭ ap Ioꝫ ap
non h; doᵐ non h; domū
Grono . Euer ap Ithel ap Groñ Dauid ap Ioꝫ Grono .
non habet doᵐ non h; domū non h; dom̃
Eden ap Dđ ap Grono Ioꝫ fraꝰ eius ⁊ Yeuan ap Ioꝫ ap
Gaū Eignon ap Canon. Grono tenent medieẗ ⁊ xxiiijᵗᵃᵐ ptem gauelł Eignoñ ap Canon . Reddendo de Tungꝭ ẗmīo Oīm Sc̄oꝫ xvj. đ qᵃ . ⁊ ꝑ pastu Princip̃ ad Natał Ðni ij. s̃ v đ ⁊ quołt alio ẗmīo de iij ẗm̃is p̃dictꝭ xix đ ⁊ ceẗa ẛuic̃ in cōi cum aliis inferius. Et ħent excamƀ in aliis villis Ita q̃d tota ista gauella in Astret reman; đno ⁊ appruatʳ inferius ut patebit.

h; domū h; doᵐ h; domu
Madokꝭ ap Eignon ap Keñ . Mourykꝭ ⁊ Ken fr̃es eius
h; domū h; doᵐ non h; doᵐ
Eignon ap Griffutħ Eden ap Griffutħ Vaghᵃn Griff ap Yenaf
non ħet domū ħet doᵐ
ap Griff Owen ap Grono ap Ken . Griffutħ ap Bletħ Loyđ
ħet doᵐ ħet doᵐ non ħet dom̃
Dauid fraꝰ eius Tuder ap Blethyn . Heillyn ap Keñ ap Bletħ
non ħet domū non ħet dom̃ non ħt dom̃
Dī gauelł Mouryk ap Canon. Eden fraꝰ eius Ioꝫ ap Griff Gogħ ⁊ Blethyn ⁊ Pythle fr̃es eius tenent iij ꝑtes dī gauelle Mourykꝭ ap Canon ⁊ duas

ptes quarte ptis eiusdem ganelle . Reddendo de Tunge̢ p
annū t̄mīo Oīm Sc̄oȝ xiij. đ qᵃ Et ꝑ pastu Princiꝑ ad Natał
Dni ij. s̃ .v. đ oƀ qᵃ Et quott alio t̄mīo de iijbȝ t̄m̄is p̄dictis
xx. đ ꝋ cetᵃ ꝫuic̄ in cōi ut supᵃ ꝋ c̄ . ꝋ h̄ent excamƀ in aliis
villis Ita q̄d dc̄a dī gaū in Astret remaneat integr̄ đno ꝋ
appruatʳ cum aliis ꝋ c̄.

     h̄ dom̄   h̄ dom̄   h̄
Mađ ap Dđ ad Eignoñ Dauid ap Lauwargh Duy Dđ ap
dom̄   h̄ dom̄   h̄ dom̄
Mouryke̢ Gogh Heillyn Cucca Yeuᵃ ap Dđ ap Mađ . ꝋ
ñ h̄ dom̄.   ñ h̄ doᵐ.   ñ h̄ doñ.
frat̄ eius ꝋ Anneys Moythin Eden ap Eignon ap Keneuth
ñ h̄ dom̄   ñ h̄ dom̄   ñ h̄ doᵐ
Griff frat̄ eius Mađ Gogh ap Ioȝ ꝋ Groñ ap Keñ Gogh tenent
duas ptes ꝋ quintā ptem dī gauelt̄ Nynyat ap Canoñ reddendo
de Tunge̢ t̄mīo Oīm Sc̄oȝ xj. đ Et ꝑ pastu Princ̄ ad Natał Dni
xvij. đ qᵃ . ꝋ quott alio t̄mīo de iij t̄m̄is p̄dictis xj. đ . oƀ qᵃ .
Et cetᵃ ꝫuicia in cōi ut patebit inferius ꝋ h̄ent excamƀ in
aliis villis Ita q̄d ista dīa gauella remanȝ integr̄ đno ꝋ appᵘatʳ
cū aliis inferius.

    s̄s Smᵃ Tunge̢ Villate de Astret p aᵐ t̄mīo Oīm Scoȝ vj. s̃
.xj. đ oƀ qᵃ.

Smᵃ pastus Princ̄ ibidem ad terminos				
Natał Dni	xij s̃ . ij đ oƀ qᵃ	s꜀	ꝑ	aᵐ
Međ xlᵐᵉ	viij s̃ ij đ oƀ qᵃ		xxxvj	s̃
Nat̄ sc̄i Johis	viij s̃ ij đ oƀ qᵃ		xj . đ.	
Exalt̄ sc̄e Cᵘis	viij s̃ ij đ oƀ qᵃ			

Et scid̄ q̄d tota villata de Astret Canoñ deuenit ad manꝰ
đni ptim p viam escaet̄ r̄one tenenc̄ qui obierunt contᵃ pacem
ꝋ ptim p viam excambioȝ et continet tota villata Dlxxiiij acr̄
De quibȝ sumuntʳ ad Maneriū de Kilforñ quod extendit̄ in
Cōmoto de Kaymergh CCvij acr̄ ꝋ xviij pt̄ic̄ ꝋ includunʳ
infra puñ pcum iuxᵃ Castᵐ de Dynbiegh lv acr̄ j. rođ dī ꝋ v.
pt̄ic̄ . Et arentantʳ ut patet inferieus Cxij acr̄ in bonat̄ ꝋ acr̄
Et sumuntʳ ad Mañiū de Astret Oweyn quod est in Cōmoto de
Kamgh xiiij acr̄ dī ꝋ iiij pt̄ic̄ ꝋ incluse fuerunt infᵃ pcū de

APP. B a.

A.D.
1335.

Lewenny que nũc arentanͬ cũ eodem p̄co p̄ut patet sup̄ius
Ciij ac͞r dĭ ꝉ xxxvj p̄tic̃ . Et sunt in viis ꝉ vastis cõib₃ . xxx
ac͞r ꝉ xvij p̄tic̃.

ꝉ iste .x.
ac͞r arent̃
fuer̃
coram
dᷠno apͩ
Wode-
stokꝉ
p .x. s̃.
p aͫ.
Videaͬ
quo
waranto
sunt
nunc ad
iij. s̃
iiij. đ.

Willm̃s del Mos tenet unam bouatam cont̃ x. ac͞r ꝉre que
põita fuit in Rentali villate de Lewenny erronice ꝉ reddit p
annum ad ꝉmĩos Pent̃ ꝉ sc̃i Mich̃is p equales porc̃ones iij. s̃
.iiij đ Et idem Wilꝉs tenet nichilomin͢ ·.x. ac͞r ꝉre p quib₃
solebat reddere p annũ iij s̃ iiij đ ꝉm̃is p̃dc̃is ꝉ nũc h̃et illas
quiet̃ alloc̃ p bouat̃ sua p̃tiñ ad Burg̃ suũ de Dynbiegh̃ infra
muros.

Adam de Rossyndale tenet unam bouatam ꝉre cont̃ .x. ac͞r
que prius erronice posit̃ fuit in Rentali villate de Lewenny
ꝉ reddit p aͫ ad duos ꝉmĩos p̃dc̃os iij. s̃ .iiij d.

Ioh̃es de Swynemoͬ ꝉ Ioh̃es fit̃ Wilꝉi Egelyne tenent j
bouat̃ ꝉre cont̃ x. ac͞r p qua solebat reddere p aͫ ad duos
ꝉmĩos p̃dc̃os iij s̃ iiij đ Et nũc allocantͬ Ioh̃i de Swynemor
quiet̃ p bouat̃ sua p̃tiñ ad Burg̃ suũ de Dynb̃ infra muros ꝉ
c̃ . Et fuit ista bouata ·pri͢ põita in Rentali villate de
Lewenny.

Ric̃us de Fermery tenet unam bouatam similt̃r cont̃ x. ac͞r
ꝉre que prius posita fuit erronice in Rentali villate de Lewenny
p qua solebat reddere p annũ ꝉm̃is p̃dictis iij s̃ iiij đ . Et nũc
tenet illam quiet̃ p bouat̃ sua ad burg̃ suũ de Dynb̃ inf͢ᵃ muros
ꝉ c̃.

Ioh̃es de Lonnesdale tenet unam bouat̃ ꝉre cont̃ x. ac͞r
que prius erronice ponebatͬ in Lewenny r̃ ꝉ p̃—iij. s̃ .iiij đ.

s̃s Sm̃ᵃ Firm̃ bouat̃—Pent̃ .v. s̃.⎫ Sic p annũ x s̃ p iij bouat̃
in ꝉm̃is—Sc̃i Mich̃ .v. s̃. ⎭ cont̃ xxx ac͞r.

Willm̃s Cͬteys tenet p Cartam dᷠni Wilꝉi de Monte Acuto
.xx. ac͞r ꝉre impp̃m p quib₃ solebat reddere p annũ xx s̃.

Ioh̃es de Mostoñ tenet iiij ac͞r ꝉre p̃c̃ ac͞r viij đ . reddendo
p annũ ad duos ꝉmĩos p̃dc̃os—ij. s̃ .viij đ . Adam le Carpenꝉ
tenet vij ac͞r ꝉre p̃c̃ ac͞r viij đ reddᷞo p annũ ad duos ꝉmĩos

ꝑdc̄os—ij ꝫ .viij đ . Willm̄s ꞇ Ioħes de Swynemor teñ ij acr̄
eiꝰđ ꝑc̄ r̄ ꝑ ꝑ xvj. đ.

Ioħes Egelyne tꝫ .ij acr̄ eiusđ ꝑc̄ r̄ p aᵐ ꝑm̄is ꝑdc̄is xvj đ.

Thomᵃs de Hultoñ tenet iiij acr̄ ꞇ dï ꝉre unde .j. acr̄ ꝑc̄
viij đ . ꞇ iij acr̄ dï ꝑc̄ acr̄ vj đ . r̄ p aᵐ ꝑ ꝑ—ij ꝫ .v. đ.

Alex̄ Danney tꝫ vj acr̄ r̄ p aᵐ ꝑm̄is ꝑdc̄is—iij. ꝫ .iij. đ.

Wilꞇs del Wode tenet j. plac̄ ꝑc̄ iiij đ ꞇ x. acr̄ ꝉre ꝑc̄
acr̄ vj đ reddendo ꝉm̄is ꝑdc̄is—v. ꝫ .iiij. đ.

Ioħes de Hoghtoñ tenet vij acr̄ ꝉre ꝑc̄ acr̄ xij đ reddendo
ꝉm̄is ꝑdictis—vij ꝫ.

Iorđ de Byngeleye tenet j acr̄ r̄ ꝉm̄is ꝑdc̄is—xij đ. [p. 79.]

Henr̄ Grym tenet iiij acr̄ ꝉre eiusdem ꝑc̄ reddo ꝉm̄is ꝑdc̄is
iiij ꝫ.

Thomᵃs de Lonnasdale tenet v. acr̄ eiusdem ꝑc̄ r̄ ꝉïs ꝑdc̄is
v. ꝫ.

Ioħes de Lonnesdale tenet v acr̄ eiusdem ꝑc̄ . r̄ ꝉ p
aᵐ .v. ꝫ.

Ric̄us de Baytoñ tenet j. plac̄ ꝑc̄ vj đ ꞇ iiij acr̄ ꝉre ꝑc̄ acr̄
xij đ . reddendo p annū ꝉminis ꝑdictis—iiij. ꝫ .vj. đ.

Smᵃ Firm̄ acr̄ de ⎱ Penꞇ xxiij ꝫ .ix đ. ⎰ Sic p annū xlvij ꝫ
Astret in terminis ⎰ Sc̄i Mich xxiij ꝫ .ix đ ⎱ .vj đ p ij plac̄ ꞇ
lxij. acr̄ ꝉre.

Et ꝑꝉea tenentʳ quieꞇ tam inꝉ bouaꞇ qᵃm inꝉ acras ut
ꝑdicitʳ—l acr̄ que solebant reddere xxx ꝫ . p annū que nunc
nichil reddunt ut supᵃ.

Et sic supsunt l acr̄ ꞇ medietas uniꝰ rode . que cedunt
in auauntagiū mensur̄ tenenciū unde dñs nullū capit annuale
ꝑficuū que si extracte fuissent valerent p aᵐ adminꝰ xxv ᴙ
oꝭ qᵃ ꝑc̄ acr̄ .v. đ.

APPENDIX B b.

Extent of the Villata of Nanthyn Canon.   Progenies of Canon
ap Lauwargh located there.

Villata de Nanthyn Canon.

Villata de Nanthyn Canon . que conᵗ in terᵲ boscę ꞇ vastę cū hamelt de Pennankyngy vᶜlxiiij acᵲ iij rođ consistit in manibȝ ꝑgenieij Canon ap Lawargĥ absꝗ Tungę ꞇ Tretĥ que est hamelt ꝑtinens ad Astret Canon ꞇ tenetʳ in iiij gauelt de quibȝ statim responʳ inposteȝ Et est porᵭo cuiuslibꞇ gauelt sᴄđm equam ꝑticipacõem Cxlj acᵲ ꞇ xxx ptiᴄ ꝑre . bosci ꞇ vasti ꞇ ᴄ̃.

Ithel Loyd ap Caduğ ꞇ coheredes ꞇ ꝑticipes sui quoȝ noĩa patent in villa de Astret Canon tenent dĩ gauelt integᵲ

que fuit Lauwargĥ Vaghᵃn ꝑ qua faᴄ̃ omĩđ ꝫuiᴄ̃ in Astret Canoñ . Et ideo nᵗ hic Et dñs nullam ħet ꝑpartem in ista dĩ gauelt ꞇ ᴄ̃.

Cadugan Butoñ ꞇ coheredes ꞇ ꝑticipes sui quoȝ noĩa patent in villa de Astret ꞇ tenent hic dĩ gauelt que fuit Ioȝ

ap Canon integᵲ faᴄ̃ ꝑ ea omĩđ ꝫuiᴄ̃ in Astret Et ideo nᵗ hic Et dñs nullam ħet ꝑpartem in ista dĩ gauelt.

Ken . Routĥ ap Iennᵃfę ꞇ coheredes ꞇ ꝑticipes sui quoȝ noĩa patent in Astret Canoñ tenent hic duas ptes gauelt que

fuit Iennᵃfę ap Canoñ faᴄ̃ ꝑ inde oṁia ꝫuiᴄ̃ in Astret Canoñ Et ĩo nᵗ hic . Et ꝑcia ps istius gauelt est escaeꞇ đni ꞃone mortuoȝ conᵃ paᴄ̃ uᵗ pȝ inferiꝰ.

Yeū Loitę ap Groñ ap Caduğ ꞇ coheredes ꞇ pcenaᵲ sui

quoȝ noĩa patent in Astret tenent hic tres ptes gaū Eigñ ap Canoñ faᴄ̃ oṁ.ia ꝫuiᴄ̃ in Astret Et ideo nichil hic . Et quarta ps eiusdem gauelł hᶜ est escae� đni . que appruatʳ cū ał esc̃

inferiuˢ.

Mađ ap Eigñ ap Keñ ꝫ pcenaꝝ sui quo� noĩa patent in
Astret Canon . teñ hic dĩ gaũ Meurᵃ ap Canon integꝝ fac̃ p
ea omĩđ ꝰuic̃ in Astret Et ideo nⁱ hic Et dñs nullā ħet Esc̃
de iᵗᵃ dĩ gaũ.

Mađ ap Dđ ap Eigñ ꝫ pcenaꝝ sui quoꝫ noĩa patent in
Astret Canon . teñ totam dimiđ gauelł Nynyat ap Canoñ fac̃
p ea omĩđ ꝰuic̃ in Astret Et ideo nⁱ hic Et dñs ñlⱦ ħet esc̃ in
iᵃ dĩ gauⱦ.

Et est ꝑpars đni ibm ꝑcia ps illius gauelł ꝫ quarta ps

xx

illius gauelł que cont̃ scđm veram ꝑporc̃õem iiij ij acꝝ .j. rođ
ꝫ xvij ptic̃ dĩ. Unde allocanđ sunt p excamƀ ꝑodarioꝫ eiusdem
ꝑgeĩj pimplenđ p eoꝫ patⁱmoniis in Astret Canon ꝫ Wen-
nannokɇ Canoñ . xxix acꝝ iij rođ di ꝫ iiij ptic̃ dĩ.

Ken . Routħ tenꝫ . vij acꝝ dĩ veteꝝ ꝑre p̃c̃ acꝝ vj. đ redđo
p annū ad ꝑmĩos Penⱦ ꝫ sc̃i Micħis—iij ꞩ .ix đ.

Idem Keñ tenꝫ in Pennanckyngy iij acꝝ ꝑre que fuerunt
Itħ Voil p̃c̃ acꝝ vj đ reddendo p annū ꝑm̃is ꝑdictis—xviij đ.

Et ꞇn hucusꝗ . nⁱ p eis reddiđ toto tempe đni nūc quia
erronice p̃õite fueꝝ in Nantħyn Sc̃oꝫ ꝫ sic fraudelenⱦ dedicte
ꝫ concellate . Ideo leuentʳ arreraꝝ ꝫ c̃ Et iacet illa ꝑra in j pec̃
circumfossaⱦ . ubi dc̃us Ithel solebat in tempe Escaeⱦ reddeꝝ.

Heillyn ap Groñ tꝫ de assarⱦ bosci j acꝝ .j. rođ dĩ ꝫ xiiij
ptic̃ p mensuꝝ Extenⱦ p̃c̃ acꝝ vj. đ reddendo p annū ad duos
ꝑmĩos ꝑdc̃os viij đ oƀ qᵃ . ꞇn hucusꝗ non reddidit nisi p una
acᵃ vj. đ.

Hugo Pygᵒot solebat tenere hic xviij acꝝ ꝑre ꝝ p aᵐ ix ꞩ p̃c̃
acꝝ vj đ quas excamƀ p pte Keñ Routħ in Wennannok Canon .
Uñ idem Hugo . ꝝ de ista firma in incꝝo ibm ꝫ Ideo nⁱ de
ista firma hic.

nãnok Canon . ꝗd si aliꝗd auanⱦ poꞏⱦit accresc̃e de
dc̃o excamƀ accrescat đno ex quo ambe ꝑtes tenēt
in inꞩr non ħent potestaⱦ fac̃ excamƀ sñ lic̃ đni

Dĩ gaũ
Meurᵃ ap
Canon.

Dĩ g aũ
Nynyat
ap
Canon.

Distincꞇo
Escaeⱦ.

Firᵃ Esc̃

[p. 87.]

Noᵃ.

Videaʳ
que fuit
ꝑporc̃o
Ken .
Routħ in
Wen-

APP. Bb.

A.D.
1335.

Hbag̃

§s. Smᵃ Firme de Nanthyn Canon in P̃minis—

Pent̃ ij. ꝫ .xj đ oƀ qᵃ

Sc̃i Micħ iij ꝫ

Sᵉ p annū v ꝫ .xj đ oƀ qᵃ cū xx đ oƀ qᵃ de incr̄o p xj acr̄
iij rođ dī xiij p̃tic̃ de incr̄o.

Et residuū ppartis đni alloc̃ p̃odar̄ de Astret Canon p eoꝫ
hered̃ iƀm ꞇ in Wennannok Canoñ p̃p̃ . xxij acr̄ dī bosci p qᵃꝫ
ħbag̃ tota cōitas ville r̄ p annū ad duos . P̃mīos p̃dc̃os ix. s.
Sᵃ pꝫ.

Ken Routħ tenꝫ ad firmam ppartem đni quam ħet in uno
Molendino aquatico eiusdem ville r̄ p annū P̃ p̃ ij ꝫ . viij đ.

Idem Keñ reddidit đno annuatim incipiendo anno viijᵒ. ut
fateʳ ij ꝫ . viij đ p licenc̃ leuand̃ unū Molend̃ fulloñ ꞇ c̃ sup
solū cōe ut dicᵗ ꞇ c̃.

§s. Smᵃ Firm̃ Molendini ad Terminos

Pent̃—ij ꝫ . viij đ ⎞
                         ⎬ Sic p aᵐ. v ꝫ iiij đ.
Sc̃i Micħis ijꝫ . viij đ ⎠

APPENDIX B c.

Extent of the Villata of Prees . Progenies of Canon ap
Lauwargh and Pithle ap Lauwargh located there.

Villata of Prees.

Villata de Prees cum suis hamellis que cont p̃ magnum

vastum quod est cõe ad oм̃es tenentes dominii de Ros et de

mͭ c

Rewaynok ꝉ Kayм̃għ viij viij lxxviij acꝛ j rođ dī que temporib₃

Principum reddidit de Tungꝑ xx ẛ oƀ idem [1] villata integᵃ fuit

in manib₃ veꝛ heređ ante forisfcuꝛ Et consistit in tenurᵃ

diūsa₂ ꝑgenie₂ tam liƀo₂ qᵃm Natiuo₂ de quib₃ patet inferius

primo de liƀis et postea de Natiuis.

De sexta ꝑte eiusdem ville que consistit in tenurᵃ ꝑgenieij

Canō ap Lauwargħ sunt iiij gauelͭ ꝉ dīa que đum fueꝛ integᵃ

reddiderunt de Tungꝑ iij. ẛ . iiij đ.

Ithel Loit ap Caduǥ ꝉ ꝑcenaꝛ sui quo₂ noīa patent in

Astret Canon teñ hic dī gauelͭ Lauwargħ Vaghᵃn integꝛ re .

de Tungꝑ adinuicem ꝑ annū ꝑmīo Oīm Sco₂ iiij đ oƀ ꝉ nulla

alia ꝫuicia hic quia eo₂ ꝫuicia una cū ꝫuic̃ oīm alio₂ de ꝑgenie

Canon ap Lauwargħ plene inscribuntʳ in villis de Astret

Canon.

Caduǥ Bottum ap Edeñ ꝉ ꝑcenaꝛ sui quo₂ noīa patent in

Astret Canon teñ dī gauelͭ Io₂ ap Canon integre reddendo de

Tungꝑ inꝑ se ꝑmīo ꝑdc̃o iiij. đ oƀ ꝉ nichil aliud hic ꝙ in

Astret Canon ꝉ c̃.

Ken . Routħ ap Ienaf ꝉ ꝑcenaꝛ sui quo₂ noīa patent in

Astret Canon teñ inꝑ se medieꞇ ꝉ ixᵃᵐ ꝑtem gauelle Iennᵃꝼ ap

APP. B c.

A.D.
1335.

[p. 89.]

Liƀe
tenenꞇ.

[p. 90.]

De
ꝑgenie
Canō ap
Lau-
wargħ.

Dī gaū
Lau-
wargħ
Vaghan.

Dī gaū
Io₂ ap
Canon.

---

[1] So in the MS.

APP. B c.

Gaū Iennaf ap Canon.

Canon hic reddendo de Tunge ꝑmīo Oīm Scoꝝ v. đ . ob̄ . Et nulla fac̄ alia ꝭuic̄ hic quia in Astret Canon . Et ꝑcia ꝑs ⁊ xviija ꝑs eiusdem gauelt hic sunt Escaet̄ đni unde respondetr inferius.

Gauelt Eigñ ap Canon.

Iennaf Loit ap Groñ ap Cadug̃ ⁊ ꝑcenar̃ sui quoꝝ nōia patent in Astret Canon tenent ij ꝑtes ⁊ quartam ꝑtem ꝑcie ꝑtis gauelt Eignoñ ap Canon . reddendo de Tunge ꝑmīo Oīm Sc̄oꝝ vj đ ob̄ qa Et nulla alia ꝭuic̄ hic quia in Astret Canon ⁊ tres p̃t . iije p̃t eiusdem gauelle hic sunt escaet̄ đni unde respondetr inferiuꝰ c̄ at esc̄ ⁊ c̄.

Dī gaū Meura ap Canon.

Mađ ap Eigñ ap Keñ ⁊ ꝑcenar̃ sui quoꝝ noīa patent in Astret Canon teñ dī gauelt Meura ap Canon hic integreređo de Tunge adinuicem .iiij. đ ob̄ ꝑmīo ꝑdc̄o Et nl aliud hic qꝫ ī Astret Cañ.

Dī gaū Nynyat ap Canon.

Mađ ap Dđ ap Eigñ ⁊ ꝑticipes sui quoꝝ nōia patent in Astret Canon teñ duas ꝑtes ⁊ ꝑciam ꝑtem ꝑcie ꝑtis dī gauelt Nynyat ap Canoñređo de Tunge ꝑmīo ꝑdc̄o iij đ ob̄ Et nl aliud hic qꝫ in Astret Canon ⁊ ij p̃t iij ꝑte eiusđ dī gaū sūt esc̄ đni uñ rr inferiꝰ.

[p. 91.]

Dī gauelt Keneuth ap Canoñ.

Et dī gauelt que fuit Keneuth ap Canon . et que reddd' de Tunge iiij đ hic est pur̃ ⁊ integr̃ escaet̄ đni r̄one mortuoꝝ conta pacē Et inde respondetr inferius cum aliis escaet̄.

Ꝺ ꝑgenie Pithle ap Lauwargh.

De sexta ꝑte eiusdem ville . que consistit in tenura ꝑgenieij Pithle ap Lauwargh sunt octo lecta . que dum fuerunt integr̃ in manibꝫ vere ħedū ante conquestum . ⁊ c̄ . reddiderunt de Tunge ꝑ annū iij. s .iiij. đ . Videlt quodlt lectū .v. đ.

Wele Ioꝝ ap Pithle.

Inde primū lectū quod fuit Ioꝝ ap Pithle ⁊ quod reddidit v. đ de Tunge . integr̃ accidit ad manꝰ đni tanqam escaet̄ r̄one mortuoꝝ conta pacem . ⁊ inde respondetr inferius cū aliis escaet̄.

non ħ domū hꝫ domū

Eigñ ap Ioꝝ ap Cadug̃ ⁊ Ieuan Vaghan ap Ieuan ap Elidur tenent mediet̄ ⁊ quintam ꝑtem de Wele Edenoweñ ap Pithle reddo de Tunge ƿmīo p̄dc̄o iij đ oƀ Et nˡ ꝓ pastu

Princ̄ hic q꜀ soluūt in Ros Ugħdulas . vidett in villa de

Tobritħ nec aliquod aliud ꝫuiciū fac̄ hic neꝗ ibi nec aliqui

alii de ista ꝑgenie nisi pastū Staloñ ꝉ garcōis lucᵃř cū canib꜀

Pennackew ꝉ Waissioñ bagħeyn . Sc̄đm quod ħuerunt domos

seu tenentes ꝑut alii liƀi de isto Cōmoto . ꝉ vᵃ ps ꝉ xᵃ ps

istius Wele sunt escaec̄ đni Unde respondetʳ inferius cum

aliis escaec̄.

App. B c.

A.D.
1335.

Wele
Eden-
oweñ
ap
Pithle.

Io꜀ ap Dđ ap Bletħ teñ međ ꝉ vᵗᵃᵐ ptem de Wele Ithon

ap Pythle reddo de Tunge ƿmīo p̄dc̄o .iij. đ oƀ ꝉ ceꝑa ꝫuic̄ ut

px̃m Wele p̃cedens ꝉ vᵃ ps ꝉ xᵃ ps istius Wele sunt escaec̄

đni Unde respondetʳ cum aliis escaec̄ inferius.

non hab꜀ domū   non ħet domū   non

Ieuᵃn ap Wyn ap Mađ Dauid ap Io꜀ Vaghᵃn ap Eigñ

ħ domū   non ħ doم̃   nō ħ domū

Gogħ ap Eignoñ Ieuᵃn ap Dđ ap Keñ Ieuᵃn ap Dđ ap Auř

nō ħet doم̃   ñ h꜀ domū

Ieuᵃn Vaghᵃn ap Ieuᵃu ap Auř ꝉ Dauid Vaghᵃn ap Dđ ap

Meurᵃ tenent međ ꝉ v ptem de Wele Kennyngħ ap Pithle

Reddo de Tunge ƿmīo p̄dc̄o iij đ oƀ adinuicem ꝉ ceꝑa ꝫuicia

ut px̃ Wele p̃cedens Et vᵃ ps ꝉ xᵃ ps istius vilie sunt escaec̄

đni Unde respondetʳ inferius cum ceꝑis escaetis.

non h꜀ domū   h꜀ domū

Hoel ap Dauid ap Doyoke M꜀꜀)eđ ap Lt ap Meilleř

non h꜀ domū   non h꜀ domū

Cađ ap Wylhym ap Cađ ꝉ Griffutħ ap Io꜀ ap Keñ tenent

međ ꝉ quintam ptem Wele Cađ ap Pythle reddo de Tunge

adinuicem ƿmīo p̄dc̄o iij đ oƀ ꝉ ceꝑa ꝫuicia ut px̃ Wele p̃cedens

Et vᵃ ps ꝉ xᵃ ps istius Wele sūt escaec̄ đni ut supᵃ . Unde

respondetʳ cum ceꝑis escaetis inferius.

h꜀ domū   habet domū

Dauid Loyt ap Lauwargħ ꝉ Tuder ap Griff ap Grono

tenēt medietatem ꝉ quintaم ptem de Wele Edeñ ap Pythle

reddo de Tunge adinuicem ƿmīo p̄dc̄o .iij. đ oƀ Et ceꝑa

ꝫuicia ut alia lecta p̃cedenc̄ ꝉ tantam pporcōem escaec̄ h꜀

đñs in iᵃ Wele sᵗ in px̃ Wele p̃ceđ.

App. B c.

Dauid ap Griff ap Ienn^{a}f tenet međ ꝉ quintam ꝑtem de Wele Rissard ap Pythle Reddendo de Tunge ꝑmīo ꝑđc̄o

Wele
Rissard
ap
Pythle.

.iij. đ oƀ et ceꝑa ꝫuic̄ ut sup^a ꝉ v^a ꝑs ꝉ x^a ꝑs istius Wele est esc̄ đni unde respondet^r inferius cū aliis escaetę ꝉ c̄.

h₃ domū
Grono ap Ieu^{a}n Goch ap Dehewynd Dauid fraꝑ eius et

nō h₃ domū

ñ h₃ domū
Madokę ap Meur^a ap Heylin teñ međ ꝉ quintam ꝑtem de

Wele
Geny-
thlyn ap
Pythle.

Wele Genythlyn ap Pithle ređđo de Tunge ꝑmīo Oīm Sc̄oꝫ .iij. đ oƀ Et ceꝑa ꝫuic̄ ut sup^a ꝉ v^a ꝑs ꝉ x^a ꝑs sunt esc̄ đni unde respondet^r inferius cū aliis escaetę ꝉ c̄.

*   *   *

[p. 100.]

De pastu Princ̄ nichil hic neꝗ de pastu famuꝉ Princ̄ neꝗ de aliis pasꞇ ꝗ om̄es tenentes istius ville faciunt hi⁹ . ꝫuic̄ in aliis villis ut patet ꞅri⁹ in siḡlis locis ꝉ villatis ꝑ se.

Et sci^d q̄d ꝑpars đni in Prees de escaeꞇ mortuoꝫ cont^a pacem . si veꝝ ꝉ directe ꝑporc̄one^r continebit in ꝑris boscis
Mꝉ
ꝉ vastis in uniůso iij lxj acꝝ xxvij ptic̄.

Et deinde diůsi ꝑodaꝝ de Lewenny . Astret Canon . Wennennokę Canon . Beryn . Talabryn ꝉ aliunde habent ꝑ eoꝫ excamƀ loco pat^{t}mōioꝫ suoꝫ in diůsis villatis ab eis captis tempe Comitę Lincolñ—Dccclxxix acꝝ ꝉ xxv ptic̄ terre ꝉ vasti . Et de residuo r^r inferi⁹.

*   *   *

APPENDIX B d.

*Extents of the Villatœ of Dennant, Grugor, Quilbreyn, Pennau-
aleth, Penglogor, Hendreuennyth, Prestelegot, and Petrual,
where the Progenies of Rand Vaghan ap Asser held.*

Rewaynokę Ughalet.

Extenta Commoti de Ughalet facta anno regni Regis Edwardi ꝓcii post conquestum viij^{uo}.

Dñs nichil habebit in đnico in Cōmoto de Ughalet
nisi escaetas de forisſcuris tenencium qui insurrexɔunt in
guerris ꝛ obierunt cont^a pacem aut de ꝑris fugitiuoꝫ aut alioꝫ
tenenciū qui reliquerunt teñ sua in mañ đni ꝑ defc̄u releū vel
aliquoꝫ ſuicioꝫ ꝑut inferi^9 patebit in singuł vilł seu locę ubi
aliquales hi^9 escaeꝯ ptinent đno.

App. B d.

A.D.
1335.

[p. 152.]

*   *   *

Et sciend est q̓d est quedam ꝓgēies libeꝙ tenenc̄ in isto
Cōmoto que vocat^r ꝓgenies Rand Vagħ ap Asseꝙ que quidem
ꝓgenies tenent in diùsę villis istius Cōmoti et tenueꝙ tempe
Princiꝑ añ conquestum videłt totam villatam de Dennantę
totam villam de Grugor . totam villam de Quilbreyn . totam
villam de Penplogor ꝛ totam villam de Pennauelet . medieꝯ
ville de Hendreuennyth . ꝓciam ptem ville de Prestegot ꝓciam
decimam ptem ville de Pet^ual . Et om̄es illas villaꝯ ꝛ pcełt
villataꝫ ꝑdictaꝫ tenuerunt in quatuor lectis videłt Wele
Ruathlon ap Rand Wele Idenerth ap Rand Wele Daniel ap
Rand ꝛ Wele Kewret ap Rand unde primū Wele diuisum est
in quatuor gauełt videlic; Gauel Guyon ap Ruathlon Gauel

[p. 154.]

[p. 155.]

App. B d.

A.D.
1335.

Bleth ap Ruathł Gauel Kewret ap Ruathlon ⁊ gauel Madokę ap Ruathlon . Scđm Wele diuiditᵣ in quatuor gauelł vidł⊋ gauel ap Io⊋ ap Idenertħ gauel Madoc ap Idenertħ gauel Allot ap Idenertħ ⁊ Gauel ap Tegwarat ap Idenertħ . Ꝃciū Wele diuiditᵣ in duas gauelł v⊋ . gauel Eigñ ap Daniel gauł Cađ ap Daniel Et quartum lectū quod est ultimū diuiditᵣ in ij gauelł videl⊋ gauelł Griffꝛ ap Kewret ⁊ gauel Kenewrekę ap Kewret . Et sequitᵣ de ꝑporc̃ tenuꝛ ⁊ Ꝗuic̃ cuiustt Wele ⁊ cuiustt eius gauelł in singuł villatę seriatim ꝑ se ⁊ de ꝑporc̃ esc̃ đni in sinğlis lccę ⁊ gauelł scđm ut statim patebit in postę⊋.

Villata de Dennantę.

Ken ap Bletħ Vaghᵃn Io⊋ ap Lewelyn ap Bletħ Ken . ap Lewelyn ap Bletħ Ken . ap Bletħ Loyd ⁊ Howel ap Bletħ Loid tenent inꝓ se duas gauelł de primo lecto integro v⊋ gauelł Guyon ap Rauthlon ⁊ gauelł Bletħ ap Rauthlon ⁊ reddunt inꝓ se de Tungę adinuicem Ꝋmïo Oĩm Sc̃o⊋ .ij � . viij đ qᵃ . v⊋ . xij đ in Dennant .v. đ oᵬ qᵃ in Grugor .v. đ in Quilbreyn . j đ oᵬ qᵃ in Penplogor j. đ oᵬ qᵃ in Pennaualet . iij đ in Hendreuennyth . ij đ oᵬ in Prestlegot ⁊ oᵬ qᵃ in Petrual . Reddunt eciam adinuic̃e ꝑ pastu Princ̃ ꝑ annū ꝑ om̃ib⊋ villis ꝓdc̃is vj ꝱ . ad Natał Ðni . ij ꝱ Ꝋmïo Medie xlᵐᵉ .xvj. đ . Ꝋmïo Nał sc̃i Ioħis Baꝓte . xvj đ et Ꝋmïo Exalł sc̃e Crucę . xvj đ . Et fac̃ alia Ꝗuicia in cõi cum aliis liᵬis de Commoto que patebunt inferius in fine Cõmoti.

[p. 156.]

Bletħ ap Yeuan ap Madok tenet Ꝃciam gauelł eiusdem lecti integꝛ . Reddđo de Tungę Ꝋmïo Oĩm Sc̃o⊋ xvj. đ . Videłt vj. đ in Dennant .ij đ oᵬ qᵃ in Grugor .ij đ oᵬ in Quilbreyn . oᵬ qᵃ in Penplogor . oᵬ qᵃ dī in Pennaualet .j đ oᵬ in Hendreuennytħ .j đ qᵃ in Prestlegot ⁊ qᵃ dī in Petrual . Reddit ꝷ ꝑ pastu Princ̃ ꝑ annū ij. ꝱ .iij đ ad quatuor Ꝋmïos ꝓdic̃ Unde ad Natał Ðni ix đ . ⁊ quołt alio Ꝋmïo vj đ . Et fac̃ alia Ꝗuic̃ cum aliis liberꝛ in cõi ut infra.

Ioꝫ ap Dd ap Mađ Keñ ap Bleth̄ ap Grono . Ken . ap Ioꝫ ap Tudeř Eden . ap Lauwař ap Tudeř ⁊ Bleth̄ fraꝰ eius tenent totam quartam gauelł eiusdem lecti ꝓꝰ inde xvj. ꝑtem que est escaẗ đni ⁊ . ř . de Tungꝭ adinuicem ꝑmīo Oīm Sc̄oꝫ .xv. đ . Uñ v. đ ob̄ qᵃ in Dennant .j. đ ob̄ qᵃ in Grugor ij đ ob̄ in Quilbreyn . ob̄ qᵃ in Penplogor . ob̄ qᵃ dī in Pennaualet .j. đ . ob̄ in Hendreuennyth .j. đ ob̄ in Prestlegot ⁊ qᵃ dī in Petrual . Et ꝑ pastu Princiꝑ ꝑ aᵐ vij. ŝ .vj. đ . ad quatuor ꝑmīos ꝓdc̄os Videłt ad Natał Dni ij. ŝ .vj. đ . ⁊ quołt alio ꝑmīo .xx. đ . ⁊ ceꝰa ꝰuic̄ cum aliis in cōi ut infra.

Eigñ Loid ap Ioꝫ Grugor ap Bleth̄ Routh̄ fř eius ⁊ Ioꝫ fraꝰ eius tenent primam gauelł sc̄di lecti que quidem gauł vocatʳ gauelł Ioꝫ ap Idenerth̄ integř . reddendo de Tungꝭ ꝑmīo Oīm Sc̄oꝫ xvj. đ . Unde .vj. đ . in Dennant ij đ ob̄ qᵃ in Grugor ij. đ ob̄ in Quilbreyn . ob̄ qᵃ in Penplogor . ob̄ qᵃ dī in Pennaualet .j. đ ob̄ in Hendreuennyth̄ .j đ qᵃ in Prestlegot ⁊ qᵃ dī in Petrual . ⁊ ꝑ pastu Princ̄ .vij ŝ .j. đ . ad quatuor ꝑmīos ꝓdc̄os . Unde ad Festum Natał Dni ij. ŝ .iiij đ . ⁊ quołt alio ꝑmīo .xix đ ⁊ ceꝰa ꝰuic̄ cū ał in cōi ut infᵃ.

Et ꝓdc̄i Eigñ Loid ⁊ Bleth̄ ⁊ Ioꝫ fr̄es eiꝰ tenent ij ꝑť sc̄de gauelł eiusdem lecti que vocatʳ Gauᴵ Madokꝭ ap Idenerth̄ [p. 157.] reddō de Tungꝭ ꝑmīo Oīm Sc̄oꝫ .x. đ . ob̄ . Unde .iij. đ qᵃ in Dennant .ij đ in Grugor .ij đ in Quilbreyn ob̄ in Penglogor . qᵃ in Pennaualet .j đ qᵃ in Hendreuennyth̄ .j đ qᵃ in Prestlegot ⁊ qᵃ in Petrual . Et ꝑ pastu Princiꝑ ꝑ annū .xv. đ ob̄ ad quatuor ꝑmīos ꝓdc̄os Unde ad Naẗ Dni .v. đ . ⁊ quołt alio ꝑmīo .iij. đ ob̄ . Et ceꝰa ꝰuic̄ in cōi ut infra.

Bleth̄ ap Ken ap Madokꝭ tenet medieẗ ꝰcie ꝑtis eiusdem gauelł reddō de Tungꝭ ꝑmīo Oīm Sc̄oꝫ .j· đ . ob̄ qᵃ . Unde ob̄ in Dennant . qᵃ in Grugor . qᵃ in Quilbreyn . dī qᵃ in Penplogor . dī qᵃ in Pennaualet . qᵃ in Hendreuennyth̄ qᵃ in Prestlegot ⁊ nichil in Petrual . Et ꝑ pastu Princ̄ ꝑ annū .ij. đ ob̄ ad quatuor ꝑmīos ꝓdictos videłt ad Naẗ Dni .j. đ . ⁊ quołt alio ꝑmīo ob̄ ⁊ ceꝰa ꝰuicia ut infra . Et alꝰa medieẗ

App. B d. — A.D. 1335.

eiusdem ꝑcie ptis gauelt est escaet̃ đni ⁊ tenetʳ in acr̃ cum ceꝑis escaetꝭ inferius.

Item ꝑdc̃us Bletħ ap Keñ ap Mađ ⁊ Eigñ ap Yeuan ap Ioꝫ . Eignon ap Mađ ap Ieuᵃn ⁊ Dauid ap Heilyn ap Ioꝫ tenent quartam ptem ꝑcie gauelt que vocatʳ gauelt Allet ap Idenertħ . reddo de Tungꝭ .iiij. đ ꝑmio Oĩm Sc̃oꝫ Uñ .j. đ qᵃ in Dennant . ob̄ qᵃ in Grugor . ob̄ qᵃ in Quilbreyn . dĩ qᵃ in Penplogor . dĩ qᵃ in Pennaualet . qᵃ in Hendreuennytħ . ob̄ in Prestlegot ⁊ qᵃ in Petrual . Et p pastu Princ̃ p aᵐ ij s ob̄ ad quatuor ꝑmios ꝑdc̃os . Unde ad Natat Dni .viij. đ ⁊ quott alio ꝑmio .v. đ ob̄ ⁊ ceꝑa ꝭuic̃ cum aliis in cõi ut infᵃ . Et .iij. ptꝭ eiusdem gavelt sunt esc̃ đni uñ rʳ inꝑ acr̃ inferiꝰ.

Bleytħ ap Eigñ Voil ap Ioꝫ tenet .ij. pt̃ quarte gauelt eiusdem lecti que vocatʳ gauel Tegwaret ap Idenerth reddendo de Tungꝭ .x. đ ob̄ qᵃ . Unde .iij. đ qᵃ in Dennant .j. đ ob̄ qᵃ in Grugor .ij đ in Quilbreyn . ob̄ in Penplogor .

[p. 158.] qᵃ in Pennaualet .j. đ qᵃ in Hendreuennyth .j. đ ob̄ in Prestlegot ⁊ qᵃ in Petrual . Et p past̃ Princ̃ p annũ .v. s .ix. đ . ad quatuor ꝑmios ꝑdc̃os . Videlt ad Natat Dni .xxij. đ . ob̄ ⁊ quott alio ꝑmio .xv. đ ob̄ . Et ceꝑa ꝭuicia in cõi ut infra . Et ꝑcia ps istius gauelt est escaet̃ đni ⁊ rʳ inde inꝑ ꝑr̃ inferius.

Ioꝫ ap Ieuan ap Keneuth . Tuder fr eius . Yeuan ap Edeñ ap Mađ . Ken . fraꝑ eius . Griffitħ ap Tuder ap Mađ . Edeñ Grono ⁊ Yenaf fr̃es eius Ioꝫ ap Eigñ ap Ioꝫ Eignoñ Gogħ ap Đd ap Eigñ . Itħ ⁊ Ken . fres eius tenent septem ptes ⁊ . lxiiijᵗᵃꝫ ptem prime gauelle ꝑcii lecti . que quidem gauella vocatʳ gauel Eignoñ ap Danyel . reddo de Tungꝭ ꝑmĩo Oĩm Scoꝫ .ij. s .iiij. đ ob̄ Uñ .xj. đ ob̄ in Dennant .v. đ qᵃ in Grugor .v. đ qᵃ in Quilbreyn .j. đ qᵃ in Penplogor .j. đ qᵃ in Pennaualet .ij. đ qᵃ in Hendreuennytħ .j. đ in Prestlegot ⁊ ob̄ qᵃ in Petrual . Et p pastu Princ̃ p annũ .vij. s .v. đ ad iiijᵒʳ ꝑmĩos ꝑdictos videlt ad Natat Dni .ij. s .v. đ . ⁊ quott alio ꝑmĩo xx. đ . Et ceꝑa ꝭuic̃ cum aliis in cõi

App. Bd.

A.D.
1335.

ut infra . Et .viijᵃ ps . eiusdem gauelł est esc̄ d̄ni p̄r̄ inde
viijᵃᵐ ptem . ꝉ respondetʳ inde inferius inꝑ firm̄ acr̄ ꝉ c̄.

Item Dd ap Ioӡ ap Cadugan . Bletħ ap Ioӡ Vaghᵃn ap
Ioӡ Grono ap Keneūth ap Ioӡ Mad fraꝺ eius Bletħ ap Mad
ap Ioӡ . Keñ fraꝺ eius Dauid ap Mad Duy ap Ioӡ ꝉ Mad Loꝝd
fraꝺ eius tenent inꝑ [se] quartam ptem . ꝉ viijᵃᵐ ptem sc̄de
gauelle eiusdem lecti que vocatʳ gauel Cad ap Danꝝel . reddo
de Tungę ꝑm̄io Oīm Sc̄oӡ xij ꝺ . Unde .iiij. ꝺ in Dennant
.ij ꝺ qᵃ in Grugor .ij ꝺ qᵃ in Quilbreyn . qᵃ dī in Penglogor .
qᵃ dī in Pennaualet .j. ꝺ in Hendreuennytħ .j. ꝺ in Prestlegot .
ꝉ oƀ in Petrual . Et ꝑ past̄ Princ̄ ꝑ annū .iij. ӡ .ij. ꝺ qᵃ ad [p. 159.]
.iiij. ꝑm̄ios ꝓdc̄os videłt ad Natał D̄ni .xij. ꝺ . oƀ qᵃ . et quołt
alio ꝑm̄io .viij. ꝺ oƀ ꝉ ceꝑa s̄uicia in cōi cum aliis infra . Et
medit̄ eiusdem gauelł est esc̄ d̄ni ꝉ respondetʳ inde inferius
inꝑ firm̄ acr̄ . Et .viijᵃ ps eiusdem gauelł est in mañ d̄ni a
tempę Comitę Lincolñ que fuit Keñ ap Mⁱ)dith ap Ioӡ qui
utlagat̄ fuit ꝑ feloñ ꝉ c̄ . Et allocatʳ illa ps filiis Yeuan ap
Lauwargħ liƀo de Lewenny in excamƀ ꝑ hereditat̄ sua iƀm.

Item de quarto lecto quod diuiditʳ in duas gauelł . prima
gauelł que vocatʳ Gauelł Griffri ap Keuret est penit⁹ in mañ
d̄ni ꝉ pur̄ Esc̄ ꝉ respondetʳ inde inferius inꝑ firmas acraӡ .
ꝉ c̄.

Item Keñ ap Lauwar̄ ap Keñ . Caduc̄ ꝉ Yeuan fr̄es eius
tenent quinꝗ ptes sc̄de gauelle eiusdem lecti que vocatʳ
gauel Keñ ap Keuret . reddo de Tungę ꝑm̄io Oīm Sc̄oӡ .ij ӡ
.iij ꝺ . oƀ qᵃ . Unde .x. ꝺ oƀ in Dennant .v. ꝺ qᵃ in Grugor
.v. ꝺ qᵃ in Quilbreyn . oƀ dī qᵃ in Penglogor . oƀ qᵃ in
Pennaualet .j. ꝺ oƀ qᵃ in Hendreuennyth .ij ꝺ in Prestlegotę
ꝉ oƀ dī qᵃ in Petrual Et ꝑ pastu Princ̄ ꝑ annū vij. ӡ .x. ꝺ . ad
iiijᵒʳ ꝑm̄ios ꝓdc̄os videłt ad Natał D̄ni .ij ӡ .vij ꝺ . ꝉ quołt
alio ꝑm̄io .xxj ꝺ . ꝉ ceꝑa suicia in cōi cum aliis ut infra . Et
vjᵗᵃ ps eiusdem gauelle est esc̄ d̄ni uñ rʳ inferius inꝑ firmas
acr̄.

ӡₐ Smᵃ Tungę ꝑgenieij Rand in diũsę villat̄ Commoti

de Ughalet p annum ᵖmino Oĩm Sc̃oჳ .xiiij. ꝰ .v. đ oƀ qᵃ .

De quibus extᵃhendi sunt ab ista smᵃ hic ꝉ ponenđ in aliis villatis ꝑut ꝑbatʳ supius in ꝑcelꝉ singulaჳ gauellaჳ—ix ꝰ . j đ oƀ qᵃ.

ꝰs Et sic restat Smᵃ tocius Tuɲgꝑ villate de Dennant ꝑ annum—v. ꝰ .iiij. đ.

ꝰs Smᵃ pastꝰ ⎰Nataꝉ Ɖni . xvj ꝰ . viij đ qᵃ⎱ Sic ꝑ aᵐ .l. ꝰ
Prĩnc̃ in ᵖmis ⎱Međ xlᵐᵉ . xj ꝰ . iij đ oƀ⎰ .vj đ oƀ qᵃ.
⎰Naꞇ sc̃i Ioħis . xj ꝰ . iij đ oƀ⎱
⎱Ex̃ sc̃e Crucꝑ . xj ꝰ. iij đ oƀ.⎰

*   *   *

Villata de Grugor.

Tota villata de Grugor que conꞇ de ᵖris ꝉ vastis .CCClviij. ac̃r dĩ ꝉ dĩ rođ consistit in tenurᵃ ꝑgenieij Rand Bagħ ap Asser in iiijᵒʳ lectꝑ ut pჳ supius in Dennant et eoჳ ꝰuic̃ plenius patent in ꝑticlis supius in Dennant . Unde ꝑgenies

Wele Rauthloñ ap Ranđ.

Rauthlon ap Rand quoჳ noĩa inscribuntʳ sr̃iꝰ in Dennant teñ hic inꝑ se ut patჳ supius ꞏꝉ totũ Wele Rauthlon ap Rand quod consistit in iiijᵒʳ gaueꝉ . reddendo de Tungꝑ ꝑut patჳ iƀm in ꝑticlis .x. đ . ꝉ nichil aliud hic q, om̃ia alia eoჳ ꝰuic̃ inseruntʳ in Dennant Et dñs nullam ħet escaeꞇ in isto Wele.

Item Wele Idenertħ ap Rand quod consistit ꝑtiꞇ in iiijᵒʳ gaueꝉ ꞏꝉ ꝑgꝑies p̃dicti Idenertħ quoჳ noĩa plenius patent in Dennant tenēt unam gaueꝉ integr̃ ꝉ quinꝗ ꝑtes sc̃de gaueꝉ

Wele Iderneħ ap Ranđ.

ꝉ quartam ꝑtem ꝑcie gaueꝉ ꝉ eciam duas ꝑtes quarte gauelle . Reddendo de Tungꝑ inꝑ se hic ꝑut pleniꝰ patet in ꝑticlis sepatꝑ in Dennant vijᵈ. oƀ ꝉ ceꝑa ꝰuic̃ in Dennant Et sic qᵃi quarta ps ꝉ .xvjᵃ. ps istius Wele vel qᵃi una gauella ꝉ quarta ps istius gauelle est escaeꞇ đni Unde respondetʳ inferius ꝉ c̃.

Wele Daniel ap Ranđ.

Item de Wele Danyel ap Rand quod consistit in ij gaueꝉ ꞏꝉ ꝑgenies p̃dicti Danyel quoჳ noĩa patent in Dennant tenent septem ꝑtes prime gaueꝉ ꝉ mediet sc̃de gaueꝉ Red-

dendo de Tungę pᵾt patȝ in ptic͠lis in Dennant .vij đ oƀ. Et Aᴘᴘ. B d.
ceᵽa ꝫuic͠ in Dennant . Et sic quarta ps ꝛ .xvjᵃ ps istius A.D.
1335.
Wele aut medieꞇ ꝛ viijᵃ ps uniꝰ gaueᵾ est esc͠ đni Unde
respondetʳ inferius ꝛ c͠.

Item de Wele Keuret ap Rand quod consistit in .ij. gaueᵾ
pgēies dicti Keuret quoꝫ noïa patent in Dennant tenent
quinque ptes istius gauelle . reddendo de Tungę pᵾt patȝ in [p. 162.]
pticˡ in Dennant .v. đ qᵃ ꝛ ceᵽa ꝫuic͠ in Dennant Et sic͠
meᵈ ꝛ vjᵗᵃ ps alᵽius medietatę istius Wele aut eciam .j.
gauᵉ. integꝝ ꝛ vjᵗᵃ. ps alᵽius gaueᵾ sunt esc͠ đni Uñ
respondetʳ inferꝰ.

Smᵃ Tungę de Grugor .ij ꝫ .vj đ qᵃ.

Et erit p̄porc͠o escaete đni de ᵽris boscę ꝛ vastę forisfc͠is
in Grugor ꝫcđm veram p̄porc͠oem .Cviij. acꝛ j. rođ ꝛ .xij. ptic͠
De quibȝ allocantʳ [&c]

Villata de Quilbreyn. [p. 163.]

Et sciend ꝗ̃d tota villata de Quilbreyn consistit in tenura
pgenieij Rand Vagᵵ supius in quatuor lectis Et quodꞇꞇ lectū
diuiditʳ in tot gauellis ꝛ totidem p̄porc͠oibȝ ꝛ p̄ easdem
p̄porc͠oes accidit escaeta đni sicut in Dennant vel Grugor
supius . Et cont͠ dc͠a villata in ᵽris boscę ꝛ vastę . Mˡ Clxviij.
acꝛ ꝛ .iij. rođ unde sequitʳ primo de ꝫuic͠ viuoꝫ ꝛ eoꝫ tenuꝝ ꝛ
postea de ᵽꝛ mortuoꝫ contᵃ pacem . que sunt escaeta đni ꝛ c͠.

Pgenies Rautᵵlon ap Rand quoꝫ nōia patent in Dennant
tenent totū Wele Rautᵵlon ap Rand in iiijᵒʳ gaueᵾ . reddendo
de Tungę .x. đ ꝛ ceᵽa ꝫuic͠ in Dennant Et nulla est escaeta
in isto Wele.

Item pgenies Idenertᵵ quoꝫ noïa patent in Dennant tenent
qᵃi medietatem ꝛ .iij. ptes quarte ptis de Wele p̄dc͠i Idenertᵵ
quod ptitʳ in .iiijᵒʳ. gauellis . reddendo de Tungę inᵽ se vij đ
oƀ ꝛ ceᵽa ꝫuic͠ in Dennant . Et sic quarta ps istius Wele ꝛ
quarta ps alᵽius quarte ptis eiusdem sūt esc͠ đni . Uñ rʳ
inferius.

Item ꝑgenies Danyel ap Rand quoꝺ noĩa patent in Dennant tenent medieť 'ꞇ iij ꝑtes quarte ꝑtis istius Wele . reddo de Tungꝉ hic vij đ oᵬ 'ꞇ ceᵱa ꝫuĩc in Dennant . Et iiijᵗᵃ ꝑs 'ꞇ .xvjᵃ. ꝑs istius Wele est esč đni   Unde respondetʳ inferius.

Item ꝑgenies Keuret ap Rand quoꝺ noĩa patent in Dennant tenent vꝫ . ꝑtes medietatis istius Wele reddendo de Tungꝉ hic .v. đ qᵃ 'ꞇ ceᵱa ꝫuĩc in Dennant   Et sic medieť 'ꞇ vjᵗᵃ ꝑs alᵗius medietatis istius Wele est escaeᵱ đni . Unde respondetʳ inferius.

Smᵃ Tungꝉ de Quilbreyn ᵱmĩo Oĩm Sčoꝺ .ij ꝫ vj đ qᵃ.

[p. 164.]   Et est ꝑpars đni in villa de Quilbreyn .CCCliij. acῖ .ix. ꝑtič dĩ que appruantʳ inferius.

*   *   *

Villata de Pennaualetħ.

[p. 165.]   Villata de Pennaualet que conť in ᵬr bosč 'ꞇ vastꝉ .vij lj acῖ dĩ consistit in oῖibꝫ porcõibꝫ in tenura ꝑgenieij Rand ap Asser   Et in tot lectꝉ 'ꞇ tot gauelᵗ sicut ꝑx̃ villaῖ ꝑcedens de Quilbreyn   Et oῖes Pˢ⁾daῖ qui tenent in Dennaut 'ꞇ Grugor 'ꞇ Quilbreyn tenent hic in quatuor lectis ut ibi   Et redđ de Tungꝉ inᵱ se ꝑ annũ ᵱmio Oĩm Sčoꝺ .vij đ oᵬ . Unde Priodaῖ de Wele Rauthlon ap Rand .iij đ oᵬ . Pˢ⁾odaῖ de Wele Idenerth ap Rand .j đ oᵬ 'ꞇ dĩ qᵃ . Priodaῖ de Wele Daniel ap Rand .j đ oᵬ 'ꞇ dĩ qᵃ 'ꞇ Priodaῖ de Wele Keuret ap Rand . oᵬ qᵃ . Et ceᵱa ꝫuĩc in Dennant   Et sunt escaeť đni hic qᵃi unũ Wele 'ꞇ viijᵃ. ꝑs 'ꞇ xijᵃ ꝑs istius Wele que continent quartam ꝑtem 'ꞇ xxxijᵈᵃᵐ ꝑtem 'ꞇ xlviijᵃᵐ ꝑtem istius ville.

ꝫs   Smᵃ Tungꝉ de Pennaualet ᵱmĩo Oĩm Sčoꝺ . vij đ oᵬ.

Et sic est porčo escaeť đni in villa de Pennaualet ꝫcđm ꝑticipacõem directam .CCxxvij. acῖ .ij. ꝑtič dĩ.

Đ quibꝫ allocantʳ diũsꝉ Priodaῖ de Arquedlokꝉ Hano-dregħhaitħ in excamᵬ ꝑ eoꝺ ¹ iᵬm .Cxlviij acῖ dĩ   Et xv acῖ ᵱre arentantʳ ut patebit inferius.

*   *   *

---

¹ So in the MS.

Villata de Penglogor.

Tota villata de Penglogor consistit in tenura p̃dc̃e ꝑgeñ ᴀᴘᴘ. ʙ d.
Rand ap Asser in tot lectꝑ sicut px̃ᵃ villata pcedens Et
iidem qui tenent villaꝟ de Denuant . Grugor . Quilbreyn . et
Pennaualet tenent inꝟ se totam istam villatam p̃ꝟ porcõem [p. 166.]
escaeꝟ dni ut patꝫ inferius ꝶ reddunt per annũ de Tungꝑ ꝑmĩo
Oĩm Sc̃oꝫ vij đ oƀ . Unde Preodaꝛ de Wele Ruathlon ap
Rand .iij đ qᵃ . Priodaꝛ de Wele Idenerth ap Rand ij. đ .
Priodaꝛ de Wele Daniel ap Rand .ij đ oƀ dĩ qᵃ ꝶ Priodaꝛ de
Wele Keuret ap Rand oƀ ꝶ dĩ qᵃ Et facient ceꝟa ꝩuic̃ in
Dennant . Et quarta ps ꝶ .xxxijᵈᵃ. ps ꝶ xlviijᵃ ps istius ville
est escaeꝟ dni uñ rʳ inferius.

ꝫs Smᵃ Tungꝑ villate de Penglogor p anñ ꝑĩo Oĩm Sc̃oꝫ
—vijᵈ oƀ.

Et conꝟ tota villata de Penglogor .Cxxviij. acꝛ Et inde
ppars escaeꝟ dni conꝟ de ꝑrꝑ ꝶ vastꝑ . ꝶ c̃ .xxxviij. acꝛ dĩ ꝶ
xxvj ꝑtic̃ dimiđ.

* * *

Villata de Hendreuennyth. [p. 167.]

Villata de Hendreuennyth conꝟ in ꝑris vastꝑ .CCix acꝛ
iij. rođ cuius medieꝟ consistit in tenura ꝑgc̃ii Rand Vaghan
supius in .iiijᵒʳ. lectꝑ ꝶ alia medieꝟ est de tenura ꝑgenieij
Rees·Gogh in .jᵒ. lecto . Unde primo sequitʳ de pparte prima
ꝶ .ijᵈᵒ. de ijᵈᵃ.

Ɖ medieꝟ villate de Hendreuennyth que consistit in
ꝑgenie Rand Eadem ꝑgenies tenet medietatem illam p̃ꝟ inde
escaeꝟ ut patebit inposteꝫ in tot lectꝑ ꝶ tot gauelꝟ put
tenent in Dennant vel aliis villatis p̃dictꝑ Et reddunt de
Tungꝑ inꝟ se put patet p ꝑticlas specificatas ꝩrꝰ in Dennant
.xv đ oƀ . Et fac̃ ceꝟa ꝩuic̃ in Dennant ꝶ c̃ . Et reddidit ista
medietas de Tungꝑ p annũ dum fuit integꝛ in mañ p̃dicꝟ ꝑgeñ
.xx. đ.

ꝫs Smᵃ Tungꝑ ꝑgeñ Rand Vagh hic—xv đ oƀ.

Y 69

Villata de Prestelegotꝭ.

App. Bd.

A.D. 1335.

[p. 169.] Villata de Prestlegotꝭ que uniu̇salit̾ cont3 .DCxxx. acr̃ t̾re bosc̃ ⁊ vast̃ fuit ptit̃ in .iij. ptes . Un̄ p^i^ma t̾cia ps consistit in tenura ꝑgeniei Ranđ Vagħ ⁊ reddid^t^ illa t̾cia ps dū fuit integ^a^ in tenura illius ꝑgēiei .xx. đ . ꝑ annū . Et alia t̾cia ps consistit in tenura ꝑgēiei Idenerth̄ que sitr dū fuit integr̃ r̃ de Tungꝭ .xx. đ . Et ultĩa t̾cia ps fuit in tenura ꝑgēiei Keneuerch̄ ap Maer ⁊ c̃ . que sitr r̃ de Tungꝭ dū fuit integr̃ .xx. đ . ꝑ annū . Et om̄s p̾dc̃e ꝑgen̄ sūt lib̃e . Un̄ seq^r^ distinctõ p^i^mo de p^i^ma ꝑgēie . sc̃do de sc̃da . t̾cõ de t̾tia.

Ppars ꝑgēiei Ranđ Vagħ. Ꝑgen̄ Ranđ Vagħ quoꝝ noĩa patent in Dennantꝭ t3 hic in .iiij. lect̃ p^i^mā ꝑpartem istius ville . Vidħt t̾ciam ptem except̃ inde .iiij^ta^. pte ⁊ .xxxij^da^. pte⁊ xlviij^a^ pte que sūt escaet̃ đni r̃one mortuoꝝ cont^a^ pacem . Et reddūt p̾dc̃i Priodar̃ nūc de Tungꝭ int̾ se ꝑ annū t̾cõ Oĩm Sc̃oꝝ ꝑut p3 ꝑ ꝑcelħ distinct̃ in Dennantꝭ .xiiij. đ q^a^ . Et n^l^ aliud hic q̥ in Dennant suꝑius.

* * *

[p. 171.] s̃s Sm^a^ Tungꝭ de Prestlegotꝭ .iij s̃ .ij đ.

s̃s Sm^a^ pastus Princip̃ in-t̾m̃is	Natal Đni	.xxiij. đ õ	Sm^a^ ꝑ a^m^ viij. .ix. đ.
	Međ xl^e^	.xxiij. đ õ.	
	Nat̃ sc̃i Ioħ	.xxiij d . õ	
	Exaltacõ sc̃e crucꝭ	.xxiij đ õ.	

Et sci^đ^ q^đ^ de p^i^ma t̾cia pte villate de Prestl̃egotꝭ que est de tenura ꝑgēiei Ranđ Vagħ ꝑtinent đno de escaet̃ ⁊ c̃ . sc̃dam[1] veram ꝑticipacōm de t̾ris bosc̃ ⁊ vastꝭ lxiij acr̃ dĩ .j. rođ dĩ ⁊ .x. ptic̃.

Distincĩo escaete. Ĩtm de .ij^da^. ꝑparte eiusđm ville que est de tenura triū lectoꝝ Madokꝭ ap Ideñtħ . Heilyn ap Ideñtħ ⁊ Eign̄ ap Ideñtħ ꝑtinent đno de escaet̃ .Cj. acr̃ dĩ ⁊ .iiij. ptic̃ t̾re bosc̃ ⁊ vast̃.

Ĩtm de ultĩa ꝑparte eiusđm ville que est de tenura Keneu̇th ap Maer ⁊ Res ap Hunytħ ꝑtinēt đno eođm m^o^ .lxxij. acr̃ .j. rođ dĩ ⁊ .x. ptic̃ . Et sic est sm^a^ tocius escaet̃

[1] So in the MS.

.ij. xxvij. acr̃ .j. rođ dī ꝯ .iiij. p̃tic̃ que appͮant͛ ut statī patebᵗ
īposterū.

*   *   *

Villata de Petrual.

[p. 180.]

Villata de Petrual que cont₃ .Mˡ.C.lxx acr̃ . consistit in
.xiij. lectis libo₃ de quib₃ statim patebit in posterū . Vidĩt de
quoĩt lecto p se.

Priodar̃ de p̃g̃eie Ranđ Vagĥ quo₃ noĩa patent in Dennant
tenent hic tantam ptem in .iiij. lect̃ qᵃntam tenent s̃rius in
Dennant . ĩn tenent hic qᵃi p uno lecto quod vocatᵃ Wele   Wele
Wiryon Ranđ . ꝫciam deciam ptem istius ville . Reddᵭo de Wyrion
Tunge͢ hic p̃ut p₃ in p̃tic̃lis specificat͢e in Dennant .iiij. đ . ob Ranđ.
ꝫmĩo oĩm Sc̃o₃ . ꝯ nˡ aliud hic quia om̃ia alia eo₃ s̃uic̃ on̂ant͛
s̃rius in Dennant . Et qᵃuis reddant hic plenū Tunge͢ ꞉ʹ nˡoᵍ
quarta ps ꝯ .xxxijᵃ. ps ꝯ .xlviijᵃ. ps istius lecti hic est escaet̃
đni . sic̃ de eo₃ tenura in aliis villis . Et iñ r̃ndet͛ inferius cū
ceteris escaet͢e ꝯ c̃.

*   *   *

APPENDIX B e.

*Extent of the Villata of Wickwere with the Hamlets of Boy-
droghyn and Kilmayl, in which the Wele of Lauwarghe ap
Kendalyk held.*

Roos Ysdulas.

APP. B e.

A.D.
1335.

[p. 201.]

Extenta Cōmoͭ de Roos Ysdulas fͨa aᵒ. Regͤ Eͤ iijᶜⁱⁱ. pᵍ
cōꝗ .viijᵒ.

Sciendͭ ꝗd dn̄s nichil ħebit de veͭi dōico nūc in d̄nico suo
nⁱ Maneriū de Dynnorbyn Vaur quod extenditͬ inferius in
serie Cōmoͭ cū villaͭ de Dynnorbyn Vaur ut inferiᵍ patebit in
suo cursu ꝛ c̄.

Villata de Wyckewere cū suis Hamellis de
Boydrogħyn ꝛ Kilmayl.

Villata de Wyckwere cū Hamelͭ de Boydrogħyn ꝛ Kylmayl consistebat tempibꝝ Iᵖⁿcipū ante conquestū in octo
lectis . Unde .vj. lecͭ fuerūt in ōibꝝ locis p̃dͨis vidͭt in
Wyckewere Boydrogħyn ꝛ Kylmayl . Et de hiis .vj. lectͤ
unū lectū fuit penitᵍ in tenura litͦꝝ quod vocatͬ Wele
Lauwargħ ap Kendelykͤ . Secundū lectu consistit vidͭt due
ptes in tenura litͦꝝ ꝛ ͭcia ps in tenura Natͭoꝝ quod lectū
vocatͬ Wele Morythe.

Tͭ)ciū lectū consistit vidꝝ due ptes in tenura litͦꝝ ꝛ ͭcia
ps in tenura Natͭoꝝ quod quidē lectū vocatͬ Wele Peidytħ
Mogħ.

Ceͭa tria lecta de p̃dͨis .vj. lectis fuerunt integre in tenura
Natͭoꝝ . Unde pⁱmū lectū vocatͬ Wele Breyntͤ . Secundū
lectū vocatͬ Wele Meynon et ͭciū vocatͬ Wele Bothloyn
ꝛ duo ultͭa lecta de p̃dͨis .viij. lectis :ᶠ fuerunt tantūmodo

in villa de Boydroghyn ꝉ consistūt pēitᵒ iu teuura Natĩoӡ .

Unde pⁱmū lectū voʳ Wele Anergh Cuyṙdyon, et ŝcđm lectū vocatʳ Wele Thlowthon . Unde sequitʳ de quoꝉt lecto ŝiatim ŝcđm q̄d ꝑmittitʳ ꝉ de nōibӡ inde teueñ cū eoӡ ŝuic̄ ꝉ deinde de ꝑporcōibӡ đui que sibi attinguut ptim r̃one teuenciū morienciū contᵃ pacem, ptim ꝑ defc̄u ŝuicioӡ ptī ꝑ defc̄u heredū in ꝑcio gᵃdu v̄l iufra ꝑciū gᵃdū ꝉ c̃.

De pⁱmo lecto quod consistit tōliꝉ in teuura liꝺoӡ ꝉ quod est in om̄ibӡ vilꝉ ꝉ hamelꝉ fuuut tria lecta seu tres gauelle vidꝉt Wele Risshard ap Lauwargh . Wele Moridykе ap Lawʰ et Wele Kandalo ap Lauwargh, et sequitʳ pⁱmo :´ de primo. sc̄do :´ de sc̄do, ꝑcio : de ꝑcio ꝉ c̃.

De Wele Risshard ap Lauwargh fiuut tres gauelꝉ, vidꝉt gauelꝉ Madokе ap Risshard gauelꝉ Kendalo ap Risshard ꝉ Gauelꝉ Keñ ap Risshard.

[p. 202.]

Gronou ap Madokе Vaghᵃn . Eynon Routh f̄r eius Heilyu ap Eynon ap Risshard . Heilyu ap Groñ ap Eyuon Bleth ꝉ Ithel fres eius ꝉ Heilyu ap Eynon Gogh tenent gauelꝉ Madokе ap Risshard integr̄ redđo de Tungе iuꝺ se ꝑ aᵐ . ꝑio oĩm Sc̄oӡ .viij. đ . Et ꝑ pasꝉ Pⁱucipis ad Naꞇ Ɗni .xij. đ . Međ .xlᵉ. vj. đ Et ad fm Naꞇ Sc̄i Iohis Bapꞇ .vij. đ . oꝺ . Et ad fu Exaltacōis sc̄e Crucis .vj.ᵈ đ . Et facient ceꝑa ŝuicia cū aliis liꝺis istius Cōmoꞇ in cōi de quibӡ patebit in fiñ istiᵒ Cōmoꞇ iuꝺ cōes consueꞇ ꝉ c̃.

In margin: Gauelꝉ Madok ap Risshard.

Madokе ap Heilyu ap Howel . Ithel ap Ioӡ ap Keudalo Griff ꝉ Tuder f̄res eius . Dauid ap Kendalo ap Ioӡ . Dauid Vaghᵃn ap Dauid ap Ioӡ ꝉ Tuder fr eius tenent gauelꝉ Kendalo ap Risshard integr̄ redđo iuꝺ se de Tungе ꝑio ꝑdc̄o .v. đ . oꝺ . Et ceꝑa ŝuic̄ iu oĩbӡ ut Gauelꝉ px̄ ꝑcedens.

In margin: Gauelꝉ Kendalo ap Risshard.

Keñ Vaghᵃn ap Keñ ap Madokе . Eynon fr eius . Ioӡ ap Madokе ap Ioӡ Iũ fr eius . Dauid Loyd ap Kendalo . Ioӡ fr eius . Mađ ap Keñ ap Eynon . Dauid ꝉ Iũ f̄res eius . Madokе ap Dauid up Eynon . Ada ꝉ Dauid f̄res eius ꝉ ꝑdc̄us Heilyu ap Eyuon ap Risshard ꝉ uepotes sui supius iu gauelꝉ Madokе

APP. B e.
—————
A.n.
1335.

Gauelt
Keñ ap
Risshard.

Wele vel
Gauelt
Moridyk
ad Lau-
wargh.

Gaū Ioӡ
ap
Kendalo.

Gaū
Kyloen

Pporčo
liboӡ de
Wele
Mo-
royth.

tenent tres ptes gauelt Keñ ap Risshard reddo inꝑ se de Tungꝑ ꝑio ꝑdco .vj. đ . Et ꝑ past Pincipis p aᵐ. ad Nat Đni .ix. đ . ꝑio Mеđ .xlᵉ . iiij. đ oꝧ . ꝑio Nat sēi Ioħis Baꝑte .v. đ oꝧ qª . Et ꝑio Exalt sēe Crucis .iiij. đ . oꝧ . Et facient ceꝑa ꝫuicia in cōi ut supª . Et qªrta ꝑs istius gauelt est escaeta đni . Unde r̄nebitʳ inferius cū ceꝑis escaetis.

Iẽm de sēdo Wele quod est extractū de Wele Lauwargħ ap Kendalykꝑ et quod supius nūcupatʳ Wele Moridykꝑ ap Lauwargħ nulla extªhitʳ gauelt ideo dicitʳ id idem Wele nisi ut una gauelt unde Kendalo ap Madokꝑ ap Eynon . Eynon ap Groñ ap Griff . Lauwargħ fr eius . Ioӡ ap Lauwargħ ap Griff ꝶ Madokꝑ ap Heylyn ap Griff tenent gauelt Moridykꝑ ap Lauwargħ integr̄ r̄ de Tunḡ inꝑ se .xij. đ . oꝧ . qª . Et ꝑ past Pincipis ad Nat Đni .xij. đ . sēdo ꝑio vj. đ . ꝑcio ꝑio .vij. đ . oꝧ . Quarto ꝑio .vj. đ . Et facient ceꝑa ꝫuicia in cōi ut supª.

Iẽm de ꝑcio Wele exªcto de Wele Lauwargħ ap Kendelyk fiunt due gauelt vidtt Gauella Ioӡ ap Kendalo ꝶ Gauelt Dauid ap Kendalo que đr Gauelt Kyloen ut statim subsequitʳ.

Groñ ap Eynon ap Madokꝑ . Eynon ap Ioӡ ꝶ Iuª fr̄es eius ꝶ Heilyn ap Eynon ap Howel tenent gauelt Ioӡ ap Kendalo integr̄ reddo de Tungꝑ inꝑ se ꝑio ꝑdco .viij. đ . Et ꝑ past Pincipis p aᵐ ad Nat Đni ꝶ quott aº ꝑio.

Iẽm Ithel ap Eynon ap Kendalo ꝶ Phelip fr eiꝰ tenent .vjtª. ptem gauelle Kyloen reddo de Tungꝑ ꝑio ꝑdco .j. đ . oꝧ . Et ꝑ past Pincipis p aᵐ. pimo ꝑio .ij. đ . sēdo ꝑio .j. đ qª . ꝶ qªrto ¹ ꝑio .j. đ . Et fač alia ꝫuič in cōi ut supª Et. vꝗ. ptes istiꝰ gauelt sunt escaeꝡ đni . Unde r̄ndebitʳ inferius ꝶ č.

De duabӡ ptibӡ sēdi lecti quod vocatʳ Wele Moroythe . quod est in villa de Wickewere ꝶ hamelt de Kilmayl ꝶ Boydroghyn sunt qªtuor vidtt due gauelt Meiller ap Morroyth ꝶ due gauelt Lauwargħ ap Morroyth . Et de ꝑcia pte istiꝰ lecti que est in tenura Natioӡ r̄ndetʳ inferiꝰ iꝑ Natios ꝶ č.

—————————————————————————————

¹ So in the MS.

Ioȝ ap Eynon ap Ienaf tenet ꝑciā ꝑtē . jᵖ . gauelł Meiller
ap Morroyth . r̄ . de Tungꝑ ꝑio ꝑdc̄o .iiij. đ . oƀ . Et ꝑ past̄
Pᶦncipis ꝑ aᵐ. vidīt pᶦmo ꝑio .iiij. đ . Secundo ꝑio .ij. đ . ꝑcio
ꝑio .ij. d . oƀ . qᵃrto ꝑio .j. đ . Et fac̄ cefa ꝫuic̄ in cōi ut supᵃ .
Et una gauelł integr̄ ꝫ .ijᵉ. ꝑtes de .ijᵇȝ. gauelł ꝑdc̄is sunt
escaeꝷ đni   Unde r̄nde ͬ inferius.

Eynon ap Kendalo ap Keñ Pithle ꝫ Ioȝ fr eius tenent
medietatē unius gauelł que fuit Lauwargh ap Moroythe . r̄ .
de Tung̃ ꝑio ꝑdc̄o .vj. đ . qᵃ . Et ꝑ pastu Pᶦncipis pᶦmo ꝑio
.vj. đ . Sc̄do ꝑio .iij. đ . ꝑcio ꝑio .iij. đ . oƀ qᵃ ꝫ q̄rto ꝑio .iij. đ .
Et cefa ꝫuicia ut supᵃ Et alfa međ eiusđm gauelle est
escaeta đni   Unde r̄ndebit ͬ inferius.

Rees ap Meiller ap Heilyn . Groñ ꝫ Lł fr̄es eius .
Meiller ap Ioȝ ap Heilyn Dauid Gronou ꝫ Ioȝ fr̄es eius .
Meiller ap Lewet ap Heilyn Eynon ꝫ M̃)edyth fr̄es eius Iñ
ap Ioȝ ap Lauwargh ꝫ Dauid fr eius tenent medietatē gauelł
Ioȝ ap Lauwargh . r̄ . de Tung̃ ꝑio ꝑdc̄o .vij. đ . Et ꝑ pastu
Pᶦncipis ad quemīt ꝑminū sicut pxᵃ gauelł ꝑcedens . Et alfa me-
dietas eiusdem gauelł est escaeta đni . Unde r̄ndebit ͬ inferius.

De duabȝ ꝑtibȝ Wele quod vocat ͬ Pidrith Moughⁿ nō fit
nᶦ una gauelł liƀoȝ unde statim subsequit ͬ . Et de ꝑcia ꝑte
eiusdem Wele que cōstitit in tenura Natïoȝ unde r̄ndebit ͬ
inferius inꝑ Natios sc̄do.

Ienaf map Ithel ap Madok . Riritħ ꝫ Gur̃g̃ fr̄es eius .
Groñ Vagh-n ap Groñ ap Madok . Groñ ap Ioȝ Loyd . Ioȝ
ap Riritħ ap Groñ . Meiller ap Rees . Groñ ꝫ Ieū fr̄es eius .
Ioȝ ap Lauwargh ap Pithle . Dauid ꝫ Riritħ fr̄es eius tenent
.vij. ꝑtes gauelł Priditħ Mough . r̄ . de Tungꝑ ꝑio ꝑdc̄o
.xxiij. đ . oƀ . qᵃ . Et ꝑ past̄ Pᶦncipis pᶦmo ꝑio .x. đ . oƀ .
Sc̄do ꝑio .v. đ . qᵃ . ꝑcio ꝑio .vj. đ . oƀ . qᵃ . Quarto ꝑio .v. đ .
qᵃ . Et cefa ꝫuic̄ in cōi ut supᵃ . Et .viijᵃ. ps eiusđm gauelł est
escaeꝷ đni . Uñ r̄ndet ͬ inferius ꝫ c̄.

Smᵃ Tungꝑ liƀor̄ de Wickewere ꝑ aᵐ ꝑio Oïm Sc̄oȝ .vj. ſ
.xjᵈ. qᵃ.

App. B e.

ijᵉ gauelł
Meiller
ap Mo-
roytħ.
[p. 203.]

Gaū
Eynon
ap Lau-
wargħ
Thletħ.

Gaū Ioȝ
ap Lau-
wargħ.

Pporc̄o
liƀoȝ de
Wele
Priditħ
Mougħ.

Gaū
Priditħ
Mougħ.

APP. B e.

A.D.
1335.

Natiui.

Smᵃ pastᵒ Pⁱn-
cip̄ l̄iꝫ

$\left\{\begin{array}{ll} \text{Nat̄ Dni} & \text{vij. ꝫ .j. đ ob̄.} \\ \text{Med̄ xlᵉ} & \text{iij. ꝫ vj. đ ob̄ qᵃ} \\ \text{Nat̄ sc̄i Iok̄is iiij. ꝫ .v. đ . ob̄ qᵃ} \\ \text{Exalt̄ sc̄e Cᵘcis iij. ꝫ .vj. đ.ob̄qᵃ} \end{array}\right\}$ Sᵉ p aᵐ xviijꝫ.
viijᵈ. ob qᵃ.

De l̄cia pte Wele Moroythe que fuit in tenura Natīoꝫ ut
supᵃ nullus remansit tenens viuus sꝫ est pēitus escaet̄ đni
rac̄one mortuoꝫ contᵃ pacem Et respondetʳ inferius cū cet̄is
escaetis ꝗ c̄.

het domū   nŏ hent domū
Eynon ap Kendalo ap Madok . Ieũ ꝗ Heilyn fr̄es eius
tenent medietatē l̄cie ptis de Wele Pridit̄h Mouḡh . r̄ . de
Tungl̄ p aᵐ l̄mīo p̄dc̄o .vj. đ . qᵃ . Et isti cū aliis paribꝫ suis
inferius ꝗ cū Nat̄is de Dynhengryn inferius reddent adinuicem
p past̄ famil̄ Pⁱncip̄ in cŏi .viij. ꝫ .j. đ . ob̄ ad .iiijᵒʳ. l̄ios
supᵃdc̄os vidīt ad Nat̄ Dni .ij. ꝫ Med̄ xlᵉ .ij. ꝫ . Nat̄ sc̄i Iok̄is
Bapte ij. ꝫ . Et ad festū Exalt̄ sc̄e Crucis .ij. ꝫ .j. đ . ob̄ . Et

Ppars
natīoꝫ de
Wele
Pridit̄h
Mouḡh.

colligitʳ ille pastus p catalt̄ et iiđm Natiui reddunt p aᵐ p
pastu equi Ragloti in cŏi ad fm Exalt̄ sc̄e Crucis .xiiij. đ ob̄ .
qui quidem pastus colligitʳ inl̄ eos p catalt̄ ꝗ c̄ . Et iiđm
Natiui cū illis de Dynhengreyn reddent adinuicem p aᵐ p
pastu dextᵃr̄ ꝗ garcōis ad l̄minū p̄dc̄m .viij. ꝫ .iiij. đ . ꝗ p
constructione Molend̄ de Bragot .iij. ꝫ p aᵐ ad l̄mīos Pent̄ ꝗ

[p. 204.]

sc̄i Mick̄is qui carcantʳ cū Molend̄ p̄dc̄o Et p eīctŏe p̄posit̄ p
aᵐ ad fm exalt̄ Sc̄e Crucis .x. ꝫ . Et quilt̄ istoꝫ Natīoꝫ hens
domū dabit .j. galt̄ ad Nat̄ Dni v̄l .j. đ . Et accidit sc̄dm maḡ
vel minᵒ put pt̄res eoꝫ habuerunt domos v̄l pauciores Et
quilt̄ eoꝫ siue domū huerit siue non . siue ptitᵒ fuit inl̄ cōes
consuetudīes in fine istius Cōmoti Et alt̄a medietatas ¹ l̄cie
ptis eiusdē Wele est escaeta đni unde r̄ndetʳ inferius.

Wele
Brento.
Wele
Both-
leyn.

Itm fuit ibi unū lectū Natīoꝫ quod vocatʳ Wele Breyntl̄ .
et aliud Natīoꝫ quod vocatʳ Wele Bothleyn Et sunt illa duo
lecta integr̄ escaet̄ đni unde respondetʳ inferius cū aliis
escaetl̄ ꝗ c̄.

---

¹ So in the MS.

Extracts from Extent of Denbigh, 1335.

het domū   nĩ teȝ adhuc ut đr   nō ht domū sȝ   App. B c.

Madok ap Ioȝ . Wilt ℣ Ioȝ Wynene fr eius Ioȝ Cam ap

est try diffyc   het domū   A.D. 1335.

Madok ap Willym Dauid ap Ithel ap Willym ℣ Madok ap

Ithel ap Groñ tenent qᵃrtā ptem de Wele Moynou . r̃ de   Wele

Tungℓ inℓ se r̃io p̃dc̄o .ix. đ . oƀ . Et ceĩa s̃uicia fac̄ in om̄ibȝ   Moynou.

ut Nati de Wele supius Pridith Mough Et tres ptes istius

Wele sunt escaeta đni   Unde r̃ndetʳ inferius.

Iĩm de duobȝ lectis Natĩoȝ que sunt penit⁹ in Boydroghyn

ut supᵃ ℣ nichil in aliis villis . pˡmū lectū quod vocatʳ Wele   Wele

Anergh Cuyr Duyon est pēit⁹ escaeta đni vidĩt medietas inde   Anergh

rac̄one mortuoȝ contᵃ pacē . Et alĩa medietas est tyrdiffyc in   Duyon.

mañ đni p defc̄u s̃uic̄ Et inde respondetʳ inferius cū ceĩis

escaetis ℣ c̃.

Et sc̃dm lectū quod vocatʳ Wele Thleytheu ℣ quod siĩr

est penit⁹ in Boydroghyn diuiditʳ in qᵘtuor gaueℓ Unde

statim subsequitʳ de qᵃℓt gaū p se.

De pˡma gaueℓ isti⁹ lecti que vocatʳ gaueℓ Pridith bolgh   Wele

que solebat reddere de Tungℓ .ix. đ . Et p .iij. vasis butir̃   Pridith

.x. s̃ . nullus remansit tenens sȝ est integr̃ escaeta đni unde   Bolgh.

r̃ndetʳ inferius ℣ c̃.

      nō ht domū   nō ht domū

Eynon Voyl ap Eynon ap Groñ . Dauid Loyd ap Ph̃ ap

      nō het dom̃   nō ht dom̃

Dauid Keñ Duy ap Cadogan ap Heilyn ℣ Kendalo ap Groñ

tenent medietatem gaueℓ map Gurnewyth . r̃ . de Tungℓ r̃io

p̃dc̄o .iiij. đ . oƀ . Et p .j. vase dĩ butir̃ .v. s̃ . eodm r̃io Et

ceĩa s̃uicia in cōi ℣ c̃ . Et isti tenentes dicunt q̃d nō soluũt

gallinas neqₚ p opibȝ autūpnalibȝ eo q̃d nullus eoȝ sedet sup

ĩram ĩn quiĩt ĩram tenens siue sederit sup ĩram siue nō :

dabit p opibus autūpnalibȝ sc̃dm dc̃m alioȝ Natĩoȝ supius ₚ   Gaū map

.iij. dietis messionis .iiijᵈ. oƀ . ĩn nˡt inde hic qȝ in gaueℓ   Gourne-

Keñ Duy inferius Et debent isti de iure cenari ad domū sup   with.

ĩram suā construendā simul cū om̄ibȝ aliis Natis domos nō

hentibȝ si habeant unde . Ideo ℣ c̃ . Et alĩa medietas isti⁹

gaueℓ est escaeta đni unde respondetʳ inferius ℣ c̃.

APP. B e.

A.D.
1335.

Gaū
Bryn
pridan.

Gaū Keñ
Duy.
[p. 205.]

inuer⁹
mēdosus,
forte.

Distincīo
escaeī.

nō ħt doñ   nō ħent doñ
Griff Bagħ ap Madokę Gogħ . Groñ ꝫ Tuder fřes eius
tenent ꝑciā ptē gauelł Brynprydan . ř . de Tungę ꞇio ꝑdᴄo
.iij. đ . Et ꝑ .j. vaš butiř eođm ꞇio .iij. š .iiij. đ . et ceꞇa ꝫuicia
ut supᵃ.

Iꞇm Ieñ ap Madokę ap Geinthlyn tenet .ixᵃᵐ. ptem
eiusdem gauelł . ř . de Tungę .j. đ . Et ꝑ .iiijᵗᵃ. pte ꝫ .viijᵃ.
pte .jᵖ. vasis butiř .xv. đ . eodē ꞇmꞺo . Et faᴄ aꞇ ꝫuicia ut supᵃ
Et sic medietas ꝫ ixᵃ. ps alꞇius medietatis sūt escaeꞇ đni unde
 řndetʳ inferius ꝫ ᴄ̄.

ħꝫ doñ   ħꝫ doñ
Iꞇm ꝑdᴄi Eynon Voyl ap Eynon . Dauid Loyd ap Pħ .

ħet doñ
Keñ Duy ap Cađ ꝫ Kendalo ap Groñ tenent ꝑciam ptem ꝫ
xviijᵃᵐ. ptem gauelł Keñ Duy . ř . de Tungę ꞇio ꝑdᴄo .iij. đ .
oꞇ . Et ꝑ .j. vase ꝫ .viijᵃ. pte .jᵖ. vasis buꞇ eođm ꞇio .iij. š
.ix. đ . Et ceꞇa ꝫuicia ut supᵃ Et medietas ꝫ .ixᵃ. ps eiusđ
gauelł sunt escaeꞇ đni unde řndetʳ inferius ꝫ ᴄ̄.

Smᵃ Tungę NatꞺoꝫ de Wickewere ꝫ Boydroghyn ꝑ aᵐ. ꞇio
Omniū Sᴄoꝫ .ij. š .iiij. đ . oꞇ . qᵃ . Unde .ij. đ diffykę.

Smᵃ gallinaꝫ ad Naꞇ Dni ut nūc .viij. galliñ ꝑᴄ .viij. đ.

Smᵃ opū autūpnaliū ut nūc .xlij. opa ꝑᴄ .v. š .vj. đ.

Smᵃ butiř ꝑ aᵐ. ꞇio Oïm Sᴄoꝫ ut nūc .iiij. vaš ꝑᴄ .xiij. š
.iiij. đ.

De aliis pastibꝫ nichil assūmantʳ hic ⸴ quia in fine Cōmoꞇ
ꝫ ᴄ̄.

Et sciend q̄d villata de Wickewere contꝫ in ꝑris boscis ꝫ
vastis . Mˡlxxij. acř .iij. rođ ꝫ dı̄ . Hamelꞇ de Kilmayl contꝫ
in oñibꝫ .Clx. acř ꝫ dı̄ . Hamelꞇ de Boydroghyn contꝫ
.MˡCCCxl. acř řre bosci ꝫ vasꞇ unde Smᵃ in uniůso MˡDlxxiij.[1]
acř .j. rođ . dı̄ . Et inde erit ꝑpars escaeꞇ đni šᴄdm veram
ꝑporcōem MˡDCxxxviij acř .j. rođ dı̄ ꝫ ᴄ̄ . De quibꝫ allocantʳ
diůsis ꝑodariis de Lewenny ꝫ Astretę Canon in excambio ꝑ
eoꝫ ꝑriōniis in dᴄis vilꞇ ꝫ ᴄ̄ . quedam ꝑporcōes diůsoꝫ tenenciū

---

[1] So in MS.

in Wickewere qui obierūt cont⁴ pacem quoʒ pporcões debent
contīere .Clxxv. acř .iij. rođ ꝑre bosc̄ ꝉ vasꞇ . Et sic supsunt
de ꝓpte đni in Wickewere . Kilmayl ꝉ Boydrogħyn
MᶦCCCClxij. acř dï ꝉ dï rođ ꝑre bosc̄ ꝉ vasꞇ que appᵘantʳ ut
patet inferius . Primo in Wickewere postea in Kilmayl ꝉ
deinde in Boydrogħyn.

APP. B e.

A.D.
1335.

Hugo de Hultoñ tenet in Wickewere medietatē .jᵐ. bouaꞇ
ꝑre contiñ .v. acř ꝑre que solebant poni in renꞇli in villaꞇ de
Lewenny ꝑ quibᷓ solebat reddere ꝑ aᵐ .xx. đ . ut patet inꝉ
bouaꞇ de Lewenny ꝉ nūc dāt͛ ꝑ cartā đni tenentʳ quiete cū
alia dimiđ bouaꞇ in Lewenny ptiñ ad Burḡ de Dynꝑeigħ infra
muros.

Bouaꞇ de
Wicke-
were.

Leweł ap Eynon Cogħ tenet .vj. acř .j. rođ ꝑre de escaeꞇ
in Wickewere ꝑc̃ acř .vj. đ . ř . ꝑ aᵐ ad ꝑios l'enꞇ ꝉ sc̄i Micħis
.iij. ᵴ .j. đ . oꞇ.

Firm̃ acř
de
Wicke-
were.

Iđm Leweł tenet .xx. acř ꝑre unde .ij. acř ꝑc̃ acř .vj. đ ꝉ
.xvij. acř ꝑc̃ acř .viij. đ . ř . ꝑ aᵐ ꝑïs ꝑdc̄is .xij. ᵴ .iiij. đ.

Ioʒ ap Eynon ap Yenaf tenet .j. acř dï . ꝑc̃ acř .viij. đ . ř .
ꝉ . ꝑdc̄o .xij. đ.

Iđm Ioʒ tenet .xij. acř .iiij. rođ dï unde .ijᵉ. acř ꝉ dï ꝉ dï
rođ ꝑc̃ acř .viij. đ ꝉ .x. acř .j. rođ ꝑc̃ acř .vj. đ . ř . ꝉ ꝑdictᶒ
.vj. ᵴ .x. đ . oꞇ.

Iđm Ioʒ tenet .iij. acř dï ꝉ .xxx. ꝑtic̄ Unde .j. acř ꝉ
xxx ꝑtic̄ ꝑc̃ acř viij. đ ꝉ ij acř dï ꝑc̃ acř vj đ . ř . ꝉ . ꝑ .ij. ᵴ .
oꞇ.

Et iđm Ioʒ tenet .iiij. acř dï ꝑre ꝑc̃ acř viij đ . ř . ꝉ . ꝑ
.iij. ᵴ.

Ithel Loyd ap Cadoḡ tenet .xvj. acř .j. rođ ꝑre unde xiij
acř dï ꝑc̃ acř .iiij. đ ꝉ ij. acř iiij. rođ ꝑc̃ acř .vj. đ . ř . ꝑ aᵐ .
ꝉ . ꝑ .v. ᵴ .x. đ oꞇ.

Iđm Ithel tenet .j. rođ ꝑre quā Eynon ap Dauid ap Groñ
tenuit . ř . ꝉ . ꝑ .ij. đ.

Iđm Ithel tenet .iiij. acř ꝑre .iij. rođ ř . ꝉ . ꝑ .ij. ᵴ .iiij. đ
oꞇ . ꝑc̃ acř .vj. đ.

App. B e.

A.D.
1335.

Eynon ap Kendal ap Keñ tenet j. acr̃ .iij. rod̃ dĩ p̃c̃ acr̃ .iiij. d̃ . r̃ . ł . p̃ .vij. d̃ . ob̃.

Id̃m Eynon ap Kendal tenet .j. acr̃ dĩ łre . r̃ . ł . p̃ .xij. d̃.

Eynon ap Kendal ap Madok tenet .j. acr̃ dĩ . r̃ . ł . p̃ .ix. d̃.

[p. 206.]

Gurg̃ ap Ithel tenet .viij. acr̃ .iij. rod̃ dĩ . Unde .j. acr̃ .j. rod̃ dĩ p̃c̃ acr̃ viij. d̃ ꝯ vij. acr̃ dĩ p̃c̃ acr̃ vj. d̃ . r̃ . ł . p̃ .iiij. � .viij. d̃.

Id̃m Gurg̃ tenet j. rod̃ dĩ . r̃ . ł . p̃ .iiij. d̃.

Ririth ap Ithel tenet vij. acr̃ .j. rod̃ Unde iij. acr̃ dĩ p̃c̃ acr̃ vj. d̃ ꝯ,iij. acr̃ .iij. rod̃ dĩ . p̃c̃ acr̃ .viij. d̃ r̃ p aᵐ . ł . p̃ .iiij. ꝫ .iiij. d̃.

Iuᵃ map Ithel tenet .iiij. acr̃ .j. rod̃ Unde .iij. acr̃ p̃c̃ acr̃ iiij d̃ ꝯ .j. acr̃ .j. rod p̃c̃ acr̃ viij. d̃ . r̃ . ł . p̃ .xxij. d̃.

Ithel ap Ioʒ tenet .j. acr̃ . r̃ . ł . p̃ .viij. d̃.

Griff ap Ioʒ tenet .ij. acr̃ dĩ łre r̃ . ł . p̃ .xx. d̃ p̃c̃ acr̃ .viij. d̃.

Rees ap Meiller tenet .viij. acr̃ łre p̃c̃ acr̃ vj. d̃ . r̃ . ł . p̃ .iiij. ꝫ.

Id̃m Rees tenet de łra que fuit Keñ ap Meiller .v. acr̃ p̃c̃ acr̃ .iiij. d̃ . r̃ . ł . p̃ .xx. d̃.

Id̃m Rees tenet .vj. acr̃ j. rod̃ łre unde dĩ acr̃ ꝯ dĩ rod̃ p̃c̃ acr̃ iiij. d̃ ꝯ v. acr̃ dĩ ꝯ dĩ rod̃ p̃c̃ acr̃ .vj. d̃ . re . ł . p̃ .iiij. ꝫ . qᵃ.

Et ĩn
valet
acr̃ vj .
d̃ . ad
minꝰ 't
ĩo melius
appᵘetʳ.

Et id̃m Rees tenet .ij. acr̃ dĩ . ꝯ dĩ rod̃ . Unde .j. acr̃ ꝯ dĩ rod̃ p̃c̃ acr̃ .vj. d̃ ꝯ .j. acr̃ ꝯ dĩ p̃c̃ acr̃ .viij. d̃ . r̃ . ł . p̃ .xviij. d̃ . ob̃ qᵃ.

Leuky que fuit uxor Kendał ap Keñ tenet .j. acr̃ .iij. rod̃ p̃c̃ acr̃ .vj. d̃ . ł . p̃ .ix. d̃.

Ead̃m Leuky tenet .ij. acr̃ .j. rod̃ dĩ łre p̃c̃ acr̃ viijᵈ. r̃ . ł . p̃ .xix. d̃.

Ead̃m Leuky tenet dĩ acr̃ łre . r̃ . ł . p̃ .iiij. d̃.

Ioʒ ap Lauwargh tenet .iiij. acr̃ ꝯ xxx ptĩc̃ łre p̃c̃ acr̃ .viij. d̃. r̃ . ł . p̃ .ij. ꝫ .ix. d̃ . ob̃.

80

Groñ Vaghᵃn ap Groñ tenet .iij. acr̃ .iij. rod t̃re p̃cii acr̃
.iiij. đ . r̃ p aᵐ ꝑ . ꝑ .xv. đ.

Iđm Groñ tenet .j. acr̃ .j. rod dĩ eiᵖđ p̃c̃ . r̃ . ꝑ . ꝑ .v. đ . oɓ.

Iđm Groñ tenet .iij. acr̃ ꞇ ꝉciam pt̃e .jᵖ. acre . r̃ . p aᵐ . in grosso ꝑ . ꝑ .ij. ꙅ .iij. đ . ut fater.

Heilyn ap Eynon tenet .iij. acr̃ ꞇ ꝉciam ptem .jᵖ. acre . r̃ . p aᵐ . in grosso ꝑ . ꝑ .ij. ꙅ .iij. đ.

Madokę ap Heilyn tenet iij. acr̃ ꞇ ꝉciam ptem .jᵖ. acre . r̃ . p aᵐ . ꝑ . ꝑ .ij. ꙅ .iij. đ.

Iđm Madokę tenet .j. acr̃ p̃c̃ .vj. đ . ꞇ dĩ acr̃ p̃c̃ .iiij. đ . r̃ . p aᵐ . ꝑ . ꝑ .x. đ.

Ĩtm p̃đc̃us Heilyn ap Eynon tenet dĩ acr̃ t̃re . r̃ . p aᵐ . ꝑ . ꝑ .iij. đ.

Kenerys uxor Madokę tenet .ij. acr̃ p̃c̃ acr̃ .vj. đ ꞇ j. acr̃ dĩ . p̃c̃ acr̃ .iiij. đ . r̃ . ꝑ . ꝑ .xviij. đ.

Ioꝛ ap Ririth ap Groñ tenet .xj. acr̃ .iij. rod Unde .vij. acr̃ iij. rod p̃c̃ acr̃ .iiij. đ . r̃ . ꝑ . ꝑ .v. ꙅ .iij. đ.

Groñ Loyd ap Ithel teꝫ v. acr̃ .iij. rod . Unde .iiij. acr̃ p̃c̃ acr̃ .viij. đ . ꞇ j. acr̃ .iij. rod . p̃c̃ acr̃ .iiij. đ . r̃ . ꝑ . ꝑ .iiij. ꙅ .iij. đ.

Meiller ap Yoruarđ tenet j. acr̃ t̃re . r̃ . ꝑ . ꝑ .iij. đ.

Eddeñ ap Griff teꝫ unā acr̃ t̃re . r̃ . ꝑ . ꝑ .viij. đ.

Eynon ap Griff tenet ij. acr̃ dĩ . p̃c̃ acr̃ vj. đ . r̃ . ꝑ . ꝑ .xv. đ.

Yeuᵃn Loyd ap Groñ tenet .j. acr̃ j. rod t̃re p̃c̃ acr̃ .viij. đ . r̃ . p aᵐ t̃is p̃đc̃is .x. đ.

Groñ ap Ioꝛ Loyđ . tꝫ unā placeam p̃c̃ . oɓ . ꞇ vij. acr̃ dĩ t̃re p̃c̃ acr̃ viij. đ . r̃ . p aᵐ . ꝑ . ꝑ .v. ꙅ . oɓ.

Tangoistel uxor Eynon tenet de t̃ra que fuit Keñ ap Meiller .v. acr̃ t̃re p̃c̃ acr̃ .iiij. đ . r̃ . ꝑ . ꝑ .xx. đ.

Dauid ap Bleth tenet .xiij. acr̃ .j. rod dĩ . Uñ .iiij. acr̃ .j. rod dĩ p̃c̃ acr̃ .viij. đ . ꞇ ix. acr̃ p̃c̃ acr̃ vj. đ . r̃ . p aᵐ . ꝑ . ꝑ .vij. ꙅ .v. đ.

APP. B e. — A.D. 1335.

Madokɼ ap Ithel tenet .ij. acr̃ dĩ ⁊ xxx ptic̃ ꝑc̃ acr̃ .viij. đ. r̃. p a^m. ꝑ. ꝑ .xxj. đ ob̃.

Madokɼ Bagħ tenet unã acr̃. r̃. ꝑ. ꝑ .vj. đ.

Bleitħ ap Eynon ap Ada tenet ꝑram Yockyn Cam natiui diffikɼ que cõtȝ .xvij. acr̃ ⁊ xxv. ptic̃ ꝑre bosc̃ ⁊ vast̃. r̃. p a^m. ꝑ. ꝑ. in grosso .v. s̃. Et n̄ro^9 r̃. p ea Tungɼ ⁊ alia viua ꝑuicia supius no^ata quousq, ꝑdict̃ Ioȝ Cam aut heredes sui

[p. 207.] veñint ⁊ satisfecint p dc̃a t̃ra rehabenđ ⁊ c̃.

Sm^a firm̃ de Wickewere ꝑis	Pent̃ .lvj. s̃ .j. đ. Sc̃i Michis .lvj. s̃ .j. đ.	s^c	p a^m .Cxij. s̃ .ij. đ p j. plac̃ ⁊ .CCxix. acr̃ j rođ dĩ ⁊ .xv. ptic̃ ꝑre.

Herbag̃. Et sic supsunt de ppte·đni in Wickewere .CCxxvij. acr̃ .iij. rođ ⁊ xv. ptic̃ ꝑre ⁊ vast̃ de quibȝ dñs nullũ capit annuale pficuũ nisi q̃d cõitas villat̃ redđ đno p a^m. pinde herbag̃ ad .ij^os. ꝑíos .xiij. s̃ .iiij. đ. Et t̃n valeret quełt acr̃ ad app^uanđ una plus ⁊ alia min^9 .iij. đ p a^m ad min^9. Et sic foret

No^a. app^uament̃ p a^m plus q^am nũc xliij. s̃ .vj. đ ob̃.

Sm^a herbag̃—xiij. s̃ .iiij. đ.

Molenđ. Et est ibi unũ Molendinũ aq^aticũ Unde q^arta ps ptinet đno quã Heilyn ap Watte tenet ad firmã. r̃. p a^m. ad ij^os. ꝑíos ꝑdc̃os .vj. s̃ .viij. đ. Et iđm Heilyn. r̃. đno p a^m. ad eosđm ꝑíos loco Priodar̃ illius vilł p attacħ stagni Molenđ .viij. s̃ .iiij. đ.

Sm^a firm̃ Molenđ cũ attacħ Stagni—viij. s̃ .iiij. đ.

Ioȝ ap Eynon tenet xxj. acr̃ .iij. rođ ꝑre in Boydroghyn Unde .v. acr̃ ⁊ dĩ. ꝑc̃ acr̃ .vj. đ. ⁊ .xv. acr̃ ⁊ dĩ ꝑc̃ acr̃ .viij. đ. r̃ ꝑis ꝑdc̃is xiij. s̃ .j. đ.

Hamelł de Boydroghyn. Ieuan ap Groñ ap Eynon tenet ix. acr̃ ꝑre ꝑc̃ acr̃ viij. đ. r̃. ꝑ. ꝑ .vj. s̃.

Groñ ap Madokɼ tenet. xiiij. acr̃ ꝑc̃ acr̃ iiij. đ. r̃. ꝑ. ꝑ .iiij. s̃ .viij. đ.

Ioȝ ap Madokɼ ap Ioȝ tȝ iiij. acr̃ eiusđm ꝑc̃. r̃. ꝑ. ꝑ xvj. đ.

Heilyn ap Groñ ap Eynon tᵹ iiij. acr̃ .iij. roď eiusďm p̃cii .
r̃ . ℓ . p̃ .xix. ď.

Arr. B e.

A.D.
1335.

Eynon Routh tenᵹ .iij. acr̃ eiusďm p̃c̃ . r̃ . ℓ . p̃ .xij. ď.

Wladus Vergh Edeneweyn tenet . dī acr̃ . r̃ . ℓ . p̃ .ij. ď.

Dauid ap Dauid Wan tenet ij. acr̃ iij. roď eiusďm p̃c̃ r̃ .
ℓ . p̃ .xj. ď.

Dauid ap Ioᵹ tenet j. acr̃ dī eiusď p̃c̃ r̃ . ℓ . p̃ .vj. ď.

Eynon Loyd tenet iiij. acr̃ eiusď p̃c̃ r̃ . ℓ . p̃ .xij. ď.

Dauid ap Ph tenet .ij. acr̃ eiusďm p̃c̃ . r̃ . ℓ . p̃ .viij. ď.

Keñ ap Conagh tenet .v. acr̃ eiusďm p̃c̃ . r̃ . ℓ . p̃ .xx. ď.

Madokᵉ ap Heilyn tenet .ij. acr̃ eiusďm p̃c̃ . r̃ . ℓ . p̃
.viij. ď.

Meiller ap Ioᵹ tenet .j. acr̃ dī eiusďm p̃c̃ . r̃ . ℓ . p̃ .vj. ď.

Madokᵉ ap Dauid Wan tenet j. acr̃ r̃ ℓ p̃ .iiij. ď.

Heilyn ap Eynon tenet .ij. acr̃ eiusďm p̃c̃ . r̃ . ℓ . p̃ .viij. ď.

Itm Heilyn ap Eynon Gogh tenet .j. acr̃ dī eiusď p̃c̃ . r̃ .
ℓ . p̃ .vj. ď.

Keñ ap Eynon tenet .ij. acr̃ eiusďm p̃c̃ . r̃ . ℓ . p̃ .viij. ď .

Eynon Voyl tenet .ij. acr̃ eiusďm p̃c̃ . r̃ . ℓ . p̃ .viij. ď.

Dauid ap Kendat ap Ioᵹ tenᵹ .ij. acr̃ eiusď p̃c̃ . r̃ . ℓ . p̃
.viij. ď.

Dauid Loyd tenet .j. acr̃ ℓre . r̃ . ℓ . p̃ .viij. ď.

Keñ Duy tenet .ij. acr̃ . r̃ p aᵐ . ℓ . p̃ .viij. ď . p̃c̃ acr̃ ut supᵃ.

Madokᵉ ap Ph tenet .j. acr̃ . r̃ . ℓ . p̃ .iiij. ď.

Omñes Natiui eiusďm vilt qui dant butir tenent gauelt
Pᵈdith bulgh integre que cont̃ .l. acr̃ dī ℓre p̃ᵉ pptõ eiusď gañ
in cõi vasto que contineret si ptita fuisset .xxvj. acr̃ dī . ꞇ
xxxij. ptic̃ redď p annū in grosso ℓminis p̃dictis—xvj. ꝯ .j. ď oƀ.

Noᵃ.

Appᵐetʳ
istᵃ ꞇra
meliꝰ q
valet p
annū .
xx . ꝯ.

[p. 208.]

Smᵃ firm̃ de
Boydroghyn.
ℓīs

{ Penꞇ   .xxvij. ꝯ .iiijᵈ. qᵃ
{ Sc̃i Mich .xxvij. ꝯ .iiij. ď . qᵃ

Sᶜ p aᵐ .liiij.
ꝯ .viij. ď p
.Cxxxix. acr̃.
.j. roď ℓre ꞇ
.xxvj. acr̃ dī
ꞇ xxxij ptic̃
vasꞇ si p̃

APP. B e.

A.D. 1335. Herbaḡ.

Noᵃ.

Molend.
ss. S3.
appᵘetʳ
meliˢ . q3
molend
est bonū
꓿ in loco
viuo ꓿ c̄.

Et cōitas eiusďm Hamelt r̄ ďno p aᵐ ad .ijᵒˢ. r̄ios p̄dc̄os p̄ herbaḡ residue p̄partis ďni iᵬm .lv. ꝫ . ꓿ cont̄ illúd residuū si ptitū fūit ꓿ extractū p̄ꝛ vastū p̄porcōis gauelt Priditħ bulgħ

c
supius .vij.l. acr̄ ꓿ xxviij. ptic̄ quaꝫ quett acr̄ valeret p aᵐ ad appᵘanď .ij. ď . Et sᶜ foret appᵘamentū p aᵐ . plus qᵃm nūc .lxx. ꝫ.

Smᵃ herbaḡ p aᵐ—lv. ꝫ.

Et est ibi unū Molendinū aqᵃticū unde . xijᵃ. ps ptiñ ďno quā Dauid ap Io3 tenet ad firmā . r̄ . ďno p aᵐ . ad .ijᵒˢ. r̄ios p̄dc̄os .xvj. ď.

Smᵃ Molenď p aᵐ—xvj. ď.

Io3 ap Eynon ap Yenaf tenet xij. acr̄ .iiij. roď r̄re mortue ꓿ j. acr̄ .j. roď dï r̄re diffikꝝ Unde ij. acr̄ ꓿ dï . ꓿ dï roď p̄c̄ acr̄ iiij. ď ꓿ .xj. acr̄ dï p̄c̄ acr̄ .vj. ď . re . ꝯ p̄ .vjˢ. viijᵈ oᵬ.

Groñ ap Maď te3 .ix. acr̄ ꝑr̄ . p̄c̄ acr̄ .viijᵈ. ꓿ iij. roď p̄c̄ .iiij. ď . oᵬ . r̄ p aᵐ ꝯ . p̄ .ijˢ. iiijᵈ oᵬ.

Eynon Loyd tenet .xiij. acr̄ r̄re . Unde .vij. acr̄ p̄c̄ acr̄ .viij. ď . ꓿ v. acr̄ .iiij. roď p̄c̄ acr̄ .xij. ď . r̄ p aᵐ . ꝯ . p̄ .x. ꝫ .vij. ď.

Heilyn ap Eynon tenet .viij. acr̄ dï . p̄c̄ acr̄ .vj. ď . r̄ . ꝯ . p̄ .iiij. ꝫ .iij. ď.

Madokꝝ ap Heilyn tenet .j. acr̄ . r̄ . ꝯ . p̄ .vj. ď.

Heilyn ap Groñ tenet .iiij. acr̄ r̄re p̄c̄ acr̄ .viij. ď ꓿ .j. roď p̄c̄ .j. ď . oᵬ . r̄ . ꝯ . p̄ .ij. ꝫ .ix. ď . oᵬ.

Tota villata tenet .ij. acr̄ r̄re p̄c̄ acr̄ x. ď . r̄ . p aᵐ . p̄m̄is p̄dc̄is .xx ď.

Smᵃ firm̄ de⎰Pent̄ .xiiij. ꝫ .iiij. ď oᵬ qᵃ⎱Sᶜ p aᵐ .xxviij.
Kilmayl r̄is⎱Sc̄i Micħis .xiiij. ꝫ .iiij. ď oᵬ qᵃ⎰ꝫ .ix. ď . ob p̄
                                                          xlvj. acr̄ dï ꓿
                                                          dï roď r̄re.

Et sic supsunt de p̄pte ďni in Kilmayl .xlvij. acr̄ dï ꓿ .x. ptic̄ r̄re ꓿ vast̄ p quaꝫ herbaḡ Cōitas vilt redď p aᵐ . ad .ijᵒˢ. r̄ios p̄dc̄os .iiij. ꝫ . et tamen si ptit̄ fuissent ꓿ extracte .

valeret quett acr̃ . una plus ⁊ alia min⁹ ad appuand̃ p aᵐ

.iij. d̃ ad min⁹ Et sᵉ foret p̃ficuū p aᵐ . plus qᵃm nūc—vij. ꝝ

.x. d̃ . ob̃.

    Smᵃ herbag̃ p aᵐ—iiij. ꝝ.

       *   *   *

    Smᵃ Tungℓ tocī⁹ Cōmoti de Ysdulas p aᵐ P̃io Oᵐ Scõꝫ— [p. 243.]
lxꝝ. iiijᵈ.

    Smᵃ denar̃ p butir̃ eod̃m P̃mīo—lxiij. ꝝ .iij. d̃ . ob̃ qᵃ.

        vj. ꝝ .ij. d̃ . ob̃ qᵃ   x. ꝝ .j. d̃
    Smᵃ denar̃ p discℓ farine ⁊ Thraū aueñ eod̃ P̃io—xvj. ꝝ
.iijᵈ. ob̃ . qᵃ p Cxlix. discℓ dī fariñ ⁊ xxx Thraū ⁊ iiijᵗᵃ pte
.j⁹. thraū.

    Smᵃ pastus Pⁱnc̃ diũsimode accidentℓ p cʳsū tⁱennalē P̃is

Smᵃ Past⁹ Pⁱnc̃ et Consue- tudines.	Anno r̃ Rℓ Eℓ . P̃cii p⁹ cōq̃m viii⁰	Nat̃ Do̅ˡ	.lij. ꝝ ix d̃ ob̃ qᵃ	sᶜ illo aᵒ	vj. lĩ
		Med̃ xlᵉ	.xxvjꝝ. .vjᵈ. ob̃ qᵃ		.xviijꝝ.
		Nat̃ sc̃i Ioħ .xxxiijꝝ. jᵈ ob̃ qᵃ			xᵈ ob̃ qᵃ
		Exalt̃ . s . Crucℓ .xxvjꝝ. .vᵈ.			dī.
		ob̃ . qᵃ			
	Anno reg- ni Reℓ P̃dc̃i no- no	Nat̃ D̃ni	.iiij. ꝝ . qᵃ	sᶜ toto illo	aᵒ .vj lĩ
		Med̃ xlᵉ	.xxvj. ꝝ .vij d̃		.xix. ꝝ .v
		Nat̃ . ꝝ . Ioħ Bapt̃ .xxxiijꝝ.			d̃ . ob̃ .
		iijᵈ qᵃ . dī.			qᵃ. dīqᵃ.
		Exalt̃ . ꝝ . Crũc̃ .xxvjꝝ. vijᵈ.			

                        Et redd̃o ad pᵐ .
                        aᵐ . ⁊ sic semp
                        decʳrendo p illā
                        differenc̃ triennalem.

    Smᵃ Past⁹ Pⁱnc̃ diũsimode accid̃ p cʳsū tⁱennalem aᵒ tũc
p̃x seq̃nt̃—

Nat̃ Do̅ˡ	.lijꝝ . iiijᵈ. qᵃ	sᶜ toto illo aᵒ .vj. lĩ .xvij. ꝝ .	
Med̃ xlᵉ	.xxvj. ꝝ .iij d̃	ob̃ . ⁊ dī qᵃ.	
Nat̃ . ꝝ . Ioħ .xxxij. ꝝ .x. d̃. qᵃ dī			
Exalt̃ . ꝝ . Cᵘcis .xxvj. ꝝ .iij. d̃.			

Sm^a Pasᵵ famiᵗ Princiᵖ exeunᵗ de Natiũ isti⁹ Cōmoti ᵗis

Naᵵ Do¹	ij. ꝫ	
Međ xl^e	ij. ꝫ	s^c. ꝑ a^m. viij. ꝫ .j. đ oƀ.
Naᵵ s . Ioħ	ij. ꝫ	
Exalᵵ . ꝫ . C^ucis .ij. ꝫ .j đ oƀ		

Et sciend q̃d omēs liƀi istius Cōmoti ᵗ eoꝫ tenentes ꝑᵗ ꝑgēiem Edeñ reddent đno in cōi ꝑ a^m. ad festũ Exalᵵ Scē

xij. ꝫ .x. đ   xx. ꝫ .j. đ   x. ꝫ . oƀ

Crucis ꝑ pastu Staloñ ᵗ garcōis luctraᵣ cũ canibꝫ ᵗ Pennackew ᵗ Waissyon bagħeyn adīuicē .xlij. ꝫ .xj. đ . oƀ . Et colligitʳ inᵗ eos ꝑ cataᵗ ᵗ c̃.

Et omēs Natiui istius Cōmoti ᵗre tenentes reddent đno

ij. ꝫ .iiij. đ   iiij. ꝫ .vj. đ

adimuicē ꝑ annũ eođm ᵗio ꝑ pastũ Staloñ ᵗ garcōis luctraᵣ cũ

ij. ꝫ .iij. đ.   ix. ꝫ .j. đ

canibꝫ Pennackew ᵗ Waissyon bagħeyn . Iᵗm omēs Natiui qui non dant butiᵣ reddũt đno adīuicē ᵗio ꝑdco ꝑ pastu

xiij đ . oƀ

dextraᵣ ᵗ garcōis ᵗ ꝑ pastu equi Ragloti .ix. ꝫ .v đ . oƀ put

plenius patet in villa de Wyckeweᵣ.

.Adhuc
de Sm^a
Past⁹
Princiᵖ
ᵗ
Consue-
tudines.

Sm^a past⁹ liƀoꝫ ᵗ Natiũ ꝑ a^m. adīuicē ꝑ

Pastu Staloñ ᵗ garcōis	xv ꝫ .ij. đ	
Pastu lucᵣ cũ canibꝫ	xxiiij ꝫ .vij đ	ad festũ Exalᵵ . ꝫ .
Pastu Pennak ᵗ Weiꝫ bagħ xij^ꝫ. iij^d oƀ		C^ucis.
Pastu dext^aᵣ ᵗ garcōis	viij. ꝫ .iiij đ	
Pastu equi Ragloti	xiij. đ . oƀ	

Et omēs liƀi istius Cōmoti reddunt đno ꝑ a^m. adīuicē ꝑ sustentacōne domoꝫ ᵗ sepiũ Manerii de Dynorbyn ad ᵗmios Penᵵ ᵗ sci Michis ꝑ eq^ales porcōes .xij. ꝫ .iiij. đ . et colligitʳ ista consuetudo inᵗ eos ꝫc ᵗm eoꝫ catalla ut dicunt.

Iᵗm omēs Natiui istius Cōmoti qui dant butiᵣ reddunt ad

v. ꝫ .viij. đ

eosđm in ᵗmios cōi pro sustentacōe domoꝫ eiusđm Manerii ᵗ

vj. ꝫ .viij. đ

sustenᵵ Molend de Meynyot ut patet supius—xiij. ꝫ .iiij. đ.

Sm^a denar̄ tū de libis q^am de Natis p—

APP. B e.

A.D.
1335.
Consue-
tudines.

Sustent̄ domoꝫ r̃is $\begin{cases} \text{Pent} & .\text{x. } \mathfrak{s} \\ \text{Sc̄i Mich} & .\text{x. } \mathfrak{s} \end{cases}$ s^c p a^m .xx. ꝫ.

Sustent̄ Molend̄ r̃is $\begin{cases} \text{Pent} & \text{iij } \mathfrak{s} \text{ .iiij. d} \\ \text{Sc̄i Mich .iij. } \mathfrak{s} \text{ .iiij. d} \end{cases}$ s^c p a^m vj^ꝫ. viijd.

Sm^a denar̄ exeunc̄ de Natis p diūsis minutę c̄osueꝵ—
Vidett.

Galtis ad Naꝵ Doⁱ ut nūc   iiij. ꝫ . p xlviij. galtis.

Cribrar̄ aueñ ad Pasch ut nūc iij. ꝫ . p xxxvj Cribr̄.

Ouis ꝓ agū eod̄m r̃io ut nūc   ix ꝫ p .viij.lxiiij. oū ꝓ xxxvj. agū.

Opibꝫ autūpnat̄ r̃ Assūpc̄ be M^e. ut īc   xxj^ꝫ p Clxviij. opibꝫ.

Accidunt iste consuedines [1] ꝺcd̄m magę ꝓ min⁹ put plur̄
fuint teñ de Natiuis vl pauciores.

Sm^a denar̄ exeunc̄ de Natis qui non dant butir̄ de fine p
offic̄ ꝓpōiture eis relaxando p annū r̃io Exalt̄ sc̄e Crucis .x. ꝫ.

Sm^a valor̄ opū arure ꝓ herciature de Natis de Meynyot .

Kilkydokę ꝓ Dynorbyn Vagh^an p estimacōem cōibꝫ annis ad
Natat̄ Dni .iij. ꝫ . Tamen accidit sub incerto ꝺcd̄m pluralit̄
Natīoꝫ habenc̄ caruc̄ ꝓ c̄.

Sm^a valor̄ busce ad sepes puc̄ienꝵ de Natis istius Cōmoti
facientibꝫ vl emendantibꝫ sepes cōibꝫ annis p estiacōem pⁱmo
die Maii—ij. ꝫ . Accidit tamen sub incerto.

Et ōmes libi ꝓ Nati isti⁹ Cōmoti reddunt d̄no adinuicē
p annū ad r̃ios Pent̄ ꝓ sc̄i Mich p past̄ Forest̄ in cōi—lx ꝫ
.viij. d.

Sm^a patet.

Et sic est Sm^a valor̄ ōim cōsuetud̄ ꝓdict̄ cōibꝫ annis xvij. lī
.vij. ꝫ .vij. d . ob q^a . dī.

Offic̄ Ragloti cū feod̄ eius valet cōibꝫ annis	C. ꝫ
Offic̄ Ryngildr̄ valet cōibꝫ annis cū feod̄ suis	iiij. lī .ij. ꝫ
Offic̄ Iudic̄ cū feod̄ suis valet cōibꝫ annis	xx. ꝫ
Offic̄ Coidar̄ cū feod̄ suis valet cōibꝫ annis	xl. ꝫ Officia
Offic̄ Seruienꝵ pacis cū feod̄ suis	lx. ꝫ

App. B c.

A.D.
1335.

Offic̄ Ragloti aduocaria꜀ cū reddu hoīm qˡ sūt ī aduocar̄⎱
dūi val꜀ cōib꜀ annis ⎰ xxꝺ

Offic̄ amobr̄ cū amobragiis istius Cōmoti valet cōib꜀ annis x lī

Smᵃ valor̄ Officio꜀ ad firm̄ r̄is—

Pen̄t   xiij lī .xij đ ⎱ sᶜ. ᵽ aᵐ .xxvj lī .ij. ꝺ.
Sc̄i Mich̄ .xiij lī .xij. đ ⎰

Pquis Cur̄.

 It̄m pquiꝺ Cur̄ cū fīñ releū intestato꜀ ꝿ ōib꜀ aliis escaet̄ estimantʳ valere cōib꜀ annis—xx lī.   Smᵃ patet.

Pqˡꝺ Fores.

It̄m pquiꝺ Cur̄ Fores̄t cū ōib꜀ escaet̄ Fores̄t istius Cōmoti estimantʳ valere cōib꜀ annis—xx. ꝺ.   Smᵃ patet.

Smᵃ valor̄ Mañ̄ii de Dynorbyn quod est ī đnico ᵽ aᵐ. — xxiiij. lī .x. ꝺ .vijᵈ. qᵃ.

Smᵃ sᵃma꜀ oīm reddituū cōsuetuđ ꝿ firm̄ istiꝰ Cōmoti uno aⁿ plꝰ ꝿ alio minꝰ iu terminis .

Oīm Sc̄o꜀	.	.vj lī .xix ꝺ .xj. đ . oƀ.⎫	
Nat̄ Dni .	.	lxxviij. ꝺ . .ixᵈ oƀ qᵃ⎮	
Međ xlᵉ .	.	. xxviij. ꝺ .v đ . qᵃ⎮	Sᶜ ᵽ aᵐ .Cliij. lī
Pasch̄ .	. .	. xij. ꝺ⎬ .vij. ꝺ .vj. đ . oƀ .
Pen̄t .	.	lxvj. lī .vj. ꝺ .j. đ qᵃ⎮ qᵃ đī.
Nat̄ . s . Ioh̄ .	.	xxxv. ꝺ .j. đ . dī qᵃ⎮	
Assūp̄c̄ ƀe Mar̄	.	. xxj. ꝺ .⎮	
Exalt̄ sc̄e Cᵘcis	.	. C. ꝺ . oƀ qᵃ⎮	
Sc̄i Mich̄is	lxvj. lī .vj. ꝺ .j. đ qᵃ⎭	

Smᵃ valor̄ exituū qˡ accidūt ꝺb inc̄to ī r̄ñis—

Arure ꝿ herciature   . iij. ꝺ.
Busc̄ ad seᵽ .   . . ij. ꝺ.
Pquiꝺ ꝿ exit̄ Fores̄t   . xx. ꝺ.
Pquiꝺ Cur̄ cū ret̄ ꝿ escaet̄ xx. lī.

Et sic est Smᵃ valoris tocius Cōmoti de Ysdulas ᵽ annū

in ōib꜀ exit̄ scđm istā extent̄—C̄ iiij . xix . lī .iij. ꝺ .ij. đ ꝿ dī qᵃ.

Et pot̄it appᵘari ᵽ annū plus qᵃm nūc put patet ᵽ ptic̄las in diūsꝑ villat̄ de—xvij. lī .viij. ꝺ .xj. đ.

88

APPENDIX B f.

Extent of the Villata of Dynorbyn Vaur.

Manⁱiū de Dynorbyn Vaur.

Situs Manerii de Dynorbyn in quo est una gᵃngia Aᴘᴘ. B f.
cōpetens ꝶ alꝑa penitˢ vastata p̃ꝶ grosꝫ maereᵐ̃ . unū gᵃnaꝛ
ꝶ unā boueria ꝶ una domˢ p feno ꝶ foraḡ debit cont uniūsaꝶr
ij acꝛ ꝶ unā ptic̃ unde aᵧsiaᵐ̃t domoꝫ ꝶ Cuꝛ valet p aᵐ .v. ꝫ .
Et est ibi unū colūbaꝛ ruinosū quod si repetʳ valebit p aᵐ
vj. ꝫ .viij. đ.

      Smᵃ valoris capit̃ Mesuagii cū colūbaꝛ—xj. ꝫ .viijᵈ.

Et sunt ibi de ꞇra arabili que potest quott aᵒ seῑari .j. acꝛ
.iij. rođ dῑ ꝶ xix. ptic̃ que valent in grosso p aᵐ iij. ꝫ .iiij. đ.
Sunt ꞇ ibi de ꞇra araꝟli cōusa in tres seisonas .CCj. acꝛ ꝶ
xxxvj. ptic̃ que valent p aᵐ ꝫcđm diūsa p̃cia .xij. lῑ .vij. ꝫ .ix. đ ·
Unde in una seisona vidꞇt in .ij. culturis in le Spitelfeld .lxvij.
acꝛ .xv. ptic̃ p̃c̃ acꝛ .xv. đ . In ꝫcđa seisona vidꝫ in duabꝫ pec̃ ex
pte occiđ del Spitelfeld .viij. acꝛ .x. ptic̃ dῑ . ꝶ in .ij. forlongꝰ Tⁱᵃra
arabit.
ex pte austᵃli del Spitelfeld usꝙ ad viam regiā subtˢ Pendinas
.lvij. acꝛ .j. rođ .xix. ptic̃ dῑ . p̃c̃ cuiusꞇt acꝛ .xv. đ . Et in
ꞇcia seisonᵃ in le Vaugꞇcleit subꞇiori ex pte boriali vie
p̃đc̃e .liiij. acꝛ dῑ ꝶ xvij. ptic̃ p̃c̃ acꝛ .xv. đ . Et ibm ex pte
australi eiusđm vie .xv. acꝛ ꝶ .xiiij. ptic̃ p̃c̃ acꝛ .xij. đ . Iꞇm
sunt ibi de veꞇi frisc̃ in cultᵃ vocaʳ ¹ le Maorderū .xl. acꝛ dῑ
ꝶ xxx. ptic̃ que non valent conūti cū aliis seisonis ꞇre arabit
ꝑpꝶ eoꝫ debilitatem qᵃppꝶ ordinantʳ de ceꞇo ađ pastʳam
bidenciū ꝶ valent p aᵐ .xx. ꝫ .iiij. đ . p̃c̃ acꝛ vj. đ.

      Smᵃ tociˢ ꞇre arabit—CCxliij acꝛ .iij. rođ dῑ ꝶ .v. ptic̃ .
vat p aᵐ—xiij. lῑ .xjꝫ. vᵈ.

[p. 214.]
Capitale
Mesuaḡ.

---

¹ So in the MS.

App. B f.

A.D.
1335.

Sunt ꞇ ibi in đnic̄ .xxij. acꞃ .iij. rođ ꞇ iij. ptic̄ pᵃti . Vidłt
in magno pᵃto sim̄l iacenꞇ .xvij. acꞃ .iij. rođ dī ꞇ viij. ptic̄ .
Et nūc p̄đc̄m pᵃtū ꞇ le Spitelfelđ cū una pua plac̄ intᵃ ꞇrā
arabilē subꝑioꞃ cultꞃe de Spitelfelđ .iiij. acꞃ .iij. rođ ꞇ .xv.
ptic̄ ꞇ valent in uniũso p aᵐ .lx. ꝫ .viij. đ . p̄c̄ acꞃ ij. ꝫ
.viij. đ.

Smᵃ acꞃ pᵃꞇ .xxij. acꞃ ꞇ xxxiij. ptic̄ qᵉ . vał p aᵐ .lx. ꝫ .viij. đ .

Et sunt ibi de pastura sepali in đnicis .lxxij. acꞃ ꞇ
.xxxiij ptic̄ que valent p aᵐ . ꝫcđm diũꝫ p̄c̄ .iiij. lī .vj. ꝫ . qᵃ .
Unde in Marisco quod vocatꞃ le Frith .lxvj. acꞃ .j. rođ di ꞇ

Pastᶜᵃ
sepał.

·x. ptic̄ p̄c̄ acꞃ .xv. đ . In quadam plac̄ inꝑ ꞃram arabił vidłt
in campo desup le Spitelfelđ j. rođ dī ꞇ xvj. ptic̄ p̄c̄ in toto
iiij. đ . Iꞇm in .j. pcelł subtus Pendinas .j. acꞃ .j. rođ ꞇ .xv.
ptic̄ p̄c̄ acꞃ .xij. đ ꞇ a bosco de Pendinas usꝙ ad porꞇ Manⁱii
ex utᵃꝙ pte le Longeclogh cū viriđ exᵃ portā .iij acꞃ .iij. rođ

[p. 215.]

dī ꞇ xiij. ptic̄ . p̄c̄ acꞃ iiij. đ.

Smᵃ acraꝫ pasture—lxxij. acꞃ ꞇ xxxiij ptic̄ qᵉ . vał p aᵐ
.iiij. lī .vjꝫ. qᵃ.

Boscus.

Est ibi unus boscus qui vocatꞃ Pendinas vestitus debili
subbosco qui cōtinꝫ .xxxiij. acꞃ .iij. rođ qui poꞇit amputari
quołt duodecio anno ꞇ tunc valebit acꞃ .iiij. ꝫ . Et sic si
subboscus pporcionetꞃ in .xij. ptes equales valebit p annū
.xj. ꝫ .iij. đ . Pastura dc̄i bosci si ita pporcionetꞃ valebit nⁱoꝫ
—ij. ꝫ .ix. đ.

Smᵃ acraꝫ bosci .xxxiij. acꞃ .iij. rođ que vał p aᵐ si
pporc̄onetꞃ—xiiij. ꝫ.

Adam Anneiesone tenet ad voluntatem de p̄dictᶜ đnic̄ .j.
plac̄ ꞃre cōꞇ .j. acꞃ .j. rođ ꞇ .xj. ptic̄ subtꝰ boscū de Pendinas

Tꞃra
arentaꞇ
ad
voluntaꞇ.

reddđo p ea p aᵐ .vj. ꝫ . ad ꞃios Penꞇ ꞇ sc̄i Michis p eqᵃles
porc̄ones.

Iꞇm Adam ap Thornlee tenet iᵬm j. plac̄ ꞃre ad voluntatē
đni que continet .iij. acꞃ . ꞇ xxv. ptic̄ . reddđo p annū ad ꞃios
p̄dc̄os .v. ꝫ . equis porc̄oiᵬꝫ.

Adam fił Ric̄i tenet iᵬm .j. plac̄ conꞇ ij. acꞃ .iij. rođ ꞇ .xiiij.
ptic̄ reddđo p aᵐ ꞃis p̄dc̄is .vj. ꝫ .vj. đ.

90

Ioħes de Rothelan tenet iƀm .iiij. acr̄ .j. rod dī ꝉ .xxvij.
ptic̄ ꝑre assar̄ī de bosc̄ de Pendinas . r̄ . p aᵐ .viij. s̄ . eisđ
ꝑis . Et Ric̄us del Nant tenet iuxᵃ le Maorđcrue quaındᵃm
plac̄ ꝑre ꝑ xvj. acr̄ ꝉ .iij. ptic̄ ꝑre . r̄ . p aᵐ ꝑis ꝑđc̄is .viij. s̄.
  Smᵃ acraꝣ ꝑre arentat̄ .xxviij. acr̄ .j. rođ dī qᵉ redđ ꝑ aᵐ
ad ijᵒˢ. ꝑios—xxxiij. s̄ .vj. đ.
  Īſm pquis̄ Cur̄ estimantʳ valere cōibꝫ annis—xiij. s̄ .iiij. đ.
                                            Smᵃ patet.
  Smᵃ valoris tocius Maneꝝ de Dynorbyn ī oĩbꝫ exiꝉ ꝑ aᵐ —
xxiiij. lī .x. s̄ .vij. đ qᵃ.

  Et est ibi quedam Hamelꝉ que ptiñ ad Maneꝝ ꝑđc̄m ꝉ
consistebat temporibꝫ Princip̄ integr̄ in manibꝫ Natīoꝣ qui
consueuerūt fade diu̅s consueꝉ ꝉ opa ad Maneꝝ de Dynorbyn
que nūc eis arenꝉ a tempore Comiꝉ Liucolñ . Ita qd omēs
Natiui eiusđm Hamelꝉ reddūt adinuicē ꝑ annū ꝑ om̄imodis
redditibꝫ . consuetud̄ ꝉ opibꝫ ad ꝑios Penꝉ ꝉ sc̄i Miċhis ꝑ
equales porc̄ones .xxxv. s̄ .x. đ . Et iiđm Custumarii teñ inꝉ se
hereditaꝛ totam illam Hamelꝉ p̄ꝉ .xl. acr̄ dī . ꝉ xxx ptic̄ que
conſtuntʳ in dōic̄ Maneꝝ supᵃđc̄i . ꝉ p̄ꝉ .xxxviij. acr̄ dī que
arenꝉ inferius ut statim paꝉ in posꝑum.

Smᵃ Reddiꝉ ꝉ cons̄ Ha-⎫ Penꝉ .xvijˢ. xj. đ. ⎫ sᶜ ꝑ aᵐ .xxxvˢ.
  melꝉ de Mayrdreue ⎬ Sc̄i Miċhis .xvijˢ. xjᵈ ⎬ xᵈ.
  arenꝉ in ꝑm̄is ⎭ ⎭

Hamelꝉ de Mayrdreue.

  Cōitas ville tenet .xiiij. acr̄ de escaeꝉ p̄c̄ acr̄ .viij. đ . r̄ .
ꝑ aᵐ ad ijᵒˢ ꝑios ꝑđc̄os .ix. s̄ .iiij. đ.
  Eadem Cōitas tenet .viij. acr̄ ꝑre eiusđm p̄c̄ . r̄ . ꝑ . p̄ .v. s̄
.iiij. đ.
  Willym Cam tenet .iij. acr̄ dī eiusđm p̄c̄ . r̄ . ꝑ . p̄ .xx. đ.
  Griff ap Iackę tenet iiij. acr̄ eiusđ p̄c̄ . r̄ . ꝑ . p̄ .ij. s̄
.viij. đ.

Hamelꝉ de Mayrdreue.

  Ioħes de Rothelan tenet .iiij. acr̄ eiusđ p̄c̄ . r̄ . ꝑ . p̄ .ij. s̄
.viij. đ.
  Ioħes de Pontefracto ꝉ Roƀtus de Castelforđ teñ qᵃndᵃm
plac̄ vocaꝉ Thle Tee Madokę que conꝉ .vj. acr̄ r̄ . ꝑ . p̄ . in
grosso .iiij. s̄.

Aᴘᴘ. B f.
A.D.
1335.

Smᵃ firm̃ de Mayrdreue t̃is { Pent̃ .xij. ſ .x. đ .
{ Sc̃i Mich̃ .xij. ſ .x. đ.

Sᶜ p aᵐ xxv. ſ .viij. đ p xxxviij acr̃ dĩ t̃re.

Et sic supsunt de ppte đni iƀm .xviij. acr̃ t̃re t̃ vasti p quaꝫ h̃bag̃ comunitas ville reddit p aᵐ . ad ijᵒˢ. t̃ios p̃dc̃os .v. ſ . Et t̃n valeret quelibet acr̃ ad appᵘand̃ p aᵐ . ad minᵍ iiij. đ . Et sic foret appᵘamentū plus qᵃm nunc .xij. đ.

Smᵃ herbag̃ p aᵐ—v. ſ.

Et sic restat clarus valor tocius Mañii cū villata de Dynorbyn Vaur p aᵐ . ĩ uniůso—xxvij. lĩ .xvij. ſ .j. đ qᵃ.

APPENDIX B g.

Extent of the Villata of Tebrith.

Ros Ughdulas.

Extenta Cōmoti de Ugħdulas facta anno regni Regis
Edwardi tercii post cōquestū .viij°.

Dominus nichil ħet in đnico in Cōmoto de Ugħdulas nisi
pporcōes que sibi acciderūt in diừsis villaī de quibȝ porcōibȝ
r̄ndebitr iferi⁹ in qualibet villaī p se . que quidem porcōes
acciderunt đno tāqªm escaeī ptim rac̄one mortuoȝ contª pacem
ptim p defc̄u seruic̄ ꝉ c̄.

Villata de Tebritħ.

Tota villata de Tebritħ cū Hamelī suis de Maencokę ꝉ
Keuenkestiltħ tenetr in quinq̨ lectis quoȝ quodlibet lectū
solebat reddere de Tungę dum fuit iutegr̄ in mañ viuoȝ tenenc̄
.iiij. ȝ . r̄mīo Oīm Sc̄oȝ . Vidīt Wele Genthlyn ap Pithle .
Wele Kemmyngę ap Pithle . Wele Cadugan ap Pithle . Wele
Edeñ ap Pithle ꝉ Wele Risshard ap Pithle Et sunt om̄es
tenentes in vilī ꝉ Hamelī p̨đc̄is liħi Pⁱodar̄ ꝉ null⁹ Natiuus ꝉ
vocantr Wyrion Pithle.

Ioȝ Gogħ ap Madok Eynon ap Yenafę ⎫
ap Pħ . Dauid ap Ieuªn Gogħ Madokę ap ⎥
Meurykę ap Heilyn tenent .iiijᵒʳ. ptes istius ⎥
Wele redđo de Tungę adinuicē r̄mīo Oïm ⎥
Sc̄oȝ .iij. ȝ .ij. đ . oħ . Et p pasī Pⁱnc̄ p annū ⎥
ad Nataī Đni .xv. đ . Et isti cū cū ¹ om̄ibȝ ⎥
aliis Priodar̄ isti⁹ ville reddunt adinuicē p ⎥
pasī Pⁱnc̄ Međ xlᵉ . ij. ȝ . ad festū Naī Sc̄i ⎭

Wele
Gen-
thlyn.

¹ So in the MS.

APP. B g

A.D.
1335.

Ioħis Bap̄te .ij. ꝝ ꝉ ad festū Exalꞇ Sc̄e Crucis
.ij. ꝝ . Et facient om̄ia alia ꝗuic̄ in cōi cū
om̄ibꝫ liꝭis istius Cōmoti, que patebunt inferius in fine istius Cōmoti . Et vᵗᵃ. ꝑs istius
Cōmoti est escaeꞇ d̄ni   Unde r̄ndetʳ inferius.

Griffç ap Đd ap Aur Madokç ap Aur
Vaghᵃn . Yeuᵃn Vaghᵃn ap Ieuan . Yeuan
ap Đd Aur . Ioꝫ Eynon ꝉ Dauid f r̄es eius
Tuder ap Ioꝫ ap Aur . Heilyn Gruff ꝉ Dauid
f r̄es eius Tuder ap Madokç Vaghᵃn . Mađ fr
eius . Yeuᵃn Guyn ap Mađ . Yeuᵃn ap Đd
ap Keñ . Yeuᵃn ap Đd ap Madokç . Bletħ
ap Ioꝫ Vaghᵃn . Dauid fr eius Dauid ap
Grono Vaghᵃn ap g̃g . Tuder fr eius Bletħ
ap Đd ap Griffry Eynon Gogħ ap Eynon ꝉ
Ithel ap Grono Gogħ tenent tres ꝑtes istiˢ
Wele excepta inde xxxvjᵗᵃ ꝑte reddo de Tungç
adinuice ꝑmīo Oīm Sc̄oꝫ iij. ꝝ .ij. đ . Et ꝑ
past̄ Pⁱnc̄ ad Natal Đni .xiij. đ qᵃ . ꝉ ceꝑa
ꝗuicia cū aliis in cōi ut supᵃ . Et .iiijᵗᵃ. ꝑs ꝉ
xxxvjᵗᵃ. ꝑs ceꝑū triū pciū istiˢ Wele sūt
escaeꞇ d̄ni   Uñ r̄ndetʳ cū ceꝑis escaetis inferius.

Wele
Ken-
nyng.

Et om̄es isti
liꝭi Priodar̄ r̄ .
adīuicē ꝑ Past̄
Staloñ ꝉ garc̄
lucr̄ cū canibꝫ
ꝉ Pennak ꝉ
Waiꝡ bag-
ħeyn p aᵐ . ad
fm Exalꞇ Sc̄e
Crucis iij. ꝝ
.x. đ . Et
colligitʳ inꝉ
eos ꝑ eoꝫ
catalla.

caue

Ioꝫ ap Willym ap Mereduth . Caduḡ ap Willym ap Caduḡ .
Lꞇ . Gogħ ap Đd . Mereduth fr eiˢ . Mereduth ap Lꞇ Meiller .
Ioꝫ ap Tudʳ ap Eynon ꝉ Keñ ap Đd Voyl ꝉ Hoel ap Đd ap
Doyokç tenent medietatē ꝉ duodecimā ꝑtē istiˢ Wele . r̄ . de
Tungç adinuicem ꝑmīo oīm Sc̄oꝫ .ij. ꝝ .iiij. đ   Et ꝑ pastu
Pⁱnciꝑ ad Natale Đni—xj. đ . Et ceꝑa ꝗuicia cū aliis in cōi ut
supᵃ . Et residuū istius Wele est escaeꞇ d̄ni . Unde respondetʳ
cū ceꝑis escaetis inferius.

Wele
Caduḡ.

Meređ ap Mađ ap Eynō . Đd Loyd ap Lauwargħ . Tuder
ap Griffuth ap Groñ Eynon Gogħ ap Đd . Groñ ap Ioꝫ Gogħ .
Bletħ ap Ioꝫ ap Groū ꝉ Griff ap Ioꝫ ap Groñ tenent totū istud

Wele
Edeñ.

Wele redďo de Tungę adinuicem P̃mīo Oĩm S̃coȥ .iiij. ȿ . Et

p pastu P¹nc̃ ad Natał Do¹ .xviij ď . Et ceᵖa ᵍuic̃ in cõi cū

aliis ut supᵃ Et dñs nullam habet escaetã in isto Wele.

Lauwargħ ap Meiller ap Caduᵹ . Dauid ap Griffri ap

Yenafę Eynon fr eius Dauid ap Edeū ap Daniel ꝉ Edeñ fr

eius tenent totū istud Wele . r̄ . de Tungę adinuicē P̃mīo oĩm

S̃coȥ .iiij. ȿ . Et p̣ pas̄t Princ̃ ad Nat̄ Ðni .xviij. ď ꝉ ceᵖa ᵍuic̃

in cõi cū aliis supius . Et dñs nullam ħet escaet̄ in isto

Wele.

Smᵃ Tungę de Tebryth p̣ aᵐ. P̃mīo Oĩm S̃coȥ—xvjˢ. viijᵈ.

oƀ.

Smᵃ pastᵒ P¹nc̃ P̃īs

$$\begin{cases} \text{Nat̄ Ðni vjˢ .iij ď . oƀ qᵃ} \\ \text{Medʰ .xlᵉ} \quad\quad\quad . \quad . \text{ ij . ȿ.} \\ \text{Nat . s . Ioħ Bapt̄ . ij . ȿ} \\ \text{Exalt̄ S̃ce Crucis . ij . ȿ} \end{cases}$$ Sic p̣ aᵐ. xijˢ .

iij ď oƀ qᵃ

Et contlet ppars escaet̄ ďni in vilł ꝉ Hamelt p̃dc̃is

.iiij.xxv. acr̄ dī P̃re bosc̄ ꝉ vast̄ que appᵘantʳ ut statim patebit

in posᵖum.

*   *   *

APPENDIX B h.

Extract from the Cymwd of Ughalet.

Et quicumq̄ eoʒ obierit filius eius ꝛ ħes dabit đno p̄ releū anteqᵃ eius hereditaꞇ optiñe possit v. ꝰ . Et si filius non ħůit tunc fraꝛ eius aut nepos aut consanguineus qui eius heres ꝑpinquior fůit videꞇt in ꝛcio gradu vel infra dabit p̄ releū suo x. ꝰ . Et qui in remocõri gradu fůit qᵃm in ꝛtio non poꝛit hereditꞇ exiḡe nᶜ optinere q̄ exᵃ ꝛ ꝑciů gradū nō est inꝛ eos descensus ħeditarius sʒ in hoc cãu erit ꝛra puꞃ escaeꞇ đni Tamen si đns velit ħiˢ ꝛram alicui tenenti dimittere cicuis dimittenda est ꝑpinquiori de sanguine illius a quo ꝛra illa sic accidit đno p̄ defectu sanguinis ꝑpinquioris qᵃm alicui extᵃnio p̄ vero valore ꝛ c̄.

Item si quis eoʒ seu quoʒcumq̄ alioʒ Naꞇioʒ istius Cōmoti filiam suam maritaůit aut quecumq̄ filiaʒ Natiū seipam maritaůit v̄l eciam sup fornicacõe conuicta fůit dabit đno p̄ amoꞇr v. ꝰ . Et si iꝑa forte non ħůit vnde solůe ꝑpinquiores pentes eius seu amici soluant p̄ ea . Et eciam si vxꝛ alicuiˢ Natiui sup adulꞇio conuicꞇ fůit maritus eius soluet p̄ ea simiꞇr p̄ amoꞇr v. ꝰ . Et ħ quocienscumq̄ alique eaʒ ꝰr huiˢmoⁱ maritaḡ Fornicacõibʒ aut adulꞇiis cum diůs ꝑsonis comisseꝶ seu iꝛateꝶ conuinci poꝛunt.[1]

[1] There is a similar statement at the end of the Extent of the Cymwd of Ros Ughdulas.

APPENDIX C.

EXTRACTS FROM EXTENT OF THE LANDS OF THE BISHOP OF ST. DAVID'S, A.D. 1326.

Additional MSS. 34135, *British Museum.*

Extent̃ oı̃m terrarũ et reddituũ đni Ep̃i Meneũ fact̃ p Magr̃m Dauid Fraunceys Cancellar̃ Meneuens̃ tempore venerabił patris đni Dauid Martyñ . Dei gr̃a Ep̃i loci Anno Đni . Milłmo .CCC^mo^. vicesimo sexto. APP. C. A.D. 1326. [Fol. 1.]

* * *

Villa de Landewybreny. [Fol. 35.]

Oweyñ ap Lł . Ythel Loyd . Gr̃ ap Ieu^a^n . Ieu^a^n Seys . Dauid ap Gruff Dun . Ieu^a^n ap Gwelowe . Ieu^a^n ap Gr̃ ap Lł . ⁊ Hõ ap Ieu^a^n iurati ibm dicunt p sacr̃m eoꝝ q̃d dñs ħet ibm unã domum in villa Et vał p annũ ad locanđ ij. s̃.

* * *

Patria de Landewybreny. [Fol. 36.]

* * *

Itm dicũt q̃d sunt ibiđ .viij. lecti qui vocant^r^ Gwely de p^i^mo Gwely Lł ap Vryeñ . Iorŭth Gogħ . Iorŭth ap Gr̃ . ⁊ descendentes ab eisđređ đno p annũ .iij. s̃ .iiij. đ ad fm sc̃i Michi . De sc̃do Gwely sunt Kediuor ap Cradoc . Gwasmyhangel ap Cradoc ⁊ descendentes ab eisđ ređ đno p annũ iij. s̃ .iiij. đ . eođ t̃mĩo . De tercio . Gwely sũt Cadog^a^n Capłłus Euer̃ fił Capłłi . Iorŭth ap Cradoc ⁊ descendentes ab eisđ ređ đno iij. s̃ .iiij. đ eođ t̃ĩo . De quarto . Gwely sũt Gronou ap Duthgu . Dauid ap Gwyon . Trah^a^rn ap Ithel ⁊ descendentes ab eisđ ređ đno p annũ iij. s̃ .iiij. đ . De Libi tenĩt.

APP. C.

A.D.
1326.

quinto . Gwely sunt Dauid ap Traharn Pħ ap Cadogañ .
Eynoñ Vagh·n ⁊ descendentes ab eisđ redđ đno p annū
iij. ꝭ .iiij. đ . eođ ℔ . De sexto . Gwely sunt Pħ ap Cadranđ .
Gurgeñ fraℓ eius Dauid Dauid frater eiusđm ⁊ descendentes
ab eisđ redđ đno p aᵐ .iij. ꝭ .iiij. đ . eođ ℔ . De septimo .
Gwely sunt Meileꝛ Capħtus Dauid ap Auel Gwas Dewy
Vagh·n . ⁊ descendentes ab eisđ redđ đno p aᵐ .iij. ꝭ .iiij đ. eođ
℔io . De octauo . Gwely sunt Dauid Coyg̃ Dauid ap Zossetħ .
Cadogañ ap Dđ . ⁊ descendentes ab eisđ redđ đno p annū
iij. ꝭ .iiij. đ . eođ ℔io . Et omͤes p̃đc̄i tenent p antiquam
tenurā vidꝫ p Acħ ⁊ Edriđ.

Smᵃ—xxvj. ꝭ .viij. đ.

Seruic̄.

Et omͤes p̃đc̄i dabūt p ħiett̄ .vij. ꝭ vj. đ . Et dabūt p
leyrwit̄ .ij. ꝭ . Et quolꝫ iijᵒ anno p cōmortħ in kt̄n Maii .viij.
vacc̄ . Et sic diuidendo quolꝫ .iijᵒ. anno est valor đno .xvij. ꝭ
.ix. đ . Et dabūt pannag̃ viꝫ ubi vij porci v̄l pꞇres fũint .j.
Et si paucͤores nℓ . Ita q̃d đns porcoꝛ eligat .ij. de uniůso ⁊
đns funuı ℔ciū Et cariare đent grossū ᶆeᶆ q̃d tᵃhi non
potest p .j. equū de foresta de Atꝓ usꝗ Maħiū de Landogy
p quinꝗ domibꝫ ibiđ facienđ viꝫ aula Caᶆa đni Coquina
staħlo ⁊ grang̃ sumptibꝫ suis Et cariare đent grosꝭ ᶆeᶆ p
molenđ quociens opus fũit . Et emendare fossam eiusđ Et
molares eiusđ cariare sumptibꝫ eoꝛ . Et fac̄ sect̄ ad molenđ
Et dicūt q̃d heredes cuiᵖlīt compelli đent ad recipienđ
ħeditat̄ post mortem pent̄ facienđ inde ꝺuic̄ debit̄ ⁊ consuet̄ .
Et ducͤe đent prisones apud villa ¹ de Landewy Et de villa usꝗ
Lawhađ quociens opus fũit sūptibꝫ suis Et fac̄ sect̄ Cuꝛ de
.iij. sept̄ in .iij. sept̄ . Et est cōe aᶆciament̄ eoꝛ .vij. ꝭ .vj. đ .

Aᶆcia-
ᶆet vij. ꝭ
.vj. đ

Et in Nunđ ibiđ fac̄ clausurā modo ⁊ locis consuet̄ cū quinꝗ
villis sequeñ sūptibꝫ suis . Et omͤes tenentes liħoꝛ de Cardiganshire solůe đent tholloñ de rebꝫ ⁊ aͤialibꝫ venđ ⁊ empt̄ .
Et valent dict̄ ꝺuic̄ ⁊ consꝭ p estimacōem

Smᵃ—

⁎ ⁎ ⁎

---

¹ So in the MS.

Extent of St. David's, 1326.

Carthely.

Iŧ dicunt q̃d pŧiŧ ⁊ pquis iɓm valent p annũ .iij. ꝸ.

Iŧ dicũt q̃d est iɓm .j. lectus qui vocatᵣ . Gwely . de quo sũt Ieuᵃn Vaghᵃn ap Ieuᵃn Wyth Lewet ap Gurgeñ . Gruff Hageᵣ ⁊ descendenŧ ab eisđ redđ đno p annũ .vj. ꝸ .viij. đ . ad fm sc̃i Mich.

Smᵃ—

Et om̃es p̃dc̃i dabũt unā vaccā quolꝛ .iij. anno in kŧñ Maii p Cõmorth . Et valꝛ porc̃o cuiuslīt anni .ij. ꝸ .ij. đ . Et facient oĩa ꝛuic̃ ⁊ conꝸ ut dc̃i tenentes de p̃ria de Landewybreny.

Llannon.

Eynon ap Wylym . Cadogañ ap Ieuᵃn ⁊ Ieuᵃn ap Howel . iurati ibiđ dicunt p sacr̃m eoꝛ q̃d pŧiŧ ⁊ pquis Cuᵣ iɓm transeũt cũ Cuᵣ de Landewy Aberarth . Iŧ dicũt q̃d est iɓm unus lectus qui dicitᵣ Gwely de quo sunt dc̃i iuraŧ cũ sequela ⁊ descendenŧ ab eisđ redđ đno p annũ .vj. ꝸ .viij. đ ad fm sc̃i Mich.

Smᵃ—

Et om̃es p̃dc̃i dabũt quolꝛ .iijᵒ. anno in kŧñ Maii unā vacc̃ p cõmorth Et valꝛ porcio cuiᵖlit anni .ij. ꝸ .ij. đ . Et fac̃ om̃ia ꝛuic̃ ⁊ consuetuđ ut p̃dc̃i tenentes de Landewybreny.

Smᵃ—

Bangor.

Iŧ dicũt q̃d sunt iɓm .iiijᵒʳ. lecti de quibꝛ pⁱmus vocatᵣ. Gwely Euewris de quo sunt tenenŧ Lewet Capŧtus Gruff ap Ieuᵃn ⁊ eoꝛ cõporc̃ Et redđ đno p aᵐ .v. ꝸ ad fm sc̃i Mich . Et sc̃dus lectus voᵣ. Gwely Oyroñ . redewyth de quo sunt tenentes Yweryth fiŧ Gronou Ieuᵃn ap Ricarđ . Res ap Gᵣ̃ ⁊ eoꝛ comporc̃. Et redđ đno p annũ .v. ꝸ eod ꝑ . Et .iijᵖ. lect⁹

---

[1] In a later hand.

A.D. 1326.
[Fol. 37.]
p̃ficua.
Liɓi.

Seruic̃.

[Fol. 38.]

Liɓi.
Infra parochiam de Llansanfrede.[1]

Seruic̃.

[Fol. 39.]
Tenenŧ iɓm.

APP. C.

———
A.D.
1326.
[Fol. 54.]
Libi.

voͬ . Oyroñ cuelyn de quo sũt tenentes Gruff ap Res . Ieuᵃn ap Adafç ꞇ eoʒ comporç . Et redđ đno p aᵐ .v. ꞩ eođm ꝉmino. Smᵃ .xx. ꞩ.

*   *   *

Arcħnatus Brechoñ . Glastoñ.

Iꞇm dicũt q̃d sunt iƀm .iij. lecti qui vulgo vocantͬ Gwele. De pᵒ Gwele est stipes Cregç ꞇ descendeutes ab eođ redđ đno p aᵐ .iiij. ꞩ . ad fm sc̃i Micħ . Et de sc̃do lecto est stipes Kenyllyn ꞇ descenđ ab eođ redđ đno p annũ .iiij. ꞩ eođ ꝉio . Et de .iij. lecto Kywryđ est stipes ꞇ descenđ ab eođ redđ đno p aᵐ .iiij. ꞩ . eođ ꝉio.

Sm —xij. ꞩ.

APPENDIX D.

INQUISITION CONCERNING THE SEIZURE BY PRINCE LLEWELYN OF LANDS HELD IN DOWER BY A WIDOW, AND CHARTERS OF GRIFFIN, SON OF MADOC, LORD OF BROMFELD, GRANTING THE VILLÆ OF HENGEMERE, LANERPANNA, AND CNOLTON, AND THE MANOR OF EYTUNE, IN MAELOR SEYSNEK, TO EMMA, HIS WIFE, FOR HER LIFE; AND CONFIRMATION BY HIS SONS MADOC, LLYWELYN, OWEN, AND GRIFFIN, A.D. 1270.

Chancery Inquisition post Mortem, 5 Edw. I., No. 78,
Public Record Office.

APP. D.

A.D.
1270.
(m. 1.)

Edwardus Dei gͬa Rex Angɫ Dn̄s Hibn ⁊ Dux Aquiⷮ dilc̃o ⁊ fideli suo Guncelino de Batelesm̃e Iustic̃ suo Cestͬ salutem . Monstrauit noꝑ Emma que fuit vx̄ Griffini fiⷮ Madocii ꝗd cum ip̄a tenuisset Maneria de Ouertoñ ⁊ Etoñ cum ꝑtiñ ⁊ quasdam ɫ̃ras ⁊ teñ in Maylor Sesnekͤ de dono ꝑdc̃i Griffini qᵒndam viri sui Habend ad totam vitam eiusdem Emme et ip̄a in pacifica seisina Mañioꝫ ɫ̃raꝫ ⁊ teñ ꝑdc̃oꝫ semp hactenus sc̃dm ꝗsuetudinē pc̃iū illaꝫ extiⷮit Balti ñri de Brumeffeud ip̄am a seisina sua Mañioꝫ ɫ̃raꝫ ⁊ teñ illoꝫ eiecerunt et ea ei adhuc detinent in ip̄ius Emme dāpnū nō modicum ⁊ gᵃuamen Nos igitͬ sup ꝑmissis c̃tiorari volentes, voꝯ mandamꝰ ꝗd p sacͬm pboꝫ ⁊ leg̃ hōiñm de ptibꝫ de Brummeffeud p quos rei veritas melius sciri poⷮit diligentꝰ inquiratis, quis Mañia illa ɫ̃ras ⁊ teñ ꝑfate Emme contulit, et si ei collata fuⷮint tenenda ad ꝉminū vite p feoffamentum ꝑfati Griffini uɫ in dotē et si ad ꝉminū vite qualiⷮ ⁊ quomodo ⁊ si in dotem qualiť ꝛ quomodo et si p balłos ñros ūl alios eiecta fůit a seisina sua p̄dc̄a et si p balłos ñros qualiť ꝛ qua de causa . et si p alios p quos ꝛ qualiť ꝛ qua de causa Et inquisicōem inde distincte ꝛ apte fc̄am sub sigillo v̄ro ꝛ sigilł eoꝛ p quos fc̄a fůit noť sine dilōe mittatis ꝛ hoc br̄e T̄ me iꝑo aꝑd Wygorñ vj die Juł anno r̄ ñ qᶦnto.

(m. 2.)   Inquiꝫ fc̄a p Guncelinū de Badelesm̄e Iustic̄ Cestr̄ die Martis pxᵃ ante festum sc̄e Margarete anno r̄ r̄ Ē. qᶦnto aꝑd Fardoñ sc̄dm tenorē br̄is d̄ni Reꝡ sibi directi p subscᶦptos videlicet Houel ab Lewelyn . Ingnon fił Lewelyñ . Yoruertħ fił Kenewrikꝯ . Joruertħ fił Griffuñ . Houa fił Pħi . Maddokꝯ fił Houel . Houa Waghan . Maddokꝯ Waghan . Kenewrikꝯ fr̄em eius . Kenewrikꝯ fił Yonas . Houen fr̄em eius . Howeyn fił Pħi . Bletħin Wicħ . Blethin fił Maddoci . Gronou fił Ythel . Kenewrikꝯ fił Lewelyn . Kenewrikꝯ fił Griffuñ ꝛ Geruasium fił Eyner . Juratos . qui dicūt sup sacr̄u suū q̄d Griffinus de Brumfeld quando Emmam fił Henr̄ de Aldetheliꝡ duxit in vx̄m dedit eidē Emme Mañiū de Oůtoñ ꝛ Malor Saysnekꝯ cū om̄ibꝫ ptiñ ad ꝑminū vite sue ꝛ eadem Emma p balliuū suū Jur̄ omnia expleł d̄ci Mañii ceꝑ ad opus suū ppᶦum toto t̄pe vite d̄ci Griffini viri sui . Requisiti ꝫ si illud Mañiū cū Malor Saysnekꝯ collatū fuit eidē nōie feofamenti v̄l dotis . dicūt q̄d p feoffamentū d̄ci Griffini ꝛ p cartam suam quam porexit ibidem . Reqᶦsiti ꝫ qᵃliť ꝛ quomodo d̄ca Emma venit ad mañiū de [E]yton dicūt q̄d d̄cm Mañiū fuit eschaeł d̄ci Griffini p mortē Howeł fr̄is eius . ꝛ postqᵃm idem Griffinus inde ħuit bonam ꝛ pacificā seiꝫ [ꝛ] Mañium p̄dc̄m dedit d̄ce Emme vx̄ sue . Reqᶦsiti . si nōie dotis v̄l feoffamenti . dicūt q̄d p feoffamentū ꝛ p quandā cartā qᵃm porrexit ibid̄ que illud idē testatʳ Simul cū cōfirmacōe hered̄ d̄ci Griffini qᵃm eidē Emme fecerūt post mortē d̄ci Griffini ꝛ cū cōfirmacōe Lewelini tunc pᶦncipis Walł que om̄es donacōes g̃firmauit . Requiꝫ ꝫ qᵃliť ꝛ q°modo . dicūt q̄d g̃suetudo Walł est q̄d vnusqᶦsꝗ Walicus ad voluntatē suā dare potest vx̄ sue terras ꝛ ten sua ante sponsalia v̄l post put sibi cederit volūtati . Reqᶦsiti ꝫ si p balłos d̄ni

102

Rege dͨa Emma eiecta fuit de ꝑris ꞇ teñ ꝑdͨis ꝟl p alios : Dicŭt q̄d post mortē dͨi Griffini eadē Emma stetit in seiͨ de omͥibȝ ꝑris ꞇ teñ ꝑdͨis usꝗ Guerram inceptam inꝑ Angꞇ ꞇ Walꞇ ꞇ extunc eo q̄d dͨa Emma fuit ad fidē dni Rege in Angꞇ dͨus Lewelinus ipsam de omͥibȝ ꝑris ꞇ teñ ꝑdͨis eiecit ꞇ dͨas ꝑrꞵs ꞇ teñ reddidit Madoco fiꞇ Griffini. Dicŭt ꞇ q̄d consuetudo Wallie taꞇ q̄d quocienscūꝗ aliquis ꝑ timore guerre ꝟl alia occͦone reliquerit ꝑram suā ꞇ recesserit de Wallia ad alias ptes bene licebit dno ꝑram illā seysire tāqͣ escaetā suam ꞇ faꝣe inde voluntatē suam.

[*Endorsed*]

> dedit x. ꞇi . redditus de Maylor Seysneke ꞇ ptē dnicaȝ de Oūtoñ sciꞇt gͣngiam in bosco ꞇ assarꞇ que eadē Emma assartauit ꞇ piscaꞃ ꞇ Molenđ.
> ˙Expectet reditū regis a Wallia.

Sciant presentes ꞇ futͥi q̄d ego Griffinus fiꞇ Madoci dñs de Bromfeld assenssu ꞇ cōsensu heređ meoꝝ dedi ꞇ cōcessi ꞇ hac presenti carta mea cōfirmaui dne Emme vxoꞃ mee legitime filie dni Henꞃ de Audidele totam patͥam que vocatͬ Maylorseysnec quoad uixerit videꞇt Maꝺium de Oūtoñ cū Molenđ ꞇ Gurgite ꞇ omͥibȝ aliis ptiñ suis, villam de Hengemͥe cū suis ptiñ . Villam de Lanerpanna cū suis ptiñ . Cnoltoñ cū suis ptiñ ꞇ omͥes villas que infra limites ꝑdͨe patͥe de Mailorseysnec cōtinentͬ put ego melius ꞇ liberiꞵ dͨam patͥam ꞁui ꞇ dare potui . ita tamen q̄d nō possit dͨam patͥam ꝟl aliqͣ pte eiusdē dare vendere ꝟl inuadiare ꝟl aliquo modo alienare . set post obitū illiꞵ ꝑdͨa patͥa ad me ꝟl heređ meos reꝰtet . Et q̄d dͨa ꝑra a dno Walꞇ nō subtͣhatͬ . Et ut hec mea donaͨo ꞇ cōcessio quoad uixerit rata ꞇ stabiꞇ pmaneat ꝑsens scͥptū sigilli mei inpressione robboraui.

Hiis testibȝ dno Aniano Epͦo de Sͨo Asaf . dno Yarwarth abꞇe de Valle crucis . Madoco . Leulino . Oweno . Griffino . filiis meis . Dno Dauid decano de Bromfeld . Nenneau fiꞇ

(m. 3.)

App. D.

A.D.
1270.
(m. 4.)

Ener . Riric fiŧ Ener . Griffry fiŧ Ener . Yeua Vawan . Gorono fiŧ Hithel . Bledint fiŧ Yarwarth ꝛ aliis.

Sciant p̃sentes ꝛ futuri q̄ ego Griffinus filius Madoci dñs de Bromfelđ assensu ꝛ consensu ħedũ meoꝫ dedi concessi ꝛ hꜹc p̃senti carta mea confᵒmaui đne Emme uxori mee legitime filie đni Henꝝ de Aldedeleᵹ totũ Mañiũ meũ de Eytune in Malauor Kemeraec cũ om̄ibꝫ ptiñ suis infra villã ꝛ extᵃ in dominiis in boscis in pcis in campis in planis in pᵃtis in pascuis in pasturis in viis in semitis aqˡs stagnis viuariis gurgitibꝫ piscariis Molendinis ꝛ in om̄ibꝫ libŧátibꝫ ꝛ aisiamentis quas ħui ũl ħ[ere] potui ꝛ in om̄ibꝫ aliis ptiñ suis p̃dc̃o Mañio spᶜtantib; vna cũ qᵃdã Terra que jaceŧ infra clausũ pci de Eytune qᵃm dñs Howelus pie memorie emit de om̄ibꝫ ħedibꝫ de Herbystoke Reddẽdo eisdem annuatim xij galones ceruiš ũl pciũ eaꝫđc̃ ad fesŧ Sc̃i Michis vna cũ quadã pticula alia Ꝑre q̄ Jacet in pco p̃dc̃o qᵃm ħedes de Erbystoke spontanea eoꝫ volũtate tᵃdiderũt Mˡ . Hñdũ ꝛ Tenenđ de Me ꝛ ħedibꝫ meis, sˡ in tota vita sua adeo libo ꝛ Integro sicuti ego umqᵃm libius ꝛ plenius illud ħui ũl ħre potui Ita tamen q̃d post decessũ p̃dc̃e đne Emme reuŧatʳ p̃dc̃m Mañiũ cũ om̄ibꝫ ptiñ suis [mihi] ꝛ heređ meis Reddendo inde annuatī Mˡ ꝛ ħedibꝫ meis ipᵃ unũ par albaꝫ cyrotecaꝫ de pc̃o uniˢ denaꝝ ad fesŧ Sc̃i Michis p omī ꝫuic̃o sc̄lari exacc̄one ꝛ demanda . Ego ꝫo dc̃us Griffinus ꝛ ħˡedes mei p̃dc̃m Mañiũ cũ om̄ibꝫ ptiñ snis sicut p̃dc̃m est p̃dc̃e đne Emme qᵃmdiu viꝛit contᵃ om̄s hoïes Warantizabimˢ ꝛ defendemˢ . In cuiˢ rei testimoñ huic scˡpto sigillũ meũ apposui.

Hiis testibꝫ fꝝe Aniano tũc Ep̃o de Sc̃o Assapħ . fꝝe Geruasio tũc Abŧe de Valle Crucis . Madoco . Lewelino . Oweyno . Griffino filiis meis . Dauiđ tũc Decano de Bromfelđ . Juna fiŧ Ahur . Ahur fiŧ Iunaf . Huna fiŧ Loreuret . Greno fiŧ Iorenert . Lewelino fiŧ Eyner . Iuna Vauehan . Nennio fiŧ Ener . Ithenanet fiŧ Dauiđ ꝛ aliis.

[*Endorsed*]   Emma filia Griff ap Madoc.

R̃ inꝓ Inquiš de A° . vj° Aui.

104

Sciant p̃seutes ꝛ futuri q̃d nos Madocus Leuueliu⁹ Oweu⁹
Griffinus filii Griffini d̃ni de Bromfeld concessim⁹ ꝛ hac p̃senti
carta n̄ra cōf'mauim⁹ d̃ne Emme mat¹ n̄re q°ad uiꝪit om̄s
t̃ras ꝛ omīa tenementa que d̃ũs Grifliu⁹ p̃r n̄r in vita sua eid̃o
dedit ꝛ cōcessit Videl; pat'am de Mailor Saisenee cũ suis
ptin. Maꝛiũ de Oũton cũ Molendino ꝛ gurgite ꝛ omīb; aliis
ptiñ . Villam de Hagneñe cũ suis ptiñ . Lannerpauna cũ suis
ptiñ Coltoñ cũ suis ptiñ ꝛ om̄s villas q̃ inf⁴ limites pat'e de
Mailor Saisenee cōtinent⁀ . Maꝛiũ de Eyton in Mailor
Kemerae cũ Molendino ꝛ peo ꝛ omīb; aliis ptiñ Et dunb;
pticulis t̃re in d̃eo peo contentis qua; unã emit domin⁹
Houuelus filius Madoci de omīb; hedib; de Herbestoe.
Reddendo eisdem annuatim xij galones Ceruisie ũl p̃ciũ
ea;dem ad fest scī Michis Aliã uo ptic̃lam tradiderũt pred̃ei
hedes de Herbestoe sponte sua d̃no G . p̃ri n̄ro Villã de
Lanarmon cũ suis ptiñ in Kenlleitoñ una cũ t̃ris illis qᵃs d̃na
Ysota auia n̄ra ex consensu d̃ni Madocí aui n̄ri ꝛ d̃ui G .
p̃ris n̄ri emit de Cadegon ꝛ Ririt ꝛ Einon filiis Doyoe que
vocant⁀ Lloytteir ꝛ p̃stimaud . H̃nda ꝛ tenenda omīa p̃dc̃a
tenementa cũ suis ptiñ de nob ꝛ hedib; n̄ris q°ad uiꝪit put
libius ꝛ melius ç̃tinent⁀ in cartis eid a p̃dc̃o G . p̃re n̄ro
cōfectis . Et ut h̃ n̄ra cōcessio ꝛ p̃seutis carte n̄re conf'mac̃o
q°ad uiꝪit rata pmaneat p̃seut̃o cartã sigillis n̄ris roborauim⁹.

Hiis testib; d̃no Aniano Ep̃o de Sc̃o Asaf . Dauid decano
de Bromfeld . F̃re Kenewrike Priore de Buthlau . d̃no
Geruasio Abbe de Valle Crucis . Nenneau fit Ener . Baric fit
Ener . Yaruorth uoyl fit Yaruorth uauhan . Madoco uauhan
fit Madoci fit Oweyn . Blethint fit Yaruorth . Huua fit Yaruorth . Madoco fit Yeinaf . Eynon fit Lewelini . Gorono fit
yaruorth . Lewelino fit Ener . Howelo fit Dauid . Yena fit
Auꝛ . Auꝛ fit Yeina . Meuric Vauhan . Ithel fit Gorono .
Yaruorth fit Wyon . Yena Vauhan ꝛ aliis . Daꞇ Dynasbriu
in cᵃstino ꞇi Thoɱ Ap̃li Anno d̃ni M° cc" lxxᵒ.

APPENDIX E.

ENFRANCHISEMENT OF A GWELY OF NATIVI HOLDING IN TREFGIFRIF IN THE VILLA OF BRYNGWYN, A.D. 1355.

App. E.
———
A.D.
1355.

Hec indentura facta inter Venerabilem Patrem dominum Iohannem Dei gratia Assaviensem Episcopum Decanum et Capitulum Assavenses ex una parte, et proprietarios et coheredes illius lecti vocati Gwely Gwarthhoet in villa de Bryngwynes . . . ex altera testatur Quod cum predicti proprietarii et coheredes semper ante hec tempora nativi vocati fuerunt et eorum terras et tenementa ibidem sub conditione trefgyfrif tenuerunt, predictus venerabilis Pater Decanus et capitulum pro se et successoribus suis ad supplicationem predictorum proprietariorum et coheredum ipsos et heredes suos et terras et tenementa ipsorum a conditione illa de cetero liberaverunt . et exoneraverunt in perpetuum et illos ejusdem conditionis sicuti et proprietarii [et coheredes] illius Lecti vocati Gwely Ithelwr in eadem villa existentis in omnibus fecerunt, ita quod predicti proprietarii et coheredes predicti lecti vocati Gwely Gwarthhoet et heredes sui de cetero in perpetuum solvant domino . . . marcas annui redditus in festo Apostolorum Philipi et Iacobi pro hac concessione habenda ubi antea quinque solidos hujus redditus in festo predicto solvere consueverunt   In cujus rei testationem predicte partes huic indenture alternatim sigilla sua apposuerunt His testibus Roberto ap Gruffud . tunc Ragloto domini Episcopi . Lew . . . ap Madoc Loyt . tunc yconomo ejusdem . Eden Moel ap Bleth Duy . tunc Ringildo ibidem . Eynon ap Ken ap Bleth . Lewarch ap Eign . Heilyn ap Bleth ap Grono et domino Ithel Duy ap David ap Lewarch et aliis multis . Datum apud Sanctum Assaphum die dominica proxima post festum Sancti Michaelis Archangeli anno Domini milessimo tricentessimo quinquegessimo quinto [1355].

INDEX.

April, 1895.

A Classified Catalogue

OF WORKS IN

GENERAL LITERATURE

PUBLISHED BY

LONGMANS, GREEN, & CO.

39 PATERNOSTER ROW, LONDON, E.C.

AND 15 EAST 16TH STREET, NEW YORK.

INDEX OF AUTHORS.

MESSRS. LONGMANS & CO.'S STANDARD AND GENERAL WORKS.

CONTENTS.

History, Politics, Polity, Political Memoirs, &c.

Abbott.—A HISTORY OF GREECE. By EVELYN ABBOTT, M.A., LL.D.
Part I.—From the Earliest Times to the Ionian Revolt. Crown 8vo., 10s. 6d.
Part II.—500-445 B.C. Crown 8vo., 10s. 6d.

Acland and Ransome.—A HANDBOOK IN OUTLINE OF THE POLITICAL HISTORY OF ENGLAND TO 1894. Chronologically Arranged. By A. H. DYKE ACLAND, M.P., and CYRIL RANSOME, M.A. Crown 8vo., 6s.

ANNUAL REGISTER, (THE). A Review of Public Events at Home and Abroad, for the year 1893. 8vo., 18s.

Volumes of the ANNUAL REGISTER for the years 1863-1892 can still be had. 18s. each.

Armstrong.—ELIZABETH FARNESE; The Termagant of Spain. By EDWARD ARMSTRONG, M.A. 8vo., 16s.

Arnold.—Works by T. ARNOLD, D.D., formerly Head Master of Rugby School.
INTRODUCTORY LECTURES ON MODERN HISTORY. 8vo., 7s. 6d.
MISCELLANEOUS WORKS. 8vo., 7s. 6d.

Bagwell.—IRELAND UNDER THE TUDORS. By RICHARD BAGWELL, LL.D. (3 vols.)
Vols. I. and II. From the first invasion of the Northmen to the year 1578. 8vo., 32s.
Vol. III. 1578-1603. 8vo. 18s.

Ball.—HISTORICAL REVIEW OF THE LEGISLATIVE SYSTEMS OPERATIVE IN IRELAND, from the Invasion of Henry the Second to the Union (1172-1800). By the Rt. Hon. J. T. BALL. 8vo., 6s.

Besant.—THE HISTORY OF LONDON. By WALTER BESANT. With 74 Illustrations. Crown 8vo., 1s. 9d Or bound as a School Prize Book, 2s. 6d.

Brassey.—Works by LORD BRASSLY.
PAPERS AND ADDRESSES.
NAVAL AND MARITIME. 1872-1893. 2 vols. Crown 8vo., 10s.
MERCANTILE MARINE AND NAVIGATION, from 1871-1894. Crown 8vo., 5s.

Brassey.—Works by LORD BRASSEY—Cont.
IMPERIAL FEDERATION AND COLONISATION FROM 1880 to 1894. Arranged and Edited by ARTHUR H. LORING and R. J. BEADON. Crown 8vo., 5s. [Nearly ready.

Bright.—A HISTORY OF ENGLAND. By the Rev. J. FRANK BRIGHT, D.D.
Period, I. MEDIÆVAL MONARCHY: A.D. 449 to 1485. Crown 8vo., 4s. 6d.
Period II. PERSONAL MONARCHY. 1485 to to 1688. Crown 8vo., 5s.
Period III. CONSTITUTIONAL MONARCHY: 1689 to 1837. Crown 8vo., 7s. 6d.
Period IV. THE GROWTH OF DEMOCRACY. 1837 to 1880 Crown 8vo., 6s.

Buckle.—HISTORY OF CIVILISATION IN ENGLAND AND FRANCE, SPAIN AND SCOTLAND. By HENRY THOMAS BUCKLE. 3 vols. Crown 8vo., 24s.

Burke.—A HISTORY OF SPAIN, from the Earliest Times to the Death of Ferdinand the Catholic. By ULICK RALPH BURKE, M.A. 2 vols. 8vo., 32s.

Chesney.—INDIAN POLITY: a View of the System of Administration in India. By General Sir GEORGE CHESNEY, K.C.B., M.P. With Map showing all the Administrative Divisions of British India. 8vo., 21s.

Creighton. — HISTORY OF THE PAPACY DURING THE REFORMATION. By MANDELL CREIGHTON, D.D., LL.D., Bishop of Peterborough. Vols. I. and II., 1378-1464, 32s. Vols. III. and IV., 1464-1518, 24s. Vol. V., 1517-1527, 8vo., 15s.

Curzon.—Works by the Hon. GEORGE N. CURZON, M.P.
PROBLEMS OF THE FAR EAST: JAPAN, COREA, CHINA. 8vo., 21s.
PERSIA AND THE PERSIAN QUESTION. With 9 Maps, 96 Illustrations, Appendices, and an Index. 2 vols. 8vo., 42s.

De Tocqueville.—DEMOCRACY IN AMERICA. By ALEXIS DE TOCQUEVILLE. 2 vols. Crown 8vo., 16s.

History, Politics, Polity, Political Memoirs, &c.—*continued.*

Ewald.—Works by HEINRICH EWALD, Professor in the University of Göttengen.
THE ANTIQUITIES OF ISRAEL. 8vo., 12s. 6d.
THE HISTORY OF ISRAEL. 8 vols., 8vo., Vols. I. and II., 24s. Vols. III. and IV., 21s. Vol. V., 18s. Vol. VI., 16s. Vol. 21s. Vol. VIII., 18s.

Fitzpatrick.—SECRET SERVICE UNDER PITT. By W. J. FITZPATRICK, 8vo., 7s. 6d.

Froude.—Works by JAMES A. FROUDE.
THE HISTORY OF ENGLAND, from the Fall of Wolsey to the Defeat of the Spanish Armada.
POPULAR EDITION. 12 vols. Cr. 8vo. 3s. 6d. each.
SILVER LIBRARY EDITION. 12 vols. Cr. 8vo. 3s. 6d. each.
THE DIVORCE OF CATHERINE OF ARAGON: the Story as told by the Imperial Ambassadors resident at the Court of Henry VIII. Crown 8vo., 6s.
THE SPANISH STORY OF THE ARMADA, and other Essays. Crown 8vo., 6s.
THE ENGLISH IN IRELAND IN THE EIGHTEENTH CENTURY.
CABINET EDITION. 3 vols. Crown 8vo., 18s.
SILVER LIBRARY EDITION. 3 vols. Cr. 8vo., 3s. 6d. each.
ENGLISH SEAMEN IN THE SIXTEENTH CENTURY. Lectures delivered at Oxford, 1893-94. 8vo., 10s. 6d. [*Nearly ready.*
SHORT STUDIES ON GREAT SUBJECTS.
CABINET EDITION. 4 vols. Cr. 8vo., 24s.
SILVER LIBRARY EDITION 4 vols. Cr. 8vo., 3s. 6d. each.
CÆSAR: a Sketch. Crown 8vo., 3s. 6d.

Gardiner.—Works by SAMUEL RAWSON GARDINER, M.A., Hon. LL.D., Edinburgh.
HISTORY OF ENGLAND, from the Accession of James I. to the Outbreak of the Civil War, 1603-1642. 10 vols. Crown 8vo., 6s. each.
A HISTORY OF THE GREAT CIVIL WAR, 1642-1649. 4 vols. Crown 8vo., 6s. each.
A HISTORY OF THE COMMONWEALTH AND THE PROTECTORATE. 1649-1660.
Vol. I. 1649-1651. With 14 Maps. 8vo., 21s.
THE STUDENT'S HISTORY OF ENGLAND. With 378 Illustrations. Crown 8vo., 12s.
Also in Three Volumes.
Vol. I. B.C. 55—A.D. 1509. With 173 Illustrations. Crown 8vo. 4s.
Vol. II. 1509-1689. With 96 Illustrations. Crown 8vo. 4s.
Vol. III. 1689-1885. With 109 Illustrations. Crown 8vo. 4s.

Greville.—A JOURNAL OF THE REIGNS OF KING GEORGE IV., KING WILLIAM IV., AND QUEEN VICTORIA. By CHARLES C. F. GREVILLE, formerly Clerk of the Council. 8 vols. Crown 8vo., 6s. each.

Hearn.—THE GOVERNMENT OF ENGLAND: its Structure and its Development. By W. EDWARD HEARN. 8vo., 16s.

Herbert.—THE DEFENCE OF PLEVNA, 1877. Written by One who took Part in it. By WILLIAM V. HERBERT. With Maps. 8vo., 18s.

Historic Towns.—Edited by E. A. FREEMAN, D.C.L., and Rev. WILLIAM HUNT, M.A. With Maps and Plans. Crown 8vo., 3s. 6d. each.
BRISTOL. By the Rev. W. HUNT.
CARLISLE. By MANDELL CREIGHTON, D.D., Bishop of Peterborough.
CINQUE PORTS. By MONTAGU BURROWS.
COLCHESTER. By Rev. E. L. CUTTS.
EXETER. By E. A. FREEMAN.
LONDON. By Rev. W. J. LOFTIE.
OXFORD. By Rev. C. W. BOASE.
WINCHESTER. By Rev. G. W. KITCHIN, D.D.
YORK. By Rev. JAMES RAINE.
NEW YORK. By THEODORE ROOSEVELT.
BOSTON (U.S.) By HENRY CABOT LODGE.

Joyce.—A SHORT HISTORY OF IRELAND, from the Earliest Times to 1608. By P. W. JOYCE, LL.D. Crown 8vo., 10s. 6d.

Lang.—ST. ANDREWS. By ANDREW LANG. With 8 Plates and 24 Illustrations in the Text by T. HODGE. 8vo., 15s. net.

Lecky.—Works by WILLIAM EDWARD HARTPOLE LECKY.
HISTORY OF ENGLAND IN THE EIGHTEENTH CENTURY.
LIBRARY EDITION. 8 vols. 8vo., £7 4s.
CABINET EDITION. ENGLAND. 7 vols. Crown 8vo., 6s. each. IRELAND. 5 vols. Crown 8vo., 6s. each.
HISTORY OF EUROPEAN MORALS FROM AUGUSTUS TO CHARLEMAGNE. 2 vols. Crown 8vo., 16s.
HISTORY OF THE RISE AND INFLUENCE OF THE SPIRIT OF RATIONALISM IN EUROPE. 2 vols. Crown 8vo., 16s.
THE EMPIRE: its Value and its Growth. An Inaugural Address delivered at the Imperial Institute, November 20, 1893, under the Presidency of H.R.H. the Prince of Wales. Crown 8vo. 1s. 6d.

History, Politics, Polity, Political Memoirs, &c.—*continued.*

Macaulay.—Works by LORD MACAULAY.

COMPLETE WORKS OF LORD MACAULAY.
CABINET EDITION. 16 vols. Post 8vo.,
£4 16.
LIBRARY EDITION. 8 vols. 8vo., £5 5s.

HISTORY OF ENGLAND FROM THE AC-
CESSION OF JAMES THE SECOND.
POPULAR EDITION. 2 vols. Cr. 8vo., 5s.
STUDENT'S EDITION. 2 vols. Cr. 8vo., 12s.
PEOPLE'S EDITION. 4 vols. Cr. 8vo., 16s.
CABINET EDITION. 8 vols. Post 8vo., 48s.
LIBRARY EDITION. 5 vols. 8vo., £4.

CRITICAL AND HISTORICAL ESSAYS, WITH
LAYS OF ANCIENT ROME, in 1 volume.
POPULAR EDITION. Crown 8vo., 2s. 6d.
AUTHORISED EDITION. Crown 8vo.,
2s. 6d., or 3s. 6d., gilt edges.
SILVER LIBRARY EDITION. Cr.8vo., 3s. 6d.

CRITICAL AND HISTORICAL ESSAYS.
STUDENT'S EDITION. 1 vol. Cr. 8vo., 6s.
PEOPLE'S EDITION. 2 vols. Cr. 8vo., 8s.
TREVELYAN EDITION. 2 vols. Cr. 8vo., 9s.
CABINET EDITION. 4 vols. Post 8vo., 24s.
LIBRARY EDITION. 3 vols. 8vo., 36s.

ESSAYS which may be had separately
price 6d. each sewed, 1s. each cloth.
Addison and Walpole.
Frederick the Great.
Croker's Boswell's Johnson.
Hallam's Constitutional History.
Warren Hastings. (3d. sewed, 6d. cloth).
The Earl of Chatham (Two Essays).
Ranke and Gladstone.
Milton and Machiavelli.
Lord Bacon.
Lord Clive.
Lord Byron, and The Comic Dramatists of
the Restoration.

MISCELLANEOUS WRITINGS
PEOPLE'S EDITION. 1 vol. Cr. 8vo., 4s. 6d.
LIBRARY EDITION. 2 vols. 8vo., 21s.

MISCELLANEOUS WRITINGS AND
SPEECHES.
POPULAR EDITION. Crown 8vo., 2s. 6d.
CABINET EDITION. Including Indian Penal
Code, Lays of Ancient Rome, and Miscel-
laneous Poems. 4 vols. Post 8vo., 24s.

SELECTIONS FROM THE WRITINGS OF
LORD MACAULAY. Edited, with Occa-
sional Notes, by the Right Hon. Sir G. O.
Trevelyan, Bart. Crown 8vo.,6s.

May.—THE CONSTITUTIONAL HISTORY OF
ENGLAND since the Accession of George III.
1760-1870. By Sir THOMAS ERSKINE MAY,
K.C.B. (Lord Farnborough). 3 vols. Crown
8vo., 18s.

Merivale.—Works by the Very Rev.
CHARLES MERIVALE, late Dean of Ely.

HISTORY OF THE ROMANS UNDER THE
EMPIRE.
Cabinet Edition. 8 vols. Cr. 8vo., 48s.
Silver Library Edition. 8 vols. Crown
8vo., 3s. 6d. each.

THE FALL OF THE ROMAN REPUBLIC:
a Short History of the Last Century of the
Commonwealth. 12mo., 7s. 6d.

Montague.—THE ELEMENTS OF ENGLISH
CONSTITUTIONAL HISTORY, from the Earliest
Time to the Present Day. By F. C. MON-
TAGUE, M.A. Crown 8vo., 3s. 6d.

O'Brien.—IRISH IDEAS. REPRINTED AD-
DRESSES. By WILLIAM O'BRIEN, M.P.
Cr. 8vo. 2s. 6d.

Prendergast.—IRELAND FROM THE RE-
STORATION TO THE REVOLUTION, 1660-1690.
By JOHN P. PRENDERGAST, Author of 'The
Cromwellian Settlement in Ireland'. 8vo.,
5s.

Seebohm.—THE ENGLISH VILLAGE COM-
MUNITY Examined in its Relations to the
Manorial and Tribal Systems, &c. By
FREDERIC SEEBOHM. With 13 Maps and
Plates. 8vo., 16s.

Sharpe.—LONDON AND THE KINGDOM:
a History derived mainly from the Archives
at Guildhall in the custody of the Corpora-
tion of the City of London. By REGINALD
R. SHARPE, D.C.L., Records Clerk in the
Office of the Town Clerk of the City of
London. 3 vols. 8vo. Vols. I. and II.,
10s. 6d. each.

Sheppard.—MEMORIALS OF ST. JAMES'S
PALACE. By the Rev. EDGAR SHEPPARD,
M.A., Sub-Dean of H.M. Chapels Royal.
With 41 Full-page Plates (8 Photo-Intaglio)
and 32 Illustrations in the Text. 2 vols.
8vo., 36s. net.

Smith.—CARTHAGE AND THE CARTHAGIN-
IANS. By R. BOSWORTH SMITH, M.A.,
Assistant Master in Harrow School. With
Maps, Plans, &c. Crown 8vo., 3s. 6d.

Stephens.—A HISTORY OF THE FRENCH
REVOLUTION. By H. MORSE STEPHENS,
Balliol College, Oxford. 3 vols. 8vo. Vols.
I. and II. 18s. each.

Stubbs.—HISTORY OF THE UNIVERSITY OF
DUBLIN, from its Foundation to the End of
the Eighteenth Century. By J. W. STUBBS.
8vo., 12s. 6d.

History, Politics, Polity, Political Memoirs, &c.—*continued.*

Sutherland.—THE HISTORY OF AUS-
TRALIA AND NEW ZEALAND, from 1606 to
1890. By ALEXANDER SUTHERLAND, M.A.,
and GEORGE SUTHERLAND, M.A. Crown
8vo., 2s. 6d.

Todd.—PARLIAMENTARY GOVERNMENT IN
THE BRITISH COLONIES. By ALPHEUS
TODD, LL.D. 8vo., 30s. net.

Wakeman and Hassall.—ESSAYS INTRO-
DUCTORY TO THE STUDY OF ENGLISH CON-
STITUTIONAL HISTORY. By Resident Mem-
bers of the University of Oxford. Edited by
HENRY OFFLEY WAKEMAN, M.A., and
ARTHUR HASSALL, M.A. Crown 8vo., 6s.

Walpole.—Works by SPENCER WALPOLE.
HISTORY OF ENGLAND FROM THE CON-
CLUSION OF THE GREAT WAR IN 1815 TO
1858. 6 vols. Crown 8vo., 6s. each.
THE LAND OF HOME RULE: being an
Account of the History and Institutions
of the Isle of Man. Crown 8vo., 6s.

Wolff.—ODD BITS OF HISTORY; being
Short Chapters intended to Fill Some
Blanks. By HENRY W. WOLFF. 8vo.,
8s. 6d.

Wylie.—HISTORY OF ENGLAND UNDER
HENRY IV. By JAMES HAMILTON WYLIE,
M.A., one of H. M. Inspectors of Schools.
3 vols. Crown 8vo. Vol. I., 1399-1404,
10s. 6d. Vol. II., 15s. Vol. III. [*In prep.*

Biography, Personal Memoirs, &c.

Armstrong.—THE LIFE AND LETTERS OF
EDMUND J. ARMSTRONG. Edited by G. F.
ARMSTRONG. Fcp. 8vo., 7s. 6d.

Bacon.—THE LETTERS AND LIFE OF
FRANCIS BACON, INCLUDING ALL HIS OC-
CASIONAL WORKS. Edited by JAMES SPED-
DING. 7 vols. 8vo., £4 4s.

Boyd.—Works by A. K. H. BOYD, D.D.,
LL.D., Author of ' Recreations of a Country
Parson,' &c.
TWENTY-FIVE YEARS OF ST. ANDREWS.
1865-1890. 2 vols. 8vo. Vol. I. 12s.
Vol. II. 15s.

ST. ANDREWS AND ELSEWHERE :
Glimpses of Some Gone and of Things
Left. 8vo., 15s.

Carlyle.—THOMAS CARLYLE : a History
of his Life. By JAMES ANTHONY FROUDE.
1795-1835. 2 vols. Crown 8vo., 7s.
1834-1881. 2 vols. Crown 8vo., 7s.

Erasmus.—LIFE AND LETTERS OF ERAS-
MUS : a Series of Lectures delivered at Oxford. By JAMES ANTHONY FROUDE. Crown
8vo., 6s.

Fabert.—ABRAHAM FABERT : Governor
of Sedan and Marshal of France. His Life
and Times, 1599-1662. By GEORGE HOOPER.
With a Portrait. 8vo., 10s. 6d.

Fox.—THE EARLY HISTORY OF CHARLES
JAMES FOX. By the Right Hon. Sir G. O.
TREVELYAN, Bart.
Library Edition. 8vo., 18s.
Cabinet Edition. Crown 8vo., 6s.

Hamilton.—LIFE OF SIR WILLIAM
HAMILTON. By R. P. GRAVES. 3 vols.
13s. each. ADDENDUM. 8vo., 6d. sewed.

Havelock.—MEMOIRS OF SIR HENRY
HAVELOCK, K.C.B. By JOHN CLARK
MARSHMAN. Crown 8vo., 3s. 6d.

Luther.—LIFE OF LUTHER. By JULIUS
KÖSTLIN. With Illustrations from Authentic
Sources. Translated from the German.
Crown 8vo., 7s. 6d.

Macaulay.—THE LIFE AND LETTERS OF
LORD MACAULAY. By the Right Hon. Sir
G. O. TREVELYAN, Bart.
POPULAR EDITION. 1 vol. Cr. 8vo., 2s. 6d.
STUDENT'S EDITION. 1 vol. Cr. 8vo., 6s.
CABINET EDITION. 2 vols. Post 8vo., 12s.
LIBRARY EDITION. 2 vols. 8vo., 36s.

Marbot.—THE MEMOIRS OF THE BARON
DE MARBOT. Translated from the French
by ARTHUR JOHN BUTLER, M.A. Crown
8vo., 7s. 6d.

Seebohm.—THE OXFORD REFORMERS—
JOHN COLET, ERASMUS AND THOMAS MORE :
a History of their Fellow-Work. By FRED-
ERIC SEEBOHM. 8vo., 14s.

Shakespeare.—OUTLINES OF THE LIFE
OF SHAKESPEARE. By J. O. HALLIWELL-
PHILLIPPS. With numerous Illustrations
and Fac-similes. 2 vols. Royal 8vo., £1 1s.

Biography, Personal Memoirs, &c.—*continued*.

Shakespeare's True Life. By James Walter. With 500 Illustrations by Gerald E. Moira. Imp. 8vo., 27s.

Stephen.—Essays in Ecclesiastical Biography. By Sir James Stephen. Crown 8vo., 7s. 6d.

Turgot.—The Life and Writings of Turgot, Comptroller-General of France, 1774-1776. Edited for English Readers by W. Walker Stephens. 8vo., 12s. 6d.

Walford.—Twelve English Authoresses. By L. B. Walford. Crown 8vo., 4s. 6d.

Verney.—Memoirs of the Verney Family. Compiled from the Letters and Illustrated by the Portraits at Claydon House, Bucks.

During the Civil War. By Frances Parthenope Verney. With a Preface by S. R. Gardiner, M.A., LL.D. With 38 Portraits, Woodcuts and Fac-simile. 2 vols. Royal 8vo., 42s.
During the Commonwealth. 1650-1660. By Margaret M. Verney. With 10 Portraits, &c. Vol. III. 8vo., 21s.

Wellington.—Life of the Duke of Wellington. By the Rev. G. R. Gleig, M.A. Crown 8vo., 3s. 6d.

Travel and Adventure, the Colonies, &c.

Arnold.—Works by Sir Edwin Arnold, K.C.I.E.

Seas and Lands. With 71 Illustrations. Cr. 8vo., 7s. 6d. Cheap Edition. Cr. 8vo., 3s. 6d.

Wandering Words: Reprinted by permission from Papers published in the *Daily Telegraph* and Foreign Journals and Magazines. With 45 Illustrations from Drawings by Ben Boothby and from Photographs. 8vo., 18s.

AUSTRALIA AS IT IS, or Facts and Features, Sketches, and Incidents of Australia and Australian Life with Notices of New Zealand. By A Clergyman, thirteen years resident in the interior of New South Wales. Crown 8vo., 5s.

Baker.—Works by Sir S. W. Baker.

Eight Years in Ceylon. With 6 Illustrations. Crown 8vo., 3s. 6d.
The Rifle and the Hound in Ceylon. 6 Illustrations. Crown 8vo., 3s. 6d.

Bent.—Works by J. Theodore Bent, F.S.A., F.R.G.S.

The Ruined Cities of Mashonaland: being a Record of Excavation and Exploration in 1891. With Map, 13 Plates, and 104 Illustrations in the Text. Crown 8vo., 3s. 6d.

The Sacred City of the Ethiopians: being a Record of Travel and Research in Abyssinia in 1893. With 8 Plates and 65 Illustrations in the Text. 8vo., 18s.

Boothby.—On the Wallaby; or, Through the East and Across Australia. By Guy Boothby. 8vo., 18s.

Brassey.—Works by the late Lady Brassey.

The Last Voyage to India and Australia in the 'Sunbeam.' With Charts and Maps, and 40 Illustrations in Monotone, and nearly 200 Illustrations in the Text 8vo., 21s.

A Voyage in the 'Sunbeam'; Our Home on the Ocean for Eleven Months.
Library Edition. With 8 Maps and Charts, and 118 Illustrations. 8vo. 21s.
Cabinet Edition. With Map and 66 Illustrations. Crown 8vo., 7s. 6d.
Silver Library Edition. With 66 Illustrations. Crown 8vo., 3s. 6d.
Popular Edition. With 60 Illustrations. 4to., 6d. sewed, 1s. cloth.
School Edition. With 37 Illustrations. Fcp., 2s. cloth, or 3s. white parchment.

Sunshine and Storm in the East.
Library Edition. With 2 Maps and 141 Illustrations. 8vo., 21s.
Cabinet Edition. With 2 Maps and 114 Illustrations. Crown 8vo., 7s. 6d.
Popular Edition. With 103 Illustrations. 4to., 6d. sewed, 1s. cloth.

In the Trades, the Tropics, and the 'Roaring Forties'.
Cabinet Edition. With Map and 220 Illustrations. Crown 8vo., 7s. 6d.
Popular Edition. With 183 Illustrations. 4to., 6d. sewed, 1s. cloth.

Three Voyages in the 'Sunbeam'.
Popular Edition. With 346 Illustrations. 4to., 2s. 6d.

Brassey.—Voyages and Travels of Lord Brassey, K.C.B., D.C.L., 1862-1894. Arranged and Edited by Captain S. Eardley-Wilmot. 2 vols. Crown 8vo., 10s.
[*Nearly ready*.

Travel and Adventure, the Colonies, &c.—*continued.*

Bryden.— KLOOF AND KAROO : Sport, Legend, and Natural History in Cape Colony. By H. A. BRYDEN. With 17 Illustrations. 8vo., 5s.

Froude.—Works by JAMES A. FROUDE.

OCEANA : or England and her Colonies. With 9 Illustrations. Crown 8vo., 2s. boards, 2s. 6d. cloth.

THE ENGLISH IN THE WEST INDIES : or, the Bow of Ulysses. With 9 Illustrations. Crown 8vo., 2s. boards, 2s. 6d. cloth.

Howitt.—VISITS TO REMARKABLE PLACES. Old Halls, Battle-Fields, Scenes, illustrative of Striking Passages in English History and Poetry. By WILLIAM HOWITT. With 80 Illustrations. Crown 8vo., 3s. 6d.

Knight.—Works by E. F. KNIGHT.

THE CRUISE OF THE 'ALERTE': the narrative of a Search for Treasure on the Desert Island of Trinidad. With 2 Maps and 23 Illustrations. Crown 8vo., 3s. 6d.

WHERE THREE EMPIRES MEET : a Narrative of Recent Travel in Kashmir, Western Tibet, Baltistan, Ladak, Gilgit, and the adjoining Countries. With a Map and 54 Illustrations. Cr. 8vo., 3s. 6d.

RHODESIA OF TO-DAY: a Description of the Present Condition and the Prospects of Matabeleland and Mashonaland. Cr. 8vo., 2s. 6d.

Lees and Clutterbuck.—B. C. 1887 : A RAMBLE IN BRITISH COLUMBIA. By J. A. LEES and W. J. CLUTTERBUCK. With Map and 75 Illustrations. Crown 8vo., 3s. 6d.

Murdoch.—FROM EDINBURGH TO THE ANTARCTIC: an Artist's Notes and Sketches during the Dundee Antarctic Expedition of 1892-93. By W. G. BURN-MURDOCH. With 2 Maps and numerous Illustrations. 8vo., 18s.

Nansen.—Works by Dr. FRIDTJOF NANSEN.

THE FIRST CROSSING OF GREENLAND. With numerous Illustrations and a Map. Crown 8vo., 3s. 6d.

ESKIMO LIFE. Translated by WILLIAM ARCHER. With 31 Illustrations. 8vo., 16s.

Peary.—MY ARCTIC JOURNAL : a Year among Ice-Fields and Eskimos. By JOSEPHINE DIEBITSCH-PEARY. With 19 Plates, 3 Sketch Maps, and 44 Illustrations in the Text. 8vo., 12s.

Smith.—CLIMBING IN THE BRITISH ISLES. By W. P. HASKETT SMITH. With Illustrations by ELLIS CARR.

Part I. ENGLAND. Fcp. 8vo., 3s. 6d.

Part II. WALES. [*In preparation.*

Part III. SCOTLAND. [*In preparation.*

Stephen.—THE PLAY-GROUND OF EUROPE. By LESLIE STEPHEN. New Edition, with Additions and 4 Illustrations. Crown 8vo., 6s. net.

THREE IN NORWAY. By Two of Them. With a Map and 59 Illustrations. Crown 8vo., 2s. boards, 2s. 6d. cloth.

Whishaw.—OUT OF DOORS IN TSARLAND : a Record of the Seeings and Doings of a Wanderer in Russia. By FRED. J. WHISHAW. Crown 8vo., 7s. 6d.

Veterinary Medicine, &c.

Steel.—Works by JOHN HENRY STEEL.

A TREATISE ON THE DISEASES OF THE DOG. With 88 Illustrations. 8vo., 10s. 6d.

A TREATISE ON THE DISEASES OF THE OX. With 119 Illustrations. 8vo., 15s.

A TREATISE ON THE DISEASES OF THE SHEEP. With 100 Illustrations. 8vo., 12s.

OUTLINES OF EQUINE ANATOMY: a Manual for the use of Veterinary Students in the Dissecting Room. Cr. 8vo., 7s. 6d.

Fitzwygram.—HORSES AND STABLES. By Major-General Sir F. FITZWYGRAM, Bart. With 56 pages of Illustrations. 8vo., 2s. 6d. net.

"Stonehenge."—THE DOG IN HEALTH AND DISEASE. By "STONEHENGE". With 84 Wood Engravings. Square cr. 8vo., 7s. 6d.

Youatt.—Works by WILLIAM YOUATT.

THE HORSE. Revised and Enlarged by W. WATSON, M.R.C.V.S. Woodcuts. 8vo., 7s. 6d.

THE DOG. Revised and Enlarged. Woodcuts. 8vo., 6s.

Sport and Pastime.
THE BADMINTON LIBRARY.
Edited by the DUKE of BEAUFORT, K.G., assisted by ALFRED E. T. WATSON.

ARCHERY. By C. J. LONGMAN and Col. H. WALROND. With Contributions by Miss LEGH and Viscount DILLON. With 195 Illustrations. Cr. 8vo., 10s. 6d.

ATHLETICS AND FOOTBALL. By MONTAGUE SHEARMAN. With 51 Illustrations. Crown 8vo., 10s. 6d.

BIG GAME SHOOTING. By CLIVE PHILLIPPS-WOLLEY, Sir SAMUEL W. BAKER, W. C. OSWELL, F. C. SELOUS, &c.

Vol. I. Africa and America. With 77 Illustrations. Crown 8vo., 10s. 6d.

Vol. II. Europe, Asia, and the Arctic Regions. With 73 Illustrations. Cr. 8vo., 10s. 6d.

BOATING. By W. B. WOODGATE. With an Introduction by the Rev. EDMOND WARRE, D.D., and a Chapter on 'Rowing at Eton,' by R. HARVEY MASON. With 49 Illustrations. Cr. 8vo., 10s. 6d.

COURSING AND FALCONRY. By HARDING COX and the Hon. GERALD LASCELLES. 76 Illustrations. Cr. 8vo., 10s. 6d.

CRICKET. By A. G. STEEL and the Hon. R. H. LYTTELTON. With Contributions by ANDREW LANG, R. A. H. MITCHELL, W. G. GRACE, and F. GALE. With 64 Illustrations. Crown 8vo., 10s. 6d.

CYCLING. By Viscount BURY (Earl of Albemarle), K.C.M.G., and G. LACY HILLIER. 89 Illustrations. Cr. 8vo., 10s. 6d.

DRIVING. By the DUKE OF BEAUFORT. With 65 Illustrations. Crown 8vo., 10s. 6d.

FENCING. BOXING, AND WRESTLING. By WALTER H. POLLOCK, F. C. GROVE, C. PREVOST, E. B. MITCHELL, and WALTER ARMSTRONG. With 42 Illustrations. Crown 8vo., 10s. 6d.

FISHING. By H. CHOLMONDELEY-PENNELL. With Contributions by the MARQUIS OF EXETER, HENRY R. FRANCIS, Major JOHN P. TRAHERNE, G. CHRISTOPHER DAVIES, R. B. MARSTON. &c.

Vol. I. Salmon, Trout, and Grayling. With 158 Illustrations. Cr. 8vo., 10s. 6d.

Vol. II. Pike and other Coarse Fish. With 133 Illustrations. Cr. 8vo., 10s. 6d.

GOLF. By HORACE G. HUTCHINSON, the Rt. Hon. A. J. BALFOUR, M.P., Sir W. G. SIMPSON, Bart., LORD WELLWOOD, H. S. C. EVERARD, ANDREW LANG, and other Writers. With 89 Illustrations. Crown 8vo., 10s. 6d.

HUNTING. By the DUKE OF BEAUFORT, K.G., and MOWBRAY MORRIS. With Contributions by the EARL OF SUFFOLK AND BERKSHIRE, Rev. E. W. L. DAVIES, DIGBY COLLINS, and ALFRED E. T. WATSON. 53 Illustrations. Crown 8vo., 10s. 6d.

MOUNTAINEERING. By C. T. DENT, Sir F. POLLOCK, Bart., W. M. CONWAY, DOUGLAS FRESHFIELD, C. E. MATHEWS, &c. 108 Illustrations. Crown 8vo., 10s. 6d.

RACING AND STEEPLE-CHASING. By the EARL OF SUFFOLK AND BERKSHIRE, W. G. CRAVEN, ARTHUR COVENTRY, &c. With 58 Illustrations. Crown 8vo., 10s. 6d.

RIDING AND POLO. By Captain ROBERT WEIR, J. MORAY BROWN, the DUKE OF BEAUFORT, K.G., the EARL OF SUFFOLK AND BERKSHIRE, &c. With 59 Illustrations. Crown 8vo., 10s. 6d.

SHOOTING. By LORD WALSINGHAM and Sir RALPH PAYNE-GALLWEY, Bart. With Contributions by LORD LOVAT, LORD C. LENNOX KERR, the Hon. G. LASCELLES, and A. J. STUART-WORTLEY.

Vol. I. Field and Covert. With 105 Illustrations. Crown 8vo., 10s. 6d.

Vol. II. Moor and Marsh. With 65 Illustrations. Crown 8vo., 10s. 6d.

SKATING, CURLING, TOBOGGANING, AND OTHER ICE SPORTS. By J. M. HEATHCOTE, C. G. TEBBUTT, T. MAXWELL WITHAM, the Rev. JOHN KERR, ORMOND HAKE, and Colonel BUCK. With 284 Illustrations. Crown 8vo., 10s. 6d.

SWIMMING. By ARCHIBALD SINCLAIR and WILLIAM HENRY. With 119 Illustrations. Crown 8vo., 10s. 6d.

TENNIS, LAWN TENNIS, RACKETS AND FIVES. By J. M. and C. G. HEATHCOTE, E. O. PLEYDELL-BOUVERIE and A. C. AINGER. With Contributions by the Hon. A. LYTTELTON, W. C. MARSHALL, Miss L. DOD, &c. With 79 Illustrations. Cr. 8vo., 10s. 6d.

YACHTING.

Vol. I. Cruising, Construction, Racing Rules, Fitting-Out, &c. By Sir EDWARD SULLIVAN, Bart., LORD BRASSEY, K.C.B., C. E. SETH-SMITH, C.B., &c. With 114 Illustrations. Cr. 8vo., 10s. 6d.

Vol. II. Yacht Clubs, Yachting in America and the Colonies, Yacht Racing, &c. By R. T. PRITCHETT, the EARL OF ONSLOW, G.C.M.G., &c. With 195 Illustrations. Crown 8vo., 10s. 6d.

Sport and Pastime—*continued.*
FUR AND FEATHER SERIES.
Edited by A. E. T. WATSON.

THE PARTRIDGE. Natural History, by the Rev. H. A. MACPHERSON; Shooting, by A. J. STUART-WORTLEY; Cookery, by GEORGE SAINTSBURY. With 11 full-page Illustrations and Vignette by A. THORBURN, A. J. STUART-WORTLEY, and C. WHYMPER, and 15 Diagrams in the Text by A. J. STUART-WORTLEY. Crown 8vo., 5s.

WILDFOWL. By the Hon. JOHN SCOTT-MONTAGU, M.P., etc. Illustrated by A. J. STUART - WORTLEY, A. THORBURN, and others. [*In preparation.*

THE GROUSE. Natural History by the Rev. H. A. MACPHERSON; Shooting, by A. J. STUART-WORTLEY; Cookery, by GEORGE SAINTSBURY. With 13 Illustrations by J. STUART-WORTLEY and A. THORBURN, and various Diagrams in the Text. Cr. 8vo., 5s.

THE HARE AND THE RABBIT. By the Hon. GERALD LASCELLES, etc. [*In preparation.*

THE PHEASANT. By A. J. STUART-WORTLEY, the Rev. H. A. MACPHERSON, and A. J. INNES SHAND. [*In preparation.*

Campbell-Walker.—THE CORRECT CARD: or, How to Play at Whist; a Whist Catechism. By Major A. CAMPBELL-WALKER, F.R.G.S. Fcp. 8vo., 2s. 6d.

DEAD SHOT (THE): or, Sportsman's Complete Guide. Being a Treatise on the Use of the Gun, with Rudimentary and Finishing Lessons on the Art of Shooting Game of all kinds, also Game Driving, Wild-Fowl and Pigeon Shooting, Dog Breaking, etc. By MARKSMAN. Crown 8vo., 10s. 6d.

Falkener.—GAMES, ANCIENT AND ORIENTAL, AND HOW TO PLAY THEM. By EDWARD FALKENER. With numerous Photographs, Diagrams, &c. 8vo., 21s.

Ford.—THE THEORY AND PRACTICE OF ARCHERY. By HORACE FORD. New Edition, thoroughly Revised and Re-written by W. BUTT, M.A. With a Preface by C. J. LONGMAN, M.A. 8vo., 14s.

Fowler. — RECOLLECTIONS OF OLD COUNTRY LIFE, Social, Political, Sporting, and Agricultural. By J. K. FOWLER ('Rusticus'), formerly of Aylesbury. With Portrait and 10 Illustrations. 8vo., 10s. 6d.

Francis.—A BOOK ON ANGLING: or, Treatise on the Art of Fishing in every Branch; including full Illustrated List of Salmon Flies. By FRANCIS FRANCIS. With Portrait and Coloured Plates. Crown 8vo., 15s.

Gibson. — TOBOGGANING ON CROOKED RUNS. By the Hon. HARRY GIBSON. With Contributions by F. DE B. STRICKLAND and 'LADY-TOBOGANNER'. With 8 Full-page Illustrations and 32 Illustrations in the Text. Crown 8vo., 6s.

Hawker.—THE DIARY OF COLONEL PETER HAWKER, Author of 'Instructions to Young Sportsmen.' With an Introduction by Sir RALPH PAYNE-GALLWEY, Bart. 2 vols. 8vo., 32s.

Lang.—ANGLING SKETCHES. By ANDREW LANG. With Illustration. Cr. 8vo., 3s. 6d.

Longman. — CHESS OPENINGS. By FREDERICK W. LONGMAN. Fcp. 8vo., 2s. 6d.

Maskelyne.—SHARPS AND FLATS: a Complete Revelation of the Secrets of Cheating at Games of Chance and Skill. By JOHN NEVIL MASKELYNE, of the Egyptian Hall. With 62 Illustrations. Crown 8vo., 6s.

Payne-Gallwey.—Works by Sir RALPH PAYNE-GALLWEY, Bart.

LETTERS TO YOUNG SHOOTERS (First Series). On the Choice and use of a Gun. With 41 Illustrations. Crown 8vo., 7s. 6d.

LETTERS TO YOUNG SHOOTERS. (Second Series). On the Production, Preservation, and Killing of Game. With Directions in Shooting Wood-Pigeons and Breaking-in Retrievers. With a Portrait of the Author, and 103 Illustrations. Crown 8vo., 12s. 6d.

Pole.—Works by W. POLE, F.R.S.

THE THEORY OF THE MODERN SCIENTIFIC GAME OF WHIST. Fcp. 8vo., 2s. 6d.

THE EVOLUTION OF WHIST: a Study of the Progressive Changes which the Game has undergone from its Origin to the Present Time. Cr. 8vo., 6s.

Proctor.—Works by RICHARD A. PROCTOR.

HOW TO PLAY WHIST: WITH THE LAWS AND ETIQUETTE OF WHIST. Cr. 8vo., 3s. 6d.

HOME WHIST: an Easy Guide to Correct Play. 16mo., 1s.

Ronalds.—THE FLY-FISHER'S ENTOMOLOGY. By ALFRED RONALDS. With coloured Representations of the Natural and Artificial Insect. With 20 coloured Plates. 8vo., 14s.

Wilcocks.—THE SEA FISHERMAN: Comprising the Chief Methods of Hook and Line Fishing in the British and other Seas, and Remarks on Nets, Boats, and Boating. By J. C. WILCOCKS. Illustrated. Cr 8vo., 6s.

Mental, Moral, and Political Philosophy.

LOGIC, RHETORIC, PSYCHOLOGY, ETC.

Abbott.—THE ELEMENTS OF LOGIC. By T. K. ABBOTT, B.D. 12mo., 3s.

Aristotle.—Works by.

THE POLITICS: G. Bekker's Greek Text of Books I., III., IV. (VII.), with an English Translation by W. E. BOLLAND, M.A.; and short Introductory Essays by A. LANG, M.A. Crown 8vo., 7s. 6d.

THE POLITICS: Introductory Essays. By ANDREW LANG (from Bolland and Lang's 'Politics'). Crown 8vo., 2s. 6d.

THE ETHICS: Greek Text, Illustrated with Essay and Notes. By Sir ALEXANDER GRANT, Bart. 2 vols. 8vo., 32s.

THE NICOMACHEAN ETHICS: Newly Translated into English. By ROBERT WILLIAMS. Crown 8vo., 7s. 6d.

AN INTRODUCTION TO ARISTOTLE'S ETHICS. Books I.-IV. (Book X. c. vi.-ix. in an Appendix). With a continuous Analysis and Notes. By the Rev. EDW. MOORE, D.D., Cr. 8vo. 10s. 6d.

Bacon.—Works by FRANCIS BACON.

COMPLETE WORKS. Edited by R. L. ELLIS, JAMES SPEDDING and D. D. HEATH. 7 vols. 8vo., £3 13s. 6d.

LETTERS AND LIFE, including all his occasional Works. Edited by JAMES SPEDDING. 7 vols. 8vo., £4 4s.

THE ESSAYS: with Annotations. By RICHARD WHATELY, D.D. 8vo., 10s. 6d.

THE ESSAYS: with Introduction, Notes, and Index. By E. A. ABBOTT, D.D. 2 Vols. Fcp. 8vo., 6s. The Text and Index only, without Introduction and Notes, in One Volume. Fcp. 8vo., 2s. 6d.

Bain.—Works by ALEX. BAIN, LL.D.

MENTAL SCIENCE. Crown 8vo. 6s. 6d.

MORAL SCIENCE. Crown 8vo., 4s. 6d.

The two works as above can be had in one volume, price 10s. 6d.

SENSES AND THE INTELLECT. 8vo., 15s.

EMOTIONS AND THE WILL. 8vo., 15s.

LOGIC, DEDUCTIVE AND INDUCTIVE. Part I. 4s. Part II. 6s. 6d.

PRACTICAL ESSAYS. Crown 8vo., 3s.

Bray.—Works by CHARLES BRAY.

THE PHILOSOPHY OF NECESSITY: or Law in Mind as in Matter. Cr. 8vo,, 5s.

THE EDUCATION OF THE FEELINGS: a Moral System for Schools. Cr. 8vo., 2s. 6d.

Bray.—ELEMENTS OF MORALITY, in Easy Lessons for Home and School Teaching. By Mrs. CHARLES BRAY. Cr. 8vo., 1s. 6d.

Crozier.—CIVILISATION AND PROGRESS. By JOHN BEATTIE CROZIER, M.D. With New Preface. More fully explaining the nature of the New Organon used in the solution of its problems. 8vo., 14s.

Davidson.—THE LOGIC OF DEFINITION, Explained and Applied. By WILLIAM L. DAVIDSON, M.A. Crown 8vo., 6s.

Green.—THE WORKS OF THOMAS HILL GREEN. Edited by R. L. NETTLESHIP.

Vols. I. and II. Philosophical Works. 8vo., 16s. each.

Vol. III. Miscellanies. With Index to the three Volumes, and Memoir. 8vo., 21s.

Hodgson.—Works by SHADWORTH H. HODGSON.

TIME AND SPACE: a Metaphysical Essay. 8vo., 16s.

THE THEORY OF PRACTICE: an Ethical Inquiry. 2 vols. 8vo., 24s.

THE PHILOSOPHY OF REFLECTION. 2 vols. 8vo., 21s.

Hume.—THE PHILOSOPHICAL WORKS OF DAVID HUME. Edited by T. H. GREEN and T. H. GROSE. 4 vols. 8vo., 56s. Or separately, Essays. 2 vols. 28s. Treatise of Human Nature. 2 vols. 28s.

Justinian.—THE INSTITUTES OF JUSTINIAN: Latin Text, chiefly that of Huschke, with English Introduction, Translation, Notes, and Summary. By THOMAS C. SANDARS, M.A. 8vo., 18s.

Kant.—Works by IMMANUEL KANT.

CRITIQUE OF PRACTICAL REASON, AND OTHER WORKS ON THE THEORY OF ETHICS. Translated by T. K. ABBOTT, B.D. With Memoir. 8vo., 12s. 6d.

INTRODUCTION TO LOGIC, AND HIS ESSAY ON THE MISTAKEN SUBTILTY OF THE FOUR FIGURES. Translated by T. K. ABBOTT. 8vo., 6s.

Killick.—HANDBOOK TO MILL'S SYSTEM OF LOGIC. By Rev. A. H. KILLICK, M.A. Crown 8vo., 3s. 6d.

Mental, Moral and Political Philosophy—*continued.*

Ladd.—Works by GEO. TRUMBULL LADD.

ELEMENTS OF PHYSIOLOGICAL PSY-CHOLOGY. 8vo., 21s.

OUTLINES OF PHYSIOLOGICAL PSYCHOL-OGY. A Text-book of Mental Science for Academies and Colleges. 8vo., 12s.

PSYCHOLOGY, DESCRIPTIVE AND EX-PLANATORY: a Treatise of the Phenomena, Laws, and Development of Human Mental Life. 8vo., 21s.

PRIMER OF PSYCHOLOGY. Cr. 8vo., 5s. 6d.

PHILOSOPHY OF MIND: an Essay on the Metaphysics of Psychology. 8vo., 16s.

Lewes.—THE HISTORY OF PHILOSOPHY, from Thales to Comte. By GEORGE HENRY LEWES. 2 vols. 8vo., 32s.

Max Müller.—Works by F. MAX MÜLLER.

THE SCIENCE OF THOUGHT. 8vo., 21s.

THREE INTRODUCTORY LECTURES ON THE SCIENCE OF THOUGHT. 8vo., 2s. 6d.

Mill,—ANALYSIS OF THE PHENOMENA OF THE HUMAN MIND. By JAMES MILL. 2 vols. 8vo., 28s.

Mill.—Works by JOHN STEWART MILL.

A SYSTEM OF LOGIC. Crown 8vo., 3s. 6d.

ON LIBERTY. Crown 8vo., 1s. 4d.

ON REPRESENTATIVE GOVERNMENT. Crown 8vo., 2s.

UTILITARIANISM. 8vo., 5s.

EXAMINATION OF SIR WILLIAM HAMIL-TON'S PHILOSOPHY. 8vo., 16s.

NATURE, THE UTILITY OF RELIGION, AND THEISM. Three Essays. 8vo., 5s.

Stock.—DEDUCTIVE LOGIC. By ST. GEORGE STOCK. Fcp. 8vo., 3s. 6d.

Sully.—Works by JAMES SULLY.

THE HUMAN MIND: a Text-book of Psychology. 2 vols. 8vo., 21s.

OUTLINES OF PSYCHOLOGY. 8vo., 9s.

THE TEACHER'S HANDBOOK OF PSY-CHOLOGY. Crown 8vo., 5s.

Swinburne.—PICTURE LOGIC: An Attempt to Popularise the Science of Reasoning. By ALFRED JAMES SWINBURNE, M.A. With 23 Woodcuts. Post 8vo., 5s.

Thomson.—OUTLINES OF THE NECESSARY LAWS OF THOUGHT: a Treatise on Pure and Applied Logic. By WILLIAM THOMSON, D.D., formerly Lord Archbishop of York. Post 8vo., 6s.

Webb.—THE VEIL OF ISIS: a Series of Essays on Idealism. By T. E. WEBB. 8vo., 10s. 6d.

Whately.—Works by R. WHATELY, D.D.

BACON'S ESSAYS. With Annotation. By R. WHATELY. 8vo. 10s. 6d.

ELEMENTS OF LOGIC. Cr. 8vo., 4s. 6d.

ELEMENTS OF RHETORIC. Cr. 8vo., 4s. 6d.

LESSONS ON REASONING. Fcp. 8vo., 1s. 6d.

Zeller.—Works by Dr. EDWARD ZELLER, Professor in the University of Berlin.

THE STOICS, EPICUREANS, AND SCEPTICS. Translated by the Rev. O. J. REICHEL, M.A. Crown 8vo., 15s.

OUTLINES OF THE HISTORY OF GREEK PHILOSOPHY. Translated by SARAH F. ALLEYNE and EVELYN ABBOTT. Crown 8vo., 10s. 6d.

PLATO AND THE OLDER ACADEMY. Translated by SARAH F. ALLEYNE and ALFRED GOODWIN, B.A. Crown 8vo., 18s.

SOCRATES AND THE SOCRATIC SCHOOLS. Translated by the Rev. O. J. REICHEL, M.A. Crown 8vo., 10s. 6d.

MANUALS OF CATHOLIC PHILOSOPHY.

(Stonyhurst Series).

A MANUAL OF POLITICAL ECONOMY. By C. S. DEVAS, M.A. Crown 8vo., 6s. 6d.

FIRST PRINCIPLES OF 'KNOWLEDGE. By JOHN RICKABY, S.J. Crown 8vo., 5s.

GENERAL METAPHYSICS. By JOHN RICK-ABY, S.J. Crown 8vo., 5s.

LOGIC. By RICHARD F. CLARKE, S.J. Crown 8vo., 5s.

MORAL PHILOSOPHY (ETHICS AND NATURAL LAW. By JOSEPH RICKABY, S.J. Crown 8vo., 5s.

NATURAL THEOLOGY. By BERNARD BOEDDER, S.J. Crown 8vo., 6s. 6d.

PSYCHOLOGY. By MICHAEL MAHER, S.J. Crown 8vo., 6s. 6d.

History and Science of Language, &c.

Davidson.— Leading and Important English Words: Explained and Exemplified. By William L. Davidson, M.A. Fcp. 8vo., 3s. 6d.

Farrar.— Language and Languages: By F. W. Farrar, D.D., F.R.S. Crown 8vo., 6s.

Graham.—English Synonyms, Classified and Explained: with Practical Exercises. By G. F. Graham. Fcp. 8vo., 6s.

Max Müller.—Works by F. Max Müller.

The Science of Language, Founded on Lectures delivered at the Royal Institution in 1861 and 1863. 2 vols. Crown 8vo., 21s.

Biographies of Words, and the Home of the Aryas. Crown 8vo., 7s. 6d.

Max Müller.—Works by F. Max Müller —*continued.*

Three Lectures on the Science of Language, and its Place in General Education, delivered at Oxford, 1889. Crown 8vo., 3s.

Roget.—Thesaurus of English Words and Phrases. Classified and Arranged so as to Facilitate the Expression of Ideas and assist in Literary Composition. By Peter Mark Roget, M.D., F.R.S. Recomposed throughout, enlarged and improved, partly from the Author's Notes, and with a full Index, by the Author's Son, John Lewis Roget. Crown 8vo. 10s. 6d.

Whately.—English Synonyms. By E. Jane Whately. Fcp. 8vo., 3s.

Political Economy and Economics.

Ashley.—English Economic History and Theory. By W. J. Ashley, M.A. Crown 8vo., Part I., 5s. Part II. 10s. 6d.

Barnett.—Practicable Socialism: Essays on Social Reform. By the Rev. S. A. and Mrs. Barnett. Crown 8vo., 6s.

Brassey.—Papers and Addresses on Work and Wages. By Lord Brassey. Edited by J. Potter, and with Introduction by George Howell, M.P. Crown 8vo., 5s.

Devas.—A Manual of Political Economy. By C. S. Devas, M.A. Crown 8vo., 6s. 6d. (*Manuals of Catholic Philosophy.*)

Dowell.—A History of Taxation and Taxes in England, from the Earliest Times to the Year 1885. By Stephen Dowell, (4 vols. 8vo.) Vols. I. and II. The History of Taxation, 21s. Vols. III. and IV. The History of Taxes, 21s.

Leslie.—Essays in Political Economy. By T. E. Cliffe Leslie. 8vo., 10s. 6d.

Macleod.--Works by Henry Dunning Macleod, M.A.
Bimetalism 8vo., 5s. net.
The Elements of Banking. Crown 8vo., 3s. 6d.
The Theory and Practice of Banking. Vol. I. 8vo., 12s. Vol. II. 14s.
The Theory of Credit. 8vo. Vol. I. 10s. net. Vol. II., Part I., 10s. net. Vol. II. Part II., 10s. 6d.

Mill.—Political Economy. By John Stuart Mill.
Popular Edition. Crown 8vo., 3s. 6d.
Library Edition. 2 vols. 8vo., 30s.

Symes.—Political Economy: a Short Text-book of Political Economy. With Problems for Solution, and Hints for Supplementary Reading. By Professor J. E. Symes, M.A., of University College, Nottingham. Crown 8vo., 2s. 6d.

Toynbee.—Lectures on the Industrial Revolution of the 18th Century in England. By Arnold Toynbee. With a Memoir of the Author by B. Jowett. 8vo., 10s. 6d.

Webb. — The History of Trade Unionism. By Sidney and Beatrice Webb. With Map and full Bibliography of the Subject. 8vo., 18s.

Wilson. — Works by A. J. Wilson. Chiefly reprinted from *The Investors' Review.*

Practical Hints to Small Investors. Crown 8vo., 1s.

Plain Advice about Life Insurance. Crown 8vo., 1s.

Evolution, Anthropology, &c.

Clodd.—Works by EDWARD CLODD.

THE STORY OF CREATION: a Plain Account of Evolution. With 77 Illustrations. Crown 8vo., 3s. 6d.

A PRIMER OF EVOLUTION: being a Popular Abridged Edition of 'The Story of Creation'. With Illustrations. Fcp. 8vo., 1s. 6d.

Huth.—THE MARRIAGE OF NEAR KIN, considered with Respect to the Law of Nations, the Result of Experience, and the Teachings of Biology. By ALFRED HENRY HUTH. Royal 8vo., 7s. 6d.

Lang.—CUSTOM AND MYTH: Studies of Early Usage and Belief. By ANDREW LANG, M.A. With 15 Illustrations. Crown 8vo., 3s. 6d.

Lubbock.—THE ORIGIN OF CIVILISATION, and the Primitive Condition of Man. By Sir J. LUBBOCK, Bart., M.P. With 5 Plates and 20 Illustrations in the Text. 8vo., 18s.

Romanes. — Works by GEORGE JOHN ROMANES, M.A., LL.D., F.R.S.

DARWIN, AND AFTER DARWIN: an Exposition of the Darwinian Theory, and a Discussion on Post-Darwinian Questions. Part I. The Darwinian Theory. With Portrait of Darwin and 125 Illustrations. Crown 8vo., 10s. 6d.

AN EXAMINATION OF WEISMANNISM. Crown 8vo., 6s.

Classical Literature and Translations, &c.

Abbott.—HELLENICA. A Collection of Essays on Greek Poetry, Philosophy, History, and Religion. Edited by EVELYN ABBOTT, M.A., LL.D. 8vo., 16s.

Æschylus.—EUMENIDES OF ÆSCHYLUS. With Metrical English Translation. By J. F. DAVIES. 8vo., 7s.

Aristophanes. — THE ACHARNIANS OF ARISTOPHANES, translated into English Verse. By R. Y. TYRRELL. Crown 8vo., 1s.

Becker.—Works by Professor BECKER.

GALLUS: or, Roman Scenes in the Time of Augustus. Illustrated. Post 8vo., 3s. 6d.

CHARICLES: or, Illustrations of the Private Life of the Ancient Greeks. Illustrated. Post 8vo., 3s. 6d.

Cicero.—CICERO'S CORRESPONDENCE. By R. Y. TYRRELL. Vols. I., II., III., 8vo., each 12s. Vol. IV., 15s.

Farnell.—GREEK LYRIC POETRY: a Complete Collection of the Surviving Passages from the Greek Song-Writting. Arranged with Prefatory Articles, Introductory Matter and Commentary. By GEORGE S. FARNELL, M.A. With 5 Plates. 8vo., 16s.

Lang.—HOMER AND THE EPIC. By ANDREW LANG. Crown 8vo., 9s. net.

Mackail.—SELECT EPIGRAMS FROM THE GREEK ANTHOLOGY. By J. W. MACKAIL, Fellow of Balliol College, Oxford. Edited with a Revised Text, Introduction, Translation and Notes. 8vo., 16s.

Rich.—A DICTIONARY OF ROMAN AND GREEK ANTIQUITIES. By A. RICH, B.A. With 2000 Woodcuts. Crown 8vo., 7s. 6d.

Sophocles.—Translated into English Verse. By ROBERT WHITELAW, M.A., Assistant Master in Rugby School; late Fellow of Trinity College, Cambridge. Crown 8vo., 8s. 6d.

Theocritus.—THE IDYLLS OF THEOCRITUS. Translated into English Verse by JAMES HENRY HALLARD, M.A. Oxon. Fcp. 4to., 6s. 6d.

Tyrrell.—TRANSLATIONS INTO GREEK AND LATIN VERSE. Edited by R. Y. TYRRELL. 8vo., 6s.

Virgil.—THE ÆNEID OF VIRGIL. Translated into English Verse by JOHN CONINGTON. Crown 8vo., 6s.

THE POEMS OF VIRGIL. Translated into English Prose by JOHN CONINGTON. Crown 8vo., 6s.

THE ÆNEID OF VIRGIL, freely translated into English Blank Verse. By W. J. THORNHILL. Crown 8vo., 7s. 6d.

THE ÆNEID OF VIRGIL. Books I. to VI. Translated into English Verse by JAMES RHOADES. Crown 8vo., 5s.

Wilkins.—THE GROWTH OF THE HOMERIC POEMS. By G. WILKINS. 8vo., 6s.

Poetry and the Drama.

Acworth.—BALLADS OF THE MARATHAS. Rendered into English Verse from the Marathi Originals. By HARRY ARBUTHNOT ACWORTH. 8vo., 5s.

Allingham.—Works by WILLIAM ALLINGHAM.
IRISH SONGS AND POEMS. With Frontis- of the Waterfall of Asaroe. Fcp. 8vo., 6s.
LAURENCE BLOOMFIELD. With Portrait of the Author. Fcp. 8vo., 3s. 6d.
FLOWER PIECES; DAY AND NIGHT SONGS; BALLADS. With 2 Designs by D. G. ROSSETTI. Fcp. 8vo., 6s. large paper edition, 12s.
LIFE AND PHANTASY : with Frontispiece by Sir J. E. MILLAIS, Bart., and Design by ARTHUR HUGHES. Fcp. 8vo., 6s.; large paper edition, 12s.
THOUGHT AND WORD, AND ASHBY MANOR: a Play. Fcp. 8vo., 6s. ; large paper edition, 12s.
BLACKBERRIES. Imperial 16mo., 6s.
Sets of the above 6 vols. may be had in uniform Half-parchment binding, price 30s.

Armstrong.—Works by G. F. SAVAGE-ARMSTRONG.
POEMS : Lyrical and Dramatic. Fcp. 8vo., 6s.
KING SAUL. (The Tragedy of Israel, Part I.) Fcp. 8vo., 5s.
KING DAVID. (The Tragedy of Israel, Part II.) Fcp. 8vo., 6s.
KING SOLOMON. (The Tragedy of Israel, Part III.) Fcp. 8vo., 6s.
UGONE: a Tragedy. Fcp. 8vo., 6s.
A GARLAND FROM GREECE : Poems. Fcp. 8vo., 7s. 6d.
STORIES OF WICKLOW: Poems. Fcp. 8vo., 7s. 6d.
MEPHISTOPHELES IN BROADCLOTH : a Satire. Fcp. 8vo., 4s.
ONE IN THE INFINITE : a Poem. Crown 8vo., 7s. 6d.

Armstrong.—THE POETICAL WORKS OF EDMUND J. ARMSTRONG. Fcp. 8vo., 5s.

Arnold.—Works by Sir EDWIN ARNOLD, K.C.I.E., Author of ' The Light of Asia,' &c.
THE LIGHT OF THE WORLD: or the Great Consummation. Cr. 8vo., 7s. 6d. net. Presentation Edition. With 14 Illustrations by W. HOLMAN HUNT, 4to., 20s. net.
POTIPHAR'S WIFE, and other Poems. Crown 8vo., 5s. net.
ADZUMA: or the Japanese Wife. A Play. Crown 8vo., 6s. 6d. net.

Beesly.—BALLADS AND OTHER VERSE. By A. H. BEESLY. Fcp, 8vo., 5s.

Bell.—CHAMBER COMEDIES : a Collection of Plays and Monologues for the Drawing Room. By Mrs. HUGH BELL. Cr. 8vo., 6s.

Björnsen.—Works by BJÖRNSTJERNE BJÖRNSEN.
PASTOR SANG : A PLAY. Translated by WILLIAM WILSON. Crown 8vo., 5s.
A GAUNTLET : a Drama. Translated into English by OSMAN EDWARDS. With Portrait of the Author. Crown 8vo., 5s.

Cochrane.—THE KESTREL'S NEST, and other Verses. By ALFRED COCHRANE. Fcp. 8vo., 3s. 6d.

Goethe.
FAUST, Part I., the German Text, with Introduction and Notes. By ALBERT M. SELSS, Ph.D., M.A. Crown 8vo., 5s.
FAUST. Translated, with Notes. By T. E. WEBB. 8vo., 12s. 6d.

Ingelow.—Works by JEAN INGELOW.
POETICAL WORKS. 2 vols. Fcp. 8vo., 12s.
LYRICAL AND OTHER POEMS. Selected from the Writings of JEAN INGELOW. Fcp. 8vo., 2s. 6d. cloth plain, 3s. cl. gilt.

Kendall.—SONGS FROM DREAMLAND. By MAY KENDALL. Fcp. 8vo., 5s. net.

Lang.—Works by ANDREW LANG.
BAN AND ARRIÈRE BAN : a Rally of Fugitive Rhymes. Fcp. 8vo., 5s. net.
GRASS OF PARNASSUS. Fcp. 8vo., 2s. 6d. net.
BALLADS OF BOOKS. Edited by ANDREW LANG. Fcp. 8vo., 6s.
THE BLUE POETRY BOOK. Edited by ANDREW LANG. With 12 Plates and 88 Illustrations in the Text by H. J. FORD and LANCELOT SPEED. Crown 8vo., 6s.
Special Edition, printed on India paper. With Notes, but without Illustrations. Crown 8vo., 7s. 6d.

Lecky.—POEMS. By W. E. H. LECKY. Fcp. 8vo., 5s.

Lytton.—Works by THE EARL OF LYTTON. (OWEN MEREDITH).
MARAH. Fcp. 8vo., 6s. 6d.
KING POPPY: a Fantasia. With 1 Plate and Design on Title-Page by ED. BURNE-JONES, A.R.A. Crown 8vo., 10s. 6d.
THE WANDERER. Crown 8vo., 10s. 6d.
LUCILE. Crown 8vo., 10s. 6d.
SELECTED POEMS. Crown 8vo., 10s. 6d.

Murray.—(ROBERT F.), Author of ' The Scarlet Gown '. His Poems, with a Memoir by ANDREW LANG. Fcp. 8vo., 5s. net.

Poetry and the Drama—*continued.*

Macaulay.—LAYS OF ANCIENT ROME, &c. By Lord MACAULAY.

Illustrated by G. SCHARF. Fcp. 4to., 10s. 6d.

——— Bijou Edition. 18mo., 2s. 6d. gilt top.

——— Popular Edition. Fcp. 4to., 6d. sewed, 1s. cloth.

Illustrated by J. R. WEGUELIN. Crown 8vo., 3s. 6d.

Annotated Edition. Fcp. 8vo., 1s. sewed, 1s. 6d. cloth.

Nesbit.—LAYS AND LEGENDS. By E. NESBIT (Mrs. HUBERT BLAND). First Series. Crown 8vo., 3s. 6d. Second Series. With Portrait. Crown 8vo., 5s.

Peek.—Works by HEDLEY PEEK (FRANK LEYTON)

SKELETON LEAVES: Poems. With a Dedicatory Poem to the late Hon. Roden Noel. Fcp. 8vo., 2s. 6d. net.

THE SHADOWS OF THE LAKE, and other Poems. Fcp. 8vo., 2s. 6d. net.

Piatt.—Works by SARAH PIATT.

AN ENCHANTED CASTLE, AND OTHER POEMS: Pictures, Portraits, and People in Ireland. Crown 8vo. 3s. 6d.

POEMS: With Portrait of the Author. 2 vols. Crown 8vo., 10s.

Piatt.—WORKS BY JOHN JAMES PIATT.

IDYLS AND LYRICS OF THE OHIO VALLEY. Crown 8vo., 5s.

LITTLE NEW WORLD IDYLS. Cr. 8vo. 5s.

Rhoades.—TERESA AND OTHER POEMS. By JAMES RHOADES. Crown 8vo., 3s. 6d.

Riley.—Works by JAMES WHITCOMB RILEY.

OLD FASHIONED ROSES: Poems. 12mo., 5s.

POEMS: Here at Home. Fcp. 8vo., 6s. *net.*

Shakespeare. — BOWDLER'S FAMILY SHAKESPEARE. With 36 Woodcuts. 1 vol. 8vo., 14s. Or in 6 vols. Fcp. 8vo., 21s.

THE SHAKESPEARE BIRTHDAY BOOK. By MARY F. DUNBAR. 32mo., 1s. 6d. Drawing Room Edition, with Photographs. Fcp. 8vo., 10s. 6d.

Sturgis.—A BOOK OF SONG. By JULIAN STURGIS. 16mo. 5s.

Works of Fiction, Humour, &c.

Anstey.—Works by F. ANSTEY, Author of 'Vice Versa'.

THE BLACK POODLE, and other Stories. Crown 8vo., 2s. boards, 2s. 6d. cloth.

VOCES POPULI. Reprinted from 'Punch'. First Series. With 20 Illustrations by J. BERNARD PARTRIDGE. Crown 8vo., 3s. 6d.

THE TRAVELLING COMPANIONS. Reprinted from 'Punch'. With 25 Illust. by J. BERNARD PARTRIDGE. Post 4to., 5s.

THE MAN FROM BLANKLEY'S: a Story in Scenes, and other Sketches. With 24 Illustrations by J. BERNARD PARTRIDGE. Fcp. 4to., 6s.

Astor.—A JOURNEY IN OTHER WORLDS. a Romance of the Future. By JOHN JACOB ASTOR. With 10 Illustrations. Cr. 8vo., 6s.

Baker.—BY THE WESTERN SEA. By JAMES BAKER, Author of 'John Westacott'. Crown 8vo., 3s. 6d.

Beaconsfield.—Works by the Earl of BEACONSFIELD.

NOVELS AND TALES. Cheap Edition. Complete in 11 vols. Cr. 8vo., 1s. 6d. each.

Vivian Grey.	Henrietta Temple.
The Young Duke, &c.	Venetia. Tancred.
Alroy, Ixion, &c.	Coningsby. Sybil.
Contarini Fleming,&c.	Lothair. Endymion.

NOVELS AND TALES. The Hughenden Edition. With 2 Portraits and 11 Vignettes. 11 vols. Crown 8vo., 42s.

Clegg.—DAVID'S LOOM: a Story of Rochdale life in the early years of the Nineteenth Century. By JOHN TRAFFORD CLEGG. Cr. 8vo., 2s. 6d.

Deland.—Works by MARGARET DELAND, Author of 'John Ward'.

THE STORY OF A CHILD. Cr. 8vo., 5s.

MR. TOMMY DOVE, and other Stories. Crown 8vo. 6s.

PHILIP AND HIS WIFE. Crown 8vo., 6s.

Dougall.—Works by L. DOUGALL.

BEGGARS ALL Crown 8vo., 3s. 6d.

WHAT NECESSITY KNOWS. Cr. 8vo., 6s.

Works of Fiction, Humour, &c.—*continued.*

Doyle.—Works by A. CONAN DOYLE.

MICAH CLARKE : A Tale of Monmouth's Rebellion. With Frontispiece and Vignette. Cr. 8vo., 3*s.* 6*d.*

THE CAPTAIN OF THE POLESTAR, and other Tales. Cr. 8vo., 3*s.* 6*d.*

THE REFUGEES: A Tale of Two Continents. Cr. 8vo., 6*s.*

Farrar.—DARKNESS AND DAWN: or, Scenes in the Days of Nero. An Historic Tale. By Archdeacon FARRAR. Cr. 8vo., 7*s.* 6*d.*

Froude.—THE TWO CHIEFS OF DUNBOY : an Irish Romance of the Last Century. By J. A. FROUDE. Cr. 8vo., 3*s.* 6*d.*

Gilkes.—THE THING THAT HATH BEEN : or, a Young Man's Mistakes. By A. H. GILKES, M.A., Master of Dulwich College, Author of 'Boys and Masters'. Crown 8vo., 6*s.*

Haggard.—Works by H. RIDER HAGGARD.

THE PEOPLE OF THE MIST. With 16 Illustrations by ARTHUR LAYARD. Crown 8vo., 6*s.*

SHE. With 32 Illustrations by M. GREIFFENHAGEN and C. H. M. KERR. Cr. 8vo., 3*s.* 6*d.*

ALLAN QUATERMAIN. With 31 Illustrations by C. H. M. KERR. Cr. 8vo., 3*s.* 6*d.*

MAIWA'S REVENGE : or, The War of the Little Hand. Cr. 8vo., 1*s.* boards, 1*s.* 6*d.* cloth.

COLONEL QUARITCH, V.C. Cr. 8vo. 3*s.* 6*d.*

CLEOPATRA. With 29 Full-page Illustrations by M. GREIFFENHAGEN and R. CATON WOODVILLE. Crown 8vo., 3*s.* 6*d.*

BEATRICE. Cr. 8vo., 3*s.* 6*d.*

ERIC BRIGHTEYES. With 17 Plates and 34 Illustrations in the Text by LANCELOT SPEED. Cr. 8vo., 3*s.* 6*d.*

NADA THE LILY. With 23 Illustrations by C. M. KERR. Cr. 8vo., 6*s.*

MONTEZUMA'S DAUGHTER. With 24 Illustrations by M. GREIFFENHAGEN. Crown 8vo., 6*s.*

ALLAN'S WIFE. With 34 Illustrations by M. GREIFFENHAGEN and C. H. M. KERR. Crown 8vo., 3*s.* 6*d.*

THE WITCH'S HEAD. With 16 Illustrations. Crown 8vo., 3*s.* 6*d.*

Haggard.—Works by H. RIDER HAGGARD. —*continued.*

MR. MEESON'S WILL. With 16 Illustrations. Crown 8vo., 3*s.* 6*d.*

DAWN. With 16 Illustrations. Crown 8vo., 3*s.* 6*d.*

Haggard and Lang.—THE WORLD'S DESIRE. By H. RIDER HAGGARD and ANDREW LANG. With 27 Illustrations by M. GREIFFENHAGEN. Cr. 8vo. 3*s.* 6*d.*

Harte.—IN THE CARQUINEZ WOODS and other stories. By BRET HARTE. Cr. 8vo., 3*s.* 6*d.*

Hornung.—THE UNBIDDEN GUEST. By E. W. HORNUNG. Crown 8vo., 3*s.* 6*d.*

Lyall.—Works by EDNA LYALL, Author of 'Donovan,' &c.

THE AUTOBIOGRAPHY OF A SLANDER. Fcp. 8vo., 1*s.* sewed.

Presentation Edition. With 20 Illustrations by LANCELOT SPEED. Crown 8vo., 2*s.* 6*d.* net.

DOREEN. The Story of a Singer. Crown 8vo., 6*s.*

Melville.—Works by G. J. WHYTE MELVILLE.

The Gladiators.	Holmby House.
The Interpreter.	Kate Coventry.
Good for Nothing.	Digby Grand.
The Queen's Maries.	General Bounce.

Cr. 8vo., 1*s.* 6*d.* each.

Oliphant.—Works by Mrs. OLIPHANT.

MADAM. Cr. 8vo., 1*s.* 6*d.*

IN TRUST. Cr. 8vo., 1*s.* 6*d.*

Parr.—CAN THIS BE LOVE ? By Mrs. PARR, Author of 'Dorothy Fox'. Crown 8vo. 6*s.*

Payn.—Works by JAMES PAYN.

THE LUCK OF THE DARRELLS. Cr. 8vo., 1*s.* 6*d.*

THICKER THAN WATER. Cr. 8vo., 1*s.* 6*d.*

Phillipps-Wolley.—SNAP: a Legend of the Lone Mountain. By C. PHILLIPPS-WOLLEY. With 13 Illustrations by H. G. WILLINK. Cr. 8vo., 3*s.* 6*d.*

Rhoscomyl.—THE JEWEL OF YNS GALON : being a hitherto unprinted Chapter in the History of the Sea Rovers. By OWEN RHOSCOMYL. Cr. 8vo., 6*s.*

Robertson. — NUGGETS IN THE DEVIL'S PUNCH BOWL, and other Australian Tales. By ANDREW ROBERTSON. Cr. 8vo., 3*s.* 6*d.*

Works of Fiction, Humour, &c.—*continued.*

Sewell.—Works by ELIZABETH M. SEWELL.

A Glimpse of the World.	Amy Herbert.
Laneton Parsonage.	Cleve Hall.
Margaret Percival.	Gertrude.
Katharine Ashton.	Home Life.
The Earl's Daughter.	After Life.
The Experience of Life.	Ursula. Ivors.

Cr. 8vo., 1s. 6d. each cloth plain. 2s. 6d. each cloth extra, gilt edges.

Stevenson.—Works by ROBERT LOUIS STEVENSON.

STRANGE CASE OF DR. JEKYLL AND MR. HYDE. Fcp. 8vo., 1s. sewed. 1s. 6d. cloth.

THE DYNAMITER. Cr. 8vo., 3s. 6d.

Stevenson and Osbourne.—THE WRONG BOX. By ROBERT LOUIS STEVENSON and LLOYD OSBOURNE. Cr. 8vo., 3s. 6d.

Suttner.—LAY DOWN YOUR ARMS (*Die Waffen Nieder*): The Autobiography of Martha Tilling. By BERTHA VON SUTTNER. Translated by T. HOLMES. Cr. 8vo., 1s. 6d.

Trollope.—Works by ANTHONY TROLLOPE.

THE WARDEN. Cr. 8vo., 1s. 6d.

BARCHESTER TOWERS. Cr. 8vo., 1s. 6d.

TRUE (A) RELATION OF THE TRAVELS AND PERILOUS ADVENTURES OF MATHEW DUDGEON, GENTLEMAN: Wherein is truly set down the Manner of his Taking, the Long Time of his Slavery in Algiers, and Means of his Delivery. Written by Himself, and now for the first time printed. Cr. 8vo., 5s.

Walford.—Works by L. B. WALFORD.

Mr. SMITH : a Part of his Life. Crown 8vo., 2s. 6d.

THE BABY'S GRANDMOTHER. Cr. 8vo., 2s. 6d.

COUSINS. Crown 8vo., 2s. 6d.

TROUBLESOME DAUGHTERS. Cr. 8vo., 2s. 6d.

PAULINE. Crown 8vo., 2s. 6d.

DICK NETHERBY. Crown 8vo., 2s. 6d.

THE HISTORY OF A WEEK. Cr. 8vo., 2s. 6d.

A STIFF-NECKED GENERATION. Cr. 8vo., 2s. 6d.

NAN, and other Stories. Cr. 8vo., 2s. 6d.

THE MISCHIEF OF MONICA. Cr. 8vo., 2s. 6d.

THE ONE GOOD GUEST. Crown 8vo., 2s. 6d.

'PLOUGHED,' and other Stories. Crown 8vo., 6s.

THE MATCHMAKER. Cr. 8vo., 6s.

West.—WORKS BY B. B. WEST.

HALF-HOURS WITH THE MILLIONAIRES : Showing how much harder it is to spend a million than to make it. Cr. 8vo., 6s.

Sir SIMON VANDERPETTER, and MINDING HIS ANCESTORS : Two Reformations. Crown 8vo., 5s.

Weyman.—Works by STANLEY WEYMAN.

THE HOUSE OF THE WOLF. Cr. 8vo., 3s. 6d.

A GENTLEMAN OF FRANCE. Cr. 8vo., 6s.

Popular Science (Natural History, &c.).

Butler.—OUR HOUSEHOLD INSECTS. An Account of the Insect-Pests found in Dwelling-Houses. By EDWARD A. BUTLER, B.A., B.Sc. (Lond.). With 113 Illustrations. Crown 8vo., 6s.

Furneaux.—Works by W. FURNEAUX, F.R.G.S.

THE OUTDOOR WORLD ; or The Young Collector's Handbook. With 18 Plates, 16 of which are coloured, and 549 Illustrations in the Text. Crown 8vo., 7s. 6d.

BUTTERFLIES AND MOTHS (British). With 12 coloured Plates and 241 Illustrations in the Text. 10s. 6d. net.

Hartwig.—Works by Dr. GEORGE HARTWIG.

THE SEA AND ITS LIVING WONDERS. With 12 Plates and 303 Woodcuts. 8vo., 7s. net.

THE TROPICAL WORLD. With 8 Plates and 172 Woodcuts. 8vo., 7s. net.

THE POLAR WORLD. With 3 Maps, 8 Plates and 85 Woodcuts. 8vo., 7s. net.

THE SUBTERRANEAN WORLD. With 3 Maps and 80 Woodcuts. 8vo., 7s. net.

Popular Science (Natural History, &c.)—*continued.*

Hartwig.—Works by Dr. GEORGE HART-
WIG—*continued.*

THE AERIAL WORLD. With Map, 8
Plates and 60 Woodcuts. 8vo., 7s. net.

HEROES OF THE POLAR WORLD.   19
Illustrations. Cr. 8vo., 2s.

WONDERS OF THE TROPICAL FORESTS.
40 Illustrations. Cr. 8vo., 2s.

WORKERS UNDER THE GROUND.   29
Illustrations. Cr. 8vo., 2s.

MARVELS OVER OUR HEADS. 29 Illustrations. Cr. 8vo., 2s.

SEA MONSTERS AND SEA BIRDS.   75
Illustrations. Cr. 8vo., 2s. 6d.

DENIZENS OF THE DEEP.   117 Illustrations. Cr. 8vo., 2s. 6d.

VOLCANOES AND EARTHQUAKES.   30
Illustrations. Cr. 8vo., 2s. 6d.

WILD ANIMALS OF THE TROPICS.   66
Illustrations. Cr. 8vo., 3s. 6d.

Hayward.—BIRD NOTES. By the late
JANE MARY HAYWARD. Edited by EMMA
HUBBARD. With Frontispiece and 15 Illus-
trations by G. E. LODGE. Cr. 8vo., 6s.

. *These notes were written by one whose quiet life
gave her exceptional opportunities of watching the ways
and manners of the birds that frequented her garden and
window sill, and have no pretension to scientific value.
They are accurate accounts, written from time to time
during many years, of the small incidents of bird life
that passed before the eyes of one qualified by artistic
training and by inherited love of birds to watch narrowly,
to understand sympathetically, what was happening.*

Helmholtz. — POPULAR LECTURES ON
SCIENTIFIC SUBJECTS. By HERMANN VON
HELMHOLTZ. With 68 Woodcuts. 2 vols.
Cr. 8vo., 3s. 6d. each.

Proctor.—Works by RICHARD A. PROCTOR.

LIGHT SCIENCE FOR LEISURE HOURS.
Familiar Essays on Scientific Subjects.   3
vols. Cr. 8vo., 5s. each.

CHANCE AND LUCK: a Discussion of
the Laws of Luck, Coincidence, Wagers,
Lotteries and the Fallacies of Gambling,
&c. Cr. 8vo., 2s. boards. 2s. 6d. cloth.

ROUGH WAYS MADE SMOOTH. Familiar
Essays on Scientific Subjects. Silver
Library Edition. Cr. 8vo., 3s. 6d.

PLEASANT WAYS IN SCIENCE. Cr. 8vo., 5s.
Silver Library Edition. Cr. 8vo., 3s. 6d.

THE GREAT PYRAMID, OBSERVATORY,
TOMB AND TEMPLE. With Illustrations.
Cr. 8vo., 5s.

NATURE STUDIES. By R. A. PROCTOR,
GRANT ALLEN, A. WILSON, T. FOSTER
and E. CLODD. Cr. 8vo., 5s. Silver
Library Edition. Crown 8vo., 3s. 6d.

Proctor.—Works by RICHARD A. PROCTOR.
—*continued.*

LEISURE READINGS. By R. A. PROC-
TOR, E. CLODD, A. WILSON, T. FOSTER
and A. C. RANYARD. Cr. 8vo., 5s.

Stanley.—A FAMILIAR HISTORY OF BIRDS.
By E. STANLEY, D.D., formerly Bishop of
Norwich. With Illustrations. Cr. 8vo.,
3s. 6d.

Wood.—Works by the Rev. J. G. WOOD.

HOMES WITHOUT HANDS: a Description
of the Habitation of Animals, classed
according to the Principle of Construction. With 140 Illustrations. 8vo., 7s.,
net.

INSECTS AT HOME: a Popular Account
of British Insects, their Structure, Habits
and Transformations. With 700 Illustrations. 8vo., 7s. net.

INSECTS ABROAD: a Popular Account
of Foreign Insects, their Structure, Habits
and Transformations. With 600 Illustrations. 8vo., 7s. net.

BIBLE ANIMALS: a Description of every
Living Creature mentioned in the Scrip-
tures. With 112 Illustrations. 8vo., 7s.
net.

PETLAND REVISITED. With 33 Illustrations. Cr. 8vo., 3s. 6d.

OUT OF DOORS; a Selection of Original
Articles on Practical Natural History.
With 11 Illustrations. Cr. 8vo., 3s. 6d.

STRANGE DWELLINGS: a Description of
the Habitations of Animals, abridged from
'Homes without Hands'. With 60 Illustrations. Cr. 8vo., 3s. 6d.

BIRD LIFE OF THE BIBLE. 32 Illustrations. Cr. 8vo., 3s. 6d.

WONDERFUL NESTS. 30 Illustrations.
Cr. 8vo., 3s. 6d.

HOMES UNDER THE GROUND. 28 Illustrations. Cr. 8vo., 3s. 6d.

WILD ANIMALS OF THE BIBLE.   29
Illustrations. Cr. 8vo., 3s. 6d.

DOMESTIC ANIMALS OF THE BIBLE. 23
Illustrations. Cr. 8vo., 3s. 6d.

THE BRANCH BUILDERS. 28 Illustrations. Cr. 8vo., 2s. 6d.

SOCIAL HABITATIONS AND PARASITIC
NESTS. 18 Illustrations. Cr. 8vo., 2s.

Works of Reference.

Maunder's (Samuel) Treasuries.

BIOGRAPHICAL TREASURY. With Supplement brought down to 1889. By Rev. JAMES WOOD. Fcp. 8vo., 6s.

TREASURY OF NATURAL HISTORY: or, Popular Dictionary of Zoology. With 900 Woodcuts. Fcp. 8vo., 6s.

TREASURY OF GEOGRAPHY, Physical, Historical, Descriptive, and Political. With 7 Maps and 16 Plates. Fcp. 8vo., 6s.

THE TREASURY OF BIBLE KNOWLEDGE. By the Rev. J. AYRE, M.A. With 5 Maps, 15 Plates, and 300 Woodcuts. Fcp. 8vo., 6s.

HISTORICAL TREASURY: Outlines of Universal History, Separate Histories of all Nations. Fcp. 8vo., 6s.

TREASURY OF KNOWLEDGE AND LIBRARY OF REFERENCE. Comprising an English Dictionary and Grammar, Universal Gazeteer, Classical Dictionary, Chronology, Law Dictionary, &c. Fcp. 8vo., 6s.

Maunder's (Samuel)Treasuries--*continued*.

SCIENTIFIC AND LITERARY TREASURY. Fcp. 8vo., 6s.

THE TREASURY OF BOTANY. Edited by J. LINDLEY, F.R.S., and T. MOORE, F.L.S. With 274 Woodcuts and 20 Steel Plates. 2 vols. Fcp. 8vo., 12s.

Roget.—THESAURUS OF ENGLISH WORDS AND PHRASES. Classified and Arranged so as to Facilitate the Expression of Ideas and assist in Literary Composition. By PETER MARK ROGET, M.D., F.R.S. Recomposed throughout, enlarged and improved, partly from the Author's Notes, and with a full Index, by the Author's Son, JOHN LEWIS ROGET. Crown 8vo., 10s. 6d.

Willich.—POPULAR TABLES for giving information for ascertaining the value of Lifehold, Leasehold, and Church Property, the Public Funds, &c. By CHARLES M. WILLICH. Edited by H. BENCE JONES. Crown 8vo., 10s. 6d.

Children's Books.

Crake.—Works by Rev. A. D. CRAKE.

EDWY THE FAIR; or, The First Chronicle of Æscendune. Crown 8vo., 2s. 6d.

ALFGAR THE DANE: or, the Second Chronicle of Æscendune. Cr. 8vo. 2s. 6d.

THE RIVAL HEIRS: being the Third and Last Chronicle of Æscendune. Cr. 8vo., 2s. 6d.

THE HOUSE OF WALDERNE. A Tale of the Cloister and the Forest in the Days of the Barons' Wars. Crown 8vo., 2s. 6d.

BRIAN FITZ-COUNT. A Story of Wallingford Castle and Dorchester Abbey. Cr. 8vo., 2s. 6d.

Lang.—Works edited by ANDREW LANG.

THE BLUE FAIRY BOOK. With 8 Full page Illustrations and 130 Illustrations in the Text by H. J. FORD and G. P. JACOMB HOOD. Crown 8vo., 5s.

THE RED FAIRY BOOK. With 4 Full page Illustrations and 96 Illustrations in the Text by H. J. FORD and LANCELOT SPEED. Crown 8vo., 6s.

Lang.—Works edited by ANDREW LANG. —*continued*.

THE GREEN FAIRY BOOK. With 11 Full page Illustrations and 88 Illustrations in the Text by H. J. FORD and L. BOGLE. Crown 8vo., 6s.

THE YELLOW FAIRY BOOK. With 22 Full page Illustrations and 82 Illustrations in the Text by H. J. FORD. Crown 8vo., 6s.

THE BLUE POETRY BOOK. With 12 Full page Illustrations and 88 Illustrations in the Text by H. J. FORD and LANCELOT SPEED. Cr. 8vo., 6s.

THE BLUE POETRY BOOK. School Edition, without Illustrations. Fcp. 8vo., 2s. 6d.

THE TRUE STORY BOOK. With 8 Full page Illustrations and 58 Illustrations in the Text, by H. J. FORD, LUCIEN DAVIS, C. H. M. KERR, LANCELOT SPEED, and LOCKHART BOGLE. Cr. 8vo., 6s.

Meade.—Works by L. T. MEADE.

DADDY'S BOY. With Illustrations. Crown 8vo., 3s. 6d.

DEB AND THE DUCHESS. With Illustrations by M. E. EDWARDS. Crown 8vo., 3s. 6d.

Children's Books—*continued.*

Molesworth.—Works by Mrs. MOLES-
WORTH.

SILVERTHORNS. Illustrated. Crown
8vo., 5*s.*

THE PALACE IN THE GARDEN. Illustrated. Crown 8vo., 5*s.*

Stevenson.—A CHILD'S GARDEN OF
VERSES. By ROBERT LOUIS STEVENSON.
Fcp. 8vo., 5*s.*

Longmans' Series of Books for Girls.

Crown 8vo., price 2*s.* 6*d.* each.

ATELIER (THE) DU LYS : or, an Art
Student in the Reign of Terror.
BY THE SAME AUTHOR.

MADEMOISELLE MORI : a Tale of Modern
Modern Rome.

THAT CHILD. With Illustrations by
GORDON BROWNE.

UNDER A CLOUD.

THE FIDDLER OF LUGAU. With Illustrations by W. RALSTON.

A CHILD OF THE REVOLUTION. With
Illustrations by C. J. STANILAND.

HESTER'S VENTURE.

IN THE OLDEN TIME: a Tale of the
Peasant War in Germany.

THE YOUNGER SISTER.

ATHERSTONE PRIORY. By L. N. COMYN.

THE THIRD MISS ST. QUENTIN. By Mrs.
MOLESWORTH.

THE STORY OF A SPRING MORNING, etc.
By Mrs. MOLESWORTH. Illustrated.

NEIGHBOURS. By Mrs. MOLESWORTH.
Illustrated.

VERY YOUNG; AND QUITE ANOTHER
STORY. Two Stories. By JEAN INGELOW.

KEITH DERAMORE. By the Author of
' Miss Molly '.

SIDNEY. By MARGARET DELAND.

LAST WORDS TO GIRLS ON LIFE AT
SCHOOL AND AFTER SCHOOL. By Mrs. W.
GREY.

The Silver Library.

CROWN 8vo. 3*s.* 6*d.* EACH VOLUME.

Arnold's (Sir Edwin) Seas and Lands. With
71 Illustrations. 3*s.* 6*d.*

Baker's (Sir S. W.) Eight Years in Ceylon.
With 6 Illustrations. 3*s.* 6*d.*

Baker's (Sir S. W.) Rifle and Hound in Ceylon.
With 6 Illustrations. 3*s.* 6*d.*

**Baring-Gould's (Rev. S.) Curious Myths of the
Middle Ages.** 3*s.* 6*d.*

**Baring-Gould's (Rev. S.) Origin and Develop-
ment of Religious Belief.** 2 vols. 3*s.* 6*d.* each.

Becker's (Prof.) Gallus : or, Roman Scenes in the
Time of Augustus. Illustrated. 3*s.* 6*d.*

Becker's (Prof.) Charicles : or, Illustrations of
the Private Life of the Ancient Greeks.
Illustrated. 3*s.* 6*d.*

**Bent's (J. T.) The Ruined Cities of Mashona-
land :** being a Record of Excavation and Exploration in 1891. With 117 Illustrations.
3*s.* 6*d.*

Brassey's (Lady) A Voyage in the ' Sunbeam '.
With 66 Illustrations. 3*s.* 6*d.*

Clodd's (E.) Story of Creation : a Plain Account
of Evolution. With 77 Illustrations. 3*s.* 6*d.*

**Conybeare (Rev. W. J.) and Howson's (Very
Rev. J. S.) Life and Epistles of St. Paul.**
46 Illustrations. 3*s.* 6*d.*

Dougall's (L.) Beggars All : a Novel. 3*s.* 6*d.*

Doyle's (A. Conan) Micah Clarke. A Tale of
Monmeutn's Rebellion. 3*s.* 6*d.*

Doyle's (A. Conan) The Captain of the Polestar,
and other Tales. 3*s.* 6*d.*

**Froude's (J. A.) Short Studies on Great Sub-
jects.** 4 vols. 3*s.* 6*d.* each.

Froude's (J. A.) Cæsar : a Sketch. 3*s.* 6*d.*

Froude's (J. A.) Thomas Carlyle : a History of
his Life.
1795-1835. 2 vols. 7*s.*
1834-1881. 2 vols. 7*s.*

Froude's (J. A.) The Two Chiefs of Dunboy : an
Irish Romance of the Last Century. 3*s.* 6*d.*

Froude's (J. A.) The History of England, from
the Fall of Wolsey to the Defeat of the
Spanish Armada. 12 vols. 3*s.* 6*d.* each.

Froude's (J. A.) The English in Ireland. 3 vols.
10*s.* 6*d.*

**Gleig's (Rev. G. R.) Life of the Duke of
Wellington.** With Portrait. 3*s.* 6*d.*

Haggard's (H. R.) She : A History of Adventure.
32 Illustrations. 3*s.* 6*d.*

Haggard's (H. R.) Allan Quatermain. With
20 Illustrations. 3*s.* 6*d.*

Haggard's (H. R.) Colonel Quaritch, V.C. : a
Tale of Country Life. 3*s.* 6*d.*

Haggard's (H. R.) Cleopatra. With 29 Full-
page Illustrations. 3*s.* 6*d.*

Haggard's (H. R.) Eric Brighteyes. With 51
Illustrations. 3*s.* 6*d.*

Haggard's (H. R.) Beatrice. 3*s.* 6*d.*

Haggard's (H. R.) Allan's Wife. With 34 Illustrations. 3*s.* 6*d.*

Haggard's (H. R.) The Witch's Head. With
Illustrations. 3*s.* 6*d.*

Haggard's (H. R.) Mr. Meeson's Will. With
Illustrations. 3*s.* 6*d.*

Haggard's (H. R.) Dawn. With 16 Illusts. 3*s.* 6*d.*

**Haggard's (H. R.) and Lang's (A.) The World's
Desire.** With 27 Illustrations. 3*s.* 6*d.*

**Harte's (Bret) In the Carquinez Woods and
other Stories.** 3*s.* 6*d.*

**Helmholtz's (Hermann von) Popular Lectures
on Scientific Subjects.** With 68 Woodcuts.
2 vols. 3*s.* 6*d.* each.

Howitt's (W.) Visits to Remarkable Places
80 Illustrations. 3*s.* 6*d.*

Hornung's (E. W.) The Unbidden Guest. 3*s.* 6*d.*

The Silver Library—*continued.*

Jefferies' (R.) The Story of My Heart: My Autobiography. With Portrait. 3s. 6d.

Jefferies' (R.) Field and Hedgerow. Last Essays of. With Portrait. 3s. 6d.

Jefferies' (R.) Red Deer. With 17 Illustrations by J. CHARLTON and H. TUNALY. 3s. 6d.

Jefferies' (R.) Wood Magic: a Fable. With Frontispiece and Vignette by E. V. B. 3s. 6d.

Jefferies (R.) The Toilers of the Field. With Portrait from the Bust in Salisbury Cathedral. 3s. 6d.

Knight's (E. F.) The Cruise of the 'Alerte': the Narrative of a Search for Treasure on the Desert Island of Trinidad. With 2 Maps and 23 Illustrations. 3s. 6d.

Knight (E. F.) Where Three Empires Meet: a Narrative of Recent Travel in Kashmir, Western Tibet, Baltistan, Gilgit, and the adjoining Countries. With a Map and 54 Illustrations. 3s. 6d.

Lang's (A.) Angling Sketches. 3s. 6d.

Lang's (A.) Custom and Myth: Studies of Early Usage and Belief. 3s. 6d.

Lees (J. A.) and Clutterbuck's (W. J.) B. C. 1887, A Ramble in British Columbia. With Maps and 75 Illustrations. 3s. 6d.

Macaulay's (Lord) Essays and Lays of Ancient Rome. With Portrait and Illustration. 3s. 6d.

Macleod's (H. D.) The Elements of Banking. 3s. 6d.

Marshman's (J. C.) Memoirs of Sir Henry Havelock. 3s. 6d.

Max Müller's (F.) India, what can it teach us? 3s. 6d.

Max Müller's (F.) Introduction to the Science of Religion. 3s. 6d.

Merivale's (Dean) History of the Romans under the Empire. 8 vols. 3s. 6d. each.

Mill's (J. S.) Principles of Political Economy. 3s. 6d.

Mill's (J. S.) System of Logic. 3s. 6d.

Milner's (Geo.) Country Pleasures: the Chronicle of a Year chiefly in a Garden. 3s. 6d.

Nansen's (F.) The First Crossing of Greenland. With Illustrations and a Map. 3s. 6d.

Phillipps-Wolley's (C.) Snap: a Legend of the Lone Mountain. With 13 Illustrations. 3s. 6d.

Proctor's (R. A.) The Orbs Around Us: Essays on the Moon and Planets, Meteors and Comets, the Sun and Coloured Pairs of Suns. 3s. 6d.

Proctor's (R. A.) The Expanse of Heaven: Essays on the Wonders of the Firmament. 3s. 6d.

Proctor's (R. A.) Other Worlds than Ours. 3s. 6d.

Proctor's (R. A.) Rough Ways made Smooth. 3s. 6d.

Proctor's (R. A.) Pleasant Ways in Science. 3s. 6d.

Proctor's (R. A.) Myths and Marvels of Astronomy. 3s. 6d.

Proctor's (R. A.) Nature Studies. 3s. 6d.

Rossetti's (Maria F.) A Shadow of Dante: being an Essay towards studying Himself, his World and his Pilgrimage. 3s. 6d.

Smith (R. Bosworth) Carthage and the Carthaginians. With Maps, Plans, &c. 3s. 6d.

Stanley's (Bishop) Familiar History of Birds. 160 Illustrations. 3s. 6d.

Stevenson (R. L.) and Osbourne's (Ll.) The Wrong Box. 3s. 6d.

Stevenson (Robert Louis) and Stevenson (Fanny van de Grift) More New Arabian Nights.— The Dynamiter. 3s. 6d.

Weyman's (Stanley J.) The House of the Wolf: a Romance. 3s. 6d.

Wood's (Rev. J. G.) Petland Revisited. With 33 Illustrations. 3s. 6d.

Wood's (Rev. J. G.) Strange Dwellings. With 60 Illustrations. 3s. 6d.

Wood's (Rev. J. G.) Out of Doors. 11 Illustrations. 3s. 6d.

Cookery, Domestic Management, etc.

Acton.—MODERN COOKERY. By ELIZA ACTON. With 150 Woodcuts. Fcp. 8vo., 4s. 6d.

Bull.—Works by THOMAS BULL, M.D.

HINTS TO MOTHERS ON THE MANAGEMENT OF THEIR HEALTH DURING THE PERIOD OF PREGNANCY. Fcp. 8vo., 1s. 6d.

THE MATERNAL MANAGEMENT OF CHILDREN IN HEALTH AND DISEASE. Fcp. 8vo., 1s. 6d.

De Salis.—Works by Mrs. DE SALIS.

CAKES AND CONFECTIONS À LA MODE. Fcp. 8vo., 1s. 6d.

DOGS; A Manual for Amateurs. Fcp. 8vo.

DRESSED GAME AND POULTRY À LA MODE. Fcp. 8vo., 1s. 6d.

DRESSED VEGETABLES À LA MODE. Fcp. 8vo., 1s. 6d.

De Salis.—Works by Mrs. DE SALIS—*cont.*

DRINKS À LA MODE. Fcp. 8vo., 1s. 6d.

ENTRÉES À LA MODE. Fcp. 8vo., 1s. 6d.

FLORAL DECORATIONS. Suggestions and Descriptions. Fcp. 8vo., 1s. 6d.

NATIONAL VIANDS À LA MODE. Fcp. 8vo., 1s. 6d.

NEW-LAID EGGS: Hints for Amateur Poultry Rearers. Fcp. 8vo., 1s. 6d.

OYSTERS À LA MODE. Fcp. 8vo., 1s. 6d.

PUDDINGS AND PASTRY À LA MODE. Fcp. 8vo., 1s. 6d.

SAVOURIES À LA MODE. Fcp. 8vo., 1s. 6d.

SOUPS AND DRESSED FISH À LA MODE. Fcp. 8vo., 1s. 6d.

SWEETS AND SUPPER DISHES À LA MODE. Fcp. 8vo., 1s. 6d.

TEMPTING DISHES FOR SMALL INCOMES. Fcp. 8vo., 1s. 6d.

WRINKLES AND NOTIONS FOR EVERY HOUSEHOLD. Crown 8vo., 1s. 6d.

Cookery and Domestic Management—*continued.*

Lear.—MAIGRE COOKERY.   By H. L.
SIDNEY LEAR. 16mo., 2s.

Poole.—COOKERY FOR THE DIABETIC. By
W. H. and Mrs. POOLE. With Preface by
Dr. PAVY. Fcp. 8vo., 2s. 6d.

West. — THE MOTHER'S MANUAL OF
CHILDREN'S DISEASES. By CHARLES WEST,
M.D. Fcp. 8vo., 2s. 6d.

Walker.—A HANDBOOK FOR MOTHERS:
being Simple Hints to Women on the
Management of their Health during Preg-
nancy and Confinement, together with
Plain Directions as to the Care of Infants.
By JANE H. WALKER, L.R.C.P. and L.M.,
L.R.C.S. and M.D. (Brux). Crown 8vo.,
2s. 6d.

Miscellaneous and Critical Works.

Allingham.—VARIETIES IN PROSE.   By
WILLIAM ALLINGHAM. 3 vols. Crown 8vo.,
18s. (Vols. 1 and 2, Rambles, by PATRICIUS
WALKER. Vol. 3, Irish Sketches, etc.)

Armstrong.—ESSAYS AND SKETCHES. By
EDMUND J. ARMSTRONG. Fcp. 8vo., 5s.

Baring-Gould.—CURIOUS MYTHS OF THE
MIDDLE AGES. By Rev. S. BARING-GOULD.
Crown 8vo., 3s. 6d.

Battye.—PICTURES IN PROSE OF NATURE,
WILD SPORT, AND HUMBLE LIFE. By
AUBYN TREVOR BATTYE, B.A. Cr. 8vo., 6s.

Baynes. — SHAKESPEARE STUDIES, and
other Essays. By the late THOMAS SPENCER
BAYNES, LL.B., LL.D. With a Biographical Preface by Professor LEWIS
CAMPBELL. Crown 8vo., 7s. 6d.

Boyd ('A. K. H. B.').—Works by A. K. H.
BOYD, D.D., LL.D.

And see Miscellaneous Theological Works, p. 24.

AUTUMN HOLIDAYS OF A COUNTRY
PARSON. Crown 8vo., 3s. 6d.

COMMONPLACE PHILOSOPHER.   Crown
8vo., 3s. 6d.

CRITICAL ESSAYS OF A COUNTRY PARSON.
Crown 8vo., 3s. 6d.

EAST COAST DAYS AND MEMORIES.
Crown 8vo., 3s. 6d.

LANDSCAPES, CHURCHES AND MORALI-
TIES. Crown 8vo., 3s. 6d.

LEISURE HOURS IN TOWN. Crown 8vo.,
3s. 6d.

LESSONS OF MIDDLE AGE. Crown 8vo.,
3s. 6d.

OUR LITTLE LIFE. Two Series. Cr.
8vo., 3s. 6d. each.

OUR HOMELY COMEDY: AND TRAGEDY
Crown 8vo., 3s. 6d.

RECREATIONS OF A COUNTRY PARSON.
Three Series. Crown 8vo., 3s. 6d. each.
Also First Series. Popular Ed. 8vo., 6d.

Butler.—Works by SAMUEL BUTLER.

EREWHON. Cr. 8vo., 5s.

THE FAIR HAVEN. A Work in Defence
of the Miraculous Element in our Lord's
Ministry. Cr. 8vo., 7s. 6d.

LIFE AND HABIT. An Essay after a
Completer View of Evolution. Cr. 8vo.,
7s. 6d.

EVOLUTION, OLD AND NEW. Cr. 8vo.,
10s. 6d.

ALPS AND SANCTUARIES OF PIEDMONT
AND CANTON TICINO. Illustrated. Pott
4to., 10s. 6d.

LUCK, OR CUNNING, AS THE MAIN
MEANS OF ORGANIC MODIFICATION ?
Cr. 8vo., 7s. 6d.

EX VOTO. An Account of the Sacro
Monte or New Jerusalem at Varállo-Sesia.
Crown 8vo., 10s. 6d.

Gwilt.—AN ENCYCLOPÆDIA OF ARCHITEC-
TURE. By JOSEPH GWILT, F.S.A. Illus-
trated with more than 1100 Engravings on
Wood. Revised (1888), with Alterations
and Considerable Additions by WYATT
PAPWORTH. 8vo., £2 12s. 6d.

Hullah.—Works by JOHN HULLAH, LL.D.

COURSE OF LECTURES ON THE HISTORY
OF MODERN MUSIC. 8vo., 8s. 6d.

COURSE OF LECTURES ON THE TRANSI-
TION PERIOD OF MUSICAL HISTORY. 8vo.,
10s. 6d.

James.—MINING ROYALTIES: their Practical Operation and Effect. By CHARLES
ASHWORTH JAMES, of Lincoln's Inn, Bar-
rister-at-Law. Fcp. 4to., 5s.

Miscellaneous and Critical Works—*continued.*

Jefferies.—Works by RICHARD JEFFERIES.

FIELD AND HEDGEROW: last Essays. With Portrait. Crown 8vo., 3s. 6d.

THE STORY OF MY HEART : my Autobiography. With Portrait and New Preface by C. J. LONGMAN. Crown 8vo., 3s. 6d.

RED DEER. With 17 Illustrations by J. CHARLTON and H. TUNALY. Crown 8vo., 3s. 6d.

THE TOILERS OF THE FIELD. With Portrait from the Bust in Salisbury Cathedral. Crown 8vo., 3s. 6d.

WOOD MAGIC: a Fable. With Frontispiece and Vignette by E. V. B. Crown 8vo., 3s. 6d.

Johnson.—THE PATENTEE'S MANUAL : a Treatise on the Law and Practice of Letters Patent. By J. & J. H. JOHNSON, Patent Agents, &c. 8vo., 10s. 6d.

Lang.—Works by ANDREW LANG.

LETTERS TO DEAD AUTHORS. Fcp. 8vo., 2s. 6d. net.

BOOKS AND BOOKMEN. With 2 Coloured Plates and 17 Illustrations. Fcp. 8vo., 2s. 6d. net.

OLD FRIENDS. Fcp. 8vo., 2s. 6d. net.

LETTERS ON LITERATURE. Fcp. 8vo., 2s. 6d. net.

COCK LANE AND COMMON SENSE. Fcp. 8vo., 6s. 6d. net.

Leonard.—THE CAMEL : Its Uses and Management. By Major ARTHUR GLYN LEONARD, late 2nd East Lancashire Regiment. Royal 8vo., 21s. net.

Max Müller.—Works by F. MAX MÜLLER.

INDIA : WHAT CAN IT TEACH US ? Crown 8vo., 3s. 6d.

CHIPS FROM A GERMAN WORKSHOP.

Vol. I. Recent Essays and Addresses. Crown 8vo., 6s. 6d. net.

Vol. II. Biographical Essays. Cr. 8vo., 6s. 6d. net.

Vol. III. Essays on Language and Literature. 6s. 6d. net.

Vol. IV. Essays on the Sciences of Language, of Thought, and of Mythology. *[In preparation.*

Macfarren.—LECTURES ON HARMONY. By Sir GEORGE A. MACFARREN. 8vo., 12s.

Mendelssohn.—THE LETTERS OF FELIX MENDELSSOHN. Translated by Lady WALLACE. 2 vols. Cr. 8vo., 10s.

Milner.—Works by GEORGE MILNER.

COUNTRY PLEASURES : the Chronicle of a Year chiefly in a Garden. Cr. 8vo., 3s. 6d.

STUDIES OF NATURE ON THE COAST OF ARRAN. With 10 Full-page Copperplates and 12 Illustrations in the Text by W. NOEL JOHNSON. Crown 8vo., 6s. 6d. net.

Poore.—ESSAYS ON RURAL HYGIENE. By GEORGE VIVIAN POORE, M.D., F.R.C.P. With 13 Illustrations. Crown 8vo., 6s. 6d.

Proctor.—Works by RICHARD A. PROCTOR.

STRENGTH AND HAPPINESS. With 9 Illustrations. Crown 8vo., 5s.

STRENGTH : How to get Strong and keep Strong, with Chapters on Rowing and Swimming, Fat, Age, and the Waist. With 9 Illustrations. Crown 8vo., 2s.

Richardson. — NATIONAL HEALTH. A Review of the Works of Sir Edwin Chadwick, K.C.B. By Sir B. W. RICHARDSON, M.D. Cr., 4s. 6d.

Rossetti.—A SHADOW OF DANTE : being an Essay towards studying Himself, his World and his Pilgrimage. By MARIA FRANCESCA ROSSETTI. With Frontispiece by DANTE GABRIEL ROSSETTI. Cr. 8vo., 10s. 6d. Cheap Edition, 3s. 6d.

Solovyoff.—A MODERN PRIESTESS OF ISIS (MADAME BLAVATSKY). Abridged and Translated on Behalf of the Society for Psychical Research from the Russian of VSEVOLOD SERGYEEVICH SOLOVYOFF. By WALTER LEAF, Litt.D. With Appendices. Crown 8vo., 6s.

Southey.—CORRESPONDENCE WITH CAROLINE BOWLES. By ROBERT SOUTHEY. 8vo., 14s.

Stevens.—ON THE STOWAGE OF SHIPS AND THEIR CARGOES. With Information regarding Freights, Charter-Parties, &c. By ROBERT WHITE STEVENS, Associate-Member of the Institute of Naval Architects. 8vo., 21s.

Van Dyke.—A TEXT-BOOK OF THE HISTORY OF PAINTING. By JOHN C. VAN DYKE, of Rutgers College, U.S. With Frontispiece and 109 Illustrations in the Text. Crown 8vo., 6s.

West.—WILLS, AND HOW NOT TO MAKE THEM. With a Selection of Leading Cases, Frontispiece. By B. B. WEST, Author of " Half-Hours with the Millionaires ". Fcp. 8vo., 2s. 6d.

Miscellaneous Theological Works.

*** *For Church of England and Roman Catholic Works see* MESSRS. LONGMANS & CO.'s *Special Catalogues.*

Balfour.—THE FOUNDATIONS OF BELIEF: being Notes Introductory to the Study of Theology. By the Right Hon. ARTHUR J. BALFOUR, M.P. 8vo., 12s. 6d.

Boyd.—Works by A. K. H. BOYD, D.D., First Minister of St. Andrews, author of ' Recreations of a Country Parson,' &c.

COUNSEL AND COMFORT FROM A CITY PULPIT. Crown 8vo., 3s. 6d.

SUNDAY AFTERNOONS IN THE PARISH CHURCH OF A SCOTTISH UNIVERSITY CITY. Crown 8vo., 3s. 6d.

CHANGED ASPECTS OF UNCHANGED TRUTHS. Crown 8vo., 3s. 6d.

GRAVER THOUGHTS OF A COUNTRY PARSON. Three Series. Crown 8vo., 3s. 6d. each.

PRESENT DAY THOUGHTS. Crown 8vo., 3s. 6d.

SEASIDE MUSINGS. Crown 8vo., 3s. 6d.

' TO MEET THE DAY' through the Christian Year : being a Text of Scripture, with an Original Meditation and a Short Selection in Verse for Every Day. Crown 8vo., 4s. 6d.

De la Saussaye.—A MANUAL OF THE SCIENCE OF RELIGION. By Professor CHANTEPIE DE LA SAUSSAYE. Translated by Mrs. COLYER FERGUSSON (*née* MAX MULLER). Crown 8vo., 12s. 6d.

Kalisch.—Works by M. M. KALISCH, Ph.D.

BIBLE STUDIES. Part I. The Prophecies of Balaam. 8vo., 10s. 6d. Part II. The Book of Jonah. 8vo., 10s. 6d.

COMMENTARY ON THE OLD TESTAMENT : with a New Translation. Vol. I. Genesis. 8vo., 18s. Or adapted for the General Reader. 12s. Vol. II. Exodus. 15s. Or adapted for the General Reader. 12s. Vol. III. Leviticus, Part I. 15s. Or adapted for the General Reader. 8s. Vol. IV. Leviticus, Part II. 15s. Or adapted for the General Reader. 8s.

Macdonald.—Works by GEORGE MACDONALD, LL.D.

UNSPOKEN SERMONS. Three Series. Crown 8vo., 3s. 6d. each.

THE MIRACLES OF OUR LORD. Crown 8vo., 3s. 6d.

A BOOK OF STRIFE, IN THE FORM OF THE DIARY OF AN OLD SOUL : Poems. 18mo., 6s.

Martineau.—Works by JAMES MARTINEAU, D.D., LL.D.

HOURS OF THOUGHT ON SACRED THINGS. Two Volumes of Sermons. Cr. 8vo., 7s. 6d.

ENDEAVOURS AFTER THE CHRISTIAN LIFE. Discourses. Crown 8vo., 7s. 6d.

THE SEAT OF AUTHORITY IN RELIGION. 8vo., 14s.

ESSAYS, REVIEWS, AND ADDRESSES. 4 Vols. Crown 8vo., 7s. 6d. each.
   I. Personal ; Political.
   II. Ecclesiastical ; Historical.
   III. Theological ; Philosophical.
   IV. Academical ; Religious.

HOME PRAYERS, with Two Services for Public Worship. Crown 8vo., 3s. 6d.

Max Müller.—Works by F. MAX MÜLLER.

HIBBERT LECTURES ON THE ORIGIN AND GROWTH OF RELIGION, as illustrated by the Religions of India. Crown 8vo., 7s. 6d.

INTRODUCTION TO THE SCIENCE OF RELIGION : Four Lectures delivered at the Royal Institution. Crown 8vo., 3s. 6d.

NATURAL RELIGION. The Gifford Lectures, delivered before the University of Glasgow in 1888. Crown 8vo., 10s. 6d.

PHYSICAL RELIGION. The Gifford Lectures, delivered before the University of Glasgow in 1890. Crown 8vo., 10s. 6d.

ANTHROPOLOGICAL RELIGION. The Gifford Lectures, delivered before the University of Glasgow in 1891. Cr. 8vo., 10s. 6d.

THEOSOPHY OR PSYCHOLOGICAL RELIGION. The Gifford Lectures, delivered before the University of Glasgow in 1892. Crown 8vo., 10s. 6d.

THREE LECTURES ON THE VEDÂNTA PHILOSOPHY, delivered at the Royal Institution in March, 1894. 8vo., 5s.

Phillips.—THE TEACHING OF THE VEDAS. What Light does it Throw on the Origin and Development of Religion ? By MAURICE PHILLIPS, London Mission, Madras. Crown 8vo., 6s.

Scholler.—A CHAPTER OF CHURCH HISTORY FROM SOUTH GERMANY : being Passages from the Life of Johann Evangelist Georg Lutz, formerly Parish Priest and Dean in Oberroth, Bavaria. By L. W. SCHOLLER. Translated from the German by W. WALLIS. Crown 8vo., 3s. 6d.

SUPERNATURAL RELIGION : an Inquiry into the Reality of Divine Revelation. 3 vols. 8vo., 36s.

REPLY (A) TO DR. LIGHTFOOT'S ESSAYS. By the Author of ' Supernatural Religion '. 8vo., 6s.

THE GOSPEL ACCORDING TO ST. PETER : a Study. By the Author of ' Supernatural Religion '. 8vo., 6s.

5000/4/95.